CAPITALIST RUSSIA AND THE WEST

*Dedicated to the memory of my father
and to Jonathan and Maggie*

Capitalist Russia and the West

JEFFREY SUROVELL
College of Aeronautics, New York

Routledge
Taylor & Francis Group

LONDON AND NEW YORK

First published 2000 by Ashgate Publishing

Reissued 2018 by Routledge
2 Park Square, Milton Park, Abingdon, Oxon OX14 4RN
711 Third Avenue, New York, NY 10017, USA

Routledge is an imprint of the Taylor & Francis Group, an informa business

Publisher's Note
The publisher has gone to great lengths to ensure the quality of this reprint but points out that some imperfections in the original copies may be apparent.

Disclaimer
The publisher has made every effort to trace copyright holders and welcomes correspondence from those they have been unable to contact.

A Library of Congress record exists under LC control number: 00134015

ISBN 13: 978-1-138-73898-0 (hbk)
ISBN 13: 978-1-315-18445-6 (ebk)

Printed in the United Kingdom
by Henry Ling Limited

Contents

Preface

If it is granted that the paramount objective of scientific analysis is explanation,[1] then the investigation of Russian foreign policy necessarily entails a focus on the key factors which motivate and shape—and thereby explain—the conduct of Russia's leaders in the international arena. In the end, amid all the confusion and chaos, after all the Russian scandals which originated in the Kremlin and in the West have died down, one factor stands out amid the welter of factors which determine Russia's foreign policy: greed. Greed, on the part of Russian and Western elites, has indeed been the defining element in Russia's relations with the West (by the "West" I mean primarily West Europe and the US and their related institutions, including NATO, the EU, etc.; Japan is included only in that it is a member of the G-7 and other organizations) in that Russia's elites have willingly implemented the neo-liberal economic agenda dictated by their Western counterparts in return for payment by the latter who, while pretending to look the other way as Russia's "robber capitalists" were engaged in the naked theft of their nation's wealth, have poured billions of dollars into Russian coffers in the form of "aid" and loans. About this we have at least some knowledge, for this tale—or at least sketches of it—has been told elsewhere.[2]

But there is another side to this sordid affair, one related to but at the same time quite distinct from the aforementioned developments in the domestic sphere and yet which, although just as crucial from the standpoint of Russian-Western relations, has gone practically unexamined by analysts. Its essence was spelled out in an unusually revealing admission by US Treasury Secretary Lawrence Summers at US Congressional Hearings on Russian corruption in September 1999 shortly after the Bank of New York scandal broke. According to Representative Barney Frank, his interrogator at the Hearings, Summers detailed how "the tacit endorsement [by the US government and the West] of high-level [Russian] government theft had actually bought the United States [and the West as a whole] some very worthwhile and palpable *foreign policy* gains," notably "Russian . . . cooperation in Bosnia and Kosovo, some dealings with Iran, some macroeconomic policy, and . . . relative quiescence in the expansion of NATO."[3]

This was a bombshell of enormous proportions, for it flew directly in the face of the prevailing assumption that, far from being quiescent and cooperative, Russia was in many respects an *opponent* of Western policy along a whole range of issues, and that Russia's leaders, particularly beginning sometime in late 1993, would "defend Russian interests vigorously in relations with the West."[4] It was thus almost a given that Russia was unalterably opposed to NATO expansion—so much so, that predictions abounded that Russian-Western relations would suffer grievously if and when expansion took place.[5] In a related sense, it was assumed that Foreign Minister Primakov, a more "hard-line opponent" of NATO than his predecessor, would fight tooth and nail against expansion.[6] Assurances by Russian leaders that Moscow was the "chief partner in the Balkans" of Yugoslav President Milosevic and the Serbs and the principal source of support for his policies in Bosnia and Kosovo which NATO and the West so vehemently opposed[7] have gone largely unquestioned in the literature (although some analyses do come closer to diverging from this line of argument by asserting that while Russian policy toward the Serbs is "not necessarily at odds with the West," Russia does seek to retain "an air of independence befitting . . . [its] great power status").[8] And it was widely predicted that the close ties with the West would "unravel" as a result of an "enraged" Russia's opposition to the US-British bombing of Iraq in December 1998.[9]

Summers' testimony should therefore have occasioned an immediate uproar, but was followed instead by a conspicuous silence. Why? The answer lies in one of this study's central arguments: that Russia's leaders, in league with their Western counterparts, have engaged in a grand *deception* to obfuscate the true nature of their relationship, which is characterized above all by Russia's acquiescence to and dependency on the West.

With their silence, politicians and specialists in the field have either been unaware of the reality around them or, cognizant of the deception, have chosen to indirectly play along with it by ignoring it, all of which only proves that the famous thesis of Marx and Engels that "the ideas of the ruling class are in every epoch the ruling ideas"—which was especially relevant to the field of Soviet studies in the West in light of the historically close ties between that field and governmental policies vis-à-vis the USSR—retains its relevance with respect to studies of post-Soviet Russia, whose mainstream line continues to be closely connected with official government circles.[10] That line holds that the downfall of the USSR and its "empire" was a positive development, that post-Soviet Russia's only hope for progress is to emulate the West and create a capitalist "market" economy and Western-style "democracy." Even most Western critics of policy toward Russia tend to accept the line, disputing not the need to institute Western-style "reforms" but rather the *manner* in which they have been implemented.[11] The present study, on the other hand, seeks to depict Russian-Western relations in such a way as to break with this conventional wisdom and, in the process, to pierce the screen of deception and expose, as it were, the emperor's new clothes.

Over the years the perpetrators of the deception have employed more sophisticated means, but have been unable to prevent the deception from becoming so transparent as to border on farce. Of the innumerable examples in this regard, a particularly memorable one came from the mouth of the director of Russia's privatization and close Yeltsin confidant Anatolii Chubais, who in September 1997 attempted to defend Russian government officials against the accusation that they were "agents of the West, of the IMF, and of the Paris Club" with the assertion that "now [that Russia was accepted as a member as compensation for its acquiescence to NATO expansion] the Paris Club itself becomes an agent of Russia . . ." Chubais' boast was so absurd that even Russian sources were compelled to expose this prevarication when they pointed out some two months later that far from being the vigorous power Chubais claimed, Russia played the role of the "poorest country" by pleading for $2 billion in Western credits.[12]

The deception has, to be sure, gone not totally unrecognized. By 1998— at least with respect to Russia's economy—it had become so obvious that what would once have been dismissed as wild conspiracy theory had become the conventional wisdom, making it possible for two US economists to argue in an article published in that year that Russia had a "virtual economy" based on "illusion" and "pretense."[13] In fact, as this study will attempt to show, Russia's illusory economy is intimately bound up with the foreign policy pretense perpetuated by Russia's leaders. It may be said for just this reason that Russia has had a "virtual foreign policy" founded on similar illusion and deception.

Having said that, the deception continues to be perpetuated by unofficial and *official* sources in Russia and the West. And even left forces in Russia—those one would assume most likely to unmask the deception— were at least until the late 1990s loathe to directly accuse the Yeltsin leadership of outright deception and sellout, even though they surely knew this to be so. Such a radical figure as Duma member Sergei Baburin skirted around the issue when he remarked that Russian authorities were "increasingly open to manipulation by internal and external forces expressing hostile interests. The Foreign Minister and the President himself are exposed to huge pressure," thus shying away from the obvious truth that they willingly sold their country out to Western interests.[14]

Nevertheless, the deception has become so obvious that since the late 1990s references to it by unofficial sources—journalists, specialists, etc.— have become almost commonplace, although they appear rather more often in Russia than in the West. One commentary thus noted in 1999 that Russian officials "pretend to be creating a law-based, market-friendly liberal democracy. We Westerners pretend to believe [them] and what's more, we pay [them] for it."[15] And the Yeltsin administration was said to have used Western money to bribe Russia's leaders to "be good—which means maintaining a low profile abroad, letting the US [and the capitalist West more broadly] have its way, and keeping the communists down."[16] Such admissions, sadly, have appeared only episodically, certainly not as the connecting thread of any full-length study.

The origins of the deception trace back to post-Soviet Russia's honeymoon period with the West, dating roughly from late 1991 to late 1993 and characterized by a Westernism on the part of the Yeltsin leadership so unabashedly obsequious that among Russians Foreign Minister Kozyrev earned the moniker of "Mr. Yes." But a seismic shift took place in August 1993 when, while on a visit to the Central and East European (CEE) capitals of Warsaw and Prague, Yeltsin openly acquiesced to the expressed desire of those governments to join NATO. The strategic implications of this demarche were so dangerous for Russia's security that the previous open acquiescence to the West which had characterized much of Russian policy was no longer an automatic option for Russia's leaders, especially in view of the ongoing and terrible effects of the pro-Western "reforms" which were impoverishing the Russian people and decimating Russia's governmental structures and armed forces. In light of these factors Russia's leaders, Westernizers through and through, undertook from this juncture a policy of concealing their pro-Westernism even as they continued to comply with Western dictates.

Thus began the grand deception perpetuated jointly by Russia and the West. The opening act of the deception drama featured the sending of a letter by the Russian government in September 1993 to the four leading

Western powers which asserted, in complete contradiction to Yeltsin's August demarche, that Russia now "opposed" NATO expansion to the east. The letter coincided with two other developments: the apogee in the political struggle between the leadership and the opposition and the sunset of the Russian elites' honeymoon with the West—*even as the former went to great lengths to preserve the marriage*, for they had not, as the conventional wisdom contends, suddenly metamorphosed into "opponents" of the West. Rather, they continued to subordinate Russia's interests to the West while camouflaging this with rhetorical and other devices.

Difficult as it may be for mainstream thinking to accept, Russia's top leaders, with their love of all things Western, have never in their heart of hearts opposed NATO expansion, the issue which has most fully embodied Russia's fruitless and painful attempt to merge with the West. This truth was brought out by a noted Russian journalist who located the explanation for Russia's leaders' "passiveness" toward the US Senate's ratification of NATO enlargement in May 1998 in the fact that "deep down in their hearts, [Russia's leaders] do not regard NATO's enlargement as an evil and a threat to their country." For this reason Russia's forceful "opposition" to NATO was dismissed as mere "bluff." Indeed, soon after the Soviet collapse it was actually commonplace for Westernizing Russians to gush adoration of NATO for its supposed support for world peace and for its being the only international security organization with extensive experience and developed political cooperation with states to its east—to whom it selflessly rendered humanitarian assistance. For these reasons, it was argued, NATO had earned the right to safeguard the security of CEE itself. Even Vice President Rutskoi as early as late 1991 welcomed NATO as the "guarantor of stability in Europe." In light of the foregoing, then, it is no wonder Dimitri Simes confessed that he is "convinced that there was more smoke than fire to Russia's anti-NATO campaign," for NATO has in reality been the *benefactor*, not the nemesis, of Russia's Westernizing elites, and they have clearly been cognizant of this and duly grateful.[17]

Russia's leaders, it is argued here, have not by the year 2000 fundamentally altered their extreme pro-Western leanings—including their love of NATO, that military bulwark of international capitalism which protects the interests of Russia's capitalist—specifically comprador—regime, in that NATO is always there to help them rebuff any attempt to rebuild a socialist Russia. A central feature of this study will be to demonstrate the accuracy of Lenin's characterization of the machinations of these Russian elites, who make up a true comprador class: "when it is a question of [capitalist] class profits," he wrote, "the [comprador] bourgeoisie will sell out their own fatherland and conclude deals contrary to the interests of their own people with any foreigner whatsoever."[18]

Russia's first post-Soviet Foreign Minister, Andrei Kozyrev, once proclaimed that only with the demise of the Soviet Union could Russia "steer the country to normal human conditions."[19] Attempts by the Westernizing leaders of Yeltsin's Russia to renew the process of (capitalist) convergence between Russia and the West were thus interrupted, he argued, by the October revolution. In this view Yeltsin emerges as the neo-liberal savior of Russia, Kerensky resurrected. But the actual, tragic state of post-Soviet Russian affairs has exploded Kozyrev's optimistic scenario for, in their frenzy for monetary enrichment, Russia's elites, having been repressed by the egalitarian restraints of socialism during the Soviet period, have displayed a mind-boggling lack of concern generally for such "unimportant" trivialities of governance as health care (one international health care expert noted that to Russia's leaders, health is no longer a concern; rather, "the new value is money—nothing else") and even for the establishment of proper institutions for the formulation and conduct of foreign policy. No wonder Kozyrev and his team, when asked how a weakened Russia would be treated after the fall of the USSR, displayed little interest and had no answers. And post-Soviet Russian foreign policy has suffered as a result: it has never had a well-defined decisionmaking mechanism nor even an overall, explicitly formulated, strategic goal. In fact, apart from its dependency on and compliance with the West, it has never had much of an explicitly defined foreign policy as such, except, apparently, to do the bidding of the capitalist West.[20]

Russian and Soviet relations with the West have long had vital importance for world affairs. In the opinion of Fareed Zakaria, Russia has been "the most important piece of American foreign policy since the end of the cold war," and Michael McFaul points out that one of the two most important issues in Russian foreign policy today is Russia's relations with the West.[21] It is surely dismaying, therefore, that the topic has not been a particularly "hot" one, as evidenced by the truly small number of works treating *Soviet* relations with the West,[22] the scanty range of writings on *post-Soviet Russian* relations with either West Europe or the US, and the fact that no full-length work on the subject has appeared.[23] This study aims to rectify this glaring lacuna.

Notes

[1] Carl G. Hempel and Paul Oppenheim, "The Logic of Explanation," in Herbert Feigl and May Brodbeck, eds., *Readings in the Philosophy of Science* (New York: Appleton-Century-Crofts, 1953), p. 319.

[2] See, for example, Lynn D. Nelson and Irina Y. Kuzes, *Radical Reform in Yeltsin's Russia: Political, Economic, and Social Dimensions* (Armonk, NY: M.E. Sharpe, 1995), and Janine Wedel, *Collision and Collusion: The Strange Case of Western Aid to Eastern Europe, 1989-1998* (New York: St. Martin's, 1998).

[3] Emphasis mine. *The eXile*, September 25, 1999. It was reported that there were virtually no followup questions to Summers' sensational statements at the Hearings.

[4] Neil Malcolm and Alex Pravda, Introduction, in Neil Malcolm, Alex Pravda, Roy Allison, and Margot Light, eds., *Internal Factors in Russian Foreign Policy* (Oxford: Oxford University Press, 1996), pp. 22-3; Angela E. Stent, *Russia and Germany Reborn: Unification, the Soviet Collapse, and the New Europe* (Princeton: Princeton University Press, 1999), p. 231. See also Mike Bowker, *Russian Foreign Policy and the End of the Cold War* (Aldershot: Dartmouth, 1997), pp. 205-16.

[5] See, for example, Peter Truscott, *Russia First: Breaking with the West* (I.B. Tauris, 1997), pp. 46-54; Stephen Covington, "Moscow's Insecurity and Eurasian Instability," *European Security*, Vol. 3, No. 4, Autumn 1995; Michael Mihalka, "Continued Resistance to NATO Expansion," *Transition*, Vol. 1, No. 14, August 11, 1995; Peter Shearman, "Russian Policy Toward Western Europe: The German Axis," in Peter Shearman, ed., *Russian Foreign Policy Since 1990* (Boulder, CO: Westview, 1995); Jonathan Deane, "NATO Enlargement: Coping With Act II," in Ted Galen Carpenter and Barbara Conry, eds., *NATO Enlargement: Illusions and Reality* (Washington, D.C.: The Cato Institute, 1998), p. 123.

[6] See Richard L. Kugler and Marianna V. Kozintseva, *Enlarging NATO: The Russia Factor* (Santa Monica, CA: Rand, 1996), p. 67, and J.L. Black, *Russia Faces NATO Expansion: Bearing Gifts or Bearing Arms?* (Lanham, MD: Rowman and Littlefield, 1999). Another work which views Primakov as a hard-liner is Dimitri K. Simes, *After the Collapse: Russia Seeks Its Place As a Great Power* (New York: Simon and Schuster, 1999), pp. 201-16.

[7] *Izvestiia*, August 11, 1995, p. 1. The typical Western view claims that Russian officials opposed sanctions against Belgrade because of the "special relationship between Russians and Serbs." See Margot Light, "Foreign Policy Thinking," in Malcolm et al, *Internal Factors*, p. 55. Although Bowker, *Russian Foreign Policy*, p. 205, contends that Russian-Western relations had "cooled" on issues including the war in Bosnia, he also contradictorily—and correctly—claims on pp. 224-5 that Russian policy vis-à-vis the Serbs remained from 1993 "within the international consensus."

[8] Mark Webber, *The International Politics of Russia and the Successor States* (Manchester: Manchester University Press, 1996), p. 266.

[9] See, for example, *The Boston Globe*, December 19, 1998, p. A2.

[10] Karl Marx and Frederick Engels, *The German Ideology* (New York: International Publishers, 1974), pp. 64-5. On ties between Soviet studies and the government, see Stephen F. Cohen, *Rethinking the Soviet Experience: Politics and History Since 1917* (Oxford: Oxford University Press, 1985).

[11] For good examples of this see Nelson and Kuzes, *Radical Reform in Yeltsin's Russia*, and Wedel, *Collision and Collusion*.

[12] *Nezavisimaia gazeta*, December 4, 1997, p. 1, December 20, 1997, p. 1, and September 26, 1997, pp. 1-2.

[13] Clifford G. Gaddy and Barry W. Ickes, "Russia's Virtual Economy," *Foreign Affairs*, Vol. 77, No. 5, September/October 1998. *Sovetskaia Rossiia*, January 7, 1999 reversed the reasoning by referring to post-Soviet Russia as a robber capitalist, virtual society whose billions had been stolen by the elites, whereas the USSR, far from being a virtual economy, had been "incredibly rich."

[14] *Pravda-5*, May 22, 1997, pp. 1, 3.

[15] *The Economist*, August 28-September 3, 1999. One study which comes the closest to the truth about the deception is Henry Trofimenko, *Russian National Interests and the Current Crisis in Russia* (Aldershot: Ashgate, 1999). Trofimenko, a leading Soviet specialist and adviser to Brezhnev, argues on pages 275-280 that "Russia will remain totally subservient to Washington, as was the case during the last six years since the demise of the Soviet Union," and that "despite his occasional 'tough talk' against NATO . . . Moscow's foreign policy line has remained fairly constant: obedience to the American [and Western] line."

[16] *The Ottawa Sun*, September 12, 1999, p. 15.

[17] Melor Sturua, *Nezavisimaia gazeta*, May 14, 1998, p. 3; *Izvestiia*, June 8, 1993, p. 4; *Nezavisimaia gazeta*, November 28, 1991, p. 2; Simes, *After the Collapse*, pp. 219-20.

[18] D.G. Tomashevskii, *Leninskie idei i sovremennye mezhdunarodnye otnosheniia* (Moscow: Izdatel'stvo politicheskoi literatury, 1971), pp. 37-8. In most general terms, the comprador bourgeoisie is that sector of the local bourgeoisie who work in the interests of the imperialists who exploit their country.

[19] Andrei Kozyrev, "Russia: A Chance for Survival," *Foreign Affairs*, Vol. 71, No. 2, Spring 1992, pp. 7. Kozyrev was Russian Foreign Minister at the time.

[20] The Russian Journal, August 30, 1999; S. Markov, Director of the Institute of Political Studies, in *RFE/RL*, June 23, 1999. See also Simes, *After the Collapse*, pp. 181, 208-9.

[21] *Newsweek*, September 27, 1999, p. 40; Michael McFaul, "A Precarious Peace: Domestic Politics in the Making of Russian Foreign Policy," *International Security*, Vol. 22, No. 3, Winter 1997/1998, p. 24.

[22] Studies of Soviet relations with the West tended to focus on specific countries, usually taking in relatively brief time frames. A partial list includes: Neil Malcolm, *Soviet Policy Perspectives on Western Europe* (London: Routledge, The Royal Institute of International Affairs, Chatham House Papers, 1989); Michael J. Sodaro, "Soviet Studies of the Western Alliance," in Herbert J. Ellison, ed., *Soviet Policy toward Western Europe: Implications for the Atlantic Alliance* (Seattle: University of Washington Press, 1983); and Robbin F. Laird and Susan L. Clark, eds., *The USSR and the Western Alliance* (Boston: Unwin Hyman, 1990).

[23] The small but growing body of studies of post-Soviet Russia and the West includes J.L. Black, *Russia Faces NATO Expansion: Bearing Gifts or Bearing Arms?* (Lanham, MD: Rowman and Littlefield, 1999); Peter Truscott, *Russia First: Breaking with the West* (London: I.B. Tauris, 1997); Angela E. Stent, *Russia and Germany Reborn. Unification, the Soviet Collapse, and the New Europe* (Princeton: Princeton University Pres, 1999); Coit D. Blacker, "After Empire: Russia and the West," in Michael Mandelbaum, ed., *The New Russian Foreign Policy* (New York: Council on Foreign Relations, 1998); Jeffrey Surovell, "Western Europe and the Western Alliance: Soviet and Post-Soviet Perspectives," *Journal of Communist Studies and Transition Politics*, Vol. 11, No. 2, 1995; and Mark Kramer, "NATO, Russia and Eastern European Security," in Uri Ra'anan and Kate Martin, eds., *Russia—A Return to Imperialism?* (New York: St. Martin's, 1996).

Acknowledgements

I wish to thank my family first of all for their loving support and encouragement in the writing of this book. I am grateful to ACTR, The American Council of Teachers of Russian, for its uncommon generosity in awarding me grants to conduct research and to teach in Russia, both of which were invaluable for this book and were also unforgettable experiences which enabled me to get to know the wonderful Soviet people. The people at ACTR were extremely gracious and helpful. I wish to emphasize that I am, of course, solely responsible for the content and the views contained in this book. I also wish to thank the staff at the Slavic Division of the New York Public Library for their uncommon kindness and consideration.

I am particularly grateful to Duncan Foley and Alex Motyl for their kindness and perceptiveness, even brilliance, on various questions of this book. They truly gave generously of themselves and were patient critics, even when they disagreed with me. Finally, I give loving thanks to Naomi Burns for her very special and helpful role in this book's creation.

List of Acronyms

ABM	Anti-Ballistic Missile
ANC	African National Congress
APC	Agreement on Partnership and Cooperation
BLFIG	Bank-Led Financial-Industrial Group
CEE	Central and Eastern Europe
CIA	Central Intelligence Agency
CFE	Conventional Forces in Europe
CFDP	Council on Foreign and Defense Policy
CIS	Commonwealth of Independent States
Cocom	Consultative Group and Its Coordinating Committee
CofE	Council of Europe
CPC	Conflict Prevention Center
CPD	Congress of People's Deputies
CPRF	Communist Party of the Russian Federation
CSCE	Conference on Security and Cooperation in Europe
EBRD	European Bank for Reconstruction and Development.
EC	European Community
EU	European Union
FIG	Financial-Industrial Group
FSU	Former Soviet Union
GATT	General Agreement on Tariffs and Trade
GKI	State Property Management Committee
IFOR	Implementation Force
ILFIG	Industry-Led Financial-Industrial Group
IMEMO	Institute of World Economy and International Relations
ISKRAN	USA-Canada Institute (of Russian Federation)
MEMO	World Economy and International Relations
NACC	North Atlantic Cooperation Council
NATO	North Atlantic Treaty Organization
OSCE	Organization on Security and Cooperation in Europe
PfP	Partnership for Peace
RFM	Russian Foreign Ministry
RRF	Rapid Reaction Force
SFOR	Stabilization Force
START	Strategic Arms Reductions Talks

STF	Systemic Transformation Facility
UN	United Nations
UNPROFOR	United Nations Protection Force
UNSC	United Nations Security Council
USAID	United States Agency for International Development
USSR	Union of Soviet Socialist Republics
WEU	West European Union
WTO	World Trade Organization

1 Introduction: Theoretical Considerations

The contradiction highlighted in the Preface—between the assumption of Russia as a hard-line opponent of the West and the reality of its dependence on the West—continues to haunt Russian foreign policy studies. It is made all the more salient because it involves a defining issue for Russian policymakers, and because only when it is fully sorted out will an understanding of the overall motivating thrust of Russian policy be possible.

But this study seeks to go beyond the elucidation of the dynamics of Russian (and to a lesser extent, Soviet) policy and the contradictions therein. Its paramount objective is to explain that policy from a particular theoretical vantagepoint which has been conspicuously absent from the literature on the Soviet Union and Russia (indeed, from most of political science) but whose time, it is here argued, has come. This became especially apparent when the 1998 crisis of global capitalism ravaged Asia, Africa, Latin America—and Russia, whose economic meltdown shattered the adulation many Russians held for the "market" and Western-style "democracy." What is more, the widespread agreement that Russia's Westernizing leaders' attempted replication of Western economic and political systems has been a spectacular failure cries out for an openness to new explanatory frameworks.

The theory alluded to is Marxism. While it is true that one would be hard put to come up with a more radical theory of politics at the dawn of the twenty-first century, it is surely also remarkable that Marxist class theory— and dependency theory, employed in this study as an adjunct to Marxism— has never been applied to explain Russian policy, particularly in light of the transparent alliance between Russia's policymakers and its economic elites and between the elites of Russia and the West.

Russia's "hostility" to Western foreign policy, as pointed out in the previous chapter, is a calculated deception orchestrated by Russia's elites in concert with their Western partners to obscure the fact that the former willingly consent to Russia's dependence on and subservience to the West and which, if openly admitted, could upend Russia's entire political order to the detriment of its elites. For their part, Western elites, although the

1

dominant parties in the relationship, depend on Russia's leaders to insure that Russia remains a bastion of pro-Westernism, that the communist "menace" is vanquished forever. An important component of their strategy is to prevent Russia from impeding their ultimate goal of penetrating and eventually dominating all of the markets of East Europe and the former Soviet Union (FSU) and their establishment of political and military control in the region. There is, therefore, a pronounced mutuality which pervades the relationship between the ruling classes of the two nations.

Because conventional theories have been deficient in explaining capitalist Russia's foreign policy—this is no more true than for Russian policy toward the West, an issue of exceeding importance for world affairs generally—we are compelled to examine Marxism and, as an adjunct, dependency theory. Relations with the West simply cannot be adequately understood without an understanding of class dynamics; they, in turn, are explained by Marxism and dependency theory. It is to these theories that we now turn.

Both theories, and especially Marxism, are, to be sure, widely viewed by mainstream scholarship as having scant validity as frameworks of analysis.[1] Marxism in particular is said to lack a general and systematic theorization of international relations—indeed, of politics more broadly.[2] Neither has ever been applied to studies of Russian (or Soviet) politics, making their application to political analysis a daunting challenge. Yet these realities, far from discouraging analysis, serve as catalysts for setting the admittedly ambitious goal of resuscitating Marxism and its adjunct, dependency theory, by way of analysis of Russian policy toward the West.

Engels noted in Chapter 52 of the third volume of Marx's *Capital* that just as Marx had begun to undertake his all-important study of classes he laid his pen down, and thus deprived the world of his analysis of the key concept in political phenomena. With this limitation in mind, this study selects those elements of Marxist theory which touch on politics, including international relations (IR). It critiques and in some cases draws on strands of mainstream theories of IR (realism, images, etc.), as well as economics and political economy, comparative politics, political culture, and sociology, and integrates elements of them into the overarching theoretical aegis of Marxism and dependency theory.

The Starting Point: Level of Analysis

The study of Soviet and post-Soviet Russian foreign policy has not been immune to the perennial level of analysis debate dividing the field of international relations.[3] One side in the debate considers the domestic level central to the determination of policy direction,[4] or at least rejects realism's emphasis on international structures and disregard of domestic factors, on the grounds that, among other things, domestic determinants of a state's external behavior are crucial in light of the blurring of distinctions between domestic and foreign policy, the growing domestic salience of social, cultural, and economic relations among states, and the post-cold war spread of "democracy" which increased the accountability of foreign policy elites.[5]

The other side abjures the domestic level for its understating such external factors, particularly salient during the late Soviet and post-Soviet periods, as transnational corporations and the foreign policy of core powers and international agencies, above all, the IMF and World Bank "whose purpose it is to influence . . . the internal developments in countries to which they give loans."[6] Other "externalists" argue that Soviet foreign policy responses "derive[d] from external sources" and emphasize the salience of nuclear weapons, the "multifaceted liberal capitalist system of states," whose economic dynamism and attractive economic model pressured the USSR to change, as did the generally "peaceful character" of the West, whose incentives and gentle pressures encouraged Soviet accommodation.[7] Indeed, the impact of international organizations—the IMF, GATT, the World Bank, etc.—on the policies of governments has, if anything, deepened in recent decades, even as the capacity of national governments (especially of the most powerful states, above all the US) to influence them has expanded. International organizations intrude in the internal affairs of nation-states by imposing economic policies on them.[8]

In response to this debate, and in the absence of a general international relations theory, many analysts are gravitating increasingly toward a cobbling together of different levels of analysis—indeed, of different theories more broadly—into a multidimensional network. For them it is not a question of *whether* but *how* to integrate both levels. Some prefer to emphasize beliefs, the international setting and the dynamic of domestic politics as most pertinent;[9] others argue that the need for a broader sweep of multidimensionality impels an even broader erasure of boundaries between comparative politics, international relations, political economy, security, culture, and political theory.[10]

Marxism and Politics

The aforementioned analytical eclecticism coincides with Lenin's dictum that a nation's foreign policy cannot be separated from, let alone counterposed to, its home policy, especially as the domestic arena is the point of policy origination.[11] Marxism thus posits that there is a dialectical interconnection between the domestic and the external levels and that the two mutually impact on each other (although the former is ultimately decisive in foreign policy decisionmaking). Indeed, as a fundamentally holistic theory,[12] Marxism answers the criterion of multidimensionality for international relations theory in that it rejects the separation of parts (economic, political, social, cultural) of the social whole and views politics as the "pervasive and ubiquitous articulation of social conflicts and particularly of class conflict," entering into virtually all social relations.[13]

One of the principal criticisms directed at previous attempts to build domestic-centered theories of foreign policy is their failure to pay attention "to the significant causal role of societal groups." Marxist analysis provides a solution to this problem in the writings, among others, of Friedrich Engels, who wrote that in the final analysis socioeconomic class, one of the components of the "economic condition," is the determining basis, the core causal factor of societal development.[14] To be sure, Marxism is frequently criticized for "reductionism" and "economic determinism," that is, for regarding economic factors as the determinants of societal development to the exclusion of others.[15] Such criticism is unfounded, however, for Marxism accepts that superstructural factors—history, political culture, psychology, ideology and the role of ideas, etc.—deeply impact on society, although they are ultimately conditioned by those factors which are causally decisive in human social relations, namely, class relations and class struggle, between capitalists and workers and between international capitals.[16] As Engels emphasized, economic factors are the overarching and determining ones *in the final analysis*.[17]

For Marxism the analytical focal point of any society's political system is the ideas and policies of politicians who function as the political agents of the ruling class and who operate in the interests of that class. In Russia today the economic and political elites are often one and the same,[18] so that to Russia's political elites what is good for Berezovskii is good for the country. It is common knowledge that these "oligarchs" wield overwhelming power in Russia's political arena since Russia's political leaders, overseen by the President, are largely beholden to and dependent on their dictates. Russia's oligarchs first came out "into the open" in the months prior to the 1996 presidential election, according to Boris Berezovskii, the most powerful and, as far as Yeltsin (and apparently Putin after him) was concerned, influential of all the oligarchs. Berezovskii admitted openly in 1996 that he had made decisions for the Yeltsin administration, including bringing Anatolii Chubais in to head Yeltsin's campaign team and conducting negotiations to bring Aleksandr Lebed into the government.[19] More, at their 1996 meeting in Davos, Switzerland just before the presidential election Russia's oligarchs floated the idea of canceling the elections if they seemed to be going badly for Yeltsin. This was not simply the idle speculation of an isolated Russian citizen.[20]

By pursuing their overriding objective of "wealth [exclusively] for themselves and their narrow constituency" of wealthy elites,[21] Russia's political leaders have sacrificed the interests of the Russian people to enrich themselves and their capitalist sponsors. Not for nothing did the World Bank in 1997 characterize Russia as a "robber capitalist" society whose wealth was "hidden, diverted or spent far from the economy in which it is produced"—all in the interests of a handful of "new Russians" completely indifferent to the needs of the masses.[22] Russia's robber capitalism can be characterized somewhat differently: in Marxist parlance, it is a peculiarly *parasitic* variant of capitalism wherein a small group of capitalists, divorced from the management of production itself, plunders the wealth created by Russia's working class, where "the motive causes of technical and, consequently, of all other progress disappear" and the section of the population engaged in services to the exploiters, in catering to their parasitic whims, steadily expands, among other things.[23]

Marxism defines social classes as

> Large groups of people different[iated] from each other by the place they occupy in a historically determined system of social production, by their relation (in most cases, fixed and formulated in law) to the means of production, by their role in the social organization of labor, and, consequently, by the dimension of the

share of social wealth of which they dispose and the mode of acquiring it. Classes are groups of people one of which [the ruling class] can appropriate the labor of another owing to the different places they occupy in a definite system of social economy.[24]

On this basis, and on the assumption that Russian society has made the transition to (a distinct form of) capitalism, I assume the existence of a post-Soviet Russian capitalist ruling class, the peculiar nature of which is discussed in greater detail in the next chapter. Having originated during the decline of the Soviet system, this nascent class eventually emerged full-blown with the assistance of Yeltsin and his fellow "democrats."[25]

The widely-held pluralist view that "national interest" takes account of the general and common benefits to society shared by all its members irrespective of individual or group preferences flies in the face of the class conflict rending Russia—indeed, all class societies.[26] To Marxists, this is a "mystification," a form of fetishism discussed below. The related idea that the state functions as a "common trustee" of society is also viewed by Marxists as a ruling class mystification to legitimize its rule.[27] Pluralism's construing the Russian executive's role as somehow representative of society's general interests is thus wide of the mark; it would be more accurate to say, following Marx and Engels, that the executive of the "modern representative state" manages the "common affairs of the whole bourgeoisie."[28] But because Russia has become a dependent state (dependency is discussed in detail in Chapter 2), the "common affairs" of its ruling class are managed not only by its political agents (and in some cases by the bourgeoisie itself) but by the latter jointly and *in conjunction with* the capitalists and their political agents of advanced capitalist countries: the US, West Europe, Japan, etc.

The assumption that the bourgeoisie dominates the state depending "on the contingent and provisional outcome of struggles to realize more or less specific 'state projects' "[29] is likewise fallacious, since the behavior of capitalist state actors is, save in exceptional instances, invariably predicated on the furtherance of the interests of the dominant bourgeoisie. As Marx demonstrated in *The Eighteenth Brumaire of Louis Bonaparte*, even in the (highly exceptional) case where a state *appears* to be independent of the economically dominant class, the modus operandi of its political leaders is to promote the interests of that class.[30]

State autonomy theory, which posits that the state and state actors function independently of social forces in society,[31] is also rejected here for its failure to explain the eternal class dynamic which underlies state behavior and societal phenomena more generally.[32] State theory also smacks of Hegelianism in its identification of the state as an autonomous sphere where the collision of private interests find their resolution,[33] and distorts Marxism when it imputes to it the claim that the expression of class interests is both automatic and solely economically determined.[34]

Marxism and International Relations

Although it is true that the creators of the doctrine formulated no explicit theory of international relations, much less a theorization of politics more broadly, a more or less cohesive framework may be strung together from various strands of Marxist theory. To begin with, Marxism holds that foreign policy is ultimately rooted in the domestic production relations of a given society, from its socioeconomic formation. The policy of any state, including its foreign policy, is thus, following the Marxist schema, conducted in the interests of the dominant class(es) of that nation or a community of interests of the ruling classes of various states.[35]

Because they are rooted in domestic processes international relations are, according to Marx and Engels, removed from but linked to the core domestic relations; they termed the former "secondary and tertiary phenomena, derived and transposed [from the national state], non-primary conditions of production."[36] Current Marxist thought holds that the imperialist phase of capitalism and its deepening economic globalization reflect an increasingly tighter interconnection between international relations and the socioeconomic processes within individual states.[37] Critics of Marxism allege, to be sure, that Marx (jointly with Engels) rejected the very idea of a states-system.[38] Such a charge is erroneous, for Marx, Engels and Lenin took great pains to analyze developments of states and to take into account their influence on world affairs as well as the influence of world affairs on states. A prime example of this was the letter from Marx to the Russian revolutionary Vera Zasulich which allowed for the possibility that underdeveloped Russia's peasant communes could enable Russia to successfully make the transition to socialism—even before the states of developed Western capitalism did.

To be sure, for Marxist analysis the nub of the issue is not so much relations between nation-states in abstract as between *national capitals*—here between the economic elites of Russia (whose interests are promoted by the political leadership) and those of the Western powers. This is a critical point, particularly since the interests of elites in capitalist nations diverge from those of the masses. Indeed, a key element of this study holds that precisely because their policies have diverged so widely from the preferences of the Russian people Russia's elites have been impelled to resort to the deception referred to earlier—to make it seem as if their foreign policy is conducted with the interests of the entire Russian people in mind when in fact they have, quite literally, sold their country out to the West. As one Western observer noted in June 1999, "the entire political class in Russia today has turned anti-Western and anti-American [catalyzed by the West's policy in Kosovo] . . . The minority school are the Yeltsinites . . . they are on the defensive" in their opposition to the mass sentiment.[39]

The activities of Russia's elites in August 1999 demonstrated that they had engaged in unheard-of levels of corruption—even for Russia, whose economy is dominated by criminal gangs. Reports of the laundering of Russian money by New York banks to the tune of tens of billions of dollars and of the Yeltsin clan receiving millions in kickbacks support this study's principal thesis that the Yeltsin-Putin leadership (Putin is essentially a creature of the Yeltsin forces) cares not one whit for the interests of the Russian people and is rather preoccupied solely with its own material enrichment and that of Russia's capitalists. The West, in turn, has willingly accommodated Russia's criminal leaders, "conspiring with the Kremlin to deceive voters" in Russia and the West by paying them off.[40]

Once again, Lenin captured the essence of this phenomenon when he wrote that Russian capitalists—he termed them "lackeys" of imperialism—hated the early Soviet government and did their utmost to undermine it. Realizing that they could not attain their objectives with forces inside Russia alone, they sought aid from abroad.[41] This study argues that today's Russian capitalists—the modern-day comprador bourgeoisie—have likewise sought aid from abroad for the purpose of enriching themselves. As a comprador bourgeoisie, they act as agents of foreign capital at the expense of Russia's working masses. And by relying on the Western capitalist powers to underwrite their pro-capitalist projects Russia's capitalists have become entangled in a web of dependency, which is the defining element of Russia's policy toward the West.

Ascertaining the link between foreign policy and class is a far from exact science. If we accept that explanation derives from the discovery of regularities (in the social sciences such regularities "cannnot be stated with the same generality and precision" as in the physical sciences),[42] then the explanatory power of Marxism and dependency theory is affirmed, for this study will demonstrate that Russia's leaders have, time after time, complied with the West's policy dictates, leading to "the loss of all [Russia's] positions and utter capitulation."[43]

Fetishism in International Relations

The Marxist conception of fetishism refers to the "direct *form of manifestation*" of relations that is reflected in our brains, but which fails to discern their real *inner connection*. It reveals the appearance of things, not their essence,[44] and is typified by the proposition that images are the "stuff of reality," that in human affairs "being and appearance are . . . one and the same."[45] A *meaningful* explanation must, to the contrary, disclose the *motive force* which underlies and impels policy and image. For Marxism, (economic) *interests* first and foremost are the motivaters of policymakers under capitalism; Western theories of politics are thus fetishized because they neglect the core factor of societal development, material production and socioeconomic classes. With their focus on nation-states and disregard for class groupings, IR theories such as realism are, according to this view, thoroughly fetishized.

In their emphasis on appearance in Russian policy vis-a-vis the West (and vice-versa), Russian policymakers have gone to extremes and resorted to outright deception. This was not always the case. During the first one-and-a-half years or so of post-Soviet Russia's existence its leaders pulled off, with minimal outcry, an open and almost total subservience to the West. Only when the crisis created by Western-style "reform" reached worrying proportions did Russia's leaders modify their policy toward the West, but only its *appearance* or *form* changed, for despite their machinations and their militant-sounding anti-Western rhetoric they could not disguise the fact that they were compliant with Western dictates.

Once again, it was Lenin who discerned the principal foreign policy aims of the capitalist class: the support, strengthening, and extension of their domination, which are masked, he argued, by "diplomatic tricks."[46] The Hungarian Marxist thinker Georg Lukacs also captured this deception in his characterization of bourgeois rule as the rule of a minority in the interests of that minority, whose "need to deceive the other classes . . . is inescapable."[47] This roughly follows Robert Jervis' observation that not only is thorough-going deception in international relations "quite common" (at least, it is argued here, by capitalist states) but that since a lie can help a state gain a dominant position in the world, it may not matter a great deal that it gains a reputation for lying. It also conforms to Jervis' thesis that if decisionmakers publicly make claims or commitments without acting accordingly, they may offend domestic public opinion or, at a minimum, will have to be wary of the public's reaction (higher political costs are generally incurred for deception in domestic politics than in international relations).[48] This is not to say that Russian policymakers are solicitous of the Russian people; it merely asserts that they must take account of mass sentiment in order to better manipulate their deception. Because there are limits to how far they can take their pro-Westernism, they must avoid even the appearance of breaching these limits.

Yeltsin's (and Putin's after him) farcical strategy of duplicity and secrecy, of concealing his dependency on the West and, conversely, the West's collaboration with Yeltsin, are central themes of this study. The lengths to which it has been taken by the Yeltsin leadership (and it seems, at the time of this writing in March 2000, the Putin government as well) is perhaps unprecedented in recent history.

Russian Foreign Policy and the Social Contract

The Russian leadership has, in conformity with the "social contract" thesis (originally applied to the USSR),[49] sought to "buy" legitimacy and compliance from the working class. But unlike Soviet leaders, who in trying to fulfil their part of the social contract made real efforts to "deliver the goods" in employment security, social welfare, and income equality, for failure to do so risked mass unrest,[50] Russia's leaders have been able to get away with policies which have eroded the standard of living and security of the people to a degree which almost defies comprehension. This is at least in part because they had the good fortune of taking power at a time when the Russian people, buffeted by repeated political and economic shocks and disappointments, had their expectations drastically lowered, their threshold for tolerance dramatically raised. The social contract thesis, when combined with the Marxist dialectical postulate that quantitative change brings about qualitative change,[51] helps to explain Russia's foreign policy deception, for the leadership's "reforms" threaten to break the social contract with the Russian people, intensifying popular unrest and forcing the leaders (with the connivance of their Western counterparts) to resort to the fiction that they are standing up for Russia against an aggressive West—especially as the Russian people identify Western-style reforms with their misfortune. The leadership knows that it must pay attention to the mass mood for, as Marxism contends, the effectiveness of the bourgeois state's foreign policy is conditioned at least in part by the degree of mass support it is able to extract.[52]

Marxist Critique of Theories of Politics

Marxism departs from and rejects the explanatory validity of the prevailing theories of politics and IR. The following is a brief critique of such theories.
Realism This study's Marxist approach radically diverges from the premises of realist theory, which regards politics as a kind of autonomous sphere held apart from other spheres.[53] Realism has come under fire from critics who attack it for its: ahistoricism, lack of a dynamic dialectic quality, extreme parsimony in explanation relative to the infinite complexity of its object of analysis,[54] tendency to make dubious assumptions about important factors of explanation, especially problematic when dealing with the seemingly self-defeating foreign policy of the USSR and of post-Soviet Russia,[55] imprecise definitions and lack of testability,[56] and above all, its unconcern with the internal structures of individual states.[57]
Institutionalism Although the "new institutionalism," which maintains that institutions play a uniquely central role in the explanation of politics, including foreign policy,[58] has become *de rigueur*, it is also fetishized and begs the central question of foreign policy explanation, namely, why do certain ideas and policies in which they are ultimately embodied prevail in a society (above all, among members of its foreign policymaking establishment) at a given time and under given circumstances, and from whence do such policies and ideas ultimately derive—that is, what are the key societal forces which impel leaders to adopt certain positions?
Institutionalism focuses on the *form* of causality instead of its *essence* by positing that "institutional frameworks define the ends and shape the

means by which interests are determined and pursued."[59] To be sure, institutions do influence interests, but the primary thrust lies with the "economic conditions of life and from social and political relations of [a] period which are in turn determined by [the] economic conditions."[60] The impulse to create, maintain, or change institutions springs from human *motivation* which is in turn determined by the material interests of people— a reflection of the socioeconomic class to which they belong.

Institutionalism cannot adequately explain why the leaders of the late USSR and especially post-Soviet Russia did not, for example, adopt a left strategy, that is, one which placed redoubled emphasis on the principles of socialism, instead of their disastrous policy of capitalist shock therapy and Western-style political "democracy." Institutionalism *reifies* institutions, making them causally central while understating the underlying socioeconomic forces which are the impetus for societal development.

Beliefs Marxism diverges radically from explanations that identify ideas and particularly the role of individual leaders as paramount. Analyses which accentuate the role of ideas in Soviet and Russian foreign policy[61] commit the Hegelian error of inverting the causal relationship. Marxism's trenchant phrase from *The German Ideology* retains its validity: "The ruling ideas are nothing more than the ideal expression of the dominant material relationships, the dominant material relationships grasped as ideas, hence of the relationships which make the one class the ruling one, therefore the ideas of its dominance."[62]

To be sure, Marxism does accord to ideas a causal influence, but to assume that such factors have preponderant causal weight, and/or to ignore the impact of the economic base—however removed it may be from the immediate phenomena being considered—misses the principal motive force in politics. Basing the explanation of the collapse of the USSR on the views and actions of individual leaders[63] is underdetermining because it fails to elucidate the critical elements of explanation, namely how and why broader and longer-term, anti-socialist trends which had been gestating in Soviet society gave Gorbachev's ideas credence among such a broad section of the elite ruling group, and without whose support they would not have ultimately prevailed. That can only be answered with reference to deeper economic and socioeconomic issues.

Learning Theory Learning at the level of cognitive integration (that is, establishing flexible but well-defined guidelines for resolving conflicts among goals) is a key precondition for coping successfully in a complex international environment; learning involves the reassessment of fundamental beliefs and values.[64] A change in fundamental (national) values does not necessarily imply learning, and one should be aware that what appears to be learning from historical experience may actually be the deliberate use of historical analogies by leaders to bolster their political preferences or rationalize bureaucratic or domestic interests.[65]

Philip Roeder correctly points out that learning theory is subjective and therefore explanatorily inadequate, because it is mainly description masked by an illusion of explanation.[66] But learning theory does serve a useful function for analysis as a gauge of policy change and its effectiveness. For as Franklyn Griffiths has noted, part of a system's "learning" involves its being able to learn to more realistically perceive the outside world, to pay greater attention to problems and the consequences of its actions, and to pursue new goals and methods.[67] As discussed in the conclusion, however, such an approach still fails to move learning theory much closer to being an explanatorily useful theory.

Notes

[1] Alvin Y. So, "Class Analysis and Radical Social Theories: Rediscovering the Missing Link," in Paul Zarembka and Ajit Sinha, *Research in Political Economy. Latest Developments in Marxist Theory*, Vol. 15 (Greenwich, CT: JAI Press, 1996), p. 24. See also Raymond Aron, "Social Structure and the Ruling Class," in Roy C. Macridis and Bernard E. Brown, eds., *Comparative Politics: Notes and Readings* (Homewood, IL: The Dorsey Press, 1972).

[2] Ralph Miliband, *Marxism and Politics* (Oxford: Oxford University Press, 1986), pp. 1-6; V. Kubalkova and A.A. Cruickshank, *Marxism and International Relations* (Oxford: Clarendon Press, 1985), pp. 1-2.

[3] Christer Pursiainen, "The Impact of International Security Regimes on Russia's Behavior: The Case of OSCE and Chechnya," in Ted Hopf, ed., *Understandings of Russian Foreign Policy* (University Park, PA: The Pennsylvania State Press, 1999), p. 123, argues that "at the moment, the demarcation line of the interaction between the level of international system and that of domestic policy remains obscure."

[4] See, for example, Jeffrey T. Checkel, *Ideas and International Political Change: Soviet/Russian Behavior and the End of the Cold War* (New Haven: Yale University Press, 1997), p. 119, which contends that the international structure is "indeterminate as a predictor of Russian and other great power behavior" in the

post-cold war world, and that Russian interests cannot be objectively inferred from its position in the international system. Janice Gross Stein, "Political Learning by Doing: Gorbachev as Committed Thinker and Motivated Learner," *International Organization*, Vol. 48, No. 2, Spring 1994, p. 160, argues that changes in international structures could not be "determining" for Soviet policy. See also R. Craig Nation, "Beyond the Cold War: Change and Continuity in US-Russian Relations," in *The United States and Russia Into the 21st Century* (Carlisle Barracks, PA: US Army War College Annual Strategic Conference, October 1997), pp. 5-6.

⁵ David Skidmore and Valerie M. Hudson, "Establishing the Limits of State Autonomy: Contending Approaches to the Study of State-Society Relations and Foreign Policy-Making," in David Skidmore and Valerie M. Hudson, eds., *The Limits of State Autonomy: Societal Groups and Foreign Policy Formulation* (Boulder: Westview, 1993), pp. 1-4.

⁶ David S. Lane, *The Rise and Fall of State Socialism: Industrial Society and the Socialist State* (Cambridge: Polity Press, 1996), p. 182.

⁷ Daniel Deudney and G. John Ikenberry, "The International Sources of Soviet Change," *International Security*, Vol. 16, No. 3, Winter 1991-92, pp 74-118. See also Sean Gervasi, "The Destabilization of the Soviet Union," *CovertAction Information Bulletin*, No. 35, Fall 1990, pp. 22-3. Deudney and Ikenberry, to be sure, acknowledge that the primary *causes* for the Soviet collapse and transition were domestic, but insist that the USSR's *response* derived from its external adaptation to a changed international environment. Others insist that there was no late Soviet economic "crisis," that its plunging economic statistics were matched by the West. See Stein, "Political Learning by Doing," pp. 157-8.

⁸ Geraint Parry, "Political Life in an Interdependent World," in Geraint Parry, ed., *Politics in an Interdependent World: Essays Presented to Ghita Ionescu* (Aldershot, Hants: Edward Elgar, 1994), p. 10.

⁹ Robert Legvold, "Soviet Learning in the 1980s," in George W. Breslauer and Philip E. Tetlock, eds., *Learning in U.S. and Soviet Foreign Policy* (Boulder, CO: Westview, 1991), p. 723. These are the standard categories used in international relations theory as defined by Kenneth Waltz. See Andrew Moravcsik, "Introduction: Integrating International and Domestic Theories of International Bargaining," in Peter B. Evans, Harold K. Jacobson, and Robert D. Putnam, eds., *Double-Edged Diplomacy: International Bargaining and Domestic Politics* (Berkeley: University of California Press, 1993), p. 5.

¹⁰ Peter J. Katzenstein, "The Role of Theory in Comparative Politics," *World Politics*, Vol. 48, No. 1, October 1995, p. 11.

¹¹ V.I. Lenin, *Collected Works*, Vol. 23 (Moscow: Progress, 1981), p. 43.

[12] "Marxism" here takes in primarily the writings of Marx, Engels, Lenin, but also includes those of other great thinkers in the Marxist tradition.

[13] Miliband, *Marxism and Politics*, p. 6.

[14] Friedrich Engels, "Letter to Heinz Starkenburg," (1894), in Howard Selsam and Harry Martel, eds., *Reader in Marxist Philosophy: From the Writings of Marx, Engels, and Lenin* (New York: International Publishers, 1963), pp. 201-2; Skidmore and Hudson, "Establishing the Limits," p. 1.

[15] One such erroneous interpretation of Marxism's supposed "reductionism," is Kenneth N. Waltz, *Theory of International Politics* (New York: McGraw-Hill, 1979), pp. 18-37. See also Theda Skocpol, "Bringing the State Back In: Strategies of Analysis in Current Research," in Peter B. Evans, Dietrich Rueschemeyer, and Theda Skocpol, *Bringing the State Back In* (Cambridge: Cambridge University Press, 1985), p. 25. Leon Aron, "The Foreign Policy Doctrine of Post-Communist Russia and Its Domestic Context," in Michael Mandelbaum, ed., *The New Russian Foreign Policy* (New York: The Council on Foreign Relations, 1998), p. 46, cautions against exaggerating the impact of "economization" on Russian foreign policy.

[16] Miliband, *Marxism and Politics*, pp. 1-9. This is the Soviet "structuralist" position, as articulated by adviser to the Soviet leadership Fyodor M. Burlatsky, in *The Modern State and Politics* (Moscow: Progress, 1978), p. 10. See also V.V. Aleksandrov, ed., *Leninskaia vneshniaia politika i razvitie mezhdunarodnykh otnoshenii* (Moscow: "Mezhdunarodnye otnosheniia," 1983), p. 10. The Marxist position on the interrelation between base and superstructure is found in Engels, "Letter to Heinz Starkenburg," pp. 201-2, and Idem, Preface to the third German edition of Karl Marx's *The Eighteenth Brumaire of Louis Bonaparte* (New York: International Publishers, 1987), p. 14.

[17] Friedrich Engels, "Letter to Joseph Bloch," in Robert C. Tucker, ed., *The Marx-Engels Reader* (New York: W.W. Norton, 1972), p. 642.

[18] This is clearly at variance with realism, which emphasizes that international actors act not out of material interest but on the basis of vague "interests defined as power." Hans J. Morgenthau and Kenneth W. Thompson, *Politics Among Nations: The Struggle for Power and Peace* (New York: McGraw-Hill, 1993), p. 5. For a good analysis of the Russian "revolving door" phenomenon, see Juliet Johnson, "Russia's Emerging Financial-Industrial Groups," *Post-Soviet Affairs*, Vol. 13, No. 4, October-December 1997, pp. 350-1. The claim by Michael McFaul, "State Power, Institutional Change, and the Politics of Privatization in Russia," *World Politics*, Vol. 47, No. 2, January 1995, p. 215, that "strong states can define and implement policies that challenge the preferences and undermine the interests of leading social interest groups, weak states cannot" certainly does not apply to Russia. Analyses which erroneously reject the political dominance of the capitalist

class in Russia include Igor Kliamkin, "The Outlook for Democracy in Russia," in Robert D. Blackwill and Sergei A. Karaganov, eds., in *Damage Limitation or Crisis? Russia and the Outside World* (Washington, D.C.: Brassey's, 1994), p. 29; Hans-Henning Schroder, "El'tsin and the Oligarchs: The Role of Financial Groups in Russian Politics Between 1993 and July 1998," *Europe-Asia Studies*, Vol. 51, No. 6, September 1999, p. 979; and Lilia Shevtsova, *Yeltsin's Russia: Myths and Reality* (Washington, D.C.: Carnegie Endowment for International Peace, 1999), pp. 218-20.

[19] *Financial Times*, October 31, 1996, p. 2.

[20] Matt Bivens and Jonas Bernstein, in Johnson's Russia List, No. 3068, February 24, 1999.

[21] Anders Aslund, "The Gradual Nature of Economic Change in Russia," in Anders Aslund and Richard Layard, eds., *Changing the Economic System in Russia* (London: Pinter, 1993), p. 33. Aslund, who I believe has been incorrect on practically every issue dealing with Soviet and post-Soviet affairs, gets this right.

[22] A good overview of Russia's robber capitalism is found in Grigory Yavlinsky, "Russia's Phony Capitalism," *Foreign Affairs*, Vol. 77, No. 3, May/June 1998, p. 70.

[23] *Fundamentals of Marxism-Leninism* (Moscow: Foreign Languages Publishing House, 1963), pp. 250-2.

[24] Lenin, *Polnoe sobranie sochinenie*, 5th ed., Vol. 39 (Moscow), p. 15, in *Great Soviet Encyclopedia*, Vol. 4 (New York: Macmillan, 1974), p. 270.

[25] I disagree with the opposition of Checkel, *Ideas and International Political Change*, p. 129, to any ideas-interest dichotomy. Checkel argues that they supplement each other, implying they are of relatively equal causal weight. The term "robber capitalism" was officially unveiled in a September 1997 World Bank report, *The State in a Changing World*. The report rated Russia the worst on fundamental measures of an efficient, credible state (the people's welfare, democracy, rule of law, etc.).

[26] For such a perspective, see Peter Shearman, "Defining the National Interest: Russian Foreign Policy and Domestic Politics," in Kanet and Kozhemiakin, *The Foreign Policy of the Russian Federation*, pp. 1-2.

[27] Miliband, *Marxism and Politics*, p. 66.

[28] Karl Marx and Friedrich Engels, *Communist Manifesto* (Chicago: The Great Books Foundation, 1955), p. 11.

[29] Bob Jessop, *State Theory: Putting the Capitalist State in its Place* (Cambridge: Polity Press, 1990), p. 9.

[30] Marx, *The Eighteenth Brumaire*, pp. 123, 131. Alan Gilbert, *Marx's Politics: Communists and Citizens* (New Brunswick, NJ: Rutgers University Press, 1981), p. 234, misinterprets Marx on this issue when he argues that Marx "saw the

Napoleonic state as typical of the development of late nineteenth-century European capitalism." On this point, see Derek Sayer and Philip Corrigan, "Late Marx: Continuity, Contradiction, and Learning," in Teodor Shanin, ed., *Late Marx and the Russian Road: Marx and the "Peripheries of Capitalism"* (London: Routledge, 1983), p. 85. Also see Derek Sayer, "The Critique of Politics and Political Economy: Capitalism, Communism and the State in Marx's Writings of the Mid-1840s," in *Sociological Review*, Vol. 33, No. 2, May 1985, and W.W. Wesolowski, "Marx's Theory of Class Domination (An Attempt at Systematization)," in Bob Jessop, ed., *Karl Marx's Social and Political Thought: Critical Assessments*, Vol. 2 (London: Routledge, 1990), pp. 177-9. See also Ralph Miliband, *The State in Capitalist Society* (New York: Basic Books, 1969), p. 93.

[31] See, for example, Skocpol, "Bringing the State Back In," p. 5; Idem, *States and Social Revolutions: A Comparative Analysis of France, Russia, and China* (Cambridge: Cambridge University Press, 1979). Lynn D. Nelson and Irina Y. Kuzes, *Property to the People: The Struggle for Radical Economic Reform in Russia* (Armonk, NY: M.E. Sharpe, 1994), p. 6, a study of Russian privatization, accepts as its frame of reference the autonomy of the state.

[32] Jessop, *State Theory*, p. 285. According to Jessop, "the various case studies advanced in favour of a statist approach . . . provide more evidence against than for statism" merely underscores this point. See also Rhonda F. Levine and Jerry Lembcke, eds., *Recapturing Marxism: An Appraisal of Recent Trends in Sociological Theory* (New York: Praeger, 1987), and especially p. 7. I disagree with the noted neo-Marxist Nicos Poulantzas, who accepted the concept of state autonomy and the state's functioning to secure the cohesion of society as a whole and not primarily of the capitalist class. The reality is that securing the cohesion of society is ultimately for the capitalists' benefit. On this point, see Simon Clarke, "The State Debate," in Simon Clarke, ed., *The State Debate* (London: MacMillan, 1991), p. 16.

[33] G. Shakhnazarov, "Sozdatel' nauki o politike," in G. Shakhnazarov et al, eds., *Marks i sovremennaia politicheskaia teoriia* (Moscow: Politizdat, 1986), pp. 8-9.

[34] See, for example, Skocpol, "Bringing the State Back In," p. 25.

[35] V.V. Aleksandrov, ed., *Leninskaia vneshniaia politika i razvitie mezhdunarodnykh otnoshenii* (Moscow: "Mezhdunarodnye otnosheniia," 1983), p. 9.

[36] *Sovremennye burzhuaznye teorii mezhdunarodnykh otnoshenii: kriticheskii analiz* (Moscow: Nauka, 1976), p. 5.

[37] A. Kortunov and A. Nikitin, "Ideinaia bor'ba vokrug metodoligicheskogo naslediia K. Marksa v sovremennoi teorii mezhdunarodnykh otnoshenii," in Shakhnazarov, et al, *Marks i sovremennaia politicheskaia teoriia*, pp. 122-3.

[38] Kubalkova and Cruickshank, *Marxism and International Relations*, p. 17.

[39] Thomas L. Friedman, *The New York Times*, June 8, 1999, p. A27.

[40] *The Economist*, August 28, 1999.

[41] V.I. Lenin, *Collected Works*, Vol. 28 (Moscow: Progress, 1981), pp. 23-6.

[42] Hempel and Oppenheim, "The Logic of Explanation," pp. 324-5.

[43] *Segodnia*, May 21, 1998, p. 6.

[44] N. Geras, "Essence and Appearance: Aspects of Fetishism in Marx's *Capital*," in Jessop, ed., *Karl Marx's Social and Political Thought*, p. 207.

[45] Christopher Smart, *The Imagery of Soviet Foreign Policy and the Collapse of the Russian Empire* (Westport, CT: Praeger, 1995), p. 22.

[46] D.G. Tomashevskii, *Leninskie idei i sovremennye mezhdunarodnye otnosheniia* (Moscow: Izdatel'stvo politicheskoi literatury, 1971), p. 36.

[47] Georg Lukacs, *History and Class Consciousness: Studies in Marxist Dialectics* (Cambridge, MA: The MIT Press, 1971), pp. 66-9.

[48] Robert Jervis, *The Logic of Images in International Relations* (New York: Columbia University Press, 1989), p. 74. For some interesting analyses of deception in foreign policy, see Ladislav Bittman, "The Use of Disinformation by Democracies," *International Journal of Intelligence and Counterintelligence*, Vol. 4, No. 2, 1990, John Pike, "Strategic 'Deception' Initiative," *Arms Control Today*, Vol. 23, No. 9, November 1993, and Gen. Akhromeev, *Pravda*, October 19, 1985.

[49] George Breslauer's theory of "welfare-state authoritarianism" comes under this rubric. See his *Khrushchev and Brezhnev as Leaders: Building Authority in Soviet Politics* (London: George Allen & Unwin, 1982). The social contract thesis was perhaps most clearly articulated by Peter Hauslohner, "Gorbachev's Social Contract," *Soviet Economy*, Vol. 3, No. 1, January-March 1987, especially pp. 55-8. Another interesting work which employs the social contract approach is Linda J. Cook, *The Soviet Social Contract and Why It Failed: Welfare Policy and Workers' Politics from Brezhnev to Yeltsin* (Cambridge, MA: Harvard University Press, 1993).

[50] Cook, *The Soviet Social Contract*, p. 3.

[51] *Osnovy Marksistkoi filosofii* (Moscow: Politizdat, 1959), pp. 223-33.

[52] Tomashevskii, *Leninskie idei*, p. 54.

[53] Morgenthau and Thompson, *Politics Among Nations*, p. 5; Robert Gilpin, *The Political Economy of International Relations* (Princeton: Princeton University Press, 1987), p. 43; Rey Kowlowski and Friedrich V. Kratochwil, "Understanding Change in International Politics: The Soviet Empire's Demise and the International System," *International Organization*, Vol. 48, No. 2, Spring 1994, pp. 217, 247.

[54] Stephen Gill, "Epistemology, Ontology, and the 'Italian School'," in Stephen Gill, ed., *Gramsci, Historical Materialism and International Relations* (Cambridge: Cambridge University Press, 1993), p. 46.

[55] Douglas W. Blum, "The Soviet Foreign Policy Belief System: Beliefs, Politics, and Foreign Policy Outcomes," *International Studies Quarterly*, Vol. 37, No. 4, December 1993, p. 374.

[56] Richard Ned Lebow, "The Long Peace, the End of the Cold War, and the Failure of Realism," *International Organization*, Vol. 48, No. 2, Spring 1994, p. 250.

[57] A particularly well-articulated and persuasive example of this position can be found in David Skidmore and Valerie M. Hudson, eds., *The Limits of State Autonomy. Societal Groups and Foreign Policy Formulation* (Boulder: Westview, 1993).

[58] Of the many works which employ such an approach in the study of Soviet and post-Soviet politics and foreign policy, the following stand out: Checkel, *Ideas and International Political Change*, pp. x-xi, 3; Blum, "The Soviet Foreign Policy Belief System"; Philip G. Roeder, *Red Sunset: The Failure of Soviet Politics* (Princeton: Princeton University Press, 1993), pp. 7-9; and Steven L. Solnick, *Stealing the State: Control and Collapse in Soviet Institutions* (Cambridge: Harvard University Press, 1998).

[59] Walter W. Powell and Paul J. DiMaggio, Introduction, in Walter W. Powell and Paul J. DiMaggio, eds., *The New Institutionalism in Organizational Analysis* (Chicago: University of Chicago Press, 1991), p. 28.

[60] Frederick Engels, "Karl Marx," in Selsam et al, eds., *The Dynamics of Social Change*, 34.

[61] Thomas Risse-Kappen, "Ideas do not Float Freely: Transnational Coalitions, Domestic Structures, and the End of the Cold War," *International Organization*, Vol. 48, No. 2, Spring 1994; Checkel, *Ideas and International Political Change*.

[62] Karl Marx and Friedrich Engels, *The German Ideology* (New York: International Publishers, 1974), p. 64.

[63] Stein, "Political Learning by Doing," takes such a position.

[64] Philip Tetlock, "Learning in U.S. and Soviet Foreign Policy: In Search of an Elusive Concept," in Breslauer and Tetlock, eds., *Learning in US and Soviet Foreign Policy*, pp. 35, 45.

[65] Jack Levy, "Learning from Experience in US and Soviet Foreign Policy," in Manus I. Midlarsky, John A. Vasquez, and Peter V. Gladkov, eds., *From Rivalry to Cooperation: Russian and American Perspectives on the Post-Cold War Era* (New York: HarperCollins, 1994), p. 75.

[66] Roeder, *Red Sunset*, p. 15.

[67] Franklyn John Charles Griffiths, "Images, Politics, and Learnings in Soviet Behaviour Toward the United States," Ph.D. diss., Columbia, 1972, p. 5. For a related approach, see also Karl Deutsch, *The Nerves of Government: Models of*

Political Communication and Control (New York: The Free Press of Glencoe, 1966), p. 164.

2 Capitalism and Dependency in Post-Soviet Russia

The previous chapter elucidated Marxism's class-based method of explanation of societal dynamics. This chapter elaborates on two aspects of class dynamics in post-Soviet Russia: the historical interconnection between the tsarist and post-Soviet variants of Russian capitalism, and dependency theory, as it involves class relations within Russia as well as between the ruling classes of Russia and the Western powers. It concludes with an assessment of how Russia's relationship with the West conforms to dependency theory.

Capitalism and the Russian Political System: Russian Capitalism Then and Now

Two events, Russia's economic meltdown of 1998 and the 1999 Bank of New York scandal, caused the debate in the West over who "lost" Russia to be joined in earnest. Of the various explanations advanced, one, from the pens of Richard Pipes and Martin Malia and widely accepted in the field, attributed Russia's corruption and overall decline to the "legacy of seventy years of communist rule."[1] As this study will argue, such a view actually stands things on their head and sidesteps the real explanation for Russia's current difficulties. A far more satisfying explanation is found in the writings of Ruth AmEnde Roosa, who correctly reminds us that an understanding of the nature of post-Soviet Russian capitalism presupposes a clear sense of its links with its *capitalist past*, since "many of the same geographical, ethnic, and cultural patterns that underlay the tsarist autocracy and made Marxism-Leninism possible in Russia from 1917 to the end of the 1980s persist today . . . any comprehensive analysis of Russia[n capitalist society today] . . . must proceed from an understanding of the functioning of capitalist institutions in the late Russian empire."[2]

The legacy of tsarist capitalism is thus a powerful one which precludes a productive, let alone humane, capitalism in Russia. And it is far more a "cause" of Russia's present-day "robber capitalism" than is Soviet communism in that, *without gainsaying the failings of Soviet socialism which was responsible for bringing about its own downfall and contributing to the problems of today's Russia*, the greed and corruption which pervades Russia's robber capitalism is in large part a *reaction to* the highly egalitarian and far more just Soviet socialism which succeeded in if not wiping out, at least repressing the greedy instincts of its would-be capitalists who are, in their present plundering activities, reverting to their rapacious pre-1917 existence. Interrupted and pent up for over seven decades in their self-serving quest, they now are, so to speak, making up for lost time and returning to the way of life interrupted by Soviet socialism. Russia is, in this sense, a victim of history reasserting and repeating itself.[3]

As historians (including Pipes himself) have documented, Russia's pre-Soviet capitalists were, like their successors in today's Russia, reactionary, self-seeking, interested only in short-term maximization of profits, placed little emphasis on honesty, industry, and thrift, tended to engage in conspicuous consumption and, most importantly, displayed an almost total disregard for the working people's interests. The net effect of such behavior was to brake Russia's economic development, weaken its position in the world economy and threaten its national self-sufficiency and independence—a result almost identical to that achieved by Russia's current capitalists. And as in today's Russia the capitalists of tsarist Russia pushed their country "to the edge of economic catastrophe."[4]

Although they aimed for self-sufficiency, by the onset of World War I Russia's capitalists were faced with the very antithesis of independence: the price of imports, consisting mainly of manufactures and industrial raw materials, rose precipitously, forcing Russia into the "colonial" position of exporter of primarily agricultural products and raw materials and importer of finished goods. Russia faced the prospect of "economic, possibly political enslavement" and its transformation into a "semicolony" of Western European powers, above all, Germany.[5]

Tsarist capitalism, like present-day Russian capitalism, was highly dependent on foreign capital, which imposed "crushingly usurious" conditions to make colossal profits and hindered Russia's own economic development.[6] Indeed, a native entrepreneurial class emerged in Russia only by the late nineteenth century. During most of the imperial period foreigners therefore filled a "crucial mediating role."[7] Foreign investment thoroughly dominated Russia's economy: from 1880-1914 alone the foreign share of Russia's total joint-stock capital rose from 17% to 47%,[8] and came to occupy a particularly strong position in key branches, such as the coal industry (almost all Donbass coal was owned by French and Belgian capital), oil (75% foreign-owned), and banks (over 75% foreign-owned).[9] In 1914 the two largest Russian industrial syndicates—Prodameta, the metallurgical group, and Produgol, the coal group—were controlled by foreign interests.[10] As discussed below, post-Soviet Russia differs from this scenario in its relatively tiny level of foreign investment.

Finally, big Russian capital was highly dependent on the tsarist state, even as the autocracy "willingly covered its eyes to the wild forms of exploitation of the industrial proletariat, satisfied the ceaseless entreaties of big capital, and permitted it to get around any rules and norms." Moreover, imperial Russia's state budget, like today's, was "exceptionally parasitic," the overwhelming part of it being devoted to supporting the dominance of the nobility and bourgeoisie and the upkeep of the tsar's family and its parasitic retainers. Like today, huge sums were paid directly from the state budget to the financial oligarchy.[11]

A significant part of the blame for tsarist Russia's technical backwardness—again, like today—lay with capital's merciless exploitation of cheap labor and use of primitive, outdated equipment.[12] And like their predecessors Russia's modern-day capitalists view as most attractive those spheres of the economy which require no large capitalist investments and produce a rapid turnover of capital. They are the very embodiment of Max Weber's "irrational" capitalist who seeks only immediate gain, lacks a work ethic,[13] cares only for power, money, and privilege, and regards Russia's working people as "simply an annoying, tiresome nuisance."[14]

Russian Capitalism and Soviet Socialism

Post-Soviet Russia's economic system is capitalist, but with a peculiarly Russian twist. While it is not the purpose of this study to enter into a polemic on the nature of the Soviet system, it is posited here that it was an amalgam of essentially socialist features mixed with some anti-socialist deformations—although the latter were understandable, given that the USSR was the world's first modern socialist society.[15] The argument that the Soviet system was fundamentally socialist is predicated above all on the fact that because the means of production in the Soviet Union were collectively and not privately owned—which made a reality of the Marxist thesis that a socialist society is one which has no class of property owners who gain income by virtue of owning property[16]—the (political) ruling groups in the USSR were prevented from viewing themselves and behaving as a distinct class. And because valuable property was held by the state, elites could not formally pass their status on to their offspring.[17]

All this changed with the demise of the Soviet Union. The USSR's established socialist structure fell victim not only to its own inherent failings, but it became increasingly susceptible during its last years to thrusts from anti-socialist cadres within its own ranks which spawned a kind of capitalist class *in embryo*. Soviet socialism nevertheless achieved undoubted successes, especially in light of the enormous obstacles it faced—not least being its having to go it alone, beset from its inception by a predatory and aggressive world capitalism, by armed occupation, economic boycott, and fascist attack. As humanity's first socialist system, it also manifested a number of the flaws which flowed from the autocratic society from whence it came.

Yet not only did the USSR's socialist economy grow at a remarkably rapid pace for much of its existence—especially impressive because it was under capitalist attack, military and otherwise, for a good part of that time,[18] but it also offered an unprecedented array of policies and programs which provided the Soviet working people with the fundamental guarantees of a decent life. On top of the USSR's attainment of a comparatively egalitarian distribution of wealth within the context of stable prices,[19] its socialist policies provided constitutional guarantees of full employment, a vast state- and enterprise-owned network of creches, kindergartens, summer camps, vacation homes, cultural centers for children and adults, paid pregnancy and maternity leave, special measures for women's safety at the workplace, educational and vocational training opportunities, relative equality in wages and job promotion, guaranteed minimum wage and pensions, free, universal access to education medical care, and many other benefits.[20] With this in mind, it was with understandable pride that Russia's Minister of Labor and Social Development M. Dimitriev told the June 1998 IMF Conference on Economic Policies and Equity of the USSR's "advanced, comprehensive, mature system," which fostered income equality and reduced poverty to a minimum.[21]

Last but not least, I designate the USSR socialist because it was the center of the proletarian internationalist movement. It expended substantial resources in support of anti-capitalist and socialist societies and movements, from Spain's anti-fascist Republican government to national liberation and socialist struggles in Africa, Asia, and Latin America, including Lumumba's Congo, Allende's Chile, South Africa's African National Congress, Angola's MPLA, the Vietnamese anti-imperialist struggle, Cuba, etc.[22]

The Russian Regime: Capitalist and Democratic?
The Economic Regime: Capitalism in the USSR and Russia

Post-Soviet Russia is a capitalist system rife with contradictions, where capitalist activity flourishes but productive investment has virtually disappeared, where traditional central planning has disintegrated but traditional economic relations are maintained, where production has declined drastically but mass unemployment has not yet appeared.[23]

The history of Russian capitalism, designated "robber capitalism" by the World Bank in 1997, is a sordid affair by any measure. Capitalism's social base developed during the latter decades of the Soviet era as the Soviet political system proved incapable of satisfying new social forces created by socioeconomic development. Indeed, the USSR experienced both the blessings and the drawbacks of its own successful modernization, which created urban centers and rapidly rising living standards but which also begat a new stratum of highly-educated workers who by the 1960s had become discontented with their comparatively shabby living conditions, inadequate services, low pay, etc. The intelligentsia also resented the ossification of cadres during the Brezhnev era and not being accommodated in the institutions of government. It felt ignored by the ruling elite, who governed largely in alliance with manual workers.[24]

Increasingly receptive to alternative conceptions of socialism—as well as to capitalism—and influenced increasingly by the "silent revolution" which exposed them to the outlook and norms of global capitalism, a development which was itself part of an increasing coalescence between epistemic communities,[25] the Soviet intelligentsia looked more and more favorably on capitalism which they believed would enable them to capitalize on their skills "in monetary terms"—that is, get rich quick and with as little expense as possible. Gorbachev and his later allies made common cause with this disgruntled stratum.[26] Having discussed for years how the transition to capitalism could be undertaken in the USSR, young pro-capitalist Soviet economists and even natural scientists began to forge links with their Western counterparts by the late 1980s.[27] Given the opportunity to witness and experience the Western lifestyle firsthand, they were receptive to that "good life" which they felt was theirs by rights.[28]

The dramatic rise in levels of mass communications thus helped to permanently alter the Russian intelligentsia's perception of life in the West, which now "became an ideal [for the Russian intelligentsia]" who had experienced a "bourgeoisification of aspirations." A sector of the political and economic elite thus developed into a latent capitalist class,[29] prompting enterprise directors by the late Soviet era to de facto seize many rights associated with property ownership.[30] The birth of the native, peculiarly Russian-style capitalism, which had been gestating for some years among sections of the elite was finally artificially and deliberately induced from above by Yeltsin's "democratic" regime, a counterrevolution of anti-socialist aspirations by the intelligentsia and the nomenklatura, the top appointed officials. All that was left for the Yeltsin government—"the godfathers of privatization"—to do was hand out property to those who would become Russia's new capitalist oligarchs.[31]

The Nature of Russian Capitalism

A distinctive feature of post-Soviet Russia's economy is that it is, much like tsarist capitalism, parasitic and, therefore, dysfunctional. Russian capitalists—above all, the big banks—display scant interest in investing in productive industrial capital, prefering instead to emphasize finance and, above all, the export of energy and raw materials. For this reason they do not easily fit into the standard Marxist image of a capitalist class which carries out its historical mission by means of the development of society's productive forces. The principal activity of Russia's capitalists is heavily skewed toward (1) the *indirect* appropriation of rental value of natural resources and energy from the world market (that is, from the world working class)—and not the labor of the Russian working class itself, and (2) the appropriation of the already accumulated surplus value produced by Soviet workers. The reproductive phase of Russian capitalism has not, at the beginning of the new millennium, taken hold, and Russia's economy has not developed to the point and in such a way that surplus value is produced via profitable production.[32]

The parasitic nature of Russia's capitalist class carries over to its relationship with international capitalist financial institutions. As McFaul notes, the financial oligarchs want Western financial institutions to remain engaged in Russia's economic reforms so that the elites do not have to pay for them. Transfers from the IMF to help close the budget deficit means the oligarchs pay that much less in taxes. "It would be irrational" for them, McFaul states, "to reject such free money."[33]

Nor has foreign investment rushed to Russia, in large part owing to the extremely unfavorable investment environment, including difficulties connected to taxation and repatriation of profits and political instability. At the same time, Russia's uncompetitiveness reduces somewhat the potential points of friction with Western capitalists which, as is discussed below, has important implications for Russia's relations with the West.

The only real success story (if only from the standpoint of those few who have actually benefited from it) in Russia's troubled and tragic transition to capitalism has been privatization, by means of which the wealth—including what was once the Soviet people's property, as well as "aid" from the West—was divided up among a handful of individuals who have become fabulously wealthy. The process was exposed as outright theft by former Finance Minister Boris Fedorov when he urged the IMF in 1997 not to give aid to Russia because no one "believes [IMF money will] be spent for the common good."[34] Indeed, it was estimated that from 1992-97 $62.3 billion were invested or deposited abroad in capital flight; others claim the actual figure is at least twice that, even as high as $300 billion.[35]

The History of Privatization in Russia

In the early stages of Russia's privatization Egor Gaidar, the "godfather" of Russian capitalism, set as one of his objectives the emulation of Russian Prime Minister Petr Stolypin who in 1907 had issued a decree to create "strong peasants" as the backbone of Russian reform. Gaidar sought to create not peasants but "strong capitalists" as the social support of the new Russian capitalism. Unlike Stolypin's Russia, however, where a class of rich peasants already existed and were helped by his decrees, Gaidar had no pre-existing capitalist class to draw on. He was therefore compelled to consciously create one "by decree" and literally from scratch.[36]

The new leaders thus acted with a furious rapidity bordering on desperation to dismantle the Soviet institutional structure and undo the accomplishments of the Soviet period. Despite his own warning in October 1991, even before the official privatization process began, that the "party-state" was already in the throes of privatization—"wildly, spontaneously, and often on a criminal basis"[37]—Yeltsin and his administration accelerated the privatization process to such a furious pace that one observer found it "surprising," given the customary snail-like slowness of the Russian bureaucracy.[38] In order to obfuscate his great robbery, Yeltsin even promised several times within the space of a few months that the worst of the reforms would be over within a year. This rapid privatization made it possible to as quickly as possible bring forth a capitalist class that would plunder the lion's share of the state's wealth while simultaneously preventing the emergence of a left opposition. Another Gadar tactic was to rapidly sever interrepublican ties as the "appropriate prelude to macroeconomic stabilization initiatives."[39]

Yeltsin, as President, oversaw the highly undemocratic privatization process. Because it did not matter to him what the "reformers" did, nor did he care one whit that the majority of the Russian people were severely harmed by the "reforms," he gave carte blanche to the designers of privatization, Gaidar and Chubais. Indeed, the latter two "were well aware that the 'voucher privatization' program [they pushed]. . . would lead to inevitable and large-scale speculative redistribution of these [voucher] checks to a small group of well-connected and well-financed indviduals."[40]

Yeltsin approved the first stage of privatization in December 1991 typically by decree and without public debate. He ignored pleas from the Supreme Soviet that privatization address improved economic performance and equity, and bypassed the latter's July 1991 law on Privatization Checks and Accounts which stipulated that investment accounts be set up for all the people so that they could buy state property. Such accounts were set up, but not until 1993, well after the most desirable enterprises had been privatized.[41] By 1993 over 70% of Russian economic output was in the private sector. And since the savings of the people had been largely wiped out by the price liberalization of January 1992 the agents for Russia's privatization, according to this scheme and as Chubais himself admitted, could only be from the nomenklatura and the "second economy," that is, criminal elements. What is more, when the voucher plan was instituted the legal requirement that those wanting to use large personal cash reserves must demonstrate that their money was acquired legally before buying property being privatized was nullified.[42] Thus was born robber capitalism.

The leadership allowed little public discussion prior to the first stage of privatization, clearly because they feared an outcry from an angry, impoverished populace. After the first privatization plan was approved by the Supreme Soviet in June 1992 Chubais proceeded within the space of four months to violate the principles of joint subordination with parliament pledged by Yeltsin by secretly preparing a very different plan, ostensibly aimed at creating a small number of "real owners."[43]

During the first wave of privatization enterprises of "strategic importance," that is, the crown jewels of the Soviet economy, were excluded from privatization; unprofitable "liabilities" were given, via vouchers, to labor collectives, who became their nominal owners. Only 10% of privatized enterprises were thus attractive investment opportunities at this stage.[44] Most voucher holders, moreover, unaware of or unconcerned with their vouchers, sold them to their bosses "for the price of a few bottles of vodka," a strategy that made sense, given that inflation had reduced the value of each voucher to the equivalent of precisely the price of a bottle of vodka.[45] More, some forty percent of Russians did not even participate in the privatization, and as early as September 1992 three-quarters of Russians expressed indifference or even opposition to the campaign.[46] Even arch-Westerner Tatiana Zaslavskaya accused Chubais, her ideological ally, of "pure deception" for knowing "perfectly well" that vouchers would lead to robbery, pure and simple.[47] The explosion of income differentials which resulted was made possible by the exclusion of the masses from the first stage of privatization.

As soon as Yeltsin signed the undemocratic decree on the new voucher plan in August 1992 laying the groundwork for rapid privatization the West's public relations machinery shifted into high gear: money funded by the US government, especially USAID, went to pay Western "experts" on economic reform to use their public relations skills to convince the Russian people that privatization was in their interests.[48] That the Western ruling circles would resort to such a deception should come as no surprise, given that even the European Bank for Reconstruction and Development's (EBRD) 1999 report on Russia acknowledged that "while paying lip service to democracy, Western governments actually favored authoritarian policies. They urged Boris Yeltsin to override opposition to his economic policies."[49]

The entire privatization process was, indeed, thoroughly undemocratic in the sense that it was carried out without mass political support and was not approved by the Duma and the people. Russians and Westerners in charge of the Russian economy even bragged after privatization had been completed that every major regulation on privatization was introduced by presidential decree.[50]

The second wave of Russian "reform" began in fall 1993 when, following Yeltsin's "coup" and subsequent abolition of parliament, decrees were issued liberalizing energy prices and trade, raising interest rates and, most importantly, accelerating privatization. The leadership's objective in all this was to meet the conditions of the IMF loan agreement Russia had signed in May.[51] By late 1994 enterprises with over 80% of the industrial labor force had already been privatized, most under insider control, while non-industrial labor remained in state hands. Subsequent privatization, completed by voucher and cash auctions, was dominated by banks and investment funds with close links to enterprise management and to local, regional, and national political authorities,[52] which lent an ironic twist to Yeltsin's promise to create "a million property owners rather than many millionaires." As one study noted with more than a little understatement, later privatization of the "large and valuable companies" was done "in a way that did not benefit ordinary Russians."[53]

Capitalism and Political Power in Russia

In December 1993 the Russian leadership resolved, on the basis of a proposal by Gaidar, to prevent the seizure of power by the opposition by making a transition to "enlightened authoritarianism," above all, based on the creation of an "evolving oligarchy," a "new political and business class created by the government."[54] This was a project far more ambitious than simply creating a capitalist class. The Yeltsin government therefore resolved to follow a strategy of promoting the development of above all so-called bank-led financial-industrial groups (BLFIGs), as opposed to industry-led financial-industrial groups (ILFIGs). With the willing cooperation of the Yeltsin "reformers," the BLFIGs achieved power on the strength of three developments: their acquisitions of the key Russian media; their roles—especially salient since the 1993 Duma elections—in financing the campaigns of "reformist" and government parties; and via the revolving door between executive positions in banks and the government. They were deliberately nourished and nudged along by the Yeltsin government, who "vilified" the ILFIGs, this in spite of Yeltsin's decree on FIGs in December 1993 which promised aid to the ILFIGs.[55]

The BLFIG leaders, along with those of the huge energy concerns Gazprom and LUKoil, have remained close to the Russian government and wielded "political power disproportionate to [their] actual economic importance and public support in Russia." Seven of them controlled, by oligarch Boris Berezovskii's 1997 estimate, at least 50% of Russia's economy.[56] Indeed, as one leading analyst points out, Russia's oligarchs became government officials or remained as "shadow figures" in the Yeltsin (and now Putin) government, demonstrating the "shameless coupling of money and power," a coupling so entrenched that, contrary to some assertions that the dominance of Russia's oligarchs somehow subsided with the accession to the presidency by Putin in December 1999, it was said to be hopelessly naïve to even imagine that Putin might "start dismantling the robber capitalist system when its most symbolic figures are key shadow players in Putin's game."[57]

Once the oligarchs solidified their positions in Russia's economy and government the bribe money began to flow freely, enabling Russia's oligarchs to amass "enormous political power" as they literally paid off the top government leaders to rule in their interests—and affirmed the precepts of Marx and Engels in the process. In late 1997, for example, it was reported that the architect of Russia's privatization, Anatolii Chubais, and four of his allies each received $90,000 from Chubais' friend and former colleague, Vladimir Potanin, head of the huge Uneximbank. Just a few months earlier Chubais had been accused—and never denied—reports that he had profited from the investment of "vast sums" of borrowed money in the state short-term bond market. These accusations against Chubais and other government officials were just the tip of the iceberg, however, and reports of bribery would surface almost daily,[58] simply part of a "natural" capitalist process, according to Russia's "reformers," in which "large banks are rich. Money, in every country, is an influential force and when the political system is not stable, everybody strives to use money as a political tool."[59] Another Russian source justified the new power of money in Russia with the claim that because the puralist, dispersed character of elite organization, a la Dahl, Sartori, Lipset, Schumpeter, et al, was a key characteristic of "democracy," the revolving door between big business and top government posts must be viewed as a boon to Russian "democracy."[60]

The leaders of the BLFIGs and directors of Gazprom and LUKoil comprise Russia's oligarchy. The initial impetus for the huge political power they wielded came from two early sources: the rapid liberalization of the Soviet financial system in the late 1980s, which allowed thousands of undercapitalized banks to establish their positions in the economy quickly, often with the direct participation of the government, and shock therapy, which enabled the best-connected bankers to make money in the highly inflationary, unstable environment while most other economic institutions were impoverished. Leading bankers were thus well-placed to expand their political influence.[61]

The legal basis for FIGs was established in November 1995, but it was the 1995 "loans-for-shares" program (see Chapter 6 for a fuller discussion) which catalyzed the BLFIGs' "leap from important players in the Russian economy to dominant financial-industrial conglomerates . . . " The loan-for-shares also contributed to the symbiotic relationship between the oligarchs and the state in that the dependence of the former on government largesse was increased and the oligarchs were encouraged to seek greater control of the government so as to reduce the risks of their dependency on state officials. It also consolidated the relationship between Chubais and the oligarchs, manifested in the latter's funding of Yeltsin's 1996 presidential election campaign.[62]

Following Yeltsin's 1993 decree on FIGs key supporters of the ILFIGs began to rapidly decline in power. In March 1997 the Yeltsin government eliminated the ILFIG-friendly Ministry of Industry and placed those allied with the BLFIGs in positions of authority,[63] a favoritism which served the purpose of enabling the BLFIG tycoons to rapidly acquire vast fortunates while it fulfilled the objectives of anti-communist leaders in Russia and the West to dismantle and destroy the industrial achievements of the socialist USSR.

A peak of BLFIG power was reached during the 1996 presidential elections, when the leading BLFIGs bankrolled Yeltsin's campaign and thus sent an unmistakable signal that the Yeltsin administration was partisan toward that class grouping. Indeed, Marx and Engels' famous thesis of the executive of the modern state as a committee managing the common affairs of the whole bourgeoisie was conclusively borne out in 1996 when an unwritten understanding was reached between the BLFIGs and their agents in the government led by Chubais, first and foremost, that they would make sure that no economic measures were introduced contradicting the interests of the natural resources sector, above all, the giant Gazprom and LUKoil companies.[64]

To be sure, harmony reigns by no means supreme among Russia's big capitalists. In fact, as the 1997 "bank war," sparked by the state sale of Sviazinvest and which led to the so-called *"semibankirshchina"* (rule of the seven banks) demonstrated, there is much recalcitrance among the members of the classs—in spite of the efforts of the executive to manage the affairs of the entire class. This also demonstrates the decisive role of the state in Russia's capitalism. The relationship between Russia's capitalist tycoons and the state is, as in all capitalist societies, a symbiotic one, but in Russia's case the capitalists are inordinately and directly dependent on the state. As Chubais' role at the February 1996 Davos meeting of the big capitalists proved, the Russian state acts as a "moderator" between the major capitalists—who are the "manufactured political base" of Chubais himself, the "creatures of his own privatization policies." What is more, in Russia official funds are managed through "authorized" commercial banks and not the central bank or state treasury. Some 90% of banking money in the market is, in fact, a free gift from the government, which enables the tycoons to purchase companies with the government's money.[65]

It should also be pointed out that the powerful role played by the Russian state in the affairs of capitalism does not at all gainsay the Marxist thesis that the capitalist state is run in the interests of the capitalist class, nor does it confirm the state autonomy thesis for, as noted in the Introduction, Marx asserted to the contrary that no matter how powerful or seemingly independent the executive governmental power, it invariably operates in the interests of the capitalists. This is certainly true of Russia.

The Nature of Russia's Political Regime

How do we characterize the Russian political system within the context of such inegalitarianism and dominance by a tiny group of wealthy capitalists? (Bourgeois) "democratic" theory is in "considerable disarray" on the question, having lagged behind the new realities of the world system.[66] Indeed, there are those who insist that because post-communist transition governments do not fit the conventional models of right-wing societies emerging from authoritarian regimes of Southern Europe and Latin America, students of post-communist political systems would be better served by not even attempting a general theory.[67]

One influential view maintains that economic development and "democracy" are positively correlated, since industrialization empowers the subordinate classes and makes it difficult to exclude them politically. Capitalist development, in this view, thus promotes "democracy."[68] With respect to Russia, another perspective argues that, however poorly it may be institutionalized, Russia allows political debate, party competition, electoral contests, and constitutional checks and balances, and is therefore at least a democratizing society.[69] To Michael McFaul, Russia meets Schumpeter's "minimalist" definition of a democracy: "the institutional arrangement for arriving at political decisions in which individuals acquire the power to decide by means of a competitive struggle for the people's vote."[70]

A contrary, Marxist, view asserts that Western or capitalist "democracy" is actually undemocratic, given the domination and control of its polity by a plutarchy of the wealthy few, which makes the goal of the Russian ruling class—creating capitalism and its political adjunct, Western "democracy"—a contradiction in terms.[71] As argued by a leading Russian political analyst, even on the basis of McFaul's Schumpeterian definition of a democratic polity Russia falls far short of being a democratic society, given the dominance of the former nomenklatura and their inaccessibility and lack of accountability to the people.[72]

To Marxists, *capitalist* democracy's *formal* freedom and equality, which makes all members of society equal *only before the law*, reflect and are patterned after the formal freedom and equality of commodity exchange. Just as the capitalist economy is controlled by a series of competitive exchanges in which members of society participate voluntarily under conditions of universal freedom and equality, so is bourgeois democracy defined by a series of competitive elections in which all members participate under those conditions. Beneath the purely formal equality, however, lurks capitalist exploitation from the ruling class monopoly over the means of production and the means of coercion by its agents. In practice, therefore, the working class is shut out of capitalist politics because as "wage slaves" they are "so crushed by need and poverty" that they "have no time for democracy" and because, unlike the bourgeoisie, they lack the financial resources for political power.[73]

Capitalist "democracy" is thus really not democratic. As one noted Russian analyst has pointed out in reference to the Russian polity:

> It was Russian executive power, with Yeltsin at the head, that was the body least interested in the development of democracy. Already by the fall of 1991, Yeltsin made an attempt to replace the existing system of his "presidential vertical," excluding other political bodies from the decision-making process. The presidential ideal was a new authoritarian regime of a liberal-technocratic orientation. Only later (in 1993) did he switch to a new orientation—more statist and more

populistic—and his autocratic style of rule became even more evident.[74]

Others, increasingly disenchanted with the "democratization" of Yeltsin's Russia, counter that not only is the Yeltsin regime authoritarian and Russia's "reformers" "profoundly undemocratic,"[75] but there has been a distinct lack of openness in the Russian political debate. This was brought to light in a report by the European Institute of the Media which concluded that candidates in the 1996 election were less free to get their views across and the voters were given less information than in the Soviet presidential election of 1991.[76] Indeed, Yeltsin himself made the glaring admission in May 1998 that the fact that only a few publications in Russia had "genuine independence" seriously impaired the "people's right to objective and truthful information."[77] In light of the above, post-Soviet Russia in no way fits the pattern described by Philippe Schmitter of the initial stage of "modern democracies" characterized by emerging compromises with no dominant group imposing its format on a hybrid regime.[78] In Russia an alliance of the "godfathers" of capital—the Yeltsins, Chubaises, et al—and the oligarchs rule with an iron grip.

If, in addition to the above, it is accepted that there can be no real political democracy without economic democracy, then the Russian regime is still less democratic. To be truly democratic it would need, at a minimum, a dominant social sector within a mixed economy and democratic regulation of the economy.[79] Even when established, Western-style "democracy" is accompanied by an extreme skewing of income distribution, by "exploitation and oppression at the workplace, within the schools . . . bureaucracies, and . . . families."[80] It thus seems to be an unfortunate reality that market "reform" can succeed only on the condition that the net benefits accrue to powerful groups who have formed dominant political coalitions, and that such politicians are insulated from punishment meted out those who bear the costs of the reform.[81]

Not only is it accepted that market reforms must precede democratic consolidation—which did not happen in post-Soviet Russia—if liberalization is to succeed, but democratic rule has tended to hinder, not help, the establishment of a market economy, and this has the grim implication that the simultaneous introduction of (Western) political "democracy" and capitalist markets in post-communist Russia is incompatible and that only Pinochet-style authoritarian regimes can force through painful capitalist reforms.[82]

In light of the foregoing it must be concluded that Yeltsin's Russia is far from democratic. It is, rather, authoritarian, following the classical definition of authoritarianism as a polity in which only a part of society must validate that polity.[83] The rejoinder that Russians have the right to vote is not convincing, for mere formal right does not at all make a polity democratic. Under the assumption that political dynamics are directly dependent on the economy, the interests of Russia's working masses under the Yeltsin-Putin regime were sacrificed to the personal (above all material) interests of the economic elites and their political agents. Contrary to the claim that privatization has given declining state firms "real owners with real desires to assert their rights as investors," the post-Soviet nomenklatura privatization[84] doomed Russia to a "quasi-parasitic capitalism with little dynamic for development" and which benefited only the wealthy.[85]

In Yeltsin's-Putin's Russia a polity has formed which, despite "official declarations in favor of democracy in the abstract, correlate[s] poorly with observable behavior affecting specific real interests and international relationships." The Russian leadership has therefore resorted to a deception consonant with O'Donnell and Schmitter's distinction between liberalization of an authoritarian regime—clearly more applicable to Russia—and full democratization: in the former, powerful minorities who seek to defend their privileges find it advantageous to adopt an appearance of sympathy for democracy.[86]

Dependent Russian Capitalism

A factor vital in the enrichment of Russia's capitalists has been Russia's alignment with—and subordination to—the West. How the new Russian elites managed this alignment in defense of their interests is a function of Russia's dependence on the West.[87] The dependency of Russia's elites on the elites of the advanced capitalist powers has enabled them to legitimize both their ideological orientation toward private gain and their policies, domestic and foreign, including the privatization of state property and foreign policies supportive of the West.

Russia and Dependency Theory. The Dependency Approach

Although it may seem obvious by the turn of the century that the l˻ ˻ders of Russia have created a state dependent on the West, no study has attempted to explain Russian foreign policy from the standpoint of dependency theory.[88] The dependency approach derives from several not entirely compatible streams in (neo-)Marxism, beginning with Paul Baran and Latin American economists, especially Raul Prebisch, associated with the UN Economic Commission for Latin America. Crystallized by the mid-1960s in the writings of Andre Gunder Frank, Teodoro dos Santos and others, it restated Marxist ideas about Latin American development with the aim of countering the theories of development articulated by such Western liberal thinkers as Walt W. Rostow, Seymour Lipset, and Gabriel Almond.[89]

Employing the dependency approach can be problematic, not least because it cannot be associated with one single theoretical position owing to the wide diversity of approaches it takes in. This is why one of the "classic" texts on dependency rejects a single, unified theory and prefers to address "situations" of dependency instead.[90] Nevertheless, especially when viewed in connection with the disarray pervading the body of international relations theory more generally, this should not be considered an invalidating condition for dependency theory.

The classical case of dependency is defined as a conditioning situation wherein the economies of poorer countries (the periphery) are determined by the development and expansion of wealthy countries (the core) and to whose dictates they largely submit. This unequal relationship entails an international division of labor between primary producers and wealthy manufacturers. In the dependent periphery the traditional export sector remains primary, limiting the development of the internal market and perpetuating backward relations of production and the dominance of the political oligarchy. The dependent state devotes considerable resources to servicing foreign debts and receives a large amount of foreign economic assistance relative to the size of its economy.[91]

The periphery is not only exploited economically, but is also dominated by the stronger militaries and government apparatuses of the core states.[92] Dependent states tend to implement anti-democratic policies, enforce strict internal security, and produce or import luxury consumption goods at the expense of more substantive development, all under the watchful eye of the core. The bulk of the population receives a comparatively small portion of the country's wealth and a lower level of social welfare than in the non-dependent states.[93] Finally, even locally-owned enterprises of dependent states provide little or no capital for industrialization because much of the profit simply goes back to foreign financial institutions to pay off loans, while what remains tends to be spent by peripheral capitalists on conspicuous consumption, especially given the meager incentives for them to invest in industrial production for the local market where wages and the number of workers in export production are low.[94]

An Assessment of Dependency Theory

The dependency approach is not without its detractors, who reject its assumption that "the more a nation's economy is penetrated by loans, investments, and aid, and reliance on external trade, the more dependent the nation is."[95] They maintain that formerly poor, dependent states such as Taiwan and South Korea—not to mention Canada—have "developed" and even achieved relative affluence. This view of "dependent development"—development within dependence—thus accepts a compatibility of foreign capital and the prosperity of dependent countries.[96]

Others correctly take issue with such suppositions. Roger Peet argues that the development of the "Asian tigers" was only "one component of the transition from Fordist to post-Fordist regimes of accumulation and is therefore not generalizable to the rest of the third world in the foreseeable future." In his view, even the most successful case of dependent development, South Korea, relies strongly on foreign capital and technology and its dependence has actually increased as a consequence of the Asian crisis of 1998. "Dependency theory may have its problems," Peet argues, but "jettisoning the entire approach on the basis of the limited achievements of [South] Korea and Brazil over the last twenty years goes too far."[97]

Marxism and Dependency

Dependency has therefore "withstood the test" in general, and its assumptions have been confirmed by reality.[98] Further, the Marxist objection to the world-system argument (which defines the domestic class struggle solely in terms of the world bourgeoisie and proletariat, and thus pays insufficient attention to the class dynamics within the dependent state) is upheld here on the grounds that the world-system approach unjustifiably relegates peripheral states to the status of passive "administrative committees" of foreign capital.[99]

Lenin's thesis of a "comprador" bourgeoisie class striking a bargain, to the detriment of its own countrypersons, with foreign capitalist interests conforms to a central tenet of dependency, namely, that the comprador bourgeoisie defends the interests of foreign domination. One of the classic works on dependency accordingly underscores the intimate linkage between the national and foreign bourgeoisies which allows the former, though dependent on international support for its survival against the forces of nationalism and revolution, to retain dominant influence in its own country.[100]

The variant of dependency theory adopted in this study is thus compatible with Marxism in that its primary, though by no means exclusive, focus is on classes rather than relations between state entities and because it accepts that those who make the ultimate decisions in the peripheral states are the elites of those countries, although as comprador bourgeoisie they are strongly influenced, even dictated to, by elites in the dominant states. In the case of Russia policymakers feel compelled at times to resist the West on at least some foreign policy issues, if only to put on a show to avoid antagonizing the Russian people, whose tolerance of the West and of Western-style "reforms" is at the breaking point as a result of the devastating effects of "reforms." Dependency therefore implies a more complex interrelationship between core and periphery: while the core ruling classes impose the terms on the dependent peripheral ruling classes, the latter willingly accept such terms as in their interests but make the final decision whether to accept them and how they are to be implemented.[101]

It is widely assumed by those who are at least minimally conversant in Marxist thought that Marx and Marxists have perceived capitalism as an inevitable but, however horrific in its effects, ultimately progressive development for the lesser developed world. Marx's writings, in this view, imply an "optimistic and unilinear determinism" which predicted that the peripheral countries would develop as a mirror-like reflection of the core.[102] It is widely accepted, according to this view, that dependency theory modified Marxism by asserting that the effects of capitalism on the periphery are negative and exploitative. Some on the left even accept that Marx (and Lenin) failed to foresee the dependency phenomenon.[103]

Contrary to the above, this study follows Robert Packenham's contention that the Marxist tradition is "broad and flexible," that dependency theory is consistent with Marxist ideas in that, like the ideas of Marx and Lenin, it accepts more broadly that capitalism is an exploitative system and must be replaced by socialism.[104] And perhaps most importantly, scholars point to Marx's writing on Russia as an example of his willingness to reject the aforementioned narrow evolutionist straitjacket which postulated the "mimicking" of the industrially advanced nations by the developing. In his fourth and final draft of an 1881 letter to the Russian revolutionary Vera Zasulich, Marx argued that its underdeveloped but socialist-oriented peasant communes could enable Russia to leap over capitalism and achieve socialism ahead of the more industrially developed West—provided the communes utilized the advanced technology of the West. From this standpoint Marx accepted that lesser-developed societies would *not necessarily* mimic those more advanced. He anticipated, at least in embryo, later ideas of global interdependence, uneven development, and the mutual impact of social transformations, and thus validated that dependency theory is consistent with the general thrust of his ideas.[105]

Dependency and Foreign Policy

Dependency theory was not originally conceived to explain the foreign policies of dependent states,[106] but it has come to be accepted that dependent states are compelled to "exhibit foreign policy compliance with the preferences of dominant countries" because of the latter's assymetric control over the former's (primarily economic) relations. The compliance of dependent states with the dictates of the core powers can also be obtained, apart from foreign investment, by political pressure, including military, and various forms of assistance.[107] Accordingly, it is a core postulate of this study that Russia—or more accurately the Russian financial oligarchy, and especially those economic elites which make the greater part of their money from foreign commercial relations—has become "greatly dependent on the leading industrialized nations," and thus has a strong incentive to maintain good relations with the West. As a result, its elites "are likely to oppose any attempt by the government to return to a foreign policy that puts [it] at odds with the West and jeopardizes [its] efforts to enter the world economy and exposes it to the danger of being cut off once again both from Western investments and from world markets."[108]

A kind of reverse dependence on the dependent state by the core state also exists, a complement to the periphery's dependence on the West. While dependent states depend on the core for assistance, purchase of raw materials, etc., the core depends on the periphery for raw materials, cheap labor, and markets—although core nations are naturally in the "position of power."[109] In Russia the core's support of—and dependence on—the dependent elites is a political one, necessary to alleviate the social costs of the transition to capitalism and guard against an authoritarian anti-Western—or, what would be a worse scenario for the elites, a socialist—Russia, "feeding off the popular dissatisfaction of economic dislocation."[110]

Dependency Theory Updated: Still Relevant?

By the 1980s the dependency paradigm had fallen out of favor, in large part because socialism, the alternative form of development to capitalism, was no longer viewed as tenable after the decline and fall of the socialist bloc. The newly-industrialized countries in the third world, on the other hand, many experiencing "democratization," seemed to demonstrate that dependency could be overcome.[111] To begin with, the assumption that socialism is untenable and that it has not done away with the effects of dependency (elimination of government services and poverty for the working people, extreme income differentials, etc.) is not confirmed by reality, as the successes of socialist Cuba—including its superior medical and educational systems available to all citizens, even under the most ferocious assaults from US capitalism—and others demonstrate. It is ironic, moreover, that almost coincident with the fading of dependency theory in the 1980s dependent countries of the Third World were squeezed even more by and became still more dependent on the industrialized powers; by the late 1990s the third world was in the throes of a deep crisis.[112]

Financial institutions demand that dependent states end government subsidies and currency devaluation to make goods more favorably priced for export, stripping trade barriers and causing mass unemployment. And the exposure of dependent states to more efficient global competition from the core nations is disastrous for their industrial production.[113] The consequences of globalization are so far-reaching, in fact, that political leaders "need to be perhaps as accountable to international market forces as they are to [their own] electorates."[114] This leads to a paradoxical situation whereby the power of governments within their own territories has never been greater even as their real power is actually reduced, since their capacity to control events in their countries and among their own populations is inhibited by developments beyond their borders,[115] a phenomenon connected to what Antonio Gramsci termed a "passive revolution" and involving, in this case, the thrusting of the "new world order" on weak states. Economic developments in such states (as Russia) tend to emanate not from the local economy but are a reflection of international developments transmitted to the periphery.[116]

Does Russia Fit the Dependency Criteria?

Russia's $150 billion debt to the West had by 1999 become an albatross around its neck, and led to a vicious cycle in which Russia required financial infusions to meet its debt service, which itself continues to grow and retards Russia's economic growth. According to one estimate, the $15-20 billion per year debt service in 1999 was so high that, if paid, it would wipe out all funds needed for the budget.[117]

The increasing share of raw materials in Russia's export structure has validated the claim that Russian "reformers" seek to neutralize their nation as a Western competitor and make it possible for Western corporations to exploit Russia's natural resources.[118] Russia has indeed become a supplier of primarily cheap raw materials and energy—substantially more so than during the Soviet era—and a supplicant for economic aid from abroad. The "massive siphoning off" of Russia's raw materials and energy has oriented each sector of the economy toward dependence on the world market.[119]

The increasing predominance of such "primitive" factors as raw materials and unskilled labor in the production of Russian exports had become "considerably worse" in 1997. Russian exports of raw materials and semi-finished goods to the "far abroad" jumped from 84% of total exports in 1992 to 90% in 1996, while finished products declined from 16% to 10%, in spite of a considerable increase in deliveries of arms and specialized equipment.[120] By 1995 Russia's production of light industry goods had fallen to crisis levels, a mere 15% of 1990. The share of imported light industry goods on the domestic market had also grown dangerously high, fully 88% of the total in 1995.[121] Russia's imports, which in 1991 made up 14% of the domestic consumer market, had risen to almost 40% by 1994[122] and by 1996, 55% of Russia's daily consumption, including food, was imported, a consequence of the government's deliberate refusal to protect Russia's collapsing national industry.[123]

The emphasis on export of primary products is especially pronounced in relation to the West. In 1996 the developing states' share of Russia's exports—overwhelmingly fuel and raw materials—was "still extremely small," that of the developed countries disproportionately large. From 1985 to 1995 alone, West Europe's share of Russia's exports rose from 27.6% to 48%, that of the USA from 0.4% to 5.2%. By contrast, the proportion of machinery, equipment, and means of transportation as a share of Russia's exports steadily fell from 13.6% in 1985 to 5% in the first half of 1995. Between 1992 and 1995 alone, the share fell almost by one-half.[124]

The boost in the share of extractive industries and exports at the expense of processing industries gives rise to the "Dutch disease," which entails the appreciation in the real exchange rate and increased opportunity cost for import-competing manufacturing industries. Over time, such factors lead to the downscaling of domestic manufacturing, although in Russia's case the crisis has been so all-embracing that *both* processing and extractive industries have declined.[125]

The reliance of dependent states on unprocessed goods can be problematic in that primary goods prices not only decline relative to manufactured goods but they also tend to fluctuate, making it "especially difficult for poor countries to protect their foreign exchange earnings from one fiscal year to the next."[126] This was particularly manifest in 1998 when falling energy prices devastated Russia's foreign earnings. The concentration of Russian exports in a small number of energy and semifabricated materials industries including oil, gas, aluminum, nickel, and lumber is a major limitation to its economic development[127] and underscores Russia's dependency on the West. The oil and gas industry has risen to special prominence, generating some 40% of total budget revenues and over half of Russia's export revenues. As a result, the oil and gas conglomerates LUKoil and Gazprom have become among the most visible and influential Russian interest groups due to their ability to earn vast amounts of hard currency, their ability to act as powerful players outside Russia, and their links to Chernomyrdin when he was Prime Minister.[128] In early 1998 one-third of the West's natural gas reserves were produced by Russia's Gazprom.[129]

Russia's dependence on the West was confirmed by German Foreign Minister Kinkel in 1995 when he brushed off fears of Russian opposition to NATO expansion with the assurance that Russia had become too closely linked economically and politically with the West for it to cut its links and seriously oppose such expansion. Kinkel's successor, Joshka Fischer, similarly predicted that Russia would "abandon Milosevic and side with the West" because Russian leaders had "no lasting interest in having their relationship with the West sidelined by the Kosovo war."[130] The overemphasis on raw materials export holds the special danger for Russia that potentially hostile forces could gain control of the principal transport arteries used for trade under conditions of the erection of a *cordon sanitaire* on Russia's western borders via NATO expansion.[131]

Perhaps the most alarming economic development connected to Russia's economic collapse and dependency on the West has been the decline in capital investment, which fell 65% from 1992 to mid-1994, with the sharpest decline in the production sphere. From 1989-1997 real capital investment had declined 92%, a fact all the more devastating in light of the reality that arresting the economic decline and starting the recovery in production will be possible only with substantial investment.[132]

Another notable consequence of dependency is the "brain drain."[133] Much research and development in Russia today is financed by the West and even owned by Westerners. This phenomenon is considered part of the brain drain because it produces an "alien" (generally Western) regulation of Russian science.[134] The other main component of the brain drain is the exodus of scientists and professionals, which by 1996 totaled 20-30,000 year, on the average and reduced Russia's high-tech output an estimated ten times.[135] An interesting development connected to the brain drain was the control of Russian research and development and its facilities by foreign companies. Procter and Gamble, for example, has rented the entire Institute of Biomedical Chemistry to employ Russian scientists for its research.[136]

Industrialization in dependent economies tends to increase income concentration and raise differentials in productivity.[137] Except for big landowners and merchants who participate in the export system—and, in the case of Russia, those involved in the FIGs, or "financial-industrial groups," which include banking, the media, and raw material and energy exporters—most of the rest of the population becomes impoverished. The effects of capitalism and dependency on Russia's working massses have indeed been cruel. According to one estimate, the payment for labor as a percentage of the population's total income, 71.2% in 1990 (it had been closer to 100% in earlier Soviet years), fell by 1995 alone to 39.5%, while income from property rose from zero to 5.2%, and entrepreneurial income doubled from 19.8% to 38.6%.[138] Real average income of working-class families in 1995 was only 25-30% that of 1990.[139] And a 1998 study of the former socialist bloc concluded that the number of poor rose some twelve times, from 4% to 45% of the population during 1993-5 alone. The Gini coefficient, a standard measurement of inequality in income distribution, rose "remarkably quickly," such that poverty in Russia, affecting only 10% in pre-"reform" times, rose to 31% in 1994, a consequence above all of the 1992 price liberalization. Finally, according to data from the World Bank, from 1992-3 there was an "astounding" 20% increase in mortality: between 1991-4 alone, life expectancy declined to an alarming 58 years for men.[140]

A History of Russian Dependency and the Class Factor

Russia's dependency derives from the workings of the class factor, which manifests itself in the political struggle between Russia's elites and the working masses. In their deliberate destruction of Soviet institutions, Russian elites have declared the aim of Russia's integration into the West, its becoming a "part of the world [capitalist] economy"[141] and the creation of a market economy and Western-style political "democracy," all under the watchful guidance of Western experts and institutions. Russia's elites have never seriously aspired to these objectives, however. Their real goal has instead been to obtain Western assistance to create and perpetuate a system that would ensure their own enrichment through economic and political power.

It is thus indicative that from late 1991 to early 1993 Western advisers, having been settled in strategically located offices in the Council of Ministers building (the former home of the CPSU Central Committee) were instrumental in the formulation of Russian economic policy.[142] What is more, Jonathan Hay and his associates from the Harvard Institute for International Development (HIID) drafted many of the Presidential decrees on privatization during this period (Hay and his associates would be charged with serious criminal activities in Russia in 1997), as did the Institute for Law-Based Economy, funded by the World Bank and USAID, which developed a legal and regulatory framework for markets. With the help of HIID and other Western advisers, Yeltsin's right-hand aide Chubais and several of his associates set up a network of aid-funded "private" organizations which enabled them to circumvent official government agencies and the Duma—the principal federal government organ which defended the Russian people.[143]

The outright foreign control of Russian policymaking was brought to light in the form of a confidential letter published in *Nezavisimaia gazeta* in 1997 from US Undersecretary of the Treasury and former Chief of the World Bank Lawrence Summers to Anatolii Chubais explicitly acknowledging Chubais' role as an "agent of a foreign power."[144] Like previous exposés in the newspaper *Den'*, the "Dear Anatolii" letter—said to be itself a suspiciously familiar form of address for an official communication between two high officials—dictated in a "commanding tone" domestic and foreign policies Russia should follow to promote US interests, in particular, the structuring of Russia's tax system in such a way as to boost the competitiveness of US goods and to make Commonwealth of Independent States (CIS) goods less competitive. As noted by one observer, not only did the letter prompt no protest from Chubais, but the proposals were implemented much more readily even than many of Yeltsin's decrees. Exposés like this led people to regard Chubais as invaluable for Yeltsin "largely because of his perceived ability to deal with the West." In fact, it was "long known" in Moscow that Chubais possessed information on Russia's economy which he made accessible to his "overseas friends."[145] And in a kind of reprise of the *Den'* exposé, it was reported in mid-December 1997 that letters dictating policy to Chernomyrdin were sent by IMF Director Camdessus and Director of the World Bank James Wolfenson attaching conditions for the issuance of a $700 million loan.[146]

The "reformers" and their Western counterparts have been motivated above all by the common objective of insuring that a socialist-led Russia or revived Soviet Union will never rise again.[147] Those who preceded the "reformers" had already begun to carry out this objective even before the Soviet collapse, as a Soviet dissident, whose activities helped lay the groundwork for the "reformers" admitted. The issue of human rights in the USSR, she revealed, had "simply been an instrument that 'we, the CIA, and the United States used as a battering ram for the destruction of the communist regime and the breakup of the Soviet Union.' "[148]

To be sure, foreign investment in Russia by the year 2000 remains quite modest.[149] The selling of assets cheaply to foreigners was considered undesirable, even for the Westernizers around Chubais,[150] and despite the fact that Russian capitalism has historically been strongly dominated by foreign capital. Substantial foreign investment, moreover, is *not* a necessary condition of dependency, as Peter Evans has pointed out in his study of the dependent states of Asia where, he notes, a "dramatic decoupling of their economies from metropolitan capital" took place well before their industrialization. In 1967 direct foreign investment in South Korea was only 2% of investment in Brazil.[151] Most importantly, foreign aid to East Asia, as with Russia, has had less to do with transnational interests than with the preservation of the domestic political status quo and support of the leadership who acted as a bulwark against the "communist threat."[152]

Although the level of foreign investment remains low, foreigners have nonetheless managed to gain control of certain sectors of Russia's economy, many strategic. By the end of the first stage of mass privatization in June 1994, for example, a London-based metals trader had gained control of two-thirds of Russia's aluminum output.[153] And it was reported in early 1998 that foreigners had acquired control of hundreds of Russia's strategic enterprises producing attack helicopters, optical equipment, spy satellites, etc. That this takeover of Russia's strategic industry was sanctioned at the highest levels of government became apparent when warnings that such control threatened Russia's security were repeatedly ignored by officials all the way up to and including the President.[154]

Russia and International Financial Institutions

International agencies (the IMF and World Bank) put "enormous pressures" on underdeveloped countries to keep their financial houses in order and to promote a favorable climate for private business. They set conditions on loans, including monetary, fiscal, and tariff policies which result in economic contraction and reduce the standard of living of the working population.[155] This is nowhere more true than in Russia. Contrary to the realist allegation that the notion that financiers rule international politics is a "newspaper fairy-tale,"[156] international financial organizations in fact play a "large actual role . . . in providing the expertise and policy guidance for economic stabilization and institutional development" in Russia,[157] which creates fertile ground for the charge that the West is "attempting to impose specific reforms and policies that reflect its own values and interests" rather than the needs of Russia.[158] In 1998 Russia was "fundamentally dependent" on international investors, particularly the IMF, for its financial stability, which was by then funding more than one-quarter of government expenditures.[159]

To be sure, Russia's leaders under Yeltsin were highly selective with respect to which IMF demands they would comply with. They imposed extreme monetarist policies with nary a peep, including freeing prices, slashing industry subsidies and military expenditures to the bone, while generally evading tax payments. In all, such policies fit the shared aims of Russian "democrats" and the IMF of making sure that the tiny group of elites were well compensated while the working masses were forced into ever greater impoverishment. In reality the "reformers" welcomed IMF pressures on Russia as a kind of alibi for the monetarist policies favored by the Gaidar team.

The History of Russia and Capitalist Financial Institutions

Contacts between Soviet officials and the IMF began in late 1988. One year later, at the September 1989 session of the UN General Assembly the USSR stated its aim of permanent membership in the IMF and World Bank. But the West did not yet fully trust the motives of the Soviet Communist leaders, viewing Russian military spending as too high and its support of Cuba, North Korea, and other "rogue" states politically unpalatable. In July 1990, however, IMF President Camdessus' visit to Moscow established direct Soviet-IMF ties. In July 1991 the USSR officially requested IMF membership; although the IMF was generally amenable, it insisted on granting associate membership first at the London G-7 meeting in July. Russian membership was further delayed by the August 1991 "coup."[160]

Even before the USSR's collapse Soviet Foreign Minister Shevardnadze requested external aid to "save" his nation from economic disaster. Russia's dependence on the West was fixed in the 1991 agreement on debt repayment between the G-7 and eight of the twelve Soviet republics, including Russia, which forced the leaders of the newly-created nations into "political [and economic] dependence and onto their knees; they need[ed] the West not just for material assistance but for leadership and authority." In order to defer some $3.6 billion in repayment to the West, the republics agreed to structural reforms under IMF tutelage. Henceforth, "the Soviets' renowned prickliness over any real or accidental intrusion into their sovereignty [was] suddenly . . . replaced by an urgent demand that intrusions be made in all spheres of life."[161]

Russia's very first economic policy statement, formally enunciated by Yeltsin in his address to the October 1991 Congress of People's Deputies (CPD), pledged Russia's preparedness to cooperate with "foreign specialists," to open up strategic data essential for the entry into international organizations, and to "accept the basic principles" set down in the charter of the IMF. He appealed to the IMF, the World Bank, and the European Bank for Reconstruction and Development to "work out a detailed plan for cooperation and participation in the economic reforms."[162] Accordingly, Russia's first official economic program, the "Memorandum on the Economic Policy of the Russian Federation"[163] adopted by the cabinet on February 27, 1992, was an "IMF shadow program" which followed IMF recommendations "to the letter," a translation from the English of the IMF requirements for a country requesting assistance.[164] It was submitted to the IMF in March 1992, just one month after Russia's application for membership. By doing so, Russia signed on to a program which gave the IMF such economic power and control that it was acknowledged in 1996 that the IMF had assumed "the rights of practically the most influential . . . member of the Russian cabinet."[165]

The Economic Memorandum was addressed exclusively to the IMF— *not* to Russia's lawmakers or its citizenry,[166] and followed Yeltsin's overall strategy of demolishing the union and its economic structures, isolating Russia from the other former Soviet republics, and implementing his own radical economic program, "the guiding principle of which was a single-minded monetarism that had been imported from the West" in the form of the "Aslund-Sachs perspectives" instead of mainstream Soviet economic thinking.[167] Indeed, when on March 31, 1992 the IMF announced that it had endorsed Russia's harsh economic reform package, thus opening the way for Russian borrowing from the Fund, observers took note that the IMF announcement had deliberately "skated over the fact" that the Russian plan had been worked out "in close cooperation with IMF experts."[168] On June 1, 1992 Russia was admitted to the IMF; its request for support was approved by the IMF on August 5.[169]

The policies of the leaders of the IMF and the West were formulated and implemented in league with their Russian "reformist" colleagues, deliberately geared to the destruction of the Russian economy and its subjugation to the West. Decisions made by Russia and the IMF in 1993, with the secret collaboration of Deputy Foreign Minister Shokhin, were "decisive in transforming the ruble from a central to a marginal role in Russian economic policy," from an instrument which integrated production and credit facilities of the FSU to an "appendage of the dollar and an inducement to capital flight." Indeed, confidential IMF memoranda in 1993 revealed that the West set the goal of placing Russia's internationally competitive industries into bankruptcy and severing Russia's economic ties with former Soviet republics, all in the name of dubious monetary and financial orthodoxy. One prominent IMF member, J. de Groote, the most senior director on the IMF board, even wrote a private memorandum which questioned whether the IMF was being used by "certain intelligence circles and by some Western media" to insure that "any weakness of Russia is advantageous for the West."[170]

In this study each of the following chapters encompasses a single year starting with 1992 and ending with 1999 (and which includes a postscript covering Putin's emergence on the political scene in late 1999 and the first months of 2000). Each chapter discusses *domestic* developments— economic, political, and social—to assess changes in the relations between the classes, between Russia's rulers and ruled. The life conditions of the Russian people, including their health, economic status, especially standard of living, etc., are examined as a gauge of the factors most directly affecting the atittudes of the Russian people toward the leadership and "reforms," and the domestic political situation, including the struggle of leadership and opposition, is assessed as cause, consequence, and reflection of foreign policy. It is assumed that as the situation in Russia deteriorated the Yeltsin leadership's pro-Western foreign policy—directly linked in the minds of the Russian people with the failed pro-Western "reforms"—also changed.

The foreign policy sections of this study address issues concerning Russia's relations with the West, including: diplomatic relations, both multilateral and bilateral; relations with NATO, especially but not exclusively as regards expansion; policy toward the former Yugoslavia, including Bosnia and Kosovo; relations with the G-7 leading capitalist industrial powers, including their yearly summits; and relations with non-Western states, including Iran, Iraq, China, India, Cuba, and others.

Notes

[1] See Richard Pipes, IntellectualCapital.com, September 9, 1999, and Martin Malia, "The Haunting Presence of Marxism-Leninism," *Journal of Democracy*, Vol. 10, No. 2, April 1999, pp. 41-6, and a similar argument in Angela E. Stent, *Russia and Germany Reborn: Unification, the Soviet Collapse, and the New Europe* (Princeton: Princeton University Press, 1999), p. 152.

[2] Ruth AmEnde Roosa, *Russian Industrialists in an Era of Revolution: The Association of Industry and Trade, 1906-1917* (Armonk, NY: M.E. Sharpe, 1997), pp. vii-viii. See also Donald Filtzer, *Soviet Workers and the Collapse of Perestroika: The Soviet Labour Process and Gorbachev's Reforms, 1985-1991* (Cambridge: Cambridge University Press, 1994), p. 222.

[3] One can encounter justifications for the worst instincts of robber capitalism, as in Rose Brady, *Kapitalizm: Russia's Struggle to Free Its Economy* (New Haven: Yale University Press, 1999), p. 45, which hails Russia's robber capitalists as "living proof that seven decades of communism had failed to obliterate the innate human drive that some people possess to take risks, to accumulate capital, to create new organizations, to strive to do better for themselves."

[4] Ia. Livshin, *Monopolii v ekonomike Rossii* (Moscow: Izdatel'stvo sotsial'no-ekonomicheskoi literatury, 1961), pp. 261-2; Thomas C. Owen, "Entrepreneurship and the Structure of Enterprise in Russia, 1800-80," in Gregory Guroff and Fred V. Carstensen, eds., *Entrepreneurship in Imperial Russia and the Soviet Union* (Princeton: Princeton University Press, 1983), pp. 63; Richard Pipes, *Russia Under the Old Regime* (Middlesex: Penguin, 1977), pp. 205-6.

[5] Roosa, *Russian Industrialists*, pp. 113-14; Livshin, *Monopolii*, pp. 143-4.

[6] Livshin, *Monopolii*, pp. 136-41.

[7] Thomas C. Owen, *Russian Corporate Capitalism from Peter the Great to Perestroika* (New York: Oxford University Press, 1995), pp. 8-9.

[8] E. Lokshin, *Ocherk istorii promyshlennosti SSSR, 1917-40* (Moscow: Gosudarstvennoe izdatel'stvo politicheskoi literatury, 1956), pp. 21-2.

[9] Ibid., p. 22.

[10] Olga Crisp, *Studies in the Russian Economy Before 1914* (London: Macmillan, 1976), pp. 125, 174-6.

[11] Livshin, *Monopolii v ekonomike Rossii*, pp. 171, 244.

[12] Ibid., pp. 310-11.

[13] H. Lapina and L. Turusova, *Rossiiskoe predprinimatel'stvo; opyt sotsiologicheskogo analiza* (Moscow: Institut nauchnoi informatsii po obshchestvennym naukam, 1993), p. 33.

[14] Peter Reddaway, testimony before the Senate Foreign Policy Subcommittee on European Affairs, May 20, 1998. For an opposing view which asserts that the traditional political culture of Russia in fact embodies "the desire to restore civil society, the rule of law, private property, free enterprise, and political pluralism," see Nicolai N. Petro, *The Rebirth of Russian Democracy: An Interpretation of Political Culture* (Cambridge: Harvard University Press, 1995), p. 2.

[15] I take issue on all counts with Michael McFaul, "Russia's Rough Ride," in Larry Diamond et al, eds., *Consolidating the Third Wave Democracies: Regional Challenges* (Baltimore: The Johns Hopkins University Press, 1997), p. 68, which states that the failure of the Soviet command system catalyzed popular demand for

radical economic change, and asks: "Should the Communist Party of the Soviet Union . . . be considered one among many political parties or is it better understood as a criminal organization that had imprisoned the nations located within Soviet territory?" The USSR, I contend, was in many respects a truly democratic and relatively egalitarian society, unlike exploitative capitalist societies. This was also projected onto the world arena in the USSR's policy of assistance to the oppressed of the world. In any case, a full treatment of this issue must be left to another study.

[16] Some left-leaning approaches deny that the USSR was socialist above all on the grounds that the means of production were *not* owned collectively. See, for example, Charles Bettelheim, *Class Struggles in the USSR: Second Period, 1923-1930* (New York: Monthly Review Press, 1978), Paul Sweezy, "The Nature of Soviet Society," *Monthly Review*, Vol. 26, No. 6, Nov. 1974, and Paresh Chattopadhyay, *The Marxian Concept of Capital and the Soviet Experience: Essay in the Critique of Political Economy* (Westport: Praeger, 1994).

[17] David M. Kotz with Fred Weir, *Revolution from Above: The Demise of the Soviet System* (London: Routledge, 1997), pp. 27-8. For an excellent rebuttal of arguments emanating from "left-wing" authors to the effect that the USSR was either a "capitalist restorationist" or a "bureaucratic exploitative" society, see David Laibman, *Value, Technical Change and Crisis: Explorations in Marxist Economic Theory* (Armonk, NY: M.E. Sharpe, 1992), especially Chapter 14.

[18] See, for example, Stanley H. Cohn, *Economic Development in the Soviet Union* (Lexington, MA: Heath Lexington Books, 1970) and Ed A. Hewett, *Reforming the Soviet Union: Economic Equality Versus Efficiency* (Washington, D.C.: The Brookings Institution, 1988).

[19] For analyses which underscore the egalitarian nature of the Soviet system, see Hewett, *Reforming the Soviet Union*, especially Chapter 2, and Alastair McAuley, *Economic Welfare in the Soviet Union: Poverty, Living Standards, and Inequality* (Madison: The University of Wisconsin Press, 1979), p. 317. According to McAuley, the USSR's "achievements have been considerable, and the Soviet experience merits careful study. Dr. Johnson once remarked that 'a decent provision for the poor is the true test of civilization'; after a quarter of a century of barbarity under Stalin, the USSR bids fair to become more civilized than the rest of Europe."

[20] Vladimir Bilenkin, "Russian Workers Under the Yeltsin Regime: Notes on a Class in Defeat," *Monthly Review*, Vol. 48, No. 6, November 1996, pp. 1-2. Because of the high level of state subsidies for basic needs and their relative economic egalitarianism, socialist societies were said to require a separate classification from first, second, or third world. See Ted C. Lewellen, *Dependency and Development: An Introduction to the Third World* (Westport, CT: Bergin and Garvey, 1995), p. 16.

[21] *RFE/RL*, June 10, 1998.

[22] It was precisely because a major aim of Soviet foreign trade was geared toward winning the sympathies of developing (anticapitalist and socialist-oriented) countries, in part through "large transfers of resources" and considerable arms transfers that post-Soviet Russia restructured its trade toward its comparative advantages and away from such "political" criteria. See Anders Aslund, "Adapting to the World Economy: Interests and Obstacles," in Stephen Sestanovich, ed., *Rethinking Russia's National Interests* (Washington, D.C.: Center for Strategic and International Studies, 1994), p. 83. According to one estimate, the USSR had given some $140 billion to former "client" states. See James Sperling and Emil Kirchner, *Recasting the European Order: Security Architectures and Economic Cooperation* (New York: Manchester University Press, 1997), p. 185.

[23] Simon Clarke, "The Enterprise in the Era of Transition," in Simon Clarke, ed., *The Russian Enterprise in Transition: Case Studies* (Cheltenham: Edward Elgar, 1996), p. 6.

[24] Sean Gervasi, "Western Intervention in the USSR," *CovertAction Information Bulletin*, No. 39, Winter 1991-2, pp. 5-6; David Lane, *The Rise and Fall of State Socialism: Industrial Society and the Socialist State* (Cambridge: Polity Press, 1996), pp. 159-61. Steven Solnick's rejection of a "societal interest" explanation of the Soviet collapse on the grounds that the causal link between "social demands" and "institutional policy responses" has not been proven seems to be unfair, especially as one cannot "prove" the societal explanation. It remains, however, the most satisfying explanation for the Soviet collapse. See Steven L. Solnick, *Stealing the State: Control and Collapse in Soviet Institutions* (Cambridge: Harvard University Press, 1998), pp. 20-2. Solnick in fact relies on societal factors when on page 245 he places his causal focus on communist leaders and cadres.

[25] On the role of epistemic communities in Soviet policy see, for example Thomas Risse-Kappen, "Ideas do not Float Freely: Transnational Coalitions, Domestic Structures, and the End of the Cold War," *International Organization*, Vol. 48, No. 2, Spring 1994, pp. 194-5. Jeff Checkel, "Ideas, Institutions, and the Gorbachev Foreign Policy Revolution," *World Politics*, Vol. 45, No. 2, January 1993, pp. 271-7.

[26] Daniel Deudney and G. John Ikenberry, "The International Sources of Soviet Change," *International Security*, Vol. 16, No. 3, Winter 1991-92, pp 106-7. Philip G. Roeder, *Red Sunset: The Failure of Soviet Politics* (Princeton: Princeton University Press, 1993), pp. 211-2; Lane, *The Rise and Fall*, pp. 159-61.

[27] Introduction, in Anders Aslund and Richard Layard, eds., *Changing the Economic System in Russia* (London: Pinter, 1993), p. xii.

[28] Risse-Kappen, "Ideas do not Float Freely," p. 195.

[29] Lane, *The Rise and Fall*, p. 161. The argument that the early Yeltsin leadership reflected "a significant degree of functional autonomy" because it was insulated from legislative oversight ignores the fact that it was the conscious agent

of the capitalist class-in-formation. See Lynn D. Nelson and Irina Y. Kuzes, *Property to the People: The Struggle for Radical Economic Reform in Russia* (Armonk, NY: M.E. Sharpe, 1994), p. 6.

[30] Michael McFaul, "State Power, Institutional Change, and the Politics of Privatization in Russia," *World Politics*, Vol. 47, No. 2, January 1995, p. 211. See also Solnick, *Stealing the State*.

[31] *Sovetskaia Rossiia*, December 20, 1997, p. 2; interview with Sergei Glaz'ev in *Vek*, No. 5, 2000. See also Michael McFaul, "A Precarious Peace: Domestic Politics in the Making of Russian Foreign Policy," *International Security*, Vol. 22, No. 3, Winter 1997/1998, pp. 22-3. Several other works argue this view of a counterrevolution from the top, including Kotz and Weir, *Revolution From Above*, and Jerry F. Hough, *Democratization and Revolution in the USSR, 1985-1991* (Washington, D.C.: Brookings, 1997).

[32] I am indebted to Duncan Foley for this insight.

[33] McFaul, "A Precarious Peace," p. 25.

[34] Peter Reddaway, *The Washington Post*, August 24, 1997, p. C1; *The eXile*, September 3, 1997.

[35] *Sovetskaia Rossiia*, December 20, 1997, p. 2.

[36] Dimitri K. Simes, *After the Collapse: Russia Seeks Its Place As a Great Power* (New York: Simon and Schuster, 1999), p. 150.

[37] Joseph R. Blasi et al, *Kremlin Capitalism: The Privatization of the Russian Economy* (Ithaca: Cornell University Press, 1997), p. 29.

[38] Ibid., p. 43.

[39] Lynn D. Nelson and Irina Y. Kuzes, *Radical Reform in Yeltsin's Russia: Political, Economic, and Social Dimensions* (Armonk, NY: M.E. Sharpe, 1995), p. 18; Simes, *After the Collapse*, p. 148.

[40] Simes, *After the Collapse*, p. 147.

[41] Ibid., pp. 44-5.

[42] Ibid., pp. 46, 53.

[43] Ibid., pp. 50-53. The argument by McFaul, "State Power," p. 228, that Russia's privatization architects believed that enterprise managers would rationalize the use and distribution of economic assets, does not ring true. It is clear that McFaul's imputing humanitarian motives to them is misplaced, since from the outset their objective was the enrichment of a greedy few at the expense of the many. McFaul, p. 230-1, even makes the ludicrous claim that Yeltsin's "doubts" about Gaidar's economic strategy in December 1992 led to the latter's removal, that the "liberals," led by Chubais, insisted that privatization should "serve the interests of all Russians," not just those at large enterprises.

[44] Clarke, "The Enterprise in the Era of Transition," pp. 39-42; Nelson and Kuzes, *Property to the People*, pp. 71-2.

[45] *Christian Science Monitor*, December 23, 1997, p. 1. See also *ETC* magazine, No. 1, 1999.

[46] Blasi et al, *Kremlin Capitalism*, pp. 78-91, 107.

[47] *Nezavisimaia gazeta*, December 9, 1997, p. 5.

[48] Ibid., p. 59. As an example, Nelson and Kuzes refer to the payment of $7 million to the US Sawyer/Miller group for a television advertising campaign to promote privatization.

[49] *The Guardian* (London), December 16, 1999, p. 19.

[50] Janine Wedel, "Rigging the U.S.-Russian Relationship: Harvard, Chubais, and the Transidentity Game," *Demokratizatsiya: The Journal of Post-Soviet Democratization*, Vol. 7, No. 4, Fall 1999, pp. 469-500.

[51] Michel Chossudovsky, *The Globalisation of Poverty: Impacts of IMF and World Bank Reforms* (London: Zed, 1997), pp. 235-7.

[52] Clarke, "The Enterprise in the Era of Transition," pp. 39-42.

[53] Blasi et al, *Kremlin Capitalism*, p. 80.

[54] Simes, *After the Collapse*, p. 161.

[55] Ibid., pp. 161-2.

[56] Juliet Johnson, "Russia's Emerging Financial-Industrial Groups," *Post-Soviet Affairs*, Vol. 13, No. 4, October-December 1997, pp. 335-48. US Congress member from Vermont Bernard Sanders reported that Gazprom and United Energy Systems alone produced over 30% of Russia's GNP. See *The Christian Science Monitor*, June 25, 1998, p. 11. See a listing of analyses which assert the autonomy of Russia's political elite from the economic elite in Introduction, fn. 18, in this study.

[57] Andrei Piontkowsky, *Russian Journal*, February 7-13, and February 14-20, 2000.

[58] *The Moscow Times*, November 22, 1997; *Nezavisimaia gazeta*, September 13, 1997, pp. 1, 6; *Sunday Telegraph*, April 16, 1995, p. 27. For a listing of the numerous cases of bribery attributed to Chubais, see Simes, *After the Collapse*, pp. 189-90.

[59] Johnson, "Russia's Emerging Financial-Industrial Groups," p. 348.

[60] O.V. Gaman-Golutvina, *Politicheskie elity Rossii: vekhi istoricheskoi evoliutsii* (Moscow: Intellekt, 1998), p. 351. The author apparently confused "democracy" with Western-style "democracy," which is not at all necessarily democratic in the generally understood sense of the term.

[61] Johnson, "Russia's Emerging Financial-Industrial Groups," p. 348.

[62] Simes, *After the Collapse*, pp. 161-2.

[63] Ibid., pp. 338-40, 348-9; G. Chernikov and D. Chernikova, *Kto vladeet Rossiei?* (Moscow: Tsentrpoligraf, 1998), p. 10.

[64] Karl Marx and Friedrich Engels, *The Communist Manifesto* (Chicago: The Great Books Foundation, 1955), p. 11; Simes, *After the Collapse*, p. 180.

[65] Simes, *After the Collapse*, p. 180.

[66] Karen L. Remmer, "New Theoretical Perspectives on Democratization," *Comparative Politics*, Vol. 28, No. 1, October 1995, pp. 104-5.

[67] Sarah Meiklejohn Terry, "Thinking About Post-Communist Transitions: How Different Are They?" *Slavic Review*, Vol. 52, No. 2, Summer 1993, pp. 333-4. For a view which dissents from the preceding, see Terry Lynn Karl and Philippe C. Schmitter, "From an Iron Curtain to a Paper Curtain: Grounding Transitologists or Students of Post Communism?" *Slavic Review*, Vol. 54, No. 4, Winter 1995, pp. 965-78.

[68] Dietrich Rueschemeyer, Preface, in Dietrich Rueschemeyer, Evelyne Huber Stephens, and John D. Stephens, eds., *Capitalist Development and Democracy* (Chicago: University of Chicago Press, 1992), p. vii.

[69] Neil Malcolm and Alex Pravda, "Democratization and Russian Foreign Policy," *International Affairs* (London), vol. 72, No. 3, July 1996, p. 539; Edward D. Mansfield and Jack Snyder, "Democratization and the Danger of War," *International Security*, Vol. 20, No. 1, Summer 1995, p. 5. One could point out that so-called "democracies"—particularly the US in the postwar period—have initiated wars, often brutal, against other "non-democracies," which have tended to be dependent countries. See a similarly sanguine analysis of post-communist "democracies" in Doh Chull Shin, "On the Third Wave of Democratization: A Synthesis and Evaluation of Recent Theory and Research," *World Politics*, Vol. 47, No. 1, October 1994, p. 136.

[70] McFaul, "A Precarious Peace," p. 14. Michael Mandelbaum, "Introduction: Russian Foreign Policy in Historical Perspective," in Michael Mandelbaum, ed., *The New Russian Foreign Policy* (New York: The Council on Foreign Relations, 1998), p. 5, reiterates the (false) cliche that Russia after 1991 "began to install a democratic polical system and create a market economy." Contrariwise, McFaul, "Russia's Rough Ride," p. 85, acknowledges elsewhere that Russia's "leading capitalists" have "no use for the democratic process."

[71] See an excellent statement of this position in Michael Parenti, *Democracy for the Few* (New York: St. Martin's, 1995), p. 48, which holds that "a [capitalist] government that pursues policies that by design or neglect are so inequitable as to deny people the very conditions of life is not democratic no matter how many elections it holds."

[72] Lilia Shevtsova, "Parliament and the Political Crisis in Russia, 1991-3," in Jeffrey W. Hahn, ed., *Democratization in Russia: The Development of Legislative Institutions* (Armonk, NY: M.E. Sharpe, 1996), pp. 32-3.

[73] Stanley W. Moore, *The Critique of Capitalist Democracy: An Introduction to the Theory of the State in Marx, Engels and Lenin* (New York: Paine-Whitman, 1957), pp. 84-92.

[74] Shevtsova, "Parliament and the Political Crisis," pp. 35-6.

[75] Nelson and Kuzes, *Radical Reform*, p. 41; Dmitri Glinski and Peter Reddaway, "Ravages of Market Bolshevism," *Journal of Democracy*, Vol. 10, No. 2, April 1999, p. 23; See also James R. Millar, "From Utopian Socialism to Utopian Capitalism: The Failure of Revolution and Reform in Post-Soviet Russia," *Problems of Post-Communism*, Vol. 42, No. 3, May-June, 1995, p. 8.

[76] L. Telen, *Moscow News*, No. 15, April 18-24, 1996, p. 2. Margot Light, "Two Cheers for Russian Democracy," *The World Today*, Vol. 52, Nos. 8-9, August-September 1996, p. 201. Acccording to Vladimir Brovkin, "The Emperor's New Clothes: Continuity of Soviet Political Culture in Contemporary Russia," *Problems of Post-Communism*, Vol. 43, No. 2, March-April 1996, p. 21, "the social, political, and cultural processes underway in Yeltsin's Russia have little to do with democratization. In hindsight, it appears that Yeltsin was not a democrat even in 1991."

[77] *RFE/RL Newsline*, Vol. 2, No. 99, Part I, May 26, 1998. This contradicts the claim by M. Steven Fish, *Democracy From Scratch: Opposition and Regime in the New Russian Revolution* (Princeton: Princeton University Press, 1995), p. 233, that a "vigorous free media has established itself as a conspicuous and powerful element of Russian political life."

[78] Philippe C. Schmitter, "The Consolidation of Democracy and Representation of Social Groups," *American Behavioral Scientist*, Vol. 35, Nos. 4 and 5, March/June 1992, p. 430.

[79] Aleksandr V. Buzgalin and Andrei Kolganov, *Bloody October in Moscow: Political Repression in the Name of Reform* (New York: Monthly Review Press, 1994), p. 208. One Western analyst acknowledges that the standard Soviet position that economic rights should be included under human rights "has a point." See Edward Dolan, President, the American Institute of Business and Economics, in *The Moscow Times*, June 16, 1998.

[80] Adam Przeworski, "Some Problems in the Study of the Transition to Democracy," in Guillermo O'Donnell, Philippe C. Schmitter, and Laurence Whitehead, eds., *Transitions from Authoritarian Rule: Comparative Perspectives* (Baltimore: The Johns Hopkins University Press, 1991), p. 63.

[81] Crawford, "Post-Communist Political Economy," pp. 4-10. On the inability of Russian workers to defend their interests, see David Ost, "Labor, Class, and Democracy: Shaping Political Antagonisms in Post-Communist Society," p. 183, in the same volume, and Filtzer, *Soviet Workers*, pp. 219-22.

[82] Beverly Crawford, "Post-Communist Political Economy: A Framework for the Analysis of Reform," in Beverly Crawford, ed., *Markets, States and Democracy: The Political Economy of Post-Communist Transformation* (Boulder: Westview, 1995), pp. 4-11, 36-8. To be sure, Crawford lays out three conditions which may favor a successful reform, but acknowledges that at least one is unlikely in post-communist societies. Igor Kliamkin, "The Outlook for Democracy in Russia," in

Robert D. Blackwill and Sergei A. Karaganov, eds., in *Damage Limitation or Crisis? Russia and the Outside World* (Washington, D.C.: Brassey's, 1994), p. 30, similarly contends that Russia is "undemocratic" because the transition to a market inevitably skews income and infringes upon the interests of the majority.

[83] To USA-Canada (ISKRAN) Director S. Rogov the Primakov era represented a new stage in Russia's history in which the "authoritarian presidential republic under Yeltsin" was replaced with a consensus regime supported by parliament. See S. Rogov, "Russia and the United States: Test By Crisis," *International* Affairs (Moscow), No. 5, May 1998, pp. 1-2.

[84] To claim that the nomenklatura was the "key opponent" of privatization, as Blasi et al, *Kremlin Capitalism*, p. 38, does, stands reality on its head.

[85] Filtzer, *Soviet Workers*, pp. 219-22; Stephen E. Hanson, "The Leninist Legacy, Institutional Change and Post-Soviet Russia," in Beverly Crawford and Arend Lijphart, eds., *Liberalization and Leninist Legacies: Comparative Perspectives on Democratic Transitions* (Berkeley: University of California at Berkeley, International Area Studies, 1997), p. 234.

[86] Laurence Whitehead, "International Aspects of Democratization," in O'Donnell et al, pp. 6-9.

[87] I accept that the USSR was not dependent. Although some, such as Christopher K. Chase-Dunn, Introduction, in Christopher K. Chase-Dunn, ed., *Socialist States in the World-System* (Beverly Hills: Sage, 1982), pp. 9-15, contend that the USSR and the socialist bloc were largely dependent on the capitalist West others, such as Albert Szymanski, "The Socialist World-System," in Ibid., pp. 58-82, maintain that the USSR was isolated from economic forces of the West.

[88] One notable exception is Glinski and Reddaway, "What Went Wrong in Russia?" p. 28, which, although not actually employing the dependency approach, at least supports its validity by conceding that Russia's "current state . . . presents plenty of evidence to support the dependency argument."

[89] Magnus Blomstrom and Bjorn Hettne, *Development Theory in Transition: The Dependency Debate and Beyond: Third World Responses* (London: Zed, 1988); Robert A. Packenham, *The Dependency Movement: Scholarship and Politics in Development Studies* (Cambridge: Harvard University Press, 1992), Chapter 1.

[90] Fernando Henrique Cardoso and Enzo Falletto, *Dependencia y desarrollo en America Latina: ensayo de interpretacion sociologica* (Mexico: Siglo Veintiuno, 1969). A similar approach is articulated in Blomstrom and Hettne, *Development Theory*, p. 70.

[91] Theotonio dos Santos, *Dependencia Economica y Cambio Revolucionario en America Latina* (Caracas: Nueva Izquierda, 1970), pp. 38-63. Santos contends that the socialist countries were able to break this syndrome of dependence.

[92] Thomas R. Shannon, *An Introduction to the World-System Perspective* (Boulder: Westview, 1996), p. 40.

[93] Vincent A. Mahler, *Dependency Approaches to International Political Economy: A Cross-National Study* (New York: Columbia University Press, 1980), p. 2.

[94] Shannon, *An Introduction to the World-System Perspective*, p. 17.

[95] Packenham, *The Dependency Movement*, p. 137.

[96] Alvin Y. So, *Social Change and Development: Modernization, Dependency, and World-System Theories* (Newbury Park, CA: Sage Publications, 1990), pp. 133-41. This has been enunciated by Fernando Cardoso in his "associated-dependent development" thesis, which stipulates "more dynamic forms of dependence than those characterizing enclave or quasi-colonial situations."

[97] Richard Peet, *Global Capitalism: Theories of Societal Development* (London: Routledge, 1991), pp. 152-64, 169. Post-Fordism is a term which describes a phase of capitalist development which began in the late 1970s and was based on automatic production control. It introduces new flexibility of production design and location, mass socialization of the conditions of life, strong totalitarian tendencies under the ideological cover of liberalism. See Ibid., pp. 154-7.

[98] See Mahler, *Dependency Approaches*, p. 147.

[99] So, *Social Change*, pp. 132-3. Peet, *Global Capitalism*, pp. 10-11. The "regional autonomy" view, expressed most succinctly in the works of Andre Gunder Frank, has been persuasively criticized by Robert Brenner, "The Origins of Capitalist Development: A Critique of Neo-Smithian Marxism," *New Left Review*, Vol. 104, July-August 1977.

[100] Dale L. Johnson, "Dependence and the International System," in James D. Cockroft, A.G. Frank, and Dale L. Johnson, eds., *Dependency and Underdevelopment: Latin America's Political Economy* (New York: Doubleday, 1972), p. 74.

[101] Harald Muller and Thomas Risse-Kappen, "From the Outside In and From the Inside Out: International Relations, Domestic Politics, and Foreign Policy," in David Skidmore and Valerie M. Hudson, eds., *The Limits of State Autonomy: Societal Groups and Foreign Policy Formulation* (Boulder: Westview, 1993), p. 31.

[102] Blomstrom and Hettne, *Development Theory*, pp. 10, 28-29; Ian Roxborough, *Theories of Underdevelopment* (Atlantic Highlands, NJ: Humanities Press, 1979), p. 43.

[103] Boris Kagarlitsky, *The Mirage of Modernization* (New York: Monthly Review Press, 1995), p. 31.

[104] Packenham, *The Dependency Movement*, pp. 120-3.

[105] Teodor Shanin, "Late Marx: Gods and Craftsmen," in Teodor Shanin, ed., *Late Marx and the Russian Road. Marx and 'the Peripheries' of Capitalism* (London: Routledge and Kegan Paul, 1983), pp. 4-13.

[106] Hey, *Theories of Dependent Foreign Policy*, p. 269.

[107] On this point see Peter Evans, "Class, State, and Dependence in East Asia: Lessons for Latin Americanists," in Frederick C. Deyo, ed., *The Political Economy of the New Asian Industrialism* (Ithaca: Cornell University Press, 1987), and Adrienne Armstrong, "The Political Consequences of Economic Dependence," *The Journal of Conflict Resolution*, Vol. 25, No. 3, September 1981, pp. 422-3.

[108] Christoph Bluth, "Russia and European Security," *The World Today*, Vol. 50, No. 4, April 1994, p. 74. For a Marxist perspective, see Vladimir Bilenkin, "The Ideology of Russia's Rulers in 1995: Westernizers and Eurasians," *Monthly Review*, Vol. 47, No. 5, October 1995, p. 24. See also Bruce D. Porter, "Russia and Europe After the Cold War: The Interaction of Domestic and Foreign Policies," in Celeste A. Wallander, ed., *The Sources of Russian Foreign Policy After the Cold War* (Boulder: Westview, 1996), p. 134.

[109] Ted C. Lewellen, *Dependency and Development: An Introduction to the Third World* (Westport, CT: Bergin and Garvey, 1995), p. 9.

[110] Mark Webber, *The International Politics of Russia and the Successor States* (Manchester: Manchester University Press, 1996), p. 301. According to another analysis, the West forgave Yeltsin for everything because, as he himself put it, he had "killed the communist monster," and because "he was going to bring the lost Russian sheep back into the capitalist fold." See K.S. Karol, "The Yeltsin Regime," in Leo Panitch, ed., *The Socialist Register 1995: Why Not Capitalism* (London: The Merlin Press, 1995), p. 136.

[111] On this point, see So, *Social Change and Development*, p. 133, and Miles Kahler, "Inventing International Relations: International Relations theory After 1945," in Michael W. Doyle and G. John Ikenberry, eds., *New Thinking in International Relations Theory* (Boulder: Westview, 1997), pp. 35-6.

[112] Kahler, "Inventing International Relations," p. 37.

[113] *The eXile*, October 9, 1997.

[114] Stephen Gill, "Gramsci and Global Politics: Towards a Post-Hegemonistic Research Agenda," in Stephen Gill, ed., *Gramsci, Historical Materialism and International Relations* (Cambridge: Cambridge University Press, 1993, p. 11.

[115] Evan Luard, *The Globalization of Politics: The Changed Focus of Political Action in the Modern World* (New York: NYU Press, 1990), pp. 3-4.

[116] Robert Cox, "Gramsci, Hegemony, and International Relations: An Essay in Method," in Stephen Gill, ed., *Gramsci, Historical Materialism and International Relations* (Cambridge: Cambridge University Press, 1993), p. 59.

[117] See Radiostantsiia Ekho Moskvy, July 29, 1999, in *FBIS*-SOV-1999-0729, July 29, 1999.

[118] Nelson and Kuzes, *Radical Reform*, p. 103.

[119] N. Petrakov, *Nezavisimaia gazeta*, March 6, 1992, p. 4. See also Leonid Abalkin, "The Economic Situation in Russia," *Problems of Post-Communism*, Vol. 42, No. 4, July-August 1995, p. 55.

[120] *Ekonomika i zhizn'*, No. 13, March 1997, p. 26.

[121] *Nezavisimaia gazeta*, May 25, 1995, pp. 1, 6; *RusData DiaLine—BizEkon News*, May 20, 1996.

[122] Leonid Abalkin, "The Economic Situation in Russia," *Problems of Post-Communism*, Vol. 42, No. 4, July-August 1995, p. 55.

[123] *The Daily Yomiuri* (Tokyo), June 9, 1996, p. 6.

[124] *Rossiiskaia gazeta*, March 30, 1996, pp. 7-8.

[125] Stefan Hedlund and Niclas Sundstrom, "The Russian Economy after Systemic Change," *Europe-Asia Studies*, Vol. 48, No. 6, September 1996, pp. 900-1.

[126] Neil R. Richardson, *Foreign Policy and Economic Dependence* (Austin: University of Texas Press, 1978), p. 21.

[127] *The Daily Yomiuri* (Tokyo), June 9, 1996, p. 6.

[128] Igor Khripinov and Mary M. Matthews, "Russia's Oil and Gas Interest Group and Its Foreign Policy Agenda," *Problems of Post-Communism*, Vol. 43, No. 3, May-June 1996, pp. 39-41; Michael McFaul, "Revolutionary Ideas, State Interests and Russian Foreign Policy," in Vladimir Tismaneanu, ed., *Political Culture and Civil Society in Russia and the New States of Eurasia* (Armonk, NY: M.E. Sharpe, 1995), pp. 41-2.

[129] *US News and World Report*, February 16, 1998, p. 53.

[130] Agence France Presse, April 13, 1995.

[131] *Nezavisimaia gazeta*, February 25, 1994, p. 2.

[132] Nelson and Kuzes, *Radical Reform*, p. 104; Igor Birman, "Gloomy Prospects for the Russian Economy," *Europe-Asia Studies*, Vol. 48, No. 5, July 1996, pp. 740-1; Stephen D. Shenfield, cited in *Business Week*, October 5, 1998.

[133] *Executive Intelligence Review*, Vol. 24, No. 29, July 18, 1997.

[134] Iu. Kormnov, "Vneshneekonomicheskie aspekty razvitiia mashinostroitel'nogo kompleksa," *Ekonomist*, No. 6, June 1996, p. 23.

[135] S. Simanovsky, M. Strepetova, and Yu. Naido, *"Brain Drain" from Russia: Problems, Prospects, and Ways of Regulation* (New York: Nova Science Publishers, 1996), p. 23.

[136] Ibid., pp. viii-ix.

[137] Fernando Henrique Cardoso and Enzo Falletto, *Dependency and Development in Latin America* (Berkeley: University of California Press, 1979), pp. xxii.

[138] Zh. Sidorova, "Izmenenie struktury dokhodov naseleniia i ee optimizatsiia," *Ekonomist*, No. 9, September 1996, p. 65. Also see the letter from Russian economist N. Petrakov in *Nezavisimaia gazeta*, March 6, 1992, p. 4.

[139] Bilenkin, "Russian Workers Under the Yeltsin Regime," p. 2.

[140] Reuters, May 23, 1998; *Russian Federation: Toward Medium-Term Viability* (Washington, D.C.: The World Bank, 1996), pp. 7-8.

[141] As Coit D. Blacker has noted, Russia's new leaders set as their "highest priority" Russia's "prompt membership in the full array of Western-sponsored institutions." See "Russia and the West," in Michael Mandelbaum, ed., *The New Russian Foreign Policy* (New York: Council on Foreign Relations, 1998), p. 170. See also "Kontseptsiia vneshnei politiki Rossiiskoi Federatsii," *Diplomaticheskii vestnik* (Special issue), January 1993, pp. 9-10, S. Neil MacFarlane, "Russian Conceptions of Europe," *Post-Soviet Affairs*, Vol. 10, No. 3, July-September 1994, p. 252, and A. Kozyrev, *Preobrazhenie* (Moscow: Mezhdunarodnye otnosheniia, 1995), pp. 210, 214-5.

[142] Anders Aslund, *How Russia Became a Market Economy* (Washington, D.C.: The Brookings Institution, 1995), pp. 19-20.

[143] Janine Wedel, "Harvard Boys Do Russia," *The Nation*, June 1, 1998, pp. 11-16. Hay was senior legal adviser to Russia's Privatization Committee, which Chubais headed.

[144] *The EXile*, October 9, 1997.

[145] *Nezavisimaia gazeta*, September 26, 1997, pp. 1-2, and December 20, 1997, p. 1; Wedel, "Harvard Boys Do Russia," pp. 11-16.

[146] *Nezavisimaia gazeta*, December 18, 1997, pp. 1-2.

[147] *Pravda*, November 17, 1992, p. 3.

[148] *The Jamestown Foundation Monitor*, Vol. 4, Issue 228, December 10, 1998.

[149] By 1913 up to 33% of Russian private capital was foreign-owned. See Nelson and Kuzes, *Property to the People*, p. 17.

[150] Reuters, December 27, 1997.

[151] Evans, "Class, State, and Dependence," pp. 206-7.

[152] Ibid., pp. 209-10.

[153] *The Economist*, January 2-27, 1995, pp. 62-3.

[154] *The eXile*, March 5, 1998.

[155] Johnson, "Dependence and the International System," pp. 95-7. Boris Kagarlitsky asserts that the IMF has imposed "openly dictatorial rule" on Russia, creating a dependent capitalism more reminiscent of Africa than of Latin America. See his *Restoration in Russia: Why Capitalism Failed* (London: Verso, 1995), p. 89.

[156] Hans J. Morgenthau and Kenneth W. Thompson, *Politics Among Nations: The Struggle for Power and Peace* (New York: McGraw Hill, 1993), p. 63.

[157] Stanislaw Gomulka, "The IMF-Supported Programs of Poland and Russia, 1990-1994: Principles, Errors and Results," *Journal of Comparative Economics*, Vol. 20, No. 3, June 1995, p. 342.

[158] Gomulka, "The IMF-Supported Programs," pp. 342-3.

[159] *The Moscow Times*, February 29, 1998.

[160] D. Smyslov, *Mezhdunarodnyi valiutnyi fond: sovremennye tendentsii i nashi interesy* (Moscow: "Finansy i statistika," 1993), pp. 168-72.

[161] *Financial Times*, November 23, 1991, p. 8.

[162] Russian Television, October 28, 1991, in *BBC Summary of World Broadcasts*, October 30, 1991.

[163] The text for the "Memorandum" can be found in *Ekonomicheskaia gazeta*, No. 10, March 1992. See also *Izvestiia*, February 28, 1992, pp. 1-2.

[164] *Kommersant-daily*, March 25, 1995, p. 2; *The Wall Street Journal*, February 27, 1992, p. A2. In IMF parlance, a "shadow program" is distinguished from a final IMF agreement. It cannot be enacted until a country becomes a full member.

[165] *Kommersant-daily*, March 28, 1996, pp. 1-2; Webber, *The International Politics of Russia*, p. 304.

[166] Nelson and Kuzes, *Radical Reform*, pp. 17-8. The text of the program was released by TASS International Service, March 4, 1992, in *FBIS*-SOV-92-044, March 5, 1992, pp. 30-38.

[167] Nelson and Kuzes, *Property to the People*, pp. 31-2, 35-6.

[168] *Russian and Commonwealth Business Law Report*, Vol. 2, No. 18, April 3, 1992; *The Guardian* (London), April 1, 1992, p. 8.

[169] Blasi et al, *Kremlin Capitalism*, p. 31.

[170] John Helmer, "The IMF and Russia—Who Pays the Piper Calls the Tune," in Johnson's Russia List, No. 3057, February 17, 1999.

3 1992: The New Regime

The Domestic Setting

The fledgling Russian government freed prices on January 2, causing them to skyrocket 345% and wiping out the savings of most Russians in the process. The economic decline did not abate, and by November consumer prices had increased some twenty-two times relative to January levels; at the same time the average wage increased only ten times, "indicating a significant impoverishment of the bulk of the Russian citizenry." The vaunted voucher program, said to herald a "democratic" and "fair" privatization, was conducted in such a way as to be concentrated in the hands of a small number of elites and "undermining the 'mass' character the designers [claimed they] had intended for the program."[1]

Economic devastation gave rise to a coalescence of political opposition almost immediately after the disbandment of the USSR. But Yeltsin, always the political brawler, won a victory in mid-April by convincing the 6th Congress of People's Deputies (CPD) to drop its demands that he relinquish additional powers by July and halt radical "reforms." He was also allowed to retain power to rule by decree through the end of 1992.[2] By the time the 7th Congress of People's Deputies convened in December the deadlocked executive and legislature had agreed to a compromise which stipulated that Parliament would appoint key governmental ministers in return for a referendum on a new constitution.[3] In an effort to regain its former status of political supremacy the CPD in December extracted from Yeltsin an agreement to replace Prime Minister Gaidar with Chernomyrdin and to sack chief Yeltsin adviser Burbulis, although the new cabinet preserved the previous cabinet's "reformist" core and even added some "liberals."[4]

The Foreign Policy Setting

Alexei Pushkov, Deputy Editor-in-Chief of *Moscow News*, discerned four political tendencies in Russia in 1994: (1) Radical Democrats (*zapadniki*), whose paramount goal was alliance with the West and gradual integration into Western institutions. Until 1993 this tendency was favored by the

64

Yeltsin team and the "democratic" media; (2) Moderate (Statist) Democrats, who emphasized the defense of Russia's national interests and favored but were skeptical about partnership with the West; (3) Statist Bureaucrats, the bulk of the state bureaucracy, the military-industrial complex, and top military officers who opposed many of Kozyrev's policies; and (4) Radicals, mainly communists and "ultranationalists," who favored a wholesale change in Russia's policy.[5] While Pushkov did not say it, in reality there was little difference between the first two and possibly the first three, all of whom shared as their foremost foreign policy objective close ties with the West—their anti-Western rhetoric notwithstanding—and thus, in effect, Russia's compliance with Western dictates.

The depth of Yeltsin's pro-Westernism was manifested during a June visit to Washington, which he described as "the greatest day in my life," a statement which was not "just political politeness," given that his foremost lifelong political objective as a Russian Westernizer (or, in Pushkov's terms, a "radical democrat") was, and remained, acceptance by the West.[6] Indeed, even before the Soviet collapse the government's foreign economic policy objectives, as set forth in Yeltsin's October 1991 economic policy speech, appealed openly to the West.[7] The Russian leadership continued to reach out to and embrace the West throughout early 1992 and in a number of instances directly translated its pro-Westernism into policy by, inter alia: declaring in late December 1991 that agreements between the USSR and Iraq, North Korea, and Cuba did not conform to Russia's "criteria of expediency," thus repudiating the anti-Westernism of its Soviet predecessors;[8] notifying Washington in January 1992 that Russia had launched a rocket from Kazakhstan's territory even before it had informed Alm-Ata;[9] sending Yeltsin's top adviser Burbulis in his place to visit India in March, a move which downgraded the importance of a non-Western ally;[10] and joining a Western flotilla in the Persian Gulf in October to help implement the pro-Western, anti-Iraq UN resolution.[11]

On January 2 Kozyrev elucidated the bedrock principles of Russia's foreign policy: a non-confrontational relationship with the US and the states of the "developed West" who were Russia's "natural allies." He asserted, with much aplomb and in a statement that would come to haunt him (although he never repudiated it in principle), that those who feared that the US aspired to be the world's superpower and to dictate its will to Russia were clinging to "outdated stereotypes." We threaten no one, Kozyrev declared, and proceed from the assumption that no "democratic" society threatens Russia[12]—essentially a reprise of his 1990 remark that as "pluralistic democracies" Western states were incapable of aggression.[13]

Kozyrev actively pursued his design of an alliance with the West when he affirmed in late March that Russia possessed all the qualifications for membership as an "equal" in the G-7—an assessment at once contradicted by Russia's position of supplicant pleading for massive aid from that body, which it received in early April in the form of a $24 billion grant.[14] Even the pro-Western *Komsomol'skaia pravda* accused Kozyrev in September 1992 of having taken Westernism to "absurd lengths," deriding as ludicrous his contention that for the first time in its history Russia had a favorable external environment and pointing to contravening evidence that Russia's neighbors were champing at the bit to hack off Russian territory even as Russian speakers in the Commonwealth of Independent States were being denied their basic rights.[15]

Kozyrev and the RFM were also sharply criticized early on for resisting the formulation of a comprehensive foreign policy concept for Russia. They defended this stand with the disingenuous argument that no blueprint could help Russia navigate the shoals of the unfamiliar new international situation—a position hardly reflective of a leadership determined to defend its people's interests. Indeed, their deliberate neglect of foreign policy conformed with the most cherished objective of Western elites: to render Russia and its foreign policy ineffectual and impotent. It was not surprising, therefore, that the "Foreign Policy Concept" the RFM finally came up with in February was so vague and excessively pro-Western that it elicited a swift rejection from parliament.[16]

In response to the growing clamor for foreign policy direction the Council on Foreign and Defense Policy (CFDP), an unofficial body composed of influential leaders, administrators, diplomats, military officers, and foreign policy experts, was compelled in August 1992 to issue its own foreign policy conception, "Strategy for Russia."[17] The Strategy's assessment of the international situation—that the solution to Russia's quandary of economic backwardness and geopolitical encirclement was strategic alliance with the West, above all, West Europe—gave Russia cold comfort, since it also warned that West Europe threatened Russia with isolation and was striving mightily to compel it to scale back its great-power strategic ambitions and return to a traditional continental strategy focused on the territory of the FSU. The report also cautioned that West European security structures (including NATO) could expand to Central and Eastern Europe without Russia.[18]

Responding only, it was clear, because its neglect of its own mission had by now become so conspicuous as to invite serious attack, the RFM in December finally issued its "Document on Russia's Foreign Policy," the central thesis of which affirmed that the West was making the transition from a politico-military alliance in the traditional sense of the term to a "world center collectively regulating the world economy and international relations." It also reiterated Russia's priority of close relations with the West, but gave a nod to the opposition with the caveat that divergent interests of Russia and the West could make it necessary for Russia to resist the US, especially if the latter relapsed into "imperialism."[19]

Russians became quickly disillusioned by the failure of their new-found Western "partners" to deliver on promised assistance. Observers noted in February that the US rejected Yeltsin's request for $17 billion, which only fostered the impression that Russia's new "allies" had no interest in really helping.[20] Even Western analysts conceded that "dribbles of support" had been approved for Russian "reforms," of which $10 billion (of the $24 billion in aid announced by the G-7 in April) was debt relief and another $6 billion was earmarked for a ruble stabilization fund. Most of the remaining $8 billion was the continuation of export credits issued in previous years.[21]

The biggest component of Western aid approved at the July G-7 meeting in Munich was earmarked for improving the safety of Soviet-built nuclear reactors. This was emblematic of Russia's relationship with the West, now largely defined by Western demands for concessions from a weakened Russia and involving, among other things, its economic restructuring under the West's watchful eye.[22] As Simon Clarke has argued, "for all its rhetoric, international capital had no interest in integrating the Russian economy into a world capitalism in crisis." Its aim, rather, was to "ring-fence" the former Soviet Union (FSU) to prevent its crisis from spilling beyond its borders[23]—and, one might add, to weaken Russia to the point that communism would never again rear its ugly head.

In 1992 Russia was accepted into Western financial institutions, including the IMF in April and the International Bank for Reconstruction and Development (IBRD) in June. In July President Bush's proposal to transform the G-7 into a G-8 was rejected by France, Germany and Japan. In his address to the G-7 meeting—which the members permitted only *after* the preparation of the agenda had been completed—Yeltsin complained of the delay in aid, proposed that repayment of the debts of the former Soviet Union be put off for two years, and pleaded with the West to open its markets to Russian goods.[24]

The Foreign Policy Line Hardens

Russia's opposition mounted a furious campaign from the outset against what it regarded as a sellout of the people's interests by the leadership's pro-Western policies, although much of the opposition, and certainly its leadership in parliament, including Khasbulatov, was itself pro-Western. Forced to respond to parliamentary resistance and because of the "great difficulty" the Russian Security Council had in formulating a position on the controversial issue, Yeltsin abruptly canceled a scheduled trip to Japan in September in an effort to squelch rumors that he was planning to return the Northern territories and South Kurile Islands.[25]

Mounting pressure for a new foreign policy caused mainstream Russian thinking on Europe during late 1992 to evolve to a "much more nuanced and differentiated perspective." It was—*only rhetorically,* it is argued here, for in practice there was little substantive change—realist and state-centric and focused on power relations, the role of the state, and the state's geopolitical position. Russia's self-awareness as a European and an Asian power was also growing,[26] a position perhaps most trenchantly articulated by leading Yeltsin adviser Sergei Stankevich, who advocated a major reorientation toward Asia.[27] The pro-Western lobby continued to predominate, however, led by Kozyrev who in August inveighed against Asianists for urging a cutoff in ties with the West and for, in his words, seeking to transform Eurasia into an "Asiatic despotism."[28]

Russia's President entered the fray, laying down the line in a speech to the Collegium of the Russian Foreign Ministry on October 27, one of the earliest of the leadership's responses to charges that it was selling the country out to the West. Admonishing the RFM for its "passivity" and "compliance," Yeltsin urged it to adopt a tougher line which emphasized "Russia's interests" and the "protection" of Russia's security. Russia, Yeltsin bellowed, "can voice its disappointment, when it has reason for this, even to the United States of America, which Andrei Kozyrev loves so much." This denunciation of Kozyrev was fraudulent in light of the fact that he was retained by Yeltsin at the Foreign Ministry for another four years. Although he did not specify, it was clear to one Western observer that Yeltsin was addressing the RFM's "acquiescence to Western proposals at the UN and in other international forums."[29] Yeltsin's charade would be unmasked in a few short months with his own acquiescence to NATO expansion, an issue which most of all threatened Russian security.

Then, coming quickly on the heels of Yeltsin's sacking of Gaidar as Prime Minister, Kozyrev on December 14 delivered his notorious "shock speech" at the Stockholm meeting of the Conference on Security and Cooperation in Europe (CSCE). In his speech Kozyrev set forth the following points (although he disavowed them later as not serious and contended they merely were intended to warn the West of what could happen if Russia's "democrats" were ousted from power): (1) although Russia would retain its goal of integration into Europe, it was constrained by its Asian traditions; (2) the goals of NATO and the West European Union (WEU)—fortification of their military presence in the Baltics and other parts of the FSU, intervention in Bosnia and the internal affairs of the former Yugoslavia—had not changed. Russia demanded that sanctions be lifted against Yugoslavia and reserved the right to defend its interests and aid its Serb allies; (3) the FSU was a "post-imperial space" not subject to norms of the CSCE; Russia had to protect its interests with "all available means," including military and economic; and (4) Russia would lead the states of the FSU in the formation of a new union.[30]

Although Kozyrev concluded his speech with a warning that those who welcomed the downfall of the USSR should not hope for the same fate for Russia, it was far from an anti-Western diatribe, which was made clear when, immediately following the speech, Kozyrev pursued a visibly "pale" US Secretary of State Eagleburger from the hall and retired with him to a separate room. When they emerged Eagleburger's demeanor had changed markedly, an indication that Kozyrev had no doubt reassured him that the speech was only rhetorical and that Russia's pro-Western line was unchanged.[31] This was confirmed days later when Kozyrev hailed the success of Russian-Western relations, which had passed the "getting acquainted" stage and was developing into a real partnership.[32]

Kozyrev's "shock speech" had several purposes, the most important being to arouse the West into complying with Russia's requests for more money, and also to induce the Western and Russian peoples to swallow the stereotypes projected by Yeltsin's team, to show Russians that their leadership was "tough" on the West.

Russian Relations with Non-Western States

Cognizant of the dangers from the mounting resistance to their extreme pro-Westernism, the Yeltsin-Kozyrev team began to place greater emphasis on relations with non-Western states.[33] An important component of Russia's foreign policy review in late 1992 was its focus on a greater balance between East and West, termed the "double-headed eagle" policy, which recognized China as its most important Eastern partner. In December Yeltsin signed a joint statement in Beijing that China and Russia would henceforth regard each other as friendly countries.[34]

Russia and NATO

It is no exaggeration to assert that in their eagerness to undo virtually all aspects of Soviet policy, Russia's Westernizing leaders regarded NATO with an affection that bordered on reverence. Even during the last days of the USSR the swelling ranks of pro-Western analysts who had, sheeplike, jumped on the conformist pro-NATO bandwagon, lauded NATO as friend and partner which, because it now lacked a direct threat from the USSR, would ineluctably metamorphose from a military into a political organization. Russia's leaders made clear that they sought membership in NATO. While pretending that they were oblivious to the ominous—and increasingly obvious—signs that NATO was contemplating an eastward expansion to fence off Russia, they supported virtually all of NATO's policies and jumped at the chance to establish any form of contact with it.

Late Soviet Relations with NATO

In the late 1980s the demise of the Warsaw Pact was presaged by the initiation of contacts between the CEE states and NATO, as delegations from the North Atlantic Assembly visited Budapest and Warsaw in 1988 and 1989 and in October 1989 the North Atlantic Assembly Subcommittee on East Europe, set up in 1986 to study East European reform, invited legislators from Poland, Czechoslovakia, and Hungary to attend a meeting of the Assembly.[35]

Despite the Warsaw Pact's declared intention in August 1989 to evolve into a "political" institution NATO showed no interest in abdicating its military role, much less in dissolving itself, as the USSR and CEE states hoped, in favor of some new structure based largely on the CSCE.[36] It was clear by the end of 1990 that this had become a moot point, for Poland, Czechoslovakia, and Hungary "were already discarding any notions they may have had about eventual neutrality and were beginning to pin their hopes on NATO." At the historic July 1990 NATO summit in London, NATO-Warsaw Pact ties warmed when NATO invited Warsaw Pact members to establish diplomatic relations. In fall 1990 Poland,

Czechoslovakia, and Hungary followed Soviet Foreign Minister Shevardnadze's suggestion to visit NATO headquarters.[37]

By 1990 Soviet dominance in East Europe was thus being phased out, the socialist bloc was crumbling, and the USSR was Europe's flashpoint. In the same way Soviet analysts extolled the virtues of the European Community (EC), they now welcomed NATO as a stabilizing factor in Europe. Leading researcher at the prestigous Institute on World Economy and International Relations (IMEMO) V. Baranovskii praised a "reformed" NATO as the future core of an all-European security system which would in the future admit former Warsaw Pact countries (including the USSR).[38] Some analysts, however, continued to urge caution regarding NATO's intentions, alluding in particular to the first draft of NATO's new doctrine which identified the USSR as the main military threat. This, they warned, was proof that NATO had failed to live up to its July 1990 proclamation that the USSR was no longer its enemy.[39]

Justifiably described as an historic event, the November 1990 CSCE summit in Paris occasioned the signing of the Conventional Forces in Europe (CFE) treaty and the Charter of Paris. The Charter foresaw a Euroatlantic space in which armed forces would be limited and their movements monitored, stipulated regular consultations on security issues, and set up a Conflict Prevention Center (CPC). Six months prior to the Paris summit the CSCE's transformation into a European security organization to replace the Warsaw Pact and NATO was proposed, which pleased the USSR, who had sought the abolition of military blocs. But when it became clear by mid-1990 that a united Germany would join NATO, "Western interest in a security role for the CSCE declined markedly"; Soviet delegates offered remarkably little protest.[40]

Even in the initial post-Paris euphoria patriotic Soviets resented the West's riding roughshod over them, and they critized Western interest in preserving NATO rather than developing joint security structures. But officials in the Soviet Foreign Ministry had by now moved so far to the right on the political spectrum that they belied their professed anti-NATO sentiments and allowed the CPC, the centerpiece of NATO's security proposals, to become "little more than an empty suite of offices charged with overseeing exchanges of military information." Indeed, the Soviet delegation to the CSCE, "primarily reactive, presenting very few original proposals and often seeming incidental to intra-Western disputes" appeared to be "absent from CSCE debates."[41] This disregard of their country's interests so shockingly displayed by late Soviet diplomats was not surprising, however, in light of their ultimate objectives for, as was shown in Chapter 2, the Westernizers were set on carrying out the destruction of the socialist USSR as quickly and thoroughly as possible.[42]

With the Kremlin exuding such seeming indifference, the North Atlantic Assembly in November 1990 invited parliamentary deputies from Czechoslovakia, Hungary, Poland, the USSR, and Bulgaria to participate in annual meetings as associate delegates.[43] And in a sign which had ominous overtones for the USSR, coming as it did just months after the August 1991 state of emergency, the Visegrad states of Poland, Hungary, and Czechoslovakia in October 1991 followed the suggestion of US Secretary of State Baker and German Foreign Minister Genscher and expressed their intention to establish "close and institutionalized" cooperation with NATO. In response, NATO set up the North Atlantic Cooperation Council (NACC), to include all former Warsaw Pact members.[44] NATO, it was clear, while not yet willing to admit the CEE states, was setting the stage for its eventual eastward expansion—without Russia. The CEE states indicated they were more than willing to join NATO: in April 1992 Polish President Walesa called for the formation of new military and economic groups in CEE to pave the way for eventual CEE membership in NATO and the EC, and in May Poland's Defense Minister Jan Parys was dismissed for resisting NATO membership.[45]

As early as April 1991 the idea of establishing direct ties with and even participation in NATO took shape in the RFM itself, a position reinforced by NATO's strong support for the Yeltsin forces during the August events. By fall 1991 the Russian government sought to develop all possible contacts with NATO,[46] and even before the final Soviet collapse expressed its desire to join NATO: Vice President Rutskoi told a delegation of NATO officials in October 1991 that Russia hoped to join NATO, a move *Izvestiia* applauded as not just a "propagandistic gesture" but a "serious political step" which found "support at the highest levels of government"; in late November 1991 S. Stepashin, leading member of the Parliamentary Security Committee (who was later named Prime Minister) urged Russia to apply for membership in NATO by 1992 so that it could guarantee Russian security and assist in converting military plants to civilian use; and in December 1991 Yeltsin himself capped off the NATO-mania by openly declaring Russia's interest in joining NATO.[47]

Russian Perspectives on NATO

Pro-NATO sentiment was by now de riguer for the *zapadniki*. Quoting approvingly from speeches of former arch-enemy US Defense Secretary

Cheney, one analyst in May 1992 even reproached Soviet leaders for having "impeded the development of normal partnership ties" with the US and its Western European allies in NATO.[48] The mainstream view in early 1992 also angrily condemned the Soviets for propagating the "tenacious political stereotype" that NATO was a purely military organization with aggressive aims, and praised NATO for promoting European stability. NATO, according to this view, had taken bold steps at its July 1990 summit conference to construct an all-European partnership.[49]

The core postulate of the standard Russian line on NATO now asserted that military-political changes in Europe would somehow shift NATO's center of gravity from the military to the political realm. Even before the collapse of the Soviet Union, S. Karaganov contended that NATO was transforming into a "demilitarized and politicized alliance."[50] And NATO was said to have shed its "enemy" image of the East to seek cooperation with the former socialist states. In keeping with such sentiment, Kozyrev applauded NATO in November 1991 for "threaten[ing] nobody—on the contrary, it . . . is becoming an increasingly more perfect instrument for preserving stability."[51]

Arch-Western advocates of a "real partnership" with NATO declared NATO membership a long-term goal and referred approvingly to Yeltsin's communique to the first session of the North Atlantic Cooperation Council (NACC) in Brussels in December 1991 which expressed that goal.[52] They also argued that Russia needed NATO and NATO needed Russia as the pivot of the CIS, the only entity capable of containing conflict in Central Asia. This, it was believed, would lay a "sound basis" for Russia's eventual inclusion in NATO.[53] The mainstream Russian view, essentially unchanged since it was first conceived in the late Soviet era, welcomed NATO as the guarantor of stability in CEE, predicted that NATO would in time consent to Russian membership,[54] and claimed that NATO attached "great importance" to strengthening the CSCE process and to developing CSCE political structures.[55] This was wishful thinking of the highest order; an article of faith of Russia's Westernizers, it would be made almost irrelevant by the West's NATO expansion campaign.

But even as Kozyrev chastized opposition deputies in September for referring to NATO as "Russia's enemy," Western analysts set off alarm bells—and confirmed opposition fears—by identifying Russia as "the principal potential threat to NATO, even if that [was] not made explicit in the new alliance strategic concept."[56] It was thus understandable that some Russians remained leary of NATO: IMEMO researcher A. Yazkova warned against unquestioning acceptance of NATO as the core of European security,[57] and even upheld some tenets of the Soviet world view; B. Khalosha, a long-time IMEMO specialist on NATO, pointed out in late 1991 that the process of unilateral "deblocization" in Europe had acquired such a headlong character that it raised doubts about NATO's stability and complicated relations with the USSR, and even wondered why NATO refused to renounce its first-strike policy;[58] *Krasnaia zvezda's* military commentator A. Golts expressed the military's suspicion of NATO when he noted that its military doctrine still upheld the notion that the principal military threat emanated from the FSU;[59] and *Pravda* capped it all off with the blunt warning that joining NATO, as was being proposed, would mark the "final step in Russia's bourgeoisification."[60]

NATO's eastward expansion would soon become Russia's overriding foreign policy concern, but even at this early period some Russian politicians and analysts expressed their opposition to NATO expansion without Russia: in March Head of the General Staff Academy I. Rodionov (who would later become Defense Minister) underscored Russia's vital interests, including *at least* the neutrality of the East European states bordering on the CIS, deemed the Baltics and CIS states vital to Russian interests, and identified the West as a threat to Russia's security;[61] and one year after after her glowing predictions for Russia-Western relations, IMEMO researcher M. Strezhneva conceded by year's end that the West would neither grant Russia the aid necessary to weather its crisis nor allow Russia into the EC or NATO.[62]

Unfortunately for Russia this pessimistic view was validated by the West's unyielding posture. At the December 20, 1991 session of the NACC, where Yeltsin announced Russia's interest in maintaining political and military contact with NATO and of joining in the future,[63] Belgian Foreign Minister Eyskens on that same day ruled out Russian membership on the grounds that it would dilute NATO's common security interests and that NATO expansion into Asia, which Russian membership would inevitably lead to, would deal NATO a fatal blow.[64] Although Yeltsin's statement disappeared from the media the next day without followup discussion, proving Russian NATO membership to be a lost cause and demonstrating the leadership's total lack of seriousness on the issue,[65] others refused to take the hint by continuing to praise NATO and even urging that it expand without Russia. President of the Institute for National Security and Strategic Studies Sergei Blagovolin, for instance, asserted that it was "time to toss out the ridiculous fears that NATO is approaching our borders"; NATO, Blagovolin insisted, "is . . . the guarantor, if you will, of our security."[66]

Russian Relations with NATO

The NATO expansion ball began rolling in earnest when NATO Secretary General Woerner declared in mid-February that all CIS members could become NATO members in the future if they created stable democracies,[67] but it quickly became clear that Russia was ruled out. And although Russian officials hastened to express their affection for NATO after the Soviet collapse, Kozyrev backtracked following a meeting with NATO Secretary General Woerner on February 24 by declaring that Russia was loathe to press NATO for membership. Because Russia shared the same values as NATO, he contended, allied relations could be established, but only sometime in the future.[68] Russian representatives nevertheless attended the May NATO conference in Banff, a first for the new nation.[69]

In the meantime, even as worshipful Russian officials were waxing rhapsodic over NATO the idea of expansion—*which indicatively did not include Russia*—was rapidly gaining ground in the West. NATO Secretary General Woerner contradicted his February 1992 declaration that NATO had put off the question of expansion[70] with the acknowledgement the following month that CEE states could join NATO, a move he insisted was necessary for CEE's security—and whose obvious subtext was that this would hedge against Russian assertiveness and communist recidivism.[71] Reports from NATO sources indicated that sentiment for expansion was proliferating in the alliance, that the Visegrad group could be admitted within a few years, and reiterated Belgian Foreign Minister Eysken's position that the line was drawn at Russia's borders.[72] After visiting Hungary in July Woerner went still further, pledging that NATO would not remain disinterested if Hungary were attacked and warned that it could extend security guarantees to CEE.[73] That this was not just idle chatter was demonstrated when NATO fulfilled an old dream by reactivating a naval fleet in the Mediterranean in April, even as it acknowledged that the dismantling of the Soviet navy had eliminated the principal threat in the region.[74]

The US, who has always been the decisive force in NATO, was also increasingly disposed to opening NATO to the CEE states. In September US NATO Ambassador Robert Hunter declared that NATO's key task was to draw Russia and other former Warsaw Pact states into the Western defense system, but that only "some Eastern European states" would actually be invited.[75] And after Polish Prime Minister Suchocka's request for NATO membership was rebuffed in October[76] top US officials, including Defense Secretary Cheney, expressed the opinion in November that Czechoslovakia, Hungary, and Poland should be admitted.[77] The stage was now set for NATO's eastward expansion—to the exclusion of Russia.

Russia and Yugoslavia

Even before the USSR's collapse Russia's leaders made it clear that their policy toward the Balkans was unambiguously pro-Western; they were as opposed to the "red" leaders in Belgrade (Milosevic et al) as they were to the leaders of the former Soviet Union. They tried to maintain the appearance of evenhandededness, however, by joining with West Europe against hard-line US proposals of air strikes against the Bosnian Serbs and insisting on Belgrade's right to be represented in international fora, but this was obviously an attempt to deceive, for Russia's Yugoslavia policy was, on balance, tilted in 1992 overwhelmingly toward the West. This was manifested by, among other things, its vote for Western-inspired United Nations Security Council (UNSC) sanctions against Belgrade.

The Late USSR and the Former Yugoslavia

In October 1991 both Gorbachev and Yeltsin met with Serbian President Milosevic and Bosnian President Tudjman in Moscow in an effort to mediate their differences, as well as to assert Moscow's waning influence in the region. Although they succeeded in brokering a ceasefire (the eighth in recent weeks) between the Serbs and Croats, fighting on the ground continued. The following month at the Hague the USSR joined the EU and US in signing a declaration supporting a leading role for the EU in settling the Yugoslav crisis. Once the new Russian government was formed, it immediately began to "obediently follow the US and EC in the Yugoslav crisis" by recognizing the independence of the Yugoslav republics just weeks after the EU did, justifying such a policy on the grounds that "after entering on a path of rapid integration with the West, [it] did not want to start off with objections to and criticisms of its Western partners."[78]

Other signs of the new Russian government's pro-Western line on Yugoslavia could be detected in Yeltsin's urging the West in November 1991 to adopt a more active posture in the Balkans. By signing a joint statement favoring "democracy" in that country, he again lined up with the West, although indirectly, in its support for the newly elected Slovenian and Croatian leaders against Belgrade. Yeltsin was backed by the "liberal"

Russian media, who called on NATO to help stop "genocide" of the Croatians by the Serbs.[79]

Yugoslavia: Russian Relations with the West

Although they made a pretense of sympathy for the leaders in Belgrade, in reality the Yeltsin team harbored a deep animus toward them which originated well before the Soviet collapse and was firmed up by Belgrade's support for the August 1991 "coup." And Russia's leaders were surprisingly candid on the issue. In his speech to the first session of the RFM's Foreign Policy Council on July 2, 1992 Kozyrev not only laid into Russia's "red-brown" forces for aiming to destroy "reform," but he thoroughly debunked the assumption that Moscow was an ally of Belgrade by asserting that the "Western countries" were "as much the natural allies of the Russian democrats as the national-Bolsheviks are foes." Russia's interests, Kozyrev reminded his listeners, were aligned with the "world community" against Iraq, Libya—and the leaders in Belgrade, "neo-communists, who have traditionally used the patronage of the CPSU Central Committee and have represented the . . . Serbs in the same way the politburo represented the Russians."[80]

While trying to make it appear that by their efforts to prevent Serbia's total political isolation they were supporters of Belgrade,[81] Russian officials actually continued to follow the West's lead in 1992, even frankly admitting—again, in July—that now that Russia had "entered the sphere of European policy which has its own rules of the game, its laws and principles" it was compelled to display solidarity with the West. According to Yeltsin's Press Secretary Kostikov, Russia was not only not "allergic" to NATO but might even send peacekeeping contingents to the Balkans, as had NATO and the WEU,[82] thus essentially confirming one Western source's characterization of Moscow's policy in the Balkans in 1992 as "virtually devoid of independent initiatives . . . [Moscow] has instead done little more than back Western moves."[83]

But the chorus of critics of Russia's Balkan policy swelled, and *Pravda* took the lead by insisting that the reality there was "dangerously different" from what was depicted in Russia's pro-government press, which "thoughtlessly copie[d] the Western press" and printed outright lies to boot, including characterizing Croatia as a "democratic state." *Pravda* emphasized, to the contrary, the transgressions of the Croatian government, including its: adoption of the fascist insignia, encouragement of destruction of anti-fascist memorials commemorating the Jewish holocaust, destruction of Serb-owned stores, persecution of Orthodox church officials, and most disturbing, its "ethnic cleansing" of almost one million Serbs. To *Pravda*, the "democratic" media's claim of Serbian "concentration camps" was a lie, since the only concentration camps in Croatia, they insisted, had been set up by the fascist Ustashi in World War II—whose evil regime the present government was rehabilitating.[84] Chair of the International Affairs Committee of the Supreme Soviet Ambartsumov also denounced Kozyrev for parroting the Western "myth" of Serb "concentration camps" and "ethnic cleansing."[85]

Russia's first major initiative on Yugoslavia came in January when it sent one thousand troops to the Bosnian region of Krajina to join the Western-led UN Protection Force, or UNPROFOR. The move, which represented the "height of Moscow's pro-Western foreign policy" to that point, was symptomatic of the Russian leadership's attempt to break completely with the USSR's anti-Western positions.[86] Kozyrev stepped up Russia's cooperation with the West by agreeing at the end of February to send additional observers and military police to Yugoslavia to join UN peacekeeping forces and announced at the March 24 CSCE meeting in Helsinki that Russia did not oppose the participation of NATO and WEU troops in CSCE peacekeeping.[87]

Russia's delegation to the May CSCE conference found itself isolated over the recognition of Belgrade as the successor to the former Yugoslavia. Objecting to the latter's treatment as a "pariah" unfairly labeled the sole aggressor in the Yugoslav conflict, Russia demanded that the conference also acknowledge Bosnia's responsibility for the conflict. So far, so good; Russia seemed to accept the mantle of Belgrade's protector. And it rejected an extremely harsh proposal advanced early in the meeting which banned Belgrade from the OSCE, voting instead for the final, softer resolution which excluded Belgrade from participating in decisions taken on Bosnia on the grounds that Belgrade had committed "clear, gross and uncorrected violations" in Yugoslavia. Russia clearly hoped that its seeming support for Belgrade would burnish its image as a Belgrade ally. And the Serbs appeared willing to believe it and played along, as was demonstrated by Bosnian Serb leader Karadzic's declaration of a unilateral ceasefire on May 12, shortly after Kozyrev sent him a telegram appealing for such a move,[88] and just one of a number of occasions when the Serbs would moderate their behavior in apparent response to the urgings of their Russian "friends."

But the perception that Russia was the Serbs' ally and protector was soon shown to be specious, and Russian policy took a dramatic, still more anti-Serb turn on May 26 when, during a visit to Sarajevo, Kozyrev joined the West in calling for Bosnian independence and urging the EC-sponsored peace conference to draft a plan for a peace settlement in the war-torn nation.[89] This "highpoint" of collaboration with the West was deepened even further when, following a Bosnian Serb mortar attack on Sarajevo which shattered a Russian-brokered truce, an outraged Yeltsin accused the Serbs of being warmongers and admonished the UNSC to impose severe sanctions—"the heavier and harder the better." He joined the RFM in proposing the establishment of a war crimes tribunal under an international commission and suggested that the UNSC be granted more authority in cases of ethnic conflict, including sanctions and "other resolute actions" against "those [Serbs] who are chiefly to blame for the bloodshed."[90]

Being in no mood to coddle their Serb "allies," Russia's leaders translated their anti-Serb temper into action. Confounding expectations that it would at least abstain, Russia's UN delegation on May 30 voted with the West on a UNSC motion imposing sanctions on the Serbs for the aforesaid attack on Sarajevo. Having thus shown that Serbia had "lost its last major friend in the world," Russian officials admitted that they had refused to abstain because doing so would have "weakened the message" to Belgrade. What is more, by voting for the harsher anti-Serb version favored by the US over milder West European versions Russia's UN delegation completely reversed the stand Russia had taken at the May CSCE session.[91]

Clearly on the defensive now, RFM spokesperson Yastrzhembskii tried to justify Russia's policy in Yugoslavia in early June by protesting that it had "ben[t] over backwards to be seen as a committed member of the international democratic establishment," but he then revealed the real rationale for Russia's policy, repeating the government's—essentially pro-Western, anti-Serb—line that "according to the world community" Belgrade shared the "bulk of the responsibility" for the situation in Yugoslavia.[92] Needless to say, Kozyrev and his RFM were roundly attacked in Russia for their support of sanctions,[93] said to be part and parcel of their general policy of acquiescing to the West in return for pecuniary gain. Kozyrev again justified Russia's support of anti-Serb sanctions on June 9 on the grounds that it was a "kind of sobering cold shower" for the Serbs, who had ignored Russia's advice to stop the violence. No wonder the official Yugoslav news agency accused Russia on June 1 of adopting "a role of an assistant in directing the Western tide against Serbia,"[94] a charge periodically rekindled in different variants up to and during the 1999 war in Kosovo.

Although the Westernizers claimed that Russia upheld an independent position on Yugoslavia as befitted Russia's presumed "great power status"[95] the opposition's mistrust of the leadership's motives increased exponentially with the publication by the newspaper *Den'* in its June 7-13 issue—on the eve of a Yeltsin-Bush summit—of a memorandum by Russia's UN Ambassador Vorontsov in which he confided that his delegation had voted for anti-Serb sanctions because they did not want to oppose the West, above all, the US, where public opinion was running strongly against Serb President Milosevic. Kozyrev implicitly admitted the document's authenticity.[96]

The controversy over Yugoslavia heated up and the Supreme Soviet, furious at the RFM's failure to consult with it, stepped up its opposition to Yeltsin's policies. Bridling at Kozyrev's June 26 request to support still tougher UN sanctions against Belgrade, the parliament passed a resolution rebuking him for his "excessive haste" to support the West and for breaching Russia's traditional pro-Serbian policy more generally. On June 26 Russia's UN delegation, with the rest of the UNSC, voted to issue an ultimatum to the Serbs to stop fighting in Sarajevo within forty-eight hours or face unspecified military action. Still leary of using force, however, the UNSC agreed on June 28 merely to strengthen economic sanctions. US and EC officials stepped up their threats to use force to repel the Serbian onslaught in Sarajevo, including a statement drawn up by EC leaders declaring that "support for the use of military means by the UN" was not excluded,[97] and which tallied with Russia's advocacy during the previous month of "more resolute" actions against the Serbs. This line would, in time, be implemented with Russia's wholehearted support.

Kozyrev answered parliament's attacks by defending his Ministry's "evenhandedness" and listing its many "accomplishments" in Yugoslavia, including the blocking of a decision based on an EU draft resolution suspending Yugoslavia from all CSCE activities, winning a month-long delay of sanctions against the Serbs, and opposing the total cutoff of supplies to the Serbs. At the same time he also revealed his anti-Serb bent by blaming Belgrade for having brought sanctions on itself and for failing to heed the demands of the international community, argued that only sanctions would force Belgrade to accept a political solution, and chided Belgrade for being unable to "find the strength to recognize the beginning of the inevitable fall of the Yugoslav government." Kozyrev also appealed to the Supreme Soviet to consider Russian participation in a UN-organized multinational force in the former Yugoslavia and ended with the familiar mantra that opposing sanctions would violate the will of the UN and the international community as a whole.[98]

Once again, Russia reverted to its tactic of "evenhandedness" at the two-day CSCE summit in Helsinki on July 9-10 by refusing to agree to a draft declaration placing "prime responsibility" on Belgrade for the violence and ethnic cleansing in Bosnia-Herzegovina on the grounds that it was too one-sided. It also opposed efforts to expel or suspend Belgrade from the Conference. Apparently Russia felt that this was a forum sufficiently safe and powerless, unlike the UNSC, for it to put on a show of opposition—however minimal—to the West. In the end, the Russian delegation agreed to the draft suspending Belgrade until October 14.[99] That same month Yeltsin gave his support to the proposed European rapid reaction force (RRF) in the former Yugoslavia, but was adamant that it be deployed in a timely way to head off bloodshed. His statement of support followed CSCE and WEU approval of an unprecedented naval operation in the Adriatic Sea, jointly coordinated by the WEU and NATO, to enforce UN sanctions against Serbia. Although Yeltsin did not directly refer to the operation in the Adriatic in the speech, Russia was "not prepared to buck its European partners" on the issue.[100]

Russia's opposition came up with a kind of smoking gun at the end of July which seemed to prove incontrovertibly the leadership's real pro-Western predilections in the Balkans in the form of transcripts of private diplomatic communications between Russia and the US during May and June and published, once again, by *Den'*. The transcripts, whose authenticity was never denied, documented how US Secretary of State Baker "advised" Kozyrev to give up Russia's position of "support" for Serbia and go along with the US-proposed temporary suspension of Belgrade from the CSCE. Baker also "suggested" to Kozyrev that although no party in the former Yugoslavia was blameless, Belgrade bore "much greater responsibility" than any other—a position Kozyrev would repeat almost verbatim months later at the London Conference on Yugoslavia. Baker also told Kozyrev precisely what he should tell Milosevic during his upcoming trip to Belgrade, expressed his "deep appreciation for Russia's support for UN [resolution 757 imposing] sanctions against Serbia," and ended by making clear that he expected "continued consultation and cooperation" from Kozyrev on foreign policy matters.[101] Russia's vote just two weeks later for a UNSC resolution legitimizing military force to ensure the delivery of humanitarian aid to Bosnia seemed to obey Baker's dictates—although diplomats acknowledged that it was unlikely that any use of force would actually result from the "vague" resolution which was to be used only "as a last resort." References to Serbian aggression were deleted on Russian insistence, clearly to sweeten the Serbs' bitter pill.[102]

At a UN-sponsored conference on the Balkans Kozyrev on August 26 sought to again display his "evenhanded" approach in the former

Yugoslavia by asserting Russia's support of "rationally-minded people in Belgrade" and its goal of isolating "aggressive forces." Having said all this, Kozyrev then placed the lion's share of responsibility for the conflict on Belgrade and hinted that Russia would support France, who was increasingly eager to take "decisive measures" against the Serbs, who were threatening UN personnel. To cap it all off, he urged the Serbs to end their "ethnic cleansing."[103]

Throughout the fall Russia maintained close cooperation with Britain and France to prevent a US-directed military action against the Serbs (although none opposed such action in principle). But Russia confounded those who assumed it to be the Serbs' protector by voting in mid-September for a UNSC resolution which took up where the May CSCE conference left off by censuring Yugoslavia and barring it from voting in the UN, a first for the UN body. Although this move came as a surprise, given Russia's prior public opposition (it had, to be sure, agreed in private that Belgrade should apply for a seat of its own), the final resolution included a minor "concession" to Russia in the form of a statement which acknowledged that no side in the conflict was blameless.[104]

Russia tried yet again to appear "evenhanded" by seeing to it that the final version of the latter resolution omitted the extreme proposal that Belgrade be completely excluded from the UN (the final version stipulated that it be excluded from the General Assembly session only). Russia's representative to the UN Vorontsov even offered as a weak justification for his vote the reassurance that Belgrade still retained its nameplate in the General Assembly. But Russia's real anti-Serb inclinations were exposed when, in the ensuing debate over who would succeed the former Yugoslavia in the UN, Belgrade's delegate to the UN tried to elicit Russian support for his country's succession by invoking a comparison between Russia after the USSR's dissolution and Serbia after the breakup of Yugoslavia—the implication being that Belgrade should take the former Yugoslavia's seat in the UN just as Russia had the USSR's. Kozyrev quickly dashed Serbia's hopes by rejecting the analogy as inapplicable on account of "fundamental differences" in the situations of the two countries.[105]

The UNSC—with Russia's assent—took another giant step in early October with the passage of Resolution 786 establishing a no-fly zone over Bosnia, although the zone was not yet enforced owing to West European fears of provoking the Serbs while West European military units were deployed in Bosnia. The West was also loathe to undermine the Yeltsin "reformers" in Russia, who would face fierce opposition if they displayed too obvious an anti-Serb bias by supporting such a policy.[106]

Forced again to defend his policy in the former Yugoslavia before the Supreme Soviet, Kozyrev on October 22 boasted that his Ministry's "firm policy" had prevented Yugoslavia's expulsion from the UN and promised that Russia would seek to ease (but not eliminate) sanctions.[107] But Kozyrev proceeded shortly thereafter to placate the West at a meeting of ambassadors from NATO states on October 28 by offering a warship to assist NATO and WEU naval forces patrolling the Adriatic Sea and the Danube River, part of the campaign to monitor the UN sanctions imposed against Serbia.[108]

A Bosnian ceasefire reached on November 10 was reinforced on November 16 by toughened UNSC sanctions and a proposed naval blockade against Yugoslavia drafted by the US, France, Britain, Belgium—and Russia, who had by now twice approved anti-Serb sanctions.[109] But when Russia also supported the West's opposition to the presidential and parliamentary victory of the Serbian Socialists in 1992,[110] such open pro-Western perfidy and duplicity by the leadership pushed parliament past the breaking point: on December 17 it demanded that the government reverse its "anti-Serb" position, and on December 30 went even further, achieving a historic first with the passage of a resolution—the opposition's first major attack against the RFM—demanding, inter alia, that sanctions be extended to all the warring sides and that Russia use its UNSC veto against any proposed military intervention. The resolution, which was rejected by the RFM as "meddling by non-professionals," followed Kozyrev's December 29 announcement that Russia had dropped its objections to a Western-backed UNSC resolution for "joint measures" with other states to finally punish violators of the no-fly zone—that is, the Serbs. After some contention, Russian officials craftily agreed to the UNSC resolution only on the condition that it not mention the Serbs by name.[111]

Notes

[1] Sheila Marnie, "Economic Reform and Poverty in Russia," *RFE/RL Research Report*, Vol. 2, No. 6, February 5, 1993, pp. 32-6; Erick Whitlock, "New Russian Government to Continue Economic Reform?" *RFE/RL Research Report*, Vol. 2, No. 3, January 15, 1993, pp. 23-4. See Chapter 2 for a more in-depth discussion of the voucher program.

[2] Alexander Rahr, "Winners and Losers of the Russian Congress," *RFE/RL Research Report*, Vol. 1, No. 18, May 1, 1992, pp. 1-3.

[3] Idem., "The First Year of Russian Independence," *RFE/RL Research Report*, Vol. 2, No. 1, January 1, 1993, p. 55.

[4] Ibid. *Nezavisimaia gazeta*, November 24, 1992, p. 2, also gives some background to the conflict.

[5] Alexei K. Pushkov, "Russia and America: The Honeymoon's Over," *Foreign Policy*, No. 93, Winter 1993-4, pp. 77-82. See a similar scheme in S. Neil MacFarlane, "Russian Conceptions of Europe," *Post-Soviet Affairs*, Vol. 10, No. 3, July-September 1994, pp. 241-50.

[6] Pushkov, "Russia and America," pp. 83-4.

[7] Anders Aslund, *How Russia Became a Market Economy* (Washington, D.C.: The Brookings Institution, 1995), p. 215. See also Christopher Smart, *The Imagery of Soviet Foreign Policy and the Collapse of the Russian Empire* (Westport: Praeger, 1995), pp. 150-1.

[8] Interfax, December 28, 1991, in *FBIS*- SOV-92-001, January 2, 1992, p. 76.

[9] *Izvestiia*, January 20, 1992, p. 1.

[10] Alexei K. Pushkov, *Moscow News*, No. 8, February 23-March 1, 1992, p. 12.

[11] *Izvestiia*, October 7, 1992, p. 4.

[12] Ibid., January 2, 1992, p. 3. Kozyrev had articulated a similar position as early as 1990. See *New Times*, October 23-9, 1990, pp. 6-8. See also TASS, February 10, 1992, in *FBIS*-SOV-92-030, February 13, 1992, p. 28.

[13] *New Times*, October 23-9, 1990, pp. 6-8.

[14] Leszek Buszynski, *Russian Foreign Policy After the Cold War* (Westport, CT: Praeger, 1996), pp. 5-6.

[15] *Komsomol'skaia pravda*, September 3, 1992, p. 3.

[16] Suzanne Crow, "Competing Blueprints for Russian Foreign Policy," *RFE/RL Research Report*, Vol. 1, No. 50, December 18, 1992, p. 46.

[17] *Nezavisimaia gazeta*, August 19, 1992, p. 4. For an analysis, see Crow, "Competing Blueprints," pp. 47-8.

[18] *Nezavisimaia gazeta*, August 19, 1992, p. 4.

[19] Interfax, December 1, 1992, in *FBIS*-SOV-92-232, December 2, 1992, p. 3; MacFarlane, "Russian Conceptions of Europe," p. 252.

[20] *Izvestiia*, February 6, 1992, p. 1, February 7, 1992, p. 1. Russia's Ambassador to the US, Vladimir Lukin, chastized the RFM for expecting to be "showered with gifts" from the West. See *Nezavisimaia gazeta*, September 10, 1992, p. 4, in *Current Digest of the Post-Soviet Press*, October 7, 1992, p. 17.

[21] *Financial Times*, August 14, 1992, p. 10.

[22] Inter Press Service, July 9, 1992.

[23] Simon Clarke, "The Crisis of the Soviet System," in Simon Clarke, Peter Fairbrother, Michael Burawoy, and Pavel Krotov, eds., *What About the Workers? Workers and the Transition to Capitalism in Russia* (London: Verso, 1993), p. 45.

[24] V. Pichugin, "Programma mnogostoronnei pomoshchi Zapada Rossii: deklaratsii ili real'noe soderzhanie?" *Rossiia v mire*, No. 1, 1993, pp. 70-1; ITAR-TASS, July 8, 1992.

[25] Leszek Busczynski, "Russia and the West: Towards Renewed Geopolitical Rivalry?" *Survival*, Vol. 37, No. 3, Autumn 1995, p. 106.

[26] MacFarlane, "Russian Conceptions of Europe," p. 235. See also the article by Kozyrev in *Nezavisimaia gazeta*, August 20, 1992, p. 4, and A. Zagorskii, A. Zlobin, S. Solodovnik, and M. Khrustalev, "Rossiia v novom mire," *Mezhdunarodnaia zhizn'*, No. 5, 1992, p. 10.

[27] *Mezhdunarodnaia zhizn'*, No. 10, 1994, p. 108.

[28] *Nezavisimaia gazeta*, August 20, 1992, p. 4.

[29] John W. R. Leppingwell, "Yeltsin Calls for Tougher Foreign Policy," *RFE/RL Research Report*, Vol. 1, No. 44, November 6, 1992, p. 17.

[30] *Izvestiia*, December 15, 1992, p. 6. The WEU is the military arm of the EU.

[31] Ibid.

[32] ITAR-TASS, December 17, 1992.

[33] See Hannes Adomeit, "Russia as a 'Great Power' in World Affairs: Images and Reality," *International Affairs* (London), Vol. 71, No. 1, January 1995, p. 45, in which Adomeit terms the Russian foreign policy shift in late 1992 "neo-imperialist."

[34] Ni Xiaoquan, "The Present Situation and Future Prospects for Sino-Russian Relations," *The Harriman Review*, July 1995, p. 36.

[35] Alfred A. Reisch, "Central and Eastern Europe's Quest for NATO Membership," *RFE/RL Research Report*, Vol. 2, No. 28, July 9, 1993, p. 34.

[36] Neil Malcolm, "Introduction: Russia and Europe," in Neil Malcolm, ed., *Russia and Europe: An End to Confrontation?* (London: Pinter, 1994), p. 19.

[37] Reisch, "Central and Eastern Europe's Quest," pp. 36-7.

[38] Vladimir Baranovskii, "Evropa: formirovanie novoi mezhdunarodno-politicheskoi sistemy," *Mirovaia ekonomika i mezhdunarodnye otnosheniia* (hereafter referred to as *MEMO*), No. 9, 1990, p. 15.

[39] *Pravda*, November 6, 1992, p. 4, in *FBIS-SOV-90-216*, November 7, 1990, p. 1.

[40] Heather F. Hurlburt, "Russia Plays a Double Game," *Transition*, Vol. 1, No. 11, June 30, 1995, pp. 10-11.

[41] Ibid., pp. 10-12.

[42] See Pavel Bogomolov's article in *Pravda*, November 19, 1991, p. 5.

[43] Reisch, "Central and Eastern Europe's Quest," p. 34.

[44] Ibid., pp. 36-8. The Visegrad three was an organization named after the town near Budapest where leaders from Poland, Czechoslovakia, and Hungary met in February 1991 to coordinate efforts to join the European Community and cooperate in economic and security affairs, especially for the purpose strengthening their bargaining hand vis-à-vis the USSR.

[45] Ibid., pp. 40-1.

[46] V. Kozin, "Novye izmereniia NATO," *Mezhdunarodnaia zhizn'*, No. 3, 1993, p. 55.

[47] A. Zagorskii and Michael Lucas, *Rossiia pered evropeiskim vyzovom* (Moscow: "Mezhdunarodnye otnosheniia," 1993), pp. 97-8. See also *Izvestiia*, October 26, 1991, p. 3, October 4, 1991, *Segodnia*, January 25, 1996, p. 2,

Nezavisimaia gazeta, November 28, 1991, p. 2, and a warning against NATO expansion without Russia in *Nezavisimaia gazeta*, October 20, 1991, p. 4.

[48] V. Kudriavtsev, "Politika NATO na perelome," *MEMO*, No. 5, 1992, pp. 46-8.

[49] Alexander Alexeyev, "The New Dimension of NATO," *International Affairs* (Moscow), No. 2, 1992, pp. 45-51; Radio Moscow, March 31, 1992, in *FBIS*-SOV-92-063, April 1, 1992, p. 8. Alexeyev was Head of the NATO Division of the European Security and Cooperation Department of the Russian Ministry of Foreign Affairs.

[50] Sergei Karaganov, "Questions Facing the Future of Europe," *International Affairs* (Moscow), No. 5, 1991, p. 39.

[51] D. Rurikov, "How It All Began: An Essay on New Russia's Foreign Policy," *Russian Security After the Cold War: Seven Views from Moscow* (Washington, D.C.: Brassey's, 1994), p. 138.

[52] Sergei Oznobishchev, "NATO skvoz' prizmu peremen," *MEMO*, No. 7, 1993, p. 152; Iu. Gusarov, "Problemy evropeiskoi bezopasnosti v svete sozdianiia novogo mirnogo poriadka," *MEMO*, No. 8, 1992, p. 111; S. Chugrov, "Rossiia mezhdu Vostokom i Zapadom," *MEMO*, No. 7, 1992, p. 81. During a January 1992 visit to Bonn, Kozyrev repeated the call for a single security space. See ITAR-TASS, January 16, 1992.

[53] Alexei Pushkov, *Moscow News*, No. 8, February 19, 1992, p. 12.

[54] Alekseyev, "The New Dimension of NATO," pp. 45-51; V. Kudriatsev, *Evoliutsiia voenno-politicheskoi strategii NATO na sovremennom etape (1967-1992 gg.) v kontekste evropeiskoi bezopasnosti*, Vol. II (Moscow: Ordena trudovogo krasnogo znamena Diplomaticheskaia Akademiia MIDRF, 1992), pp. 184-6. See also Iu. Gusarov, "Problemy evropeiskoi bezopasnosti," pp. 110-11.

[55] Kudriavtsev, "Politika NATO," pp. 54-5. See also S. Kirshin, "Metamorfozy v NATO," *SShA*, No. 9, 1992, p. 60. Later analyses would attribute such late 1991-early 1992 pro-Western optimism to the excessive "romantic enthusiasm" of the "democrats." See S. Karaganov, "Rossiia i Evropa," in *Budet li sushchestvovat' Evropa bez Rossii?* (Moscow: Mezhdunarodnyi tsentr finansogo-ekonomicheskogo razvitii, 1995), p. 102.

[56] *Defense News*, September 21-7, 1992, p. 24.

[57] A. Yazkova, "From Eastern Europe into a United Europe," *International Affairs* (Moscow), No. 10, 1991, p. 140. Yazkova was head of the Sector of General Problems on International Relations at the Institute for International Economics and Political Studies.

[58] Boris Khalosha, "Novaia voenno-politicheskaia situatsiia v Evrope," *MEMO*, No. 11, 1991, pp. 71-2. A similar unease regarding NATO's expressed need for a "counterweight" to the USSR was voiced by Alekseyev, "The New Dimension of NATO," p. 52.

[59] *Krasnaia zvezda*, January 15, 1992, p. 3.

[60] *Pravda*, January 18, 1992, p. 4. See also the piece in *Nezavisimaia gazeta*, March 11, 1992, p. 2, by Alexei Arbatov, Director of the Center on Disarmament and Strategic Stability of the Foreign Policy Association, which asserted that NATO would never admit Russia into its ranks.

[61] Trevor Taylor, *European Security and the Former Soviet Union: Dangers, Opportunities and Gambles* (London: The Royal Institute of International Affairs, 1994), p. 9. See also A. Grachev, *Moscow News*, No. 13, March 29-April 5, 1992, p. 13.

[62] Marina V. Strezhneva, "Security-Political Aspects of the Relations Betwen EC and Russia," in Hans-Georg Erhart, Anna Kreikemeyer and Andrei V. Zagorski, eds., *The Former Soviet Union and European Security: Between Integration and Re-Nationalization* (Baden-Baden: Nomos, 1993), pp. 58, 61. Strezhneva was a leading researcher at IMEMO. See also Sergei Karaganov, *Russia: The New Foreign Policy and Security Agenda* (London: Brassey's, The Centre for Defence Studies, 1992), pp. 27-9.

[63] B. Yeltsin, "Obrashchenie k uchastnikam sessii soveta severoatlanticheskogo sotrudnichestva," *Diplomaticheskii vestnik*, No. 1, January 15, 1992, pp. 12-13.

[64] Reuters, December 20, 1992.

[65] *The Independent* (Moscow), May-June, 1993, p. 14.

[66] *Izvestiia*, January 22, 1992, p. 5.

[67] ITAR-TASS, February 14, 1992, in *FBIS*-SOV-92-032, February 18, 1992, p. 7. See a similar view by Yeltsin adviser Burbulis in ITAR-TASS, May 9, 1992, in *FBIS*-SOV-92-091, May 11, 1992, pp. 12-13.

[68] Interfax, February 24, 1992, in *FBIS*-SOV-92-036, February 24, 1992, p. 25.

[69] Reuters, May 14, 1992.

[70] *Nezavisimaia gazeta*, March 10, 1992, p.4. While in Moscow in late February Woerner made a thinly-veiled warning to Russia that NATO did not "intend to come undone" despite its resolve to "reform," as it was the only organization capable of maintaining international order and security. See Interfax, February 25, 1992, in *FBIS*-SOV-92-038, February 26, 1992, p. 23.

[71] Reuters, March 9, 1992.

[72] Ibid., March 4, 1992.

[73] *Izvestiia*, July 20, 1992, p. 5.

[74] Ibid., April 30, 1992.

[75] Ibid., September 23, 1992.

[76] Ibid., October 7, 1992.

[77] Reisch, "Central and Eastern Europe's Quest," p. 43, fn. 51.

[78] TASS, October 16, 1991; *The Daily Telegraph*, October 17, 1991, p. 12; N. Arbatova, "Uroki Iugoslavii dlia Rossii i Zapada," *MEMO*, No. 2, 1995, pp. 46-8. See also Mike Bowker, *Russian Foreign Policy and the End of the Cold War* (Aldershot: Dartmouth, 1997), p. 230.

[79] Andrei Edemskii, "Russian Perspectives," in Alex Danchev and Thomas Halverson, eds., *International Perspectives on the Yugoslav Conflict* (New York: St. Martin's, 1996), p. 32.

[80] Kozyrev's speech on foreign policy, July 2, 1992, *Diplomaticheskii vestnik*, No. 15-16, August 15-31, 1992, pp. 62-3. See also a similar argument by Kozyrev in *Nezavisimaia gazeta*, August 20, 1992, p. 4. A concurring Western view identifies the "reactionary communist-nationalist forces" as the core of the anti-"liberal government" tendency in Russia which seeks to form a Russian-Serb partnership. See Allen Lynch and Reneo Lukic, "Russian Foreign Policy and the Wars in the Former Yugoslavia," *RFE/RL Research Report*, Vol. 2, No. 41, October 15, 1993, p. 25.

[81] Lynch and Lukic, "Russian Foreign Policy," p. 28.

[82] TASS, July 13, 1992.

[83] Inter Press Service, August 24, 1992.

[84] *Pravda*, January 13, 1992, p. 4.

[85] Lynch and Lukic, "Russian Foreign Policy," p. 27; *Diplomaticheskii vestnik*, No. 17-18, September 15-30, 1992, pp. 40-1, articulates the Russian government position.

[86] Bowker, *Russian Foreign Policy*, pp. 230-1.

[87] Speech by Russian Permanent Representative to the UN Security Council, Yurii Vorontsov, Yeisradio, Helsinki, March 25, 1992, in BBC Summary of World Broadcasts, March 30, 1992, February 29, 1992; Yugoslav News Agency, February 26, 1992.

[88] *Izvestiia*, May 13, 1992, p. 6; *Financial Times*, May 13, 1992, p. 22; Agence France Presse, May 12, 1992; The Associated Press, May 12, 1992.

[89] Suzanne Crow, "Russia's Response to the Yugoslav Crisis," *RFE/RL Research Report*, Vol. 1, No. 30, July 24, 1992, pp. 31-2.

[90] *The Los Angeles Times*, May 31, 1992, p. A1.

[91] *Izvestiia*, June 1, 1992, pp. 1, 4.

[92] Agence France Presse, June 2, 1992; *Izvestiia*, June 1, 1992, pp. 1, 4; Official Kremlin International News Broadcast, June 2, 1992.

[93] Lynch and Lukic, "Russian Foreign Policy," p. 29; ITAR-TASS, May 30, 1992, in *FBIS*-SOV-92-105, June 1, 1992, p. 11; Agence France Presse, June 2, 1992; The Reuter Library Report, May 29, 1992.

[94] *The Daily Telegraph*, June 1, 1992, p. 11; *Komsomol'skaia pravda*, June 9, 1992, p. 3.

[95] Mark Webber, *The International Politics of Russia and the Successor States* (Manchester: Manchester University Press, 1996), p. 266.

[96] Crow, "Russia's Response to the Yugoslav Crisis," p. 32.

[97] E. Ambartsumov, *Izvestiia*, June 29, 1992, p. 3. See also Lynch and Lukic, "Russian Foreign Policy," p. 29, and *The Boston Globe*, June 28, 1992, p. 1.

[98] ITAR-TASS, June 30, 1992, in *FBIS*-SOV-92-127, July 1, 1992, p. 23; Buszynski, *Russian Foreign Policy*, p. 71; *Izvestiia*, June 27, 1992, p. 1; Interfax, June 26, 1992.

[99] *Financial Times*, July 11, 1992, p. 3; Crow, "Russia's Response to the Yugoslav Crisis," pp. 33-4. Russia had taken an identical position at the May CSCE session. See Ibid., p. 33.

[100] Reuters North American Wire, July 10, 1992.

[101] *Den'*, July 26-August 1, 1992, No. 30, pp. 1-2.

[102] Associated Press, August 13, 1992.

[103] Lynch and Lukic, "Russian Foreign Policy," pp. 30-1; *Nezavisimaia gazeta*, August 29, 1992, p. 1; Suzanne Crow, "Reading Moscow's Policies Toward the Rump Yugoslavia," *RFE/RL Research Report*, Vol. 1, No. 44, November 6, 1992, p. 14; Inter Press Service, August 24, 1992; *Komsomol'skaia pravda*, August 27, 1992, p. 3.

[104] Lynch and Lukic, "Russian Foreign Policy," pp. 30-1; *Izvestiia*, September 21, 1992, p. 1; The Reuter Library Report, September 19, 1992; Crow, "Reading Moscow's Policies," p. 15; The Associated Press, September 19, 1992.

[105] Ibid.

[106] Lynch and Lukic, "Russian Foreign Policy," pp. 31-2; Bowker, *Russian Foreign Policy*, p. 233.

[107] Kozyrev October 22, 1992 speech to the Supreme Soviet, in *Diplomaticheskii vestnik*, No. 21-22, November 15-30, 1992, p. 26.

[108] The Reuter Library Report, October 29, 1992.

[109] *The New York Times*, November 17, 1992, p. A3; Webber, *The International Politics of Russia*, p. 261.

[110] S. Samuilov, "SShA, NATO, Rossiia i bosniiskii krizis," *SShA*, No. 7, 1995, p. 23.

[111] Karen Dawisha and Bruce Parrott, *Russia and the New States of Eurasia: The Politics of Upheaval* (Cambridge: Cambridge University Press, 1994), p. 205; *Izvestiia*, December 18, 1992, p. 4; *The Independent* (London), December 31, 1992, p. 1.

4 1993: The Deception Begins in Full Swing

The Domestic Setting

Opposition to the Yeltsin-Kozyrev foreign policy line continued to mount in 1993, spurred on by the "spectacular failure" of Russian economic "reform."[1] According to a World Bank report released in August 1995 average real income in Russia declined 43% between 1991-93, while only 40% of workers in 1993 (and 1994) were paid fully and on time.[2] Health care was in crisis, hygiene was abysmal, funding for medicine and equipment was scarce, and diseases long since eradicated reappeared with a vengeance,[3] all of which led opposition economist Sergei Glaz'ev to conclude from a report on the economy that the regime's overemphasis on raw materials export seriously undermined the position of domestic industry. His warning that Russia was courting disaster and future deindustrialization[4] was countered by Yeltsin economic aide A. Livshits, who confidently predicted that Russia's economic policies would improve its export structure. He even welcomed capital flight as a blessing which would "pave the way for future Russian exports."[5]

Economic troubles translated into political strife, as relations between Yeltsin and his opponents deteriorated to the point of bloodshed. In February Yeltsin broke an uneasy truce with parliament when, after having agreed with parliamentary Chair Khasbulatov that an extraordinary session of the CPD would be convened to ratify the division of powers, he proposed an expansion of Presidential powers and the adoption of a new constitution. Yeltsin continued throughout 1993 to pursue a policy of direct announcements to the nation over the head of parliament. For their part, the Western powers did not retreat from their staunch defense of Yeltsin, even when he openly flouted the most basic of democratic principles.[6]

Then on March 2 Yeltsin threw down the gauntlet by announcing that he was no longer obliged to observe the constitution on the grounds that it had been radically altered since he took office. In response to hints that he might institute emergency rule to bypass parliament, the Supreme Soviet on

March 3 threatened to declare emergency rule and strip Yeltsin of his powers. After several extraordinary sessions of the CPD, Yeltsin made good on his threat by declaring "special rule" on March 20 and suspending legislative powers pending new elections. But the Constitutional Court judged this action unconstitutional, and when the decree was published all references to special rule had been excised. Claiming to have garnered more than 50% of the vote in the April referendum on his Presidency, Yeltsin pressed on with the promulgation of his new constitution, secure in the knowledge that he had the support of the chief EU powers and also NATO, which indirectly lent its backing by refusing comment on his imposition of "special rule." French President Mitterand even went so far as to make sure that a few days before the decree's publication a photograph was taken of him standing conspicuously next to Yeltsin.[7]

Following statements by Presidential spokesperson V. Kostikov in March that Yeltsin was seriously considering direct presidential rule, it was reported that Yeltsin had asked "several Western leaders" if they would back his "emergency measure" to disband Parliament. Their answer was made clear by their unconditional support for Yeltsin in March and October, when he used force against parliament.[8] Indeed, Western diplomats admitted in private conversations that because there was no alternative to Yeltsin they would approve any steps, including unconstitutional, he might take.[9] German officials were particularly candid, declaring on March 21, for example, that they "welcomed with understanding" Yeltsin's March declaration of presidential rule because it "avert[ed Russia's] political crisis."[10] On March 27 an EU delegation hastened to Moscow to discuss ways of accelerating the signing of the Agreement on Partnership and Cooperation (APC), which gave Russia minimal trading and other advantages and was an important element in the EU's strategy of drawing Russia closer to Europe.[11]

Although several billion dollars in IMF and World Bank support were to have been given to Russia in 1992, only a fraction of that was actually disbursed on account of Russia's failure to meet the stringent targets on inflation and deficit reduction normally required by the IMF. Frightened by vigorous resistance to Yeltsin's policies at the eighth CPD on March 13-20, however, Mitterand and Kohl called an emergency G-7 meeting to discuss aid to Russia, an unusual move given that Western aid to Russia had until then been "mainly negative in character."[12] It was therefore no coincidence that the idea for a $3 billion specialized IMF loan, the Systemic

Transformation Facility (STF), earmarked specially for Russian "market reforms" and aimed at affording Russia and successor states easier access to funds to cover balance-of-payments deficits, was officially agreed on April 23 at the G-7 meeting in Tokyo, just two days before Yeltsin's referendum on his presidency. The loan—which reflected the IMF's eagerness to help the Yeltsin forces resist the surging opposition by, among other things, pacifying strikers and politically unstable regions—was disbursed in a form never before offered by the IMF, to be made available immediately with only a "mild commitment" on Russia's part. In May the Ministry of Finance and Central Bank reached agreement with the IMF on the STF.[13]

Hostilities between the Yeltsin forces and the opposition reached a climax in late September-early October when Yeltsin issued patently illegal decrees dissolving the Russian legislature, mandated that its powers be transferred to a new bicameral Federal Assembly, and suspended the old constitution. In the ensuing attack on the legislature ordered by Yeltsin government troops killed possibly hundreds who were defending democracy in the White House. Yeltsin then crushed the local soviets, had most of their powers transferred to appointed Heads of Administration, and ordered elections for the new lower chamber, named the State Duma.[14]

The cynical intervention of the Western powers in the March and October 1993 "coups" prompted one Russian journalist to condemn Yeltsin for having "secured his [Western] masters' support" by brutal and undemocratic means. Even Russian conservatives had cautioned the West against such support, warning that siding with Yeltsin against parliament risked further alienating a nation already hit hard by Western "reforms."[15] Nevertheless, when the violence was over European Commission President Delors gave Yeltsin a firm vote of confidence for having warded off civil war and EU experts deemed Yeltsin's draft constitution quite "acceptable," a "convincing victory for democracy in Russia." While crying crocodile tears over the "loss of life" in the October violence, they pointed the finger at "elements hostile to the democratization process" for provoking it.[16]

Foreign Policy Developments: The Origins of the "Hard" Line

In the wake of the suppression of the October "uprising" the heads of the main "power ministries"—Defense Minister Grachev, head of the Ministry of Internal Affairs Viktor Erin, head of the Ministry of Security Nikolai

Golushko, and Main Protection Administration Chief M. Barsukov, as well as Commander of Yeltsin's political bodyguard, B. Kursakov, all received awards or promotions. Most analyses contend that their increased influence on policymaking was inevitable and that after the October events Russian policy became more hard-line and anti-Western.[17] But the truth was that once parliament was bombed out of existence an important "reform" wave ensued, as right-wing radicals reasserted their preeminence in the government and Yeltsin issued radical decrees on private land ownership, accelerated privatization, and reduced subsidized credits. Moreover, after the "October massacre" the pro-Western RFM was strengthened, "hard-liner" Iu. Skokov was removed as head of the Security Council, and his replacement, Oleg Lobov, had little interest in foreign policy. In addition, Sergei Stankevich, a major critic of Foreign Minister Kozyrev, resigned from the RFM to head the Security Council's Foreign Policy Commission and was replaced by arch-Westerner D. Riurikov.[18]

By 1993 the bubble had burst for many pro-Western Russian analysts and politicians, their hopes for quick rewards from the West—payment for the pro-Western Yeltsin-Kozyrev line—ingloriously dashed. According to many analysts this disillusionment, coupled with the disastrous economy and persistent pressure from the opposition, prompted Russia's leaders to institute the aforementioned "assertive" foreign policy in 1993.[19] Others locate the origins for Russia's supposed assertiveness in the December parliamentary elections, which was a clear defeat for the Yeltsin forces[20] as Zhirinovskii's Liberal Democrats and the Communists both fared well while the pro-Yeltsin "democrats" did poorly, and producing a Duma hostile to the Yeltsin-Kozyrev forces.[21] Still others contend that the "hardening" of Russian policy began in October: "robust, confident, and deliberate," it centered around the reassertion of Russian hegemony over the FSU and, to a lesser extent, CEE states, whose incorporation into NATO, the WEU, and the EU Moscow firmly rejected. According to this line of analysis the contrast between Russia's "foreign-policy chaos before mid-1993 . . . and the disciplined, coherent foreign policy" which followed was "no less than stunning."[22]

Contrary to the above, however, the October "massacre" was followed by a "reform" wave which indicated that the Russian leadership intended to institute a "hard-line" and anti-Western foreign policy more in spirit than in essence. Any "assertiveness" was in actuality largely "more rhetorical than real," and aimed at parrying charges that the "reformist" leaders had sold their country out to comply with the West's objective of breaking up the USSR.[23] One important element which is typically missing from analysts' lists of salient factors responsible for Russia's mainly "rhetorical" assertiveness at this time is NATO expansion, which came to the fore as an issue after Yeltsin's August sanction of NATO membership for CEE states.

To be sure, Russia did abstain on a vote for a Western-inspired resolution on Yugoslavia in the UNSC for the first time in April—it had unswervingly voted in favor of all Western motions until then—and would occasionally abstain on such votes in the future. But by refusing to use its veto (save for one vote in December 1994) it continued to support the West. And Russia did pursue a somewhat more independent policy in the near abroad and with respect to trade and economic relations with nations (Cuba, Iran, Iraq, etc.) treated as pariahs by the US. Following a period of steady deterioration in relations with Iran during 1990-92, for example, when the Russian partnership with the West exacerbated Iranian fears for its geostrategic position, by 1993 a warming trend in Russian-Iranian relations had set in, part of Russia's overall reorientation as a Eurasian power, its renewed focus on Asia, and a general effort to reestablish Russian influence in the FSU.[24] Although it may on appearances have seemed to have represented an anti-Western backlash this was, as the following shows, by no means the case.

The "Hard Line" Implemented

In the first of many policy statements on the subject, Yeltsin on February 28 staked out an interventionist line in the CIS with the assertion that Russia had a responsibility to prevent conflict in the region and promised to protect by force, if necessary, Russian minorities who lived beyond Russia's frontiers. In the ensuing outcry he was vigorously defended by the RFM against accusations of "neo-imperialism" by some former Soviet states.[25] The following month Russia submitted a draft proposal to the UN Committee on the UN Charter advocating regional versus global approaches to peacekeeping, thus implicitly appealing for international support for a free hand for its own actions in the CIS and reversing Kozyrev's previous statements that peacekeeping responsibilities in the CIS be relegated to international organizations.[26] On September 22 Kozyrev repeated his pledge that Russia itself would conduct peacekeeping in the near abroad. In an address to the UN the same month, he requested approval for the deployment of Russian troops in CIS "hot spots," but was rebuffed on grounds that the UN Charter prohibits peacekeeping by states with a special interest in the conflict.[27]

Unfortunately for Yeltsin and the Russian leadership, however, the newspaper *Den'* poked an unexpected stick in their supposedly anti-Western policy wheel with the publication at this time of its third exposé, which even the Kremlin acknowledged was based on the original transcript of private conversations held in the Kremlin on January 3, 1993 between US President Bush and the Russian President. The article described how Yeltsin had treated the US President with polite "deference" but referred to the presidents of the CIS countries with "condescension," and detailed Yeltsin's reporting to Bush that he had carried out his "request" to keep Kozyrev on as Foreign Minister, a move which flew directly in the face of the enormous enmity felt by most Russians toward Kozyrev for his extreme pro-Westernism. Yeltsin also confirmed to Bush that Russian foreign policy would "regard the USA as [its] basic partner," and was promised $400 million in US aid to help Russia destroy its nuclear weapons if Russia agreed to ratify START-2, a fact which Yeltsin, understandably, urged not be "publicised at the moment."[28]

Russian Relations with Non-Western States

In early January a US-led coalition, including Russia, France, and Britain, warned Iraq that it must remove its missiles from positions north of the thirty-second parallel in forty-eight hours or face air strikes. Such open support for Western policy exacerbated domestic political tensions and compelled Kozyrev to modify somewhat Russia's policy toward Iraq by voicing concern that the US-led effort was exceeding its UN mandate and calling for an emergency meeting of the UNSC to be held on January 19. But this seemingly forceful anti-Westernism quickly evaporated for, despite their militant-sounding words, Russia's leaders "remain[ed] firm" in their determination to join their Western partners and make Saddam comply with the UN's harsh measures. An RFM statement on allied air strikes against Iraq on January 17 and 18 squarely placed the blame on Baghdad and warned in no uncertain terms that it must adhere to UNSC resolutions.

Russia also sent two warships to the Persian Gulf in a show of support for UN sanctions against Baghdad.[29]

Parliament revived the political struggle with the Yeltsin leadership on June 27 by voting to condemn US rocket attacks against Iraq and repudiating the Foreign Ministry's explicit endorsement of the raids. But the Russian government was not prepared to deliver on its anti-Western rhetoric; in contrast to its more restrained response to similar attacks in January, and hoping to avoid a worsening of already strained relations with Washington on the eve of Yeltsin's meeting in Tokyo with President Clinton,[30] it once more displayed solidarity with the West in November by retracting its veto threats and voting for the UNSC resolution imposing economic sanctions on Libya.[31]

Russia and NATO

Until late 1993 official Russian policy—which was widely endorsed by specialists—continued on its pro-NATO path. Russian analysts followed the government's lead by promoting the idea that NATO was gradually transforming into a primarily political, democratic organization, and even welcomed the supposedly positive role NATO played for Europe. Russian-NATO contacts, though minimal, also deepened. And most importantly, in conformity with the NATO-friendly trend Yeltsin, on visits to Warsaw and Prague in late August, took the momentous step of openly acceding to CEE membership in NATO. By so doing he dramatically reshaped the relationship between Russia, NATO, and the West.

Yeltsin's behavior in Warsaw was an open surrender to NATO, and Russian officials knew it. Clearly realizing that the President had gone too far this time, they knew that they must backtrack even though they remained fervently pro-NATO. But they could no more change their orientation than a leopard could its spots; they had until now worshipped NATO and been eager to do its bidding and would continue to do so. Because Yeltsin had forced their hand, they would pursue an elaborate deception, portraying themselves as "opponents" of NATO expansion. For their part, the Western powers worked with an unwavering determination to put into effect their most cherished strategic goal of ensuring that communism would not return to the FSU, and a principal component of this strategy was to maintain their NATO expansion course, although moderating the pace just enough to avoid undercutting Russia's leaders. Until now the Russian government had only occasionally resorted to deception. It now became a constant and regular feature of Russian policy and would hereafter color all of Russia's relations with the West.

Russian Perspectives on NATO

Russian analysts in early 1993 (prior to Yeltsin's August demarche) continued to adhere to the standard line enunciated during the previous year that "positive changes" were transforming NATO, athough this was just another obvious ploy to legitimize the leadership's acquiescence to this most aggressive of alliances. Most important in this respect was the "politicization" of NATO, said to be an imperative if it hoped to prevent its own eventual obsolescence after the disappearance of the Soviet "threat."[32] This alleged "mellowing" of NATO was used by the leadership to legitimize Russia's "interest in the long-term existence of NATO," even a relationship of partnership. As Russia gravitated toward NATO it also increasingly commended the thrust of NATO's policies. In a major article in *Mezhdunarodnaia zhizn'* Senior RFM official V. Kozin, for example, praised NATO for: promising to guarantee stable transatlantic (West European-US) ties, which were vital for the joint defense of a "huge part of the earth's surface" (and were, by implication, in Russia's interest); interacting with key European organizations and participating actively in European security; playing a crucial role in disarmament and arms control; functioning as the "connecting link" for the East-West exchange of views on military-political problems; conducting research for peaceful uses; regulating national and ethnic conflicts in Europe; and actively pursuing global environmental protection. NATO's new military structure was also said to place greater emphasis on conventional weapons and it was reducing its strategic, tactical and conventional weapons in Europe.[33]

Russian Relations with NATO

As the Russian leadership hastened to embrace NATO a "new phase" in Russian-NATO relations was ushered in, marked by the filtering of contacts down to the lowest levels. Following a four-day series of meetings Defense Minister Grachev and Chair of the US Joint Chiefs of Staff Shalikashvili jointly announced at a press conference on January 30 that Russian and

NATO forces would cooperate to prevent local conflicts and combat the spread of nuclear weapons. Joint staff exercises and training of Russian service personnel by NATO's military training institutions were also being considered.[34] Kozyrev also announced Russia's support for NATO's December 1992 proposal to allow the use of its military-technical equipment, personnel, and infrastructure for international peacekeeping, although he cautioned, somewhat unconvincingly, that the UNSC had ultimate peacekeeping responsibility and that only the CSCE could truly express all-European interests.[35]

Suddenly, like a bolt from the blue, the most momentous event in post-Soviet Russia's brief history took place when President Yeltsin, on a visit to the Polish capital on August 25, responded to entreaties from Polish President Walesa by signing a joint Polish-Russian declaration abjuring hegemony and non-intervention and affirming that their mutual relations were defined by equality and partnership. Yeltsin capped it off by declaring Russia's "understanding" of Poland's position (to join NATO), pronouncing it not in "conflict with the interests . . . of Russia."[36] The consent to NATO expansion coincided, not accidentally, with Russia's pro-Western fall diplomatic offensive.

Many in Russia and the West have expressed bafflement at NATO's motives for expansion, especially given that it was no longer threatened by the USSR, its age-old nemesis. It was even argued that NATO no longer had a raison d'etre and should and would eventually dissolve. But NATO's raison d'etre has always gone far beyond keeping the Soviets out of, the US in, and the Germans down in Europe. It has been and remains the military organization of international capital whose function is to ensure the interests of that class, directly or indirectly putting down crises by intervening in individual states to suppress working-class forces with the ultimate goal of controlling markets.[37] Since the collapse of the USSR a primary NATO objective has been to expand into CEE, including the former Yugoslavia, ultimately to dominate markets there. Its principal geostrategic focus has been directed at the creation of a bulwark capable of stifling left-led movements, above all in Russia because, as the heart of the former socialist bloc, it is there that the possibility for the recreation of such a movement lingers most strongly. Until 1993 one key piece was still needed for the success of that project: approval by the Russian leadership of NATO's eastward expansion. On August 25, 1993 NATO got it.

Russia and the NATO Expansion Controversy

Russian and Western specialists have pronounced Yeltsin's August 1993 concession an "improvisation" and an "anomaly." Others, like Dimitri Simes, even allege that Yeltsin's "impromptu remark" was made "under the influence of alcohol,"[38] while another observer asserts that it was "difficult to say to what degree the possible resonance of [the] Warsaw declaration was anticipated and taken into account by the creators of Russia's present policy, whose attention has been focused above all on . . . internal affairs."[39] Yeltsin's behavior in Warsaw, it is argued here, was neither an anomaly nor an improvisation—it was rather the product of cold calculation, part of his plan to attain his foremost objectives from his Western "allies" in the form of a quid pro quo: in return for their political backing and for IMF funding of the Russian government (the lion's share of which would ultimately line the pockets of Russia's economic and political elites), he would vanquish the left-wing menace, continue Russia's march toward a market economy, eliminate parliamentary opposition and, most importantly, sanction NATO expansion. Indeed, virtually all major Russian policy shifts have been initiated by the leadership to extort concessions, almost invariably in the form of monetary payment, from the West.

Tracing the developments which foreshadowed Yeltsin's fateful Warsaw demarche lays bare his strategy toward NATO. In early July Russian officials became anxious that Western support would dry up when a $4 billion fund, termed by President Clinton in April the "keystone for the privatization of Russian industry," was reduced by one-half and greater reliance was placed on trade credits, all reflecting "a reduced sense of Western urgency about Russia now that Yeltsin ha[d] survived the April referendum on his presidency."[40] Then, in response to Yeltsin's May decree that Chubais' State Property Management Committee (GKI) circumvent ministerial authority, Parliament undertook to stymie the inequitable privatization process pushed by Yeltsin and his privatization minister Chubais by voting in July to transfer authority over privatization from the GKI to the Council of Ministers.[41]

Concerned about these potential setbacks to his agenda Yeltsin hastened on July 1 to ingratiate Russia to the IMF by annulling a law requiring that Russian exporters sell 30% of their hard-currency profits to the Central Bank.[42] To be sure, he also displayed characteristically erratic behavior by alienating IMF officials with his refusal to sack Central Bank head

Gerashchenko, who in July had ordered the withdrawal from circulation of all pre-1993 cash rubles without consulting the IMF.[43]

Statements emanating from Yeltsin's office in mid-August anticipated a "decisive battle" with parliament in September, prompting Yeltsin to threaten to disband parliament if did not support his demand for fall elections.[44] As the struggle raged, mounting domestic instability in Russia, combined with what was perceived as Russia's "neoimperial" policy abroad, aroused the Visegrad bloc to press NATO for membership in August. Indeed, on the day before Yeltsin's August 25 Warsaw agreement, Richard Lugar, leader of the Republicans in the Senate Foreign Relations Committee, heard a plea from Lech Walesa that CEE states be incorporated into European structures and NATO.[45] More, in late August speakers at an IMF-organized seminar in Moscow warned that support for Russian reform would be cut off if Yeltsin agreed to parliament's proposal for budget deficits far higher than what the IMF deemed appropriate.[46]

As noted above, deep down Russia's Westernizers have been supportive of NATO as the main security bulwark of both the West *and Russia*. And like other pro-Western officials, Yeltsin did not see NATO as a military threat and did not oppose NATO expansion in principle. His main concern, in fact, connected with softening Russia's image as a "neoimperialist state," was that NATO expansion might provoke an anti-NATO and anti-Western backlash among the Russian masses, a development which would be deleterious to his twin goals of dismantling the remnants of Soviet socialist society and Russia's Westernization and, most importantly, it would endanger his enrichment and that of his capitalist allies.[47] On the other hand, giving away NATO expansion could be quite lucrative for Russia's elites in the long run in that they would be handsomely reimbursed for such a service by the West. Hence given such high stakes—the survival of his administration, the planned privatization of state property, the disbursal of substantial IMF funds, and also the considerable pressure from CEE and the West to consent to NATO expansion, Yeltsin apparently came up with a plan to cut the Gordian knot in one stroke. By offering NATO the last key to NATO expansion, its most cherished strategic objective, he hoped to guarantee Western support for all his objectives.

Yeltsin had conducted the negotiations with the Poles in Warsaw "without any particular aggressiveness," and continued to pursue his conciliatory stance toward NATO even after the signing of the August 25 agreement, stating at a Warsaw press conference subsequent to the signing that "the time when the Polish authorities turned to Moscow for advice and vice-versa are past, as are the days when . . . the leaders of the former Soviet Union . . . used to come here to give instructions . . . Now there are two sovereign states and I must respect their stands."[48] Kozyrev echoed Yeltsin's capitulation on August 26 by declaring that Russia had "no objections" to Polish membership in NATO[49] and continued to placate the alliance by affirming that same day in Prague—as did Yeltsin—that Russia had no right to hinder the Czech Republic's membership in any organization, thus indicating, to one Western analyst, that "Moscow would not object to a possible accommodation to NATO by the Czech Republic."[50]

Others displayed more caution. Yeltsin's Press Secretary Kostikov averred Russia's "respect" for Polish membership in European institutions (including NATO) while reminding the West that such membership would be assessed from the standpoint of Russian strategic interests.[51] And because Yeltsin's Warsaw "stunt" contradicted the RFM's stated policy, his words were soon disavowed by Kozyrev, who issued a statement which, although attempting to cast Yeltsin's words in a different light, did not in essence repudiate them: before accepting Polish membership, Kozyrev insisted, Russia would expect NATO to "change its role" and that NATO expansion must be done "at a suitable time."[52]

Russian officials meanwhile had embarked on a coverup in order to limit the damage: Yu. Kashlev, Russia's Ambassador to Poland, tried to explain away Yeltsin's "gaffe" by insisting that Polish membership in NATO should take place only in the distant future and within the context of the erection of a European security structure; Defense Minister Grachev whined that it would be "unfortunate" if CEE membership in NATO were to lead to Russia's isolation;[53] and E. Ambartsumov, Chair of parliament's Committee on Foreign Affairs, correctly predicted that Yeltsin's statement would be "reinterpreted."[54]

The Russian government's strategy of deception was taken to a new level at this point, spurred by the awareness that maneuvering was imperative if it was to succeed in covering up the fact that by gratuitously conceding NATO's most sought-after objective Yeltsin had placed under threat Russia's most vital security interests. Because his action could not be easily explained away the Russian government was forced to project an image of irreconcilable opposition to NATO expansion. The first and most important step in the charade came in September when the Russian government sent a letter to the four leading Western governments laying out its security concerns over expansion and recalling that the 1990 agreement on German unification barred NATO from admitting new members.[55] The Visegrad states responded with statements of support for Yeltsin in his battle with parliament but also criticized the letter's opposition to NATO expansion.[56]

Russian diplomacy then shifted into high gear, hurriedly putting up a façade of opposition to NATO expansion, which the President had just encouraged. In early September Evgenii Primakov, then head of Russia's Foreign Intelligence Service, visited Warsaw where he met with President Walesa and Prime Minister Suchocka, presumably to discuss Polish NATO membership.[57] On September 20 Kozyrev told British Foreign Secretary Rifkind that "undue haste" to expand NATO would be ill-advised. Rifkind agreed, declaring that NATO still had much work to do on expansion, although at a meeting with S. Stepashin, Chair of Russia's Defense and Security Commission, he expressed his belief that it was "inconceivable" that Russia would not "participate" in NATO in the long term.[58]

Making the charade even more transparent was the fact that as the uproar intensified the Russian government continued its policy of conciliation toward NATO, expressing opposition to NATO expansion but refusing to "portray NATO enlargement as deeply inimical to an orderly future." Not until the passing of the September-October crisis did Russia put an end to this somewhat ambivalent image and harden its position, at least rhetorically.[59] Kozyrev also met with French Defense Minister Leotard, who agreed that Russian and French military doctrines should be based on reasonable sufficiency and the absence of a potential enemy.[60]

The October 22 meeting of the NATO Council approved the US proposal for the Partnership for Peace (PfP; see below), raising tensions with the US over European security and prompting Russia to seek improved military-strategic ties with Britain and France during the fall of 1993. The first step in Russia's strategic game came when French Prime Minister Balladur arrived in Moscow on November 1-2 for discussions on NATO Council decisions. To one Russian observer, not only did France support Russia's "opposition" to NATO expansion, but Balladur's being the first Western politician to be familiarized with Russia's new military doctrine was a measure of the firmness of Russian-French relations and the extent to which Russia relied on France's voice in the West.[61] On November 3 Balladur disclosed that France and Russia had agreed that the CSCE should be the central organization for European peace and stability, implying a demotion of NATO's status.[62] But France's proposals were rhetorical, and France would prove to be one of NATO expansion's biggest promoters.

Speaking in London on October 27 Kozyrev cautioned NATO that expansion could be viewed as an attempt to partition Russia off from Europe, and suggested instead a "vertical political responsibility" for peace embracing the UN, CSCE, NACC, NATO, WEU, and the CIS. Kozyrev also urged that joint peacekeeping be organized by Russia and NATO—"partners in cooperation."[63] A typical Russian Westernizer, Kozyrev eschewed any characterization of NATO as a strategic threat—even after August 25—and preferred to base his "opposition" to NATO expansion on the rationale that it could spark the revival of "neoimperialist, nationalist forces" in Russia. Indeed, even while refusing to "view NATO as a threat to its security" Kozyrev at the same time sought to allay anti-NATOism in Russia by criticizing "supervigilantes" who "still see the enemy the moment NATO is mentioned."[64]

In like manner, other officials saw the main danger from NATO emanating not from the West's military threat but from the "political and psychological" mindset of the Russian people, who increasingly suspected NATO of harboring ill intentions toward their country.[65] This oft-heard rationale against NATO expansion, promoted assiduously by the Westernizers, was understandably decried in 1997 by Insitute of Europe specialist Pavel Kandel as contrary to Russia's national interests: "one would have to be extremely flippant," he asserted, "to reduce to a psychological problem the worsening of Russia's military parameters of security and its strategic situation in the West, its political isolation in Europe and the appearance of armed instruments of pressure on the country in the post-Soviet territory."[66] Kandel clearly implied that the leadership's flippancy covered up an unwillingness to oppose NATO expansion.

Indeed, had the Westernizers paid closer attention to statements from the NATO Nuclear Planning Group meeting at Gleneagles, Scotland in late October 1992 they would have discerned NATO's real intentions from a warning by US Defense Secretary Cheney against neglecting the long-term significance of NATO, which he insisted must be prepared to use force anywhere. They also could have detected the threat to their country's security in British Defense Minister Rifkind's appeal to the members at the same gathering not to make the mistake of viewing Russia as a "friendly country" and defending against its powerful military with "toy airplanes." NATO's menacing intent vis-à-vis Russia was evident from Secretary

General Woerner's March offer to help Albania create "modern armed forces" to safeguard its independence and become NATO's partner.[67]

In an attempt to assuage Russian concerns about NATO expansion the Western propaganda machine went into action with a campaign so effective that even Russian military analyst N. Ponomarev seemed taken in when he welcomed in early December the "serious warning" from the Paris session of the United Assembly, the WEU's supreme organ, that it would be premature for NATO to offer East Europe security guarantees on the eve of NATO's summit on expansion.[68] NATO also tried to put a damper on talk of immediate expansion by sending a delegation to Moscow in early September with the message that it desired cooperation with Moscow— although it refused to rule out CEE (and CIS) membership in the alliance.[69]

Russia's long-postponed military doctrine, finally published in November, warned of the "widening of military blocs." Almost simultaneously Foreign Intelligence Service head Primakov issued an unusually frank warning against NATO's expansion. Addressing a press conference on November 25 at the Russian Information Agency building on Moscow's Zubovsky Bul'var, he launched the opening shot by Russia's "power structures" (the general staff and the intelligence services) in the struggle over policy on NATO expansion. Laying out possible NATO expansion scenarios, Primakov cautioned the West that the materialization of such scenarios would arouse Russian suspicions that NATO sought to impinge on Russia's geopolitical interests.[70]

Primakov's warning came in response to a speech by NATO Secretary General Woerner at an October 29 conference in Madrid which had declared one of NATO's chief functions to be the projection of stability to CEE and Central Asia—areas in Russia's traditional sphere of influence. Acknowledging the existence of "tactical, interdepartmental" differences, Primakov noted that his speech had received the approval of the Ministry of Defense and the General Staff—and the less-than-unanimous and "indirect" support of the RFM.[71] With these words, *Izvestiia* wrote, Primakov was engaging in an "open polemic" with the RFM for "favoring NATO expansion and the rapid establishment of partnership with NATO."[72]

The next day Presidential Press Secretary Kostikov revealed that Yeltsin had "approved" Primakov's report.[73] Although Kozyrev days later claimed victory for having convinced the December 3 NACC Foreign Ministers' meeting's to "bur[y] immediate NATO expansion," A. Pushkov pointed out that, to the contrary, the NATO Defense Ministers' decision to admit the Visegrad states in the future came irrespective of Russia's position and in fact squelched any hope Moscow entertained of vetoing NATO expansion. "The move" of admitting new states, one analysis noted, "indicates that earlier provisions [of] the Partnership for Peace were designed to give NATO the freedom of manoeuvre in . . . its . . . enlargement, rather than to serve for keeping Eastern Europeans outside of the Alliance, as the RFM tried to present it."[74]

Kozyrev nevertheless continued to proffer carrots to the West, affirming in late September that Russia regarded NATO as an ally, that it was his "impression" that partnership with "the former enemy" was a NATO priority. He proudly cited instances of his Ministry's cooperation with NATO, including the December 1992 NATO Council resolution approving the diversification of military ties and military conversion, and the "notable example" of joint maneuvers in the Baltic Sea. And by pointedly "wish[ing] to remind [his] readers" that one of the first steps taken by the new Russia was its renunciation of the Brezhnev doctrine in East Europe—as reflected in Yeltsin's "recent visit to Poland"[75]—Kozyrev seemed to indirectly approve Yeltsin's cave-in to NATO.

Although this could hardly be interpreted as opposition to NATO expansion Russians along much of the political spectrum declared their displeasure at NATO's intentions to enlarge. Kozyrev himself joined the issue in the February 1993 issue of *NATO Review* with a plea to the West not to create a buffer zone between East and West Europe.[76] In fact, on the day before Yeltsin's arrival in Warsaw, Kozyrev had cautioned the Visegrad three against joining NATO, since CEE "has never ceased to be an area of interest for Russia."[77] And in January the RFM's first attempt at formulating its "Basic Conceptions of Russian Foreign Policy" contained a warning that Russia's "strategic task is to prevent the transformation of East Europe into a kind of buffer zone isolating us from the West. Nor can Russia's displacement by the Western powers from the East European region be permitted."[78]

Western and Russian analysts alike pointed out that until August 1993 neither NATO nor the WEU was interested in expanding.[79] This was confirmed in late March 1991, for example, when NATO officials informed a disappointed President Havel of Czechoslovakia that they were not yet willing to make a commitment toward CEE.[80] Be this as it may, the West had long before 1993 made it plainly evident that it was laying the groundwork for CEE membership in NATO and justifying it with the oft-heard rationale that NATO must be kept relevant and effective in maintaining security in Europe—that is, aimed at Russia.[81] That Russia's leaders could not but have been aware of NATO's plans all along made Yeltsin's sanction of NATO expansion that much more questionable.

Evidence of NATO's real plans was plain to see. Even as the USSR was collapsing Soviet leaders tried in vain to undermine NATO-CEE ties. A January 1991 report by the CPSU Central Committee International Department called for "vigorous action to oppose the entry of our former military allies into other military blocs or groupings, above all into NATO," and was followed by a series of articles warning of dire consequences if East Europe threatened vital Soviet interests. The Soviets also tried, unsuccessfully, to conclude bilateral military treaties with CEE states to prevent them from joining a military-political alliance against the USSR.[82] But it was clearly too late, as there were simply too many pro-Western, pro-NATO elements within the Soviet government; the pro-NATO momentum had simply gathered too much strength for any meaningful opposition to succeed.

To be sure, in spring 1991 NATO agreed to extend indirect security commitments to East Europe but, fearful of a Soviet backlash, discouraged formal membership. Accordingly, NATO Secretary General Woerner stated that East European membership in NATO could harm NATO's relations with the USSR. But Woerner also spoke in April 1993 about NATO's need to project stability to the countries of Central and East Europe," and warned West Europe against making dangerously deep cuts in its armed forces since Russia (and Ukraine) "remain important military powers."[83]

East European states had already been purchasing weapons and equipment from NATO countries—a policy actually begun in 1990—to eliminate their logistical dependence on the Soviet Union.[84] Indeed, that their membership in NATO was only a matter of time became clear as early as June 1991, when the Copenhagen NATO Foreign Ministers meeting took a "cautious step toward underwriting the security of the new democracies in Central and Eastern Europe" by pledging that its own security was inseparably linked to other states in Europe.[85] But they walked a fine line in trying to pull off the trick of making the Soviets and the world think that they wanted the same kind of relationship with the USSR. This would, in various permutations, remain a central element in NATO's and the West's strategy toward Russia throughout the 1990s.

Signals of NATO's intent to expand to CEE could be detected again in December 1992 when NATO agreed to conduct joint peacekeeping operations in Europe at UN or CSCE request and as a prelude to eventual discussions on East European membership. The following month, in a "real sea change," NATO held "discreet discussions" on the admission of the Visegrad and other East European states, signaling that it was "moving [still] closer toward extending the security umbrella eastward into parts of the new Europe." And in February 1993—*well before Yeltsin's Warsaw concession*—Secretary General Woerner disclosed for the first time that the Visegrad countries were under consideration for membership, even as he ruled out Russia as a potential inductee.[86]

In March 1993 German Defense Minister Ruehe, the most vociferous of German—and indeed West European—advocates of NATO expansion, became the first Western leader to openly urge expansion (Foreign Minister Kinkel would soon follow). He repeated his call for membership for the Visegrad group (comprised of four states after the breakup of Czechoslovakia) at the North Atlantic Assembly meeting in Berlin the following May. French Assembly President Bouvard concurred, urging the acceptance by NATO of East European states "as soon as possible."[87]

The earliest signal of US support came in September 1992 when US Ambassador to NATO Robert Hunter announced that the US accepted that certain East European states would be admitted to NATO at some unspecified date.[88] US Secretary of Defense Aspin went further in early June 1993 by urging NATO to work out the "actual modalities" and "conditions and timing" for the accession of the CEE states, while throwing in a meaningless consolation prize to Russia in the form of vapid thanks for being a "key factor in shaping the future security environment" for the US and Europe. Aspin's statement reflected the US effort to reassert its leadership in the alliance; Secretary of State Christopher continued those efforts one week later by affirming that NATO should expand ties with East Europe. That same day Senator Richard Lugar called on NATO to admit the Visegrad states as soon as possible.[89]

As long as Russia objected to NATO expansion, the West could ignore CEE entreaties and temporize on declaring it openly as a goal. After the August 1993 events in Warsaw, however, the very rationale for keeping CEE out of NATO—fear of antagonizing Russia—was undercut by the Russian head of state himself. As Dimitri Simes put it, for the US, who had the last word in NATO decisions, to refuse East Europe's admission after

Yeltsin's sanction would have made it "holier than the Pope," i.e., it would be seen as defending Russia even more than Moscow itself did.[90] A. Pushkov similarly acknowledged that it was Yeltsin's Warsaw agreement that had "set going" the "Brussels express," which had until then been "standing deep on the sidetrack."[91] And Poland was so appreciative that its jet fighters escorted Yeltsin's plane from Warsaw's airport on August 26, the highest honor accorded a leader of another state in years.[92]

Once Yeltsin had nullified the pretext for NATO to ward off CEE membership—Russian opposition to NATO expansion[93]—the issue of NATO expansion as a threat to Russian security became the central focus of Russia's European and global strategy.[94] For its part, the West wasted no time in taking advantage of Yeltsin's Warsaw statement. On September 10 Secretary General Woerner made it official: NATO was not a "closed shop" and must expand and, in apparent deference to Russia, Woerner qualified his advocacy of expansion "to reflect the *supposed changes* in Russia's sensibilities," adding that he was "happy that President Yeltsin also sees it this way."[95]

Nevertheless, in early September German Foreign Minister Kinkel's restatement of his government's support for CEE integration with (West) European institutions, including NATO, the EU, and the WEU—"without alienating Russia"[96]—was closely followed by a proposal by US Defense Secretary Aspin at an informal NATO Defense Ministers' meeting in Travemunde on October 20 to establish the Partnership for Peace (PfP), a kind of anteroom to possible eventual NATO membership which all CSCE members could join, and which was a clear attempt to forestall CEE demands for quick accession to NATO, although Aspin did declare that NATO must expand.[97] Yeltsin and Kozyrev immediately expressed their support for the plan, even though its very purpose was not to preclude but merely to defer expansion.[98]

NATO Defense Ministers wasted no time on the issue of expansion at their two-day meeting of early December by agreeing that the Visegrad states could be admitted in the future *irrespective of opposition from Russia*. They also agreed to share military information and undertake joint operations with CEE states and to decide more specifics on the question of expansion at the upcoming January NATO summit. At the meeting German Defense Minister Ruehe was reportedly told by US Defense Secretary Aspin that NATO membership for the Visegrad group was not a question of "if" but of "when" and "how." Ruehe also ruled out giving Russia the right to veto NATO expansion. But German Foreign Minister Kinkel played the "good cop" to Defense Minister Ruehe's "bad cop"—clearly one of the West's tactics to disarm Russian opposition to expansion—by cautioning a few days later that if done too hastily NATO expansion could endanger European security and impinge dangerously on Russian security interests. Russian officials had days earlier proposed to a NATO Foreign Ministers meeting that Russia be granted membership in NATO and urged the alliance to avoid undue haste in light of the "existing set of geopolitical factors" and the need to "examine all the possible consequences before taking such a step." But Kinkel "ruled out" Russian membership.[99]

In this connection, Kozyrev announced after a meeting with US Secretary of State Christopher in early December that Russia supported the Clinton administration proposal of a *gradual* expansion of NATO to the east, thus "shoot[ing] down for the moment the growing perception that Moscow was opposed to the idea" of NATO expansion.[100] To be sure, weeks prior to the summit Yeltsin and the Russian government had made considerable efforts to show that their position on NATO expansion was hardening, but this was just another obvious ploy for the runup to the December Duma elections.[101] The stage was now set for the eruption of the NATO expansion controversy, and given their pro-Western leanings, there was little doubt with whom Russia's leadership would ultimately side.

During a visit to Moscow on March 23, 1994 Kinkel agreed with Kozyrev that the erection of new barriers in Europe must be avoided, adding that Germany would assist Russia obtain membership more quickly in the Council of Europe (CofE) and promote the APC.[102] Some Russians were reassured by such "dissenting" voices in West Europe, which were said to include French Defense Minister Leotard, who declared in late August 1993 that the question of NATO expansion was "not topical now."[103] France's concurrence with Italy's warning in November 1993 that "relentless Eastern European pressure to join [NATO] could prove counterproductive" was also welcomed by Russia.[104]

Nevertheless, NATO's true anti-Russian intent soon belied its tranquilizing rhetoric. As an intended "warning" to Russia, British Foreign Secretary Hurd and his Italian counterpart Andreatta told EU Foreign Ministers in late December that West Europe should *accelerate* the forging of political ties with former Warsaw Pact states to calm their fears aroused by the success of Zhirinovskii in the Duma elections.[105] Woerner followed suit, urging in the wake of Zhirinovskii's victory in the Russian elections that NATO must remain "vigilant" toward Moscow.[106]

Russia and Yugoslavia

Although Russia's Yugoslavia policy was conducted in such a way as to make it *appear* that it was ally and protector of the Serbs against the West—it also sought to project an image of "evenhandedness" toward all sides in the Balkan conflict—when all was said and done, Russia's policymakers aligned closely with the West. In fact, Russia's leaders used the UNSC, the principal forum for implementing Western policy in the Balkans, to *bolster* the West's position by refusing to use Russia's power of veto on such issues as the lifting of sanctions and air strikes against the Bosnian Serbs. To be sure, Russia did side with West Europe against early US efforts to launch air strikes, but once the strikes were launched in early 1994—not incidentally with much prodding from West European hard-liners—Russia gave its approval. Although Russia proposed the lifting of sanctions, as Parliament urged, it refused to follow through in the UNSC.

Yugoslavia: Russian Relations with the West

At a joint Russian-US press conference in early January Yeltsin affirmed Russia's support for a Western-inspired UNSC resolution mandating enforcement of the no-fly zone in Bosnia, this despite reports that Russia would abstain, while boasting that Russia "had so far supported US positions" on the UN Security Council and would "continue to follow that line."[107] On January 17 Kozyrev exposed Russia's real anti-Serb inclinations by warning the Bosnian Serb parliament that a rejection of the Vance-Owen plan and continued violation of the no-fly zone would prompt "resolute action."[108] That same month, as part of an effort to make it appear that he was softening Russia's anti-Serb line, Kozyrev urged the UN to lift economic sanctions against the Serbs and promised parliament that Russia's defense of the near abroad, not better relations with the West, would be Russia's top foreign policy priority.[109] Russia's UN representative Vorontsov also got into the "evenhandedness" act when, after feeling the heat from Russia's parliament for his delegation's pro-Western stance, he warned Zagreb that if it failed to comply with a UNSC resolution demanding that it halt military operations, Russia would demand equal sanctions against Yugoslavs and Croats.[110]

This was shown to be all smoke and no fire when in early February Kozyrev and other RFM officials talked up the Vance-Owen peace plan for Bosnia-Herzegovina (which the EU also supported) and called for the imposition of sanctions against violators of the plan, a move clearly aimed at the Serbs. At the same time Kozyrev rejected a parliamentary resolution calling on Russia to lift economic sanctions against Serbia and Montenegro and impose them on Croatia and insisted pointedly that Russia would not place exclusive reliance on the Serbs.[111] *Moskovskaia pravda* stirred the mud up to expose Russia's Balkan policy as a calculated deception aimed at eluding the outrage provoked by Russia's pro-Western tilt before the upcoming April 25 referendum on Yeltsin's policies. The government sought, in its view, to make it appear that it was treating Belgrade more softly by advocating a crackdown on the Croats and Muslims, a policy it had no intention of implementing.[112]

In a move aimed likewise at fostering his carefully crafted image of nonpartisanship, Kozyrev told the Danish Foreign Policy Association in late February that Russia rejected "double standards" in the former Yugoslavia and suggested that Croatia's failure to comply with UNSC Resolution 802 should be criticized just as strongly as violations by the Serbs, a position which echoed his January demand that the UN impose sanctions against Croatia if it did not cease its "aggression."[113] But Kozyrev's own RFM quickly proved this to be empty rhetoric by consenting on March 2 to have Russian planes fly relief supplies to Bosnia from NATO airfields,[114] thus ushering in a stage of closer, anti-Serb cooperation with the West.

The West, willing as ever to work with Russia's leaders to cover up their machinations, agreed on three separate occasions during the week of Monday, March 27 to postpone a discussion in the UNSC of Resolution 816 authorizing the use of force against violators—overwhelmingly Bosnian Serb—of Bosnia's no-fly zone on the request of Russia, which was anxious to avoid putting its UN delegation in the position of having to vote for a resolution "that most observers consider to be anti-Serbian" just before the 9th CPD, to be held from March 26-29—especially because it was well known that they would support it. The resolution was finally approved on March 31 with only China abstaining. The West did consent to Russia's request that the resolution specify that the air strikes would not hit ground targets, including airfields, but this, too was an obvious strategem to help

Russia's Westernizers, whose real preference for the use of force by the West against the Serbs was affirmed in a warning from Russia's UN representative Vorontsov to the Bosnian Serbs in early April that if they persisted in their military offensive an even harsher resolution could be approved. And the real significance of the resolution itself was, according to *Izvestiia*, an "additional means of exerting pressure" on the Bosnian Serbs, who, by refusing to sign the Vance-Open plan, laid the groundwork for "harsher steps" should they continue their stonewalling.[115]

Russia's leaders were clearly not averse to fabrication to obfuscate their pro-Western policies, as Kozyrev made clear when he claimed that Russia opposed the use of force in Bosnia but did accept "limited military interference," and reassured critics that the resolution was in any case not anti-Serb because the Croats had been the biggest violators of the no-fly zone—an assertion flatly contradicted by *Izvestiia*, which pointed out on April 2 that the resolution was *anti*-Serb precisely because the Bosnian Serbs had committed a majority of the airspace violations.[116]

The previous month's scenario was repeated down to practically the very last detail during the week of Monday, April 5 when the Russian government again asked the West to delay a vote in the UNSC, this time on a measure toughening sanctions against the Serbs. On April 13 Russia requested, in a confidential letter to President Clinton, a second postponement and threatened to use its veto power in the UNSC for the first time since 1984 if the West did not comply. In return, Russia promised to support the measure for tightened sanctions—and assuming the Bosnian Serbs rejected the Vance-Open plan, which seemed likely. Russia's first request postponed the date to April 26, the day after Yeltsin's referendum on his presidency and a time when Yeltsin sought to avoid aggravating relations with the opposition by being forced into a position of having to vote on a measure which, like the previous one, was widely viewed as anti-Serb. Russian UN Ambassador Vorontsov also resorted to duplicity on the issue when he "dismissed as an unrelated coincidence" the timing of the postponement.[117]

But the Bosnian Serbs besieged the Muslim town of Srebrenica, and when its fall seemed imminent by April 17 threw a monkey wrench into the works, impelling the Western powers, on France's request, to brush aside Russia's postponement request and call an emergency session of the UNSC. In addition to further tightening sanctions on the Serbs, the session's final resolution—on which Russia abstained for the first time since 1984—

demanded the withdrawal of Bosnian Serb forces from Srebrenica and permission from the Serbs to increase UN peacekeeping troops in the region, and invoked Chapter 7 of the UN Charter authorizing the use of force.[118]

By early April all West European countries—except Britain, who feared for the safety of its blue helmets on the ground—had, under intense US pressure, come around to supporting the US policy of military strikes against the Serbs. German Foreign Minister Kinkel even took it upon himself to caution Russia in mid-April against "one-sidedly" supporting the Serbs.[119] After Russia's abstention on the April 17 UNSC vote for toughened sanctions against Serbia, Kinkel continued to badger Russia by demanding its "solidarity with Europe in this hard period," especially in light of Europe's "support" for Russia in its recent travails. Aid, Kinkel warned, was conditional on Russia's "at least behav[ing] within the international community as one is entitled to expect."[120]

As if prompted by Kinkel, V. Churkin, special Russian representative in Yugoslavia, held a news conference on April 19 where he criticized the Bosnian Serbs for not agreeing to the Vance-Owen plan and for their relentless siege of Srebrenica and also warned that the fall of Srebrenica would have "the most serious consequences." He affirmed that Russia had favored postponing the UNSC vote on new Yugoslav sanctions and disclosed that Russia had not used its veto against UNSC resolutions because it opposed "confrontation with the international community."[121] On April 27 Kozyrev conveyed a similar sentiment when he expressed regret for Russia's having abstained on the April 17 vote and blamed pressure from "nationalist forces" for the government's having acted contrary to what he contended were its true inclinations. Russia, he assured the West, had always been and remained with the West; in future it would vote only with "those who support civilized solutions" to problems. Yeltsin also changed his tone on the same day, reversing what had been anti-Serb rhetoric by signaling an interest in solidarity with the West.[122]

Russia also stepped up its peace efforts in the region at this time. During a euphoric but brief period the Russian media lauded Russian diplomats for having supposedly seized the initiative in the Balkans with their call for a UNSC Foreign Ministers' meeting on the future of peacekeeping. But on May 17 the US dashed any optimism Russia may have had by rejecting the proposal and declaring it inopportune to even discuss such operations.[123] When Russia complied with the US suggestion that it scrap its proposal, its Balkan policy seemed to have "returned to square one."[124] But Kozyrev, undeterred, stepped up his efforts to bring about a settlement by launching a much-ballyhooed six-day globetrotting mission on May 17 which took him to Belgrade, Rome, Washington, and New York. Intended as a "counterpunch" to US efforts to forestall growing Russian influence in the Balkans and to oppose the US' favored policy of force against the Serbs, the trip enabled Kozyrev to drum up support for the four-point Vance-Owen plan which included implementation of UN sanctions, sealing the Serbia-Bosnia border, cessation of security havens in Bosnia, and an international war crimes tribunal in the former Yugoslavia.[125]

On May 21 Russia and the US—who was now amenable to certain concessions—agreed to forge a common strategy with their allies on the Bosnia question by abandoning a central element of the Vance-Owen plan that proposed a rollback of half the territorial gains made by the Bosnian Serbs. This prepared the ground for the adoption in Washington on the following day of a "joint action program" by Russia and Western states, the fruit of Kozyrev's diplomatic efforts and ideas, notably his plan for "safe havens" for Bosnian Muslims, which had been initially rejected by the US. The program—which stipulated the provision of US air cover for UN forces guarding safe areas, the threat of sanctions against Croatia if it supported attacks by the Bosnian Croats or Muslims, insurance that Serbia would not send arms to its Bosnian brothers and sisters, and provision for international monitors in Macedonia and Kosovo to prevent the conflict from spreading—represented a major US concession to Russia and "most Western European states," who were said to be still locked in a "transatlantic rift" with their US overlord over its demands that the program include approval for air strikes against the Bosnian Serbs and the lifting of the arms embargo on the Muslims. In an indication of the depth of opposition to the US, even the UN commander in overall charge of Yugoslavia, Gen. Lars Eric Wahlgren, opposed lifting the arms embargo.[126] Others in the West were critical of the program, including the British Labor Party, which derided it as a "climbdown" given the Bosnian Serbs' past rejection of the Vance-Open plan. One source noted that "the implied climbdown" was admitted even by Kozyrev in his acknowledgement that "the main motive" behind the program had been to "patch up differences between America and Europe."[127]

The seeming triumph of the joint action program was interpreted by Russians as a diplomatic coup, and an overjoyed Russian media trumpeted the "success of Russian diplomacy" for having "stood down the Clinton administration."[128] Pro-government media declared Russia's policy in the Balkans an unqualified success while exulting that it proved Russia to be a "key player" in the Balkans and helped strengthen Russian relations with Europe, and also criticized US sabre-rattling as harmful to the peace process.[129] A major policy shift was indeed afoot as the US, indecisive and intransigent, watched while its influence in Europe seemed to dwindle. Moscow's policies, on the other hand, were said to be increasingly well-received, a consequence of Russia's "first muscle-flexing after the chaotic fragmentation of the Soviet Union."[130]

On June 4 the UNSC finally voted to send reinforcements of international troops to protect Bosnian Muslim enclaves—"safe areas"—and to use force, including air strikes, if necessary, against the Bosnian Serbs, part of the joint action plan agreed on two weeks earlier. Days later the vote was unanimous for an overtly anti-Serb proposal by Russia calling on the UN Secretary General to draw up options for deployment of troops on the borders of Bosnia to stop the flow of arms and goods from Serbia to the Bosnian Serbs.[131] Meanwhile, on June 11 France, the last holdout within NATO on the use of force in the former Yugoslavia, finally gave its consent at the Athens NATO meeting to use NATO air power to protect UN forces and Muslim safe areas in Bosnia. This set the stage for the use of NATO force for a Western-imposed settlement in the region.[132]

But trouble was brewing for the peace plan, and it came from Moscow itself as Russia categorically refused to provide troops to protect the safe areas, and despite the fact that Moscow had been a principal backer of the joint action program. EC officials reacted to Russia's decision by terming it a "sad setback" for the peace process in Bosnia.[133] On the other hand, the UNSC could not agree on the proposal by Russia to monitor Bosnia's borders to stop the flow of arms and goods from Serbia. As a result, Russia was the only country to offer to send troops for the mission.[134]

At the Vienna Conference on Human Rights held in late June a resolution sponsored by the Islamic countries to condemn "genocide" by the Serbs against Bosnian Muslims was defeated by a Russian veto—and by the Western powers, who helped to scuttle the resolution with their "furious opposition."[135] Russia's supposed pro-Serbian position was belied once again on August 3, however, when, after stating its opposition to NATO's announcement that it would prepare for possible air strikes against the Bosnian Serbs in Sarajevo, RFM spokesperson G. Karasin pointedly refused to comment on whether Russia would use its UNSC veto.[136] His silence meant only one thing: Russia would under no circumstances veto such a Western-inspired, anti-Serbian policy, certainly not at this time. Indeed, Russia's main concern seemed to be not the use of force against the Serbs but rather the West's failure to consult with Moscow on the action. This was made clear on August 3 when Karasin expressed Russia's concerns about the growing number of attacks on UN troops in Bosnia and the Bosnian Serb blockade of Sarajevo, but insisted that any plan for the use of force must be presented to the UN and that any decision to launch strikes must be done only "after consultation with" the UNSC members. Karasin at no time rejected air strikes on principle.[137]

By this time acceptance of US proposals for NATO military action in Yugoslavia, until now rejected by the West European allies, looked increasingly inevitable in light of the near-universal agreement that the failed strategies in Bosnia made more forceful measures imperative. This applied especially to France, Russia's purported chief ally in West Europe. The passage in October 1992 of UNSC Resolution 781 creating a no-fly zone had indeed "represented the beginning of a growing convergence between the French and American governments over policy toward the former Yugoslavia." France, moreover, had dropped its "vehement" opposition to US calls for air strikes against the Bosnian Serbs in August and September 1993 as a result of the gradual hardening of its (France's) position. This hardening in France's position was the result, above all, of the realization by French leaders that inaction in the face of the deteriorating situation in Sarajevo would undermine its status as a great power.[138] Russia would take no steps to oppose the West's more aggressive stance, as Kozyrev demonstrated in his September 15 statement pledging Russia's readiness to assist by shipping gas to Sarajevo, where energy was scarce as a result of the siege by the Bosnian Serbs.[139]

In fall 1993 Russian diplomacy became particularly active around Yugoslavia: in September Kozyrev defended Serbian rights in Krajina, the Serb-held territory in Croatia, whereas Yeltsin—in apparent gratitude for Western support during his battle with parliament—on October 5 reversed Russia's declared opposition to the US-backed plan for extending the UN peace-keeping mandate in the former Yugoslavia for another six months;[140] on November 2 Russia sent a letter to the UNSC proposing that Russia sell natural gas to Serbia and Montenegro on humanitarian grounds; and in mid-November Deputy Foreign Minister Churkin engaged in shuttle diplomacy to lift economic sanctions against the Serbs, clearly for the sole purpose of making a show of Moscow's policy of "evenhandedness."

Notes

[1] Ben Slay, "The Post Communist Economic Transition: Barriers and Progress," *RFE/RL Research Report*, Vol. 2, No. 39, October 1, 1993, p. 36.

[2] *Financial Times*, August 19, 1995, p. 2.

[3] Christopher M. Davis, "The Former Soviet Union," *RFE/RL Research Report*, Vol. 2, No. 40, October 8, 1993, pp. 36-40.

[4] *Rossiiskie vesti*, April 21, 1993, p. 4.

[5] *Segodnia*, May 14, 1993, p. 10.

[6] Wendy Slater, "Russia: The Return of Authoritarian Government?" *RFE/RL Research Report*, Vol. 3, No. 1, January 7, 1994, p. 22; *RFE/RL News Briefs*, September 20-4, 1993, p. 7.

[7] Slater, "Russia: The Return of Authoritarian Government?" pp. 22-3; Wendy Slater and Vera Tolz, "Yeltsin Wins in Moscow but May Lose to the Regions," *RFE/RL Research Report*, Vol. 2, No. 40, October 8, 1993, pp. 1-4; Alexander Rahr, "Yeltsin's Ups and Downs," *RFE/RL Research Report*, Vol. 2, No. 14, April 2, 1993, p. 1; *The New York Times*, March 22, 1993, p. A9; *The Guardian* (London), March 22, 1993, p. 6; Lynn D. Nelson and Irina Y. Kuzes, *Property to the People: The Struggle for Radical Economic Reform in Russia* (Armonk, NY: M.E. Sharpe, 1994), p. 89.

[8] Julia Wishnevsky, "Constitutional Wrangle While Some Voice Concern on the West," *RFE/RL Research Report*, Vol. 2, No. 14, April 2, 1993, pp. 5-7; *Rossiiskaia gazeta*, April 21, 1993, p. 7; *RFE/RL Daily Report*, No. 48, March 11, 1993, p. 2, and No. 49, March 12, 1993, p. 1. German Chancellor Kohl said that he had not discussed the possibility of Yeltsin's imposing direct presidential rule if the CPD made decisions unfavorable to Yeltsin, although one should probably take his words with a grain of salt, especially after the Christian Democratic scandal of 1999, which deeply implicated him for lying. Interfax, March 3, 1993. In mid-March, Mitterand also flew to the Russian capital to demonstrate French support for Russian "reforms and democracy." See ITAR-TASS, March 15, 1993, in *FBIS*-SOV-93-049, March 16, 1993, p. 3.

[9] *Izvestiia*, March 18, 1993, p. 4. See also *Rossiiskaia gazeta*, April 21, 1993, p. 7.

[10] ITAR-TASS, March 21, 1993.

[11] Ibid., March 27, 1993.

[12] *Krasnaia zvezda*, March 20, 1993, p. 2.

[13] *Segodnia*, July 2, 1993, p. 1; Anders Aslund, *How Russia Became a Market Economy* (Washington, D.C.: The Brookings Institution, 1995), pp. 55-6; Inter Press Service, April 23, 1993; Jiji Press Ticker Service, April 15, 1993.

[14] Richard Sakwa, "The Russian Elections of December 1993," *Europe-Asia Studies*, Vol. 47, No. 2, March 1995, p. 195; *RFE/RL News Briefs*, September 20-24, 1993, p. 7; Wendy Slater and Vera Tolz, "Yeltsin Wins in Moscow but May Lose to the Regions," *RFE/RL Research Report*, Vol. 2, No. 40, October 8, 1993, pp. 1-4. For a left-wing perspective on the events of September-October 1993 see Alexander Buzgalin and Andrei Kolganov, *Bloody October in Moscow: Political Repression in the Name of Reform* (New York: Monthly Review Press, 1994).

[15] Wishnevsky, "Constitutional Wrangle," pp. 5-7; *Rossiiskaia gazeta*, April 21, 1993, p. 7; *RFE/RL Daily Report*, No. 48, March 11, 1993, p. 2, and No. 49, March 12, 1993, p. 1.

[16] *European Political Cooperation*, Press Release, Brussels, "Community and Its Member States Declaration of Russia," October 4, 1993, p. 96/93.

[17] Victor Yasmann, "The Role of the Security Agencies in the October Uprising," *RFE/RL Research Report*, Vol. 2, No. 44, November 5, 1993, p. 13. A dissenting view which argues that the "hard-liners" did not prevail at this time is found in Allison K. Stanger, "Courting the Generals: The Impact of Russia's Constitutional Crisis on Yeltsin's Foreign Policy," in Michael Kraus and Ronald D. Liebowitz, eds., *Russia and Eastern Europe After Communism: The Search for New Political, Economic, and Security Systems* (Boulder: Westview, 1996), p. 298. See also S. Neil MacFarlane, "Russia, the West and European Security," *Survival*, Vol. 35, No. 3, Autumn 1993, p. 17.

[18] Leszek Buszynski, *Russian Foreign Policy After the Cold War* (Westport, CT: Praeger, 1996), p. 34; Many analyses, such as Jack Snyder, "Russian Backwardness and the Future of Europe," *Daedalus*, Vol. 123, No. 2, Spring 1994, pp. 179-85, saw a hardening of Russia's foreign policy line following the December Duma elections.

[19] Reuters, May 9, 1997. See also Josef Joffe, *Sueddeutsche Zeitung*, May 27, 1997, p. 4, in *FBIS*-WEU-97-147; Michael Mihalka, "Continued Resistance to NATO Expansion," *Transition*, August 11, 1995; Peter Shearman, "Russian Policy Toward Western Europe: The German Axis," in Peter Shearman, ed., *Russian Foreign Policy Since 1990* (Boulder: Westview, 1995), pp. 100-102; Stephen Covington, "Moscow's Insecurity and Eurasian Instability," *European Security*, Vol. 4, No. 3, Autumn 1995; Mark Kramer, "NATO, Russia, and East European Security," in Uri Ra'anan and Kate Martin, eds., *Russia—A Return to Imperialism?* (New York: St. Martin's, 1996), p. 123; Laszlo Valki, "Russia and the Security of East-Central Europe," *European Security*, Vol. 5, No. 3, Autumn 1996, pp. 452-3.

[20] See Richard L. Kugler and Marianna V. Kozintseva, *Enlarging NATO: The Russian Factor* (Santa Monica, CA: Rand, 1996), p. 33. Kugler and Kozintseva also took note of signs of a shift in late September 1993 as well, when Kozyrev asserted special Russian prerogatives in Eurasia and the CIS. See Ibid.

[21] See, for example, Alexander Rahr, "New Focus on Old Priorities," *Transition, 1994 in Review*, Part II, February 15, 1995, p. 9.

[22] Suzanne Crow, "Russia Asserts Its Strategic Agenda," *RFE/RL Research Report*, Vol. 2, No. 50, December 17, 1993, pp. 1-2, 7. Idem, "Why Has Russian Foreign Policy Changed?" *RFE/RL Research Report*, Vol. 3, No. 18, May 6, 1994, p. 1, concedes that "while many attempts have been made to explain [the recent] change [in Russian foreign policy], none is fully satisfactory." See also Bruce D. Porter, "Russia and Europe After the Cold War: The Interaction of Domestic and Foreign Policies," in Celeste A. Wallander, ed., *The Sources of Russian Foreign Policy After the Cold War* (Boulder: Westview, 1996), pp. 138-9. Following NATO's first air strikes against the Bosnian Serbs in March 1994, Yeltsin's spokesperson Kostikov pronounced Russia's romance with the West over.

[23] Statement of Peter Reddaway, in *Impact of IMF/World Bank Policies Toward Russia and the Russian Economy* (Hearing Before the Committee on Banking, Housing, and Urban Affairs, U.S. Senate, 103rd Congress, 2d Session, February 8, 1994, p. 34. Some Western observers even discerned a moderating trend in Russian foreign policy beginning in 1993, including Hannes Adomeit, "Russia as a 'Great Power' in World Affairs: Images and Reality," *International Affairs* (London), Vol. 71, No. 1, January 1995, pp. 37-8. To Paul Marantz, "Neither Adversaries Nor Partners: Russia and the West: Search for a New Relationship," in Roger E. Kanet and Alexander V. Kozhemiakin, eds., *The Foreign Policy of the Russian Federation* (New York: St. Martin's, 1997), p. 86, "the language in which Russian foreign policy towards the West is defended has changed, but the policy remains largely intact." See a smiilar argument by Michael McFaul, "A Precarious Peace. Domestic Politics in the Making of Russian Foreign Policy," *International Security*, Vol. 22, No. 3, Winter 1997/1998, p. 24.

[24] Shireen T. Hunter, "Closer Ties for Russia and Iran," *Transition*, Vol. 1, No. 24, December 29, 1995, pp. 43-5.

[25] Crow, "Russia Asserts Its Strategic Agenda," pp. 2-3.

[26] Suzanne Crow, "Russia Seeks Leadership in Regional Peacekeeping," *RFE/RL Research Report*, Vol. 2, No. 15, April 9, 1993, pp. 28-30. See also Eugene B. Rumer, *Russian National Security and Foreign Policy in Transition* (Santa Monica: Rand, 1995), p. 25, and Heather F. Hurlburt, "Russia Plays a Double Game," *Transition*, Vol. 1, No. 11, June 30, 1995, p. 14.

[27] *Nezavisimaia gazeta*, September 22, 1993, p. 1. Kozyrev reiterated his "tough" stand in October. See Ibid., October 13, 1993, p. 1.

[28] *The Daily Telegraph*, February 23, 1993, p. 12; *The Guardian* (London), January 27, 1993, p. 8. Government spokesperson A. Orfyonov said the transcript contained "serious distortions," but "declined to identify" what they were. See *The Washington Post*, January 27, 1993, p. A15.

[29] United Press International, January 7, 1993; *The Christian Science Monitor*, January 20, 1993, p. 7; *RFE/RL Daily Report*, No. 11, January 19, 1993.

[30] *Izvestia*, June 29, 1993, pp. 1, 3, June 30, 1993, p. 3, in *Current Digest of the Post-Soviet Press* (hereafter referred to as *CDPSP*), July 28, 1993, p. 14; *Sovetskaia Rossiia*, July 1, 1993, p. 1.

[31] *Segodnia*, November 13, 1993, p. 1.

[32] V. Mikheev, "Novye podkhody v evropeiskoi politike Vashingtona," *MEMO*, No. 2, 1993, pp. 24-7. See a similar perspective in *Izvestiia*, June 8, 1993, p. 4.

[33] V. Kozin, "Novye izmereniia NATO," *Mezhdunarodnaia zhizn'*, No. 3, 1993, pp. 55-7. Kozin, to be sure, expressed his discomfort with NATO's eastward expansion, but merely suggested that any such expansion not be done without Russian "participation" in NATO, thus stopping short of insisting on full Russian membership. Ibid., p. 59.

[34] *Nezavisimaia gazeta*, January 30, 1993, p. 1; *RFE/RL Daily Report*, No. 20, February 1, 1993, p. 1.

[35] *Diplomaticheskii vestnik*, No. 5-6, March 1993, p. 11.

[36] ITAR-TASS, August 25, 1993, in *FBIS-SOV-93-163*, August 25, 1993, p. 3; *Nezavisimaia gazeta*, August 25, 1993, p. 1; *Segodnia*, August 27, 1993, p. 1.

[37] *Bol'shaia sovetskaia entsiklopediia* (Moscow: "Sovetskaia Entsiklopediia," 1974), Vol. 18, p. 480. See also *Christian Science Monitor*, October 4, 1995, p. 20.

[38] Dimitri K. Simes, *After the Collapse: Russia Seeks Its Place As a Great Power* (New York: Simon and Schuster, 1999), p. 219. On this point, also see Suzanne Crow, "Russian Views on an Eastward Expansion of NATO," *RFE/RL Research Report*, Vol. 2, No. 41, October 15, 1993, p. 22. To be sure, Crow admits the possibility that Yeltsin meant what he said in Warsaw. See Ibid., p. 23.

[39] A. Zagorskii, "Kren ot SBSE k NATO? Bol'she vnimaniia k evropeiskim delam," *Mezhdunarodnaia Zhizn'*, No. 12, 1993, p. 19.

[40] *The St. Louis Post-Dispatch*, July 4, 1993, p. A8.

[41] Lynn D. Nelson and Irina Y. Kuzes, *Radical Reform in Yeltsin's Russia: Political, Economic, and Social Dimensions* (Armonk, NY: M.E. Sharpe, 1995), p. 25.

[42] *Journal of Commerce*, July 1, 1993, p. A3.

[43] *Financial Times*, August 2, 1993, p. 1.

[44] *Pravda*, August 18, 1993, p. 6.

[45] Ibid., August 27, 1993, p. 3; Warsaw PAP, August 24, 1993, in *FBIS-EEU-93-163*, August 25, 1993, p. 26.

[46] Nelson and Kuzes, *Radical Reform*, p. 25.

[47] *Pravda*, August 27, 1993, p. 3.

[48] Warsaw TVP Television First Program, August 25, 1993, in *FBIS*-EEU-93-164, August 26, 1993, p. 12; *Segodnia*, August 27, 1993, p. 1.

[49] *The New York Times*, August 26, 1993, p. A3.

[50] De Weydenthal, "Russia Mends Fences," p. 34; James W. Morrison, *NATO Expansion and Alternative Future Security Alignments* (Washington, D.C.: Institute for National Strategic Studies, McNair Paper 40, April 1995), p. 22.

[51] ITAR-TASS, August 25, 1993.

[52] De Weydenthal, "Russia Mends Fences, p. 34.

[53] Crow, "Russian Views," pp. 21-2; Idem, "Russia Asserts Its Strategic Agenda," p. 6. See also *Rossiiskaia gazeta*, September 8, 1993, p. 7.

[54] *RFE/RL Daily Report*, No. 178, September 16, 1993, p. 3.

[55] Reuters, September 30, 1993; *Izvestiia*, October 2, 1993, p. 4; Michael Mihalka, "Squaring the Circle: NATO's Offer to the East," *RFE/RL Research Report*, Vol. 3, No. 12, March 25, 1994, p. 3.

[56] See, e.g., the statement by Czech President Havel's spokesperson L. Spacek in Prague CTK, October 1, 1993, in *FBIS*-EEU-93-189, October 1, 1993, p. 6.

[57] ITAR-TASS, September 2, 1993.

[58] Interfax, September 20, 1993, in *FBIS*-SOV-93-181, September 21, 1993, p. 9; Ibid., pp. 9-10.

[59] Kugler and Kozintseva, *Enlarging NATO*, p. 62; *The Washington Post*, October 6, 1993, p. A24.

[60] ITAR-TASS, October 21, 1993, in *FBIS*-SOV-93-203, October 22, 1993, p. 7.

[61] V. Cherviakov, "Rasshirenie NATO i izmenenie balansa sil v Evrope," *Svobodnaia mysl'*, No. 6, April 1994, pp. 40-1. On Russia's new military doctrine, see Stephen Foye, "Updating Russian Civil-Military Relations," *RFE/RL Research Report*, Vol. 2, No. 46, November 19, 1993, p. 45.

[62] Mayak Radio, November 3, 1993, in *FBIS*-SOV-93-211, November 3, 1993, pp. 5-6.

[63] *Diplomaticheskii vestnik*, No. 21-22, November 1993, pp. 22-3.

[64] Warsaw, *Polityka*, September 4, 1993, in *FBIS*-SOV-93-172, September 8, 1993, p. 21. Kozyrev had made a similar argument on August 24. See de Weydenthal, "Russia Mends Fences," p. 34, and A. Kozyrev, *Moskovskie novosti*, No. 43, October 24, 1993, p. A15.

[65] S. Karaganov, *Moskovskie novosti*, No. 38, September 19, 1993, p. A7. See a similar view in *Nezavisimaia gazeta*, October 21, 1993, p. 1.

[66] *The Moscow Times*, May 17, 1997, p. 8.

[67] *Izvestiia*, October 21, 1992, p. 4; *Pravda*, March 20, 1993, p. 3.

[68] *Krasnaia Zvezda*, December 2, 1993, p. 3.

[69] ITAR-TASS, September 2, 1993, in *FBIS*-SOV-93-170, September 3, 1993, p. 1.

[70] Mayak Radio, November 25, 1993, in *FBIS*-SOV-93-226, November 26, 1993, p. 5; *RFE/RL News Briefs*, November 18, 1993, p. 1; *Kommersant-daily*, November 26, 1993, p. 3; *Izvestiia*, November 26, 1993, p. 4.

[71] *Nezavisimaia gazeta*, November 26, 1993, p. 1; Official Kremlin International News Broadcast, November 26, 1993.

[72] *Izvestiia*, November 25, 1993, p. 1. Others maintained that the RFM had agrreed with the Primakov report. See *Kommersant-daily*, November 26, 1993, p. 3.

[73] *Segodnia*, November 27, 1993, p. 2.

[74] Alexei Pushkov, *Moscow News*, No. 50, December 10, 1993.

[75] Kozyrev also stressed that Russia's acknowledgement of a nation's right to choose did not mean that it rejected dialogue, or accepted an East European "cordon sanitaire." See *Moskovskie novosti*, No. 39, September 26, 1993, p. 7A.

[76] Andrei Kozyrev, "The New Russia and the Atlantic Alliance," *NATO Review*, Vol. 41, No. 1, February 1993, p. 3. See also Kozyrev's February 26, 1993 speech to the Foreign Policy Association of Denmark, in *Diplomaticheskii vestnik*, No. 5-6, March 1993, pp. 11-12.

[77] Crow, "Russian Views," pp. 22-3; de Weydenthal, "Russia Mends Fences," p. 34.

[78] "O suti kontseptsii vneshnei politiki Rossii," *Mezhdunarodnaia zhizn'*, No. 1, 1993, p. 20. See also *Diplomaticheskii vestnik*, January 1993, special issue, p. 4. A. Zagorskii correctly notes that the "Basic Positions" contain little reference to NATO. See his "Rossiia i Evropa: formulirovanie 'bol'shoi Evropy'," in *Ot reformy k stabilizatsii . . . vneshniaia, voennaia i ekonomicheskaia politika Rossii (analiz i prognos), 1993-5* (Moscow: MGIMO, "Promyshlennyi vestnik Rossii," 1995), p. 37. See a similar perspective in Kozin, "Novye izmereniia NATO," pp. 58-9, and O. Prikhodko and P. Smirnov, "Rossiia i problemy evropeiskoi bezopasnosti," *SShA*, No. 4, 1993, p. 48. Prikhodko and Smirnov were researchers at ISKRAN.

[79] See, for example, Andrei Zagorskii and Michael Lucas, *Rossiia pered evropeiskim vyzovom* (Moscow: "Mezhdunarodnye otnosheniia," 1993), p. 99.

[80] *The Washington Post*, March 22, 1991, p. A18.

[81] Reuters, September 23, 1993.

[82] Kramer, "NATO, Russia and East European Security," pp. 115-16.

[83] *The Independent* (London), April 22, 1993, p. 10.

[84] Kramer, "NATO, Russia and East European Security," p. 113.

[85] *Defense News*, June 10, 1991; Kramer, "NATO, Russia and East European Security," p. 139.

[86] Reuters, February 10, 1993.

[87] Crow, "Russian Views," p. 24; John Borawski, "Partnership for Peace and Beyond," *International Affairs* (London), Vol. 71, No. 2, April 1995, p. 237, and

Ole Diehl, "Opening NATO to Eastern Europe?," *The World Today*, Vol. 49, No. 12, December 1993, p. 222.

[88] Reuters, September 23, 1993.

[89] Alfred A. Reisch, "Central and Eastern Europe's Quest for NATO Membership," *RFE/RL Research Report*, Vol. 2, No. 28, July 9, 1993, pp. 45-6.

[90] Dimitri Simes, *Moscow News*, No. 17, April 29-May 5, 1994, p. 4. See also Mihalka, "Squaring the Circle," pp. 2-3, and Zagorskii, "Kren ot SBSE," p. 18, which notes that the Warsaw document "created an important and irreversible precedent; 'taking it back' was impossible." See also P. Felgengauer, *Segodnia*, June 23, 1995, p. 9.

[91] Alexei Pushkov, *Moscow News*, January 17, 1994, p. 4.

[92] *Trud*, August 31, 1993, p. 3.

[93] Mihalka, "Squaring the Circle," p. 3.

[94] See *Geopoliticheskie peremeny v Evrope, politika Zapada i al'ternativy dlia Rossii* (Moscow: Institute of Europe, 1995), p. 9.

[95] Emphasis mine. Mihalka, "Squaring the Circle," p. 3.

[96] *Financial Times*, September 11, 1993, p. 24.

[97] Ibid., October 22, 1993, p. 2.

[98] *RFE/RL Daily Report*, No. 205, October 22, 1993, p. 2.

[99] Emphasis mine. Alexei Pushkov, *Moscow News*, No. 50, December 10, 1993, p. 1; Idem, No. 51, December 17, 1993, p. 4; The Associated Press, December 8, 1993; *Diplomaticheskii vestnik*, No. 1-2, January 1, 1994, pp. 5-6, 22; *Izvestiia*, December 4, 1993, p. 1; ITAR-TASS, December 10, 1993; PAP, December 2, 1993.

[100] United Press International, December 3, 1993.

[101] *The Independent* (London), December 5, 1993, p. 12.

[102] Reuters, December 26, 1993.

[103] Belgrade, Tanjug, August 27, 1993, in *FBIS*-EEU-93-166, August 30, 1993, p. 22.

[104] Reuters, November 28, 1993.

[105] *The Times*, December 21, 1993.

[106] *The Jerusalem Post*, December 16, 1993, p. 6.

[107] *RFE/RL Daily Report*, January 4, 1993, p. 1; Agence France Presse, January 3, 1993.

[108] *Izvestiia*, January 18, 1993, p. 2.

[109] Vera Tolz, "The Burden of the Imperial Legacy in Russia," *RFE/RL Research Report*, Vol. 2, No. 20, May 14, 1993, p. 45.

[110] *Izvestiia*, January 26, 1993, p. 3.

[111] *RFE/RL Daily Report*, No. 24, February 5; No. 25, February 8; No. 31, February 16, 1993; Ostankino Television, February 7, 1993, in *FBIS*-SOV-93-024, February 8, 1993, p. 7.

[112] *Diplomaticheskii vestnik*, No. 7-8, April 1993, p. 13; *Moskovskaia pravda*, February 6, 1993, p. 1.

[113] *Diplomaticheskii vestnik*, No. 5-6, March 1993, p. 11; Inter Press Service, February 25, 1993. The West's policy of singling out Belgrade for its transgressions was blatantly discriminatory in light of the Croats severing their alliance in 1993 with the Bosnian Muslims and instituting ethnic cleansing.

[114] *The New York Times*, March 3, 1993, p. A12.

[115] *Izvestiia*, April 2, 1993, p. 3.

[116] ITAR-TASS, April 1, 1993; *Izvestiia*, April 2, 1993, p. 3.

[117] *The Christian Science Monitor*, April 19, 1993; *The Times*, April 13, 1993; *The Ottawa Citizen*, April 13, 1993, p. A6; *The Gazette* (Montreal), April 13, 1993, p. A1.

[118] *The Independent* (London), April 17, 1993, p. 1; *The Christian Science Monitor*, April 19, 1993.

[119] Hamburg DPA, April 14, 1993, in *FBIS*-WEU-93-070, April 14, 1993, p. 11; *Le Monde*, January 5, 1993, p. 1, in *FBIS*-WEU-93-003, January 6, 1993, pp. 13-4.

[120] Berlin ADN, April 16, 1993, and Berlin DDP, April 18, 1993, in *FBIS*-WEU-93-073, April 19, 1993, p. 16. Even Britain threatened air strikes against Serbian forces in Srebrenica. See *The Daily Telegraph*, April 26, 1993, p. 11.

[121] *Diplomaticheskii vestnik*, No. 9-10, May 1993, p. 21.

[122] ITAR-TASS, April 26, 1993; The Associated Press, April 28, 1993; Allen Lynch and Reneo Lukic, "Russian Foreign Policy and the Wars in the Former Yugoslavia," *RFE/RL Research Report*, Vol. 2, No. 41, October 15, 1993, p. 32.

[123] Agence France Presse, May 18, 1993.

[124] *Izvestiia*, May 21, 1993, p. 3.

[125] Agence France Presse, May 18, 1993; *The Daily Telegraph*, May 18, 1993, p. 1.

[126] *Izvestiia*, May 25, 1993, p. 1; The Reuter Economic Community Report, May 25, 1993; Stephanie Anderson, "EU, NATO, and CSCE Responses to the Yugoslav Crisis: Testing Europe's New Security Architecture," *European Security*, Vol. 4, No. 2, Summer 1995, pp. 347-8; Agence France Presse, May 21 and 26, 1993.

[127] *The Daily Telegraph*, May 23, 1993.

[128] *Izvestiia*, May 24, 1993.

[129] Mayak Radio, May 23, 1993; *Izvestiia*, May 25, 1993, pp. 1, 3.

[130] *The Washington Times*, May 20, 1993, p. A9; *The Herald* (Glasgow), May 21, 1993, p. 11.

[131] *Financial Times*, June 5, 1993, p. 1; UPI, June 10, 1993.

[132] Press Association Newsfile, June 11, 1993.

[133] Agence France Presse, June 8, 1993.

[134] UPI International, June 10, 1993.

[135] *The Guardian* (London), June 25, 1993, p. 11.

[136] UPI, August 3, 1993.

[137] ITAR-TASS, July 30, 1993.

[138] Pia Christina Wood, "France and the Post Cold War Order: The Case of Yugoslavia," *European Security*, Vol. 3, No. 1, Spring 1994, pp. 138-48.

[139] Agence France Presse, September 15, 1993.

[140] Allen Lynch, "After Empire: Russia and Its Western Neighbors," *RFE/RL Research Report*, Vol. 3, No. 12, March 25, 1994, pp. 10-2.

5 1994: The Zapadniki Retreat

The Domestic Setting

Alarmed by the impact of "reforms," one analyst typically characterized Russian capitalism in 1994 as a "horror . . . nasty, thieving, and . . . foreign."[1] Others underscored the fundamental clash of Russian and Western cultural values, which threw into stark contrast the West's mean-spirited, market-encouraged individualism, as compared to Russia's intrinsic and more humane "togetherness" (i.e., collectiveness).[2] Director of ISKRAN Georgii Arbatov criticized the "reforms" as a "failure practically everywhere," and took to task Russia's leaders for adopting them in a society "with totally different economic and social conditions from those prevailing in Third World countries," the intended locale of most IMF-supported "reforms."[3]

Extreme Westernizers, on the other hand, welcomed Western approval of the policies of Russian leaders, whose "submi[ssion] . . . to the discipline of the IMF . . . augurs well for [Russia's] dealings with the West."[4] Economics Minister Yasin, for one, pronounced IMF demands that Russia liberalize and maintain a tough fiscal policy "well-founded . . . [They answer] our interests."[5] The IMF in late March was indeed so enthusiastic about Russia's policy that it signed an agreement on the basic parameters of the budget,[6] and in December Yasin announced an "improved" budget draft for 1995 which included slashing the deficit to 8%, cancelling benefits and reducing spending on a number of items.[7]

To critics like economist Sergei Glaz'ev this was an outright sellout to foreign interests. He lambasted the government accordingly for its "comprador policy in the interests of foreign and speculative capital" which, he charged, had been responsible for an 80% decline in the share of domestic goods on the Russian market during the previous three years, an almost 75% drop in productive investments, and a 40-50% fall in investment in science-intensive branches.[8] The insidious effects of the reforms were also reflected in statistics which showed that the ratio of the income of Russia's poorest 10% to richest 10% had risen from an egalitarian 1:3-1:4 at the beginning of 1992 (just after the USSR disbanded) to 1:26 in 1994.

The trajectory of political developments was also a far from democratic one. A special team empowered by Yeltsin to review the results of the December 1993 parliamentary elections and constitutional referendum concluded that the turnout had been substantially less than that claimed by the Central Election Commission, thus making the referendum invalid. Its findings were, needless to say, ignored by the leadership.[9] The December 1993 election for the Duma was indeed a sobering lesson for the Yeltsin forces: in all, the three main anti-"reform" blocs won 182 seats, the "reform" blocs only 164.[10] Despite the limited power of the new Duma to shape policy, its criticism was potent enough to compel the Yeltsin-Kozyrev forces to distance themselves somewhat—if only rhetorically—from their pro-Western foreign policy line.

The period from November 29 to December 11, 1994 was the "apogee of the power and influence of the party of war," a time when Russian policy seemed to reflect the preeminence of such "militants" as influential Yeltsin aides Aleksandr Korzhakov, Head of Yeltsin's Security Service, and Deputy Prime Minister Oleg Soskovets and their policy of "imperial muscle-flexing in relations with . . . Western democracies." A most significant development in post-Soviet Russian history, the first military incursion into Chechnya, also took place at this time, coming on the heels of NATO's declaration to expand. One of the principal watersheds in post-Soviet Russian policy, NATO's decision to expand in turn brought out in the open the West's intention of isolating, not befriending, Russia. For Russia's policymakers it meant that one of the main inhibitions against their resort to force in Chechnya—Western disapproval—was precluded since the West was unconcerned with Russia's sensibilities in any case. Apparently feeling that it had nothing to lose, that it could ignore the West just as it had been ignored, Russia informed neither its Western "partners" nor the CSCE of its invasion plans beforehand.[11]

The Modification of Russia's Foreign Policy

In mid-January Kozyrev delivered a speech to Russian diplomatic representatives in the CIS and Baltic countries which spelled out a "hardened" Russian foreign policy line. Identifying the CIS as a "vital" strategic priority, he insisted his government would defend with force the rights of Russians in the near abroad, thus contradicting his former espousal of the withdrawal of Russian troops from the CIS.[12] In his State of the

Nation speech to the Federal Assembly on February 23 Yeltsin adopted an equally belligerent posture when he rejected NATO expansion, insisted that Russia would make no foreign policy concessions, especially on defense, and warned that he would get tough with neighbors who discriminated against ethnic Russians.[13] Time would prove these threats to be hot air.

Kozyrev responded to charges that he was soft on the West by attacking it, thus departing from his former habit of focusing his attacks almost exclusively against "red and brown" forces in Russia. Thus, in a March analysis he attributed the failure to create a "firm partnership" with West Europe to, among other things, "discrimination" of Russian goods on West European markets, West Europe's "sharp turn" in policy toward the former Yugoslavia (it had supported the ultimatum on Sarajevo without consulting Russia), and its enthusiasm for NATO expansion.[14]

In an equally sharp departure from late Soviet and early Russian perspectives which had warmly welcomed the West's "stabilising" influence in Europe, Yeltsin promised Russia's Foreign Intelligence Service in late April that the government would, inter alia, intensify efforts to integrate the former Soviet space and create a perimeter of "zones of stability" around Russia.[15] Those hostile to Russia's pro-Western policies, however, saw a double game in this and in like-sounding statements on the Partnership for Peace (PfP): they reprimanded Russia for its attempts to create "difficulties for appearances' sake" then promptly agreeing to join PfP without any reservations.[16] Others blamed Gorbachev and Shevardnadze for having given the US carte blanche in the past to act as "world gendarme" and for making one-sided concessions to the West, who then expected a humiliated Russia to follow its lead.[17] One analyst even asserted that the purpose of the PfP—indeed, of NATO's very "genetic code"—was the USSR's disintegration, the weakening of Russia's military-political positions, and its subordination to the West.[18]

In response to this rising crescendo of anti-Westernism the CFDP in May issued its second "Theses," the "Strategy for Russia" (the first, it will be recalled, had appeared in August 1992), whose main point was to raise concern that public opinion was shifting dramatically in favor of the "Communists and nationalists" even as it conceded anti-Western sentiment had "made its point." Disparaging great-power rhetoric, it urged a reaffirmation of partnership with the West.[19]

The liberal *Kommersant-daily* voiced similar anxiety that Russia's more "assertive" policy proved that Kozyrev's Stockholm "joke" of December

1992 had finally become reality and was manifested in Russia's "support" for the Serbs and for Iraq.[20] But this assessment was clearly inaccurate, since Russia's policy was, as is discussed below, essentially pro-Western and anti-Serb, and since Russia's "support" for Iraq reflected not so much some sort of hard-line tangent as a simple desire to line up with other UNSC members—China, France and Britain, who also sought to restore commercial and political ties with Iran. If Russia *appeared* to be more assertive in its foreign policy, in reality it continued to kowtow to the West in the most critical areas. Even Western analysts realized that Yeltsin's policies were mere periodic "displays of independence" from the West which proved tactically successful in that they did "Yeltsin good" in the face of the mounting challenges to his agenda.[21]

Russia and NATO

The waning popularity of Russia's "reformers" was accompanied by the increasingly negative mainstream perception of the West. Perhaps the most perceptible evidence of this change was the almost overnight mutation of the approach toward NATO from one which welcomed its presence in the FSU to one of guarded suspicion. With its unbending determination to expand and its unwillingness to brook any resistance to expansion, NATO, one might add, did not exactly help its own position.

One of the most contentious issues facing Russia in 1994 was whether to accept NATO's offer to join the PfP. After NATO's decision to expand in January NATO relations became the touchstone of Russia's relations with the West. Knowing that immediate acceptance of NATO's offer to join the PfP would make them appear too eager to work with the very organization that threatened Russia's security but also unwilling to abandon their Western patrons, Russia's leaders decided to temporize on their decision to join. In the meantime they continued to interact with NATO and participate in NATO-led exercises.

Russian Perspectives on NATO

A measure of the recent and abrupt sea change in the mainstream Russian perception of NATO could be gauged by the conclusion in a monograph by the Institute of Europe which, in contrast to its previous praise of NATO for its benevolence and desire to peacefully transform, now emphasized that "the Atlantic alliance has maintained its positions and remains the chief military support for European security." By asserting that the change originated in the US-West European agreement made sometime in 1990-3 "to strengthen NATO and expand,"[22] however, it completely ignored Yeltsin's August 1993 sanction of NATO expansion. This (rhetorical) hardening of the position on NATO was so complete that some analysts now couched their writings in terms which recalled the Soviet line. Iu. Stroev, for example, warned that because the US needed NATO to protect its own interests NATO could, given its current direction, eventually expand all the way to Smolensk.[23]

Russian Relations with NATO

The PfP, which Kozyrev had disingenuously insisted was "not an anteroom for NATO membership," was both pilloried and praised during the heated controversy over whether Russia should join. Critics attacked it, contending that it: (1) did not reject but merely delayed NATO expansion; (2) would encourage NATO to absorb the states of the FSU; (3) marginalized all-European institutions, especially the OSCE and NACC; and (4) would deprive Russia of a traditional arms market because it encouraged new NATO members to adapt their military technique to NATO standards.[24] Loyal oppositionist A. Migranian warned in addition that NATO sought through the PfP to block political-military consolidation in the FSU, and predicted that membership in it would weaken Russia and deprive it of strategic freedom of maneuver. Aleksandr Rutskoi warned that rapprochement with NATO through the PfP would have "dangerous" consequences.[25] In March the Committee on Foreign and Defense Policy (CFDP) also gave a negative assessment of the PfP, as did most of the Russian press;[26] and Lt. Gen. L. Ivashov, Secretary of the Council of Defense Ministers of the CIS, cautioned that NATO sought to covertly expand via the PfP, to "mov[e] NATO's forward lines right up to Russia's western borders."[27]

Pro-Western analysts emphasized to the contrary that not joining PfP would isolate Russia, a position shared by most Western analysts.[28] I. Lagunina defended PfP membership and even chided Kozyrev—"Mr. Yes"—for being *too critical* of NATO and for failing to acknowledge the positive things it had done for Russia.[29] Other Westernizers judged NATO expansion legitimate in light of the "threat" Russia posed to CEE.[30] Western commentators acknowledged that PfP was a ploy to stall NATO expansion and avoid provoking Russia during the delicate period which followed Yeltsin's "bloody suppression of his political opponents."[31]

Kozyrev lauded NATO in August for responding to Yeltsin's December 1991 appeal to NATO to develop ties and to "radically transform" relations, which would have been "simply inconceivable" a few years earlier.[32] That this was sheer theatrics was borne out by Kozyrev's own admission in February that Russia would not be granted NATO membership any time soon, if ever. At a press conference following the December Budapest CSCE summit Yeltsin gave a new twist to Russia's position on its own membership in NATO: it might eventually apply for membership in NATO's *political* organization to achieve a status in NATO similar to France.[33] If Russia's request for membership in NATO was not serious it nevertheless promoted *NATO's* expansion agenda by legitimizing the membership of *other* states, a fact which was not lost six years later on Russian observers who, clearly on to the machinations of Russia's Westernizing leaders, denounced President Putin for employing the very same tactic (see Chapter 10).

Even as they tried to brake somewhat the NATO expansion momentum in early 1994 the Western powers were launching a campaign to pressure Russia. President Clinton implicitly promised East European states on January 11 that NATO would defend them if attacked[34] and US Defense Secretary Perry pledged support for Russian reform on February 5 while warning that NATO would defend against a Russian threat.[35] In early February Chancellor Kohl advised Russia to respect the integrity of its neigbors, pointing out that NATO had refrained from accepting CEE members out of respect for Moscow's security concerns, and then issued a thinly-veiled warning: "we expect Russia to continue a foreign policy marked by constructive participation in solving international problems."[36] But Russian leaders seemed—or rather pretended—not to hear. In his February 24 State of the Union Address to Parliament, a forum where moderate rhetoric was clearly inappropriate, Yeltsin cast aside his earlier temperate talk of Atlanticism and dependence on the West to rail stridently against CEE membership in NATO.[37]

But Kozyrev, who always had tricks up his sleeve to obscure Russia's unwillingness to oppose NATO, unveiled his proposal in March for a new European security system which envisioned the merger of the CSCE and

NACC into a single independent body closely tied to the CSCE and urged that the two jointly coordinate NATO, the EC, the CofE, the WEU, and the CIS. The plan also entailed a joint guarantee of the security of the CEE states by Russia and West Europe.[38] Throughout the fall of 1994 the Russian government persisted in its attacks on NATO and expansion, but betrayed its fidelity to the alliance by agreeing for the first time in October to take part in PfP naval exercises, named "Cooperative Venture 94," in Stavenger, Norway (Russia had been only an observer at the first PfP ground exercises, "Cooperative Bridge 94," at Poznan in September).[39]

In November the Clinton administration announced it would formally approve CEE membership in NATO, despite warnings from West Europeans that such a move could isolate Russia. France and Germany, in particular, feared that admitting new members to NATO before they joined the EU would hamper efforts to shore up the WEU. The crucial NATO Foreign Ministers meeting on December 1 nevertheless finally declared expansion necessary and agreed on a one-year schedule to inform NATO applicants about what steps they must take to join. The apparently unsuccessful attempt by France and Germany to persuade the US not to set the schedule[40] led to accusations that the US was "riding roughshod over its allies," negotiating terms with the East Europeans and presenting NATO with faits accomplis.[41] But this was no cause for joy to A. Pushkov, who alluded to Western divisions over NATO expansion stemming from West Europe's "big doubts" about expansion, for he was resigned to the fact that all would come to naught, since however much it criticized the US, West Europe in the end "always followed in the wake of the United States"[42]——a phrase reminiscent of Soviet assessments of "interimperialist" relations.

Then, in a particularly forceful demarche Kozyrev shocked the world by refusing to sign the Individual Partnership Program with NATO at its December 1 meeting and also voiced Russia's objections to the provisions of NATO's announcement on expansion made earlier that day.[43] Although this seemed the most explicit demonstration yet of Russian "opposition" to NATO expansion, Kozyrev never really intended to block it. Indeed, Western observers put the lie to the assumption that the move had been "unexpected" when they dismissed it as just another "carefully prepared piece of theatre" aimed at the "domestic audience." The "outlines of NATO plans for faster enlargement were well known to Russia" for some time prior to the meeting, they charged, "despite Mr. Kozyrev's claim that he had found dubious elements in the NATO plan 'at first glance'."[44]

In an equally "militant" followup gesture on December 5 Yeltsin's address to the CSCE meeting in Budapest lashed out at NATO's expansion plans by cautioning that the alliance must under no circumstances reach the borders of Russia. If NATO did expand, he thundered, Europe would be plunged into a "cold peace." Yeltsin also demanded recognition of the CIS as an international organization guaranteeing security in the FSU that was, in effect, Russia's sphere of influence. To all appearances, Russia now seemed willing to take its "opposition" to NATO to the limit.[45] NATO Secretary-General Claes, for one, was not taken in by the rhetoric, and he expressed confidence that Russia would in time come around to signing the PfP, thus demonstrating to one Russian analyst that Russia's "toughness" toward the West was part of an effort to deal with the "wimp factor," that is, to dispel Kozyrev's image as a "tame pro-Western [Foreign] Minister."[46] As it turned out, even as Russian leaders were issuing threats, they joined with West Europe and the US in Budapest to sign an agreement to exchange detailed information on the status of their armed forces.[47]

Apologists for the government termed Russia's policy a success, arguing that while "far from everything" was achieved in Budapest a "practical beginning" had been made. Russian critics, however, skeptical about their leaders' apparent anti-NATO bombast, charged that Yeltsin's pro-Western policy was "unconvincing and simply pathetic," and pointed out that the sole result of the December Budapest CSCE summit was a "meager" declaration on political partnership.[48] Kozyrev soon proved the skeptics right by assuaging Western fears about Yeltsin's threat of a "cold peace": it was only rhetoric, he explained, and Russia would never allow a "cold peace" as long as it retained its foremost foreign policy objective of strengthening partnership with the US (and the West).[49] On December 7 Kozyrev again sought to reassure the West by affirming that Russia did not wish to "erect barriers" to expansion, but merely sought to prevent it from being carried out too hastily.[50]

Such meekness in the face of the West's increasingly ominous behavior seemed particularly incongruous in view of the advice Jacques Delors gave the US as he stepped down as European Commission President in December: it should not, he cautioned, "propose *at this point* a widening of the Atlantic alliance to the East, which in my view complicates the task of consolidating relations between the US, the EU and Russia."[51] Significantly, he did not rule out NATO expansion.

The Partnership for Peace

Presidents Clinton and Yeltsin signed a joint endorsement of PfP in January. At the news conference following the signing, Yeltsin expressed satisfaction that a precipitous NATO decision to expand had been forestalled.[52] And contrary to the claim that the Russian military rejected PfP and that Yeltsin had to force it on them[53] in January the Ministry of Defense and the Security Council both backed PfP membership.[54] Given the Yeltsin leadership's firm endorsement of PfP so early on, therefore, one is compelled to question whether the vacillation and contentiousness within the leadership in the ensuing debate over Russian membership was genuine—i.e., whether it was a matter of protecting Russian security or, what is likely, whether the leaders were torn as to how best to obfuscate their inevitable capitulation to NATO. The latter hypothesis seems borne out by the fact that the idea for the PfP was originally hatched in fall 1993 during a "friendly conversation" between Kozyrev and US Secretary of State Christopher after the Visegrad states made a formal request for NATO membership.[55]

The course of Russia's eventual decision to sign the PfP was tortuous and confusing. Defense Minister Grachev and Prime Minister Chernomyrdin both told US Defense Secretary Perry in mid-March that Russia would soon sign the agreement, but days later RFM officials denied that Russia would do so even by the end of March. And on March 31 Yeltsin's Press Secretary confirmed that Russia would not sign for 6-7 months, but Kozyrev, alleging a misunderstanding, agreed the next day that Russia would sign sometime during the next month. On April 4, Grachev reported that Yeltsin favored PfP membership, but within days NATO air strikes against Bosnian Serbs outside Gorazde galvanized Kozyrev, in a seeming display of pique, into refusing to sign the PfP in Brussels on April 20 as planned.[56]

In early May Grachev termed NATO's proposals on PfP unacceptable and presented instead a four-point plan for a formal Russian-NATO security relationship which would confer on Russia and NATO equal responsibility. German Defense Minister Ruehe implicitly rejected the plan by tepidly characterizing it as "intriguing." That month Yeltsin visited Germany, where he also insisted Russia would not sign the PfP without a special protocol. The West agreed to discuss a special status for Russia, but not outside the standard PfP framework, as Russia insisted.[57]

The veritable three-ring circus finally came to an end on May 30 when it was reported that RFM officials expressed their eagerness to join the PfP before Yeltsin's arrival at the G-7 Naples summit in early July. Grachev also announced in late May that Russia would soon join the PfP,[58] despite NATO's immediate response that it would likely reject Russia's suggestion to hold regularized consultations and proposed instead the signing of a looser "gentleman's agreement," by means of which Russia's views would be sought on issues *NATO* thought appropriate. NATO officials also affirmed that they were not ready to commit to talks with Russia on expansion and rejected Russia's proposal for a European security structure which subordinated NATO to the CSCE.[59]

Yeltsin termed the PfP "brilliant" and "terrific," but the reality was that the PfP protocol was nothing less than a stunning defeat for Russian diplomacy. It granted few of Russia's demands—Russia sought a mechanism for the aforementioned automatic Russia-NATO consultation on matters of mutual interest—and failed to establish a blueprint for a new European security system which Russia so fervently sought. NATO did not even sign it. At most, the PfP "sweeten[ed] the NATO expansion pill" for Russia by consenting to the minor reinforcement of CSCE structures.[60]

The signing of the PfP in Brussels on June 22 was yet another affirmation of Russia's acceptance of NATO expansion in principle— although Kozyrev insisted that he opposed any haste in the process. Russia *did not*, however, sign the separate bilateral Russia-NATO agreement; that would have to wait until the following year.[61] In an indication of the depth of opposition to the leadership's policies a June 22 amendment invalidating Russia's accession to the PfP as a betrayal of Russian national interests fell short of passage in the Duma by a mere nine votes.[62] The vote was significant enough, however, to provoke Kozyrev into calling supporters of the motion "traitors" and defending the PfP because it established a Russia-NATO partnership instead of a "Yalta-II."[63] In a similar vein, arch-Westernizer Vitalii Churkin declared the following week that Russia-NATO differences had been "exaggerated." And another reported reason Russia had decided to sign was because it felt that eliminating a "cold war relic" (i.e., military competition and opposition) before the Naples G-7 summit would help to ensure Russia's acceptance in that club of the world's richest (capitalist) industrial nations.[64] Russia's leaders, in other words, were willing to sacrifice their country's strategic interests just so they could hobnob with the "elite" of the world's wealthiest nations—in what had become a largely meaningless organization, to boot.

Crowing over the "breakthrough" at the G-7 summit in Naples which supposedly "formalized Russia's emergence as a respected world power"[65] Yeltsin in early July pronounced Russia an "equal partner" with the West—in bilateral relations, in the UNSC, and in the newly-formed "political G-8," as he termed it. Russian observers were convinced that Russia's "successes" formed a "sound basis for dialogue" with the G-7.[66] The exaggeration of such "achievements" was calculated to make the leadership's policies—which had decimated Russia—seem a major victory. And the failures of Russia's Westernizers were manifested no more clearly than in their policy toward the former Yugoslavia.

Russia and Yugoslavia

Russia's Balkan policy, not surprisingly, faced vigorous resistance in 1994. Apart from the most pro-Western of analysts, whose sympathies lay with the West and against the Serbs, few Russians were deceived by the leadership's pretense of hostility to the West. As a result, accusations leveled at the leadership for its subservience to the West became quite commonplace. Indeed, while on appearances it seemed that Russia worked to prevent NATO air strikes against the Bosnian Serbs, in fact Russia gave unswerving support once strikes were launched in early February and broke with the Bosnian Serbs. Russia's pretensions to be the savior of the Serbs all but vanished when it refused to use its veto against crucial anti-Serb sanctions in the UNSC—it even authored the proposed sanctions resolution. Also obviously duplicitous was the display of Russian "support" for the Serbs in its veto of anti-Serb resolutions at the December OSCE meeting, a forum where it could well afford to put on a *show* of toughness because of that forum's toothlessness compared with the G-7 or the UNSC. Russia did, to be sure, use its veto against a relatively minor anti-Serb resolution in the UNSC in early December, but this was a clear aberration, the first and last time Russia would dare to veto a UNSC resolution on Yugoslavia.

Perspectives on Yugoslavia

The increasingly widespread perception that Russian policy in the former Yugoslavia was pro-Western was encapsulated in Alexei Arbatov's accusation that Russian policymakers were shamelessly following the West's lead.[67] N. Arbatova of IMEMO also pointed out that by fall 1994 (and prior to its veto of the aforementioned anti-Serb UNSC resolution in early December) Russia had voted for all US-led UNSC resolutions—except for its abstention in April 1993 on the question of new sanctions against Yugoslavia as punishment for Serb actions in Srebrenica. Even in this case, she noted, the vote violated the agreement with Russia not to raise the issue until later (see Chapter 4).[68]

Yugoslavia: Russian Relations with the West

The carnage resulting from the bombing of the Sarajevo market on February 5 spurred France, who assumed Serb responsibility, to push through a UNSC ultimatum demanding that the Serbs withdraw heavy weapons from the area or face NATO air strikes. EU foreign ministers concurred, voting on February 10—one day after NATO issued its ultimatum and without prior consultation with Russia—that it would use all means necessary to lift the siege.[69] Serb President Milosevic and Yeltsin Presidential envoy Vitalii Churkin condemned the ultimatum and urged that negotiations be the focus for a settlement of the conflict, but Churkin also underscored that the Bosnian Serb siege of Sarajevo must be lifted.[70]

West Europeans had by August 1993 changed their minds about air strikes, persuaded by US arguments that only the threat of force would compel the Serbs to alter their behavior. As a consequence, Britain and France were in total accord with Clinton's advocacy of forceful military action at the NATO January 1994 summit in Brussels. With vociferous French support, the summit's concluding document affirmed NATO's "willingness" to carry out air strikes against the Bosnian Serbs in Sarajevo. But such resolve quickly "vaporized in a cloud of indecision" over whether to use force against the Serbs, with the US playing the role of spoiler by rejecting French entreaties that it send troops to secure the Tuzla airport.[71]

Given his government's claim of evenhandedness toward all sides in the Balkan conflict, Yeltsin's response on February 10 to NATO's muscle-flexing—he merely termed NATO's ultimatum that the Bosnian Serbs pull back from Sarajevo or face military strikes "one-sided"—was remarkably mild.[72] On February 9 Deputy Foreign Minister Adamishin also condemned the possible use of air strikes and criticized UN Secretary General Boutros Ghali's decision to grant NATO the prerogative of such strikes, protesting that only the UN, and not NATO, had the right to make ultimatums. Russia threatened to call an emergency UNSC meeting on the issue where it would propose to place Sarajevo under UN control.[73]

Along the same lines, Pro-government Russian television displayed sympathy for Serb claims that the bombing of the Sarajevo market was a terrorist act committed by Muslims. Even arch-Westerner Churkin seemed to concur when he implied that the Muslims bore at least some responsibility for the crisis. But in a harbinger of what was to come Russia quickly reversed gears and dropped its opposition to NATO air strikes the very next day. Even more telling was President Clinton's report after his conversation with Yeltsin that the two leaders had "no reason to believe . . . there is a serious problem with our going forward" with the NATO plans. What is more, UN Ambassador Vorontsov told reporters that Moscow would not insist on UNSC approval of the strikes and even conceded that Boutros-Boutros Ghali was within his rights to order strikes. "Who said that we are stopping anything?" Vorontsov asked rhetorically in answer to those who worried that Russia might carry through on its threats to block the strikes. Even *The Washington Post* was compelled to dismiss this "surprising reversal" as one more example of Russian officials "talk[ing] tough against NATO at home [while] taking moderate action in diplomatic practice."[74] Other Western sources admitted that Moscow's "hard line" against NATO had seemed prior to the lightning turnabout "aimed primarily at satisfying domestic interests," since "virtually every significant political figure has lined up . . . to denounce" NATO's threat of force.[75]

While Yeltsin was meeting with British Prime Minister Major days later presidential spokesperson V. Kostikov warned on February 15 that Russia would view NATO air strikes against the Bosnian Serbs as a "false start" for the PfP and Russian relations with the West as a whole, prompting Major to reassure Russia that it had been subject to a "certain misunderstanding of the essence of the NATO decision." But Yeltsin himself indicated that he was not really concerned about NATO's use of force so much as the fact that it had not consulted with Russia beforehand when he emphasized later that the Bosnian question should not be resolved "without the participation of Russia." He even affirmed that Russia would approve air strikes in retaliation for Serb attacks on UN forces. Although the RFM's UN office issued a statement opposing the ultimatum against the Serbs and denied that NATO had the authority to decide air strikes by itself, all this diplomatic infighting was just a cover for Yeltsin's real strategy, "designed . . . to undermine support for" his opponents. Indeed, an even more insidious element in the strategy was a "trade-off" in which the West confirmed its support for Russian participation in the G-7 in return for Moscow's "accepting NATO action" in Bosnia.[76]

Having been on the political sidelines for two years, Russian diplomats swung into action to convince the Bosnian Serbs in Sarajevo to place their weapons under UN control and prevent NATO from carrying through on its bombing ultimatum. Their promise to underpin this with the deployment of Russian peace-keeping forces in Sarajevo finally succeeded in convincing the Serbs on February 17 to withdraw—although it also coincided, not accidentally, with a meeting of top NATO and UN commanders in Zagreb to finalize plans for NATO's ultimatum on the use of force. In the ensuing orgy of self-congratulatory bravado over their successful intervention with the Serbs, Russian officials claimed a momentous victory, boasting that their diplomacy had triumphed over NATO's threat of force and that Russia could no longer be ignored in any international event. It was, they declared, a diplomatic "milestone" which restored Russia to the "heart of European diplomacy" and marked the transition from a largely pro-Western to a more independent foreign policy.[77] Even Western officials alluded to a new era of collaboration between Russia and the West.[78] Here, it seemed, was a tangible success by Russian diplomacy which could now be paraded around to show how the successful the policies of the Westernizing leaders were.

As usual, however, events overtook them, proving this mistaken, for even as he congratulated Russia for its success in the Bosnian Serb withdrawal German Foreign Minister Kinkel was implicitly saying the opposite and belittling Russian diplomacy by identifying NATO's "massive" military threat as the real key to defusing the crisis. German Defense Minister Ruehe also disparaged Russia's action as a "limited and important success" which failed to resolve the conflict.[79] And when the US, Russia, France, Britain, and Germany met to discuss extending the ceasefire to other parts of Bosnia days later, Yeltsin's proposal for a five-nation summit on Bosnia was met "coolly" by the other participants, who viewed it as a Russian attempt to reinforce its recent success in scotching NATO's ultimatum. In any case, Russia's efforts to settle the conflict without the use of force did not run counter to the West's strategy, as senior US officials made clear when they admitted on February 24 that "on balance, President Clinton asked [the Russians] to do exactly what they did . . . Yeltsin basically responded very favorably."[80] The West, in other words, was willing to allow the Serbs to peacefully comply with their demands, if that worked. And it was advantageous to the West in that it bolstered Russia's Westernizers, their agents in the Kremlin, by giving them grounds to parade their international "success" as well as ammunition with which to attack the opposition.

However the US and the West may have welcomed diplomatic Russia's services, they were nevertheless unwilling to countenance Russia's occupying the political high ground for long. Russia's diplomatic success, however limited, aroused extreme circumspection in the West vis-à-vis its former antagonist who, for all its seeming "toothlessness," appeared all of a sudden to be pulling the strings in the Balkans. With an elegant countermove—a signal it was still in charge (and which would be repeated in December 1998 and in March 1999 in Kosovo)—NATO conducted its first military action since 1949, downing four Serbian fighters in the Bosnian no-fly zone on February 28. Claims by NATO spokespersons that the downed jets just happened to be the first ones NATO detected, that the downing was not the "result of any new resolve" by NATO—these in spite of reports that Serb planes had bombed many times before but were never attacked—were contradicted by specialists who contended that the action was the consequence of a "new resolve [on NATO's part] to get tough." What is more, approval by Bonn and Paris for this move proved that dissent within the Alliance's ranks was far less consequential than had been assumed.[81]

And as they had done so often in the past, Russian diplomats displayed firm support for the strikes, which they deemed consistent with the October 1992 UNSC resolution banning unauthorized flights over Bosnia. Kozyrev reassured the West that Russia would not allow the Balkan crisis to "divert it from the path of strategic partnership with the U.S. and the other Western countries"—this despite Grachev's complaint that there was "much to be clarified" on the question and notwithstanding criticism by Speaker of the Lower House Rybkin that NATO's action was unjustified. Moreover, on the day of the dogfight over Bosnia V. Churkin, in a sign more of acquiescence than resistance, made a concession by announcing Russia's readiness to sign the separate bilateral PfP agreement it had previously rebuffed. No wonder *Izvestiia* conceded that the downing of the planes made the Serbs realize not only that the West was ready to use force but that Moscow would not "quarrel with NATO on account of the Serbs."[82]

NATO launched air strikes against Bosnian Serb positions in Gorazde on April 10 and 11. That it did so, once again, without prior consultation with the Russian government was further confirmation to Russia, especially after the February events, that the West had little interest in cooperating with impotent Russia. And it flew in the face of the Russian government's claim that the February negotiation of the Bosnian Serb withdrawal from Sarajevo and the March ceasefire between Croats and Serbs in Croatia had established Russia as a major player in Bosnia.[83] On April 11 Yeltsin protested the West's refusal to consult with Moscow: "We want this matter discussed at the UNSC," he thundered, adding that Russia would "insist" that such decisions "not be taken without prior consultation between the US and Russia." Seconded by Kozyrev and Grachev, Yeltsin also warned that the air strikes could prompt Russia to reconsider signing the PfP—as if this were a fearsome threat to the West. And the Duma demanded a halt to NATO military strikes and the convocation of an emergency UNSC session. V. Churkin, on the other hand, reproached the Bosnian Serbs for their untrustworthiness and for failing to heed Russian warnings that they refrain from stepping up military operations around Gorazde,[84] indicating to *Izvestiia* that if forced to choose between ties with the West and the Serbs Russia would never imperil relations with the former. An RFM spokesperson was compelled to defend Churkin's statement with the convoluted explanation that he had meant to say that discussions with the Bosnian Serbs over Gorazde should be stopped, not that Russia should wash its hands of them altogether—yet within days Churkin would advocate precisely the latter. Coming on the heels of its recent "sensational success," Russia found itself confronting quite a conundrum.[85]

Yet another exposé of the Russian government's conspiring with the West came to light, this time revealing how Kozyrev had flown to Belgrade for talks with Milosevic immediately after receiving a telephone call from US Secretary of State Christopher in early April. This action, *Sovetskaia Rossiia* argued, demonstrated that Kozyrev was willing to accede to NATO's air strikes and would refuse to use its veto in the UNSC to lift the "genocidal economic sanctions" against the Serbs imposed by "the USA and other Western countries."[86]

A week later Kozyrev blamed the Bosnian Muslims for "clearly provoking the Serbs" *and* the Serbs for responding. A report by ITAR-TASS on April 16 that Russia had succeeded in blocking additional air strikes against the Bosnian Serbs was denied by NATO, who had apparently called off the strikes not on account of Russia but due to poor visibility. And in a statement issued on April 20 Yeltsin called on the Bosnian Serbs to withdraw from Gorazde so that UN forces could enter the area. True to form, he refrained from criticizing NATO air strikes and instead praised the UN and "other members of the international community."[87]

The next day Clinton threatened to authorize air strikes to protect UN-designated safe areas for Muslims in Bosnia. Although West Europeans were leary of using force, which they feared would alienate Russia and put UN ground troops at risk,[88] Russia was by now apparently fed up with Bosnian Serb "intransigence" and its bombardment of civilian targets in Gorazde. While not yet willing to completely sever ties with the Bosnian Serbs, Kozyrev and Churkin nevertheless threatened to do so, while Yeltsin issued a statement accusing the Bosnian Serbs of aggression and genocide and demanded that they withdraw from Gorazde.[89] As a result, the focus of Russia's support now shifted from the Bosnian Serbs toward Belgrade. Indeed, President Milosevic himself would formally cut economic and political ties with Pale after the latter's rejection of the peace plan in August, as would Moscow.[90] Although Presidential spokesperson Kostikov denied on April 21 that Russia was reassessing its attitude toward the Serbs, Yeltsin's statement left "no doubt about the direction of the [anti-Serb] evolution of the Russian approach to Bosnia." Moscow in fact recalled its ambassador to Belgrade for consultations in the possibility that the latter was complicit with the Bosnian Serbs and giving, according to one Russian analyst, the "green light to NATO's actions in Bosnia."[91]

In light of Russia's aforementioned policy shift vis-à-vis the Bosnian Serbs, when the UNSC, on Russia's request, met in emergency session on April 23 to discuss the situation in Gorazde, all fifteen members, *including Russia*, agreed to NATO's ultimatum that the Bosnian Serbs must withdraw from Gorazde or face NATO air strikes. Declaring Russia's position on the issue "very close" to that of the West, Kozyrev termed NATO's ultimatum a "reasonable response" to the Bosnian Serbs' "criminal" actions in Gorazde.[92] In a complete reversal of the Russian position taken just two months ago Russian UN Ambassador Vorontsov urged the UNSC to stop the "human tragedy" inflicted by the Bosnian Serbs—who, he stressed, had broken their promises to Russia and continued their assaults in Gorazde—if not by political measures "then . . . by other means."[93]

The government had gone so far to accommodate the West this time that even shocked pro-Western media took sharp issue with it, accusing it of a "sensational change of position" on April 19. *Moscow News* insisted that the shelling of Gorazde took place only after the Serbs had been provoked by the Muslim forces and that the Serbian defensive thrust had been used by NATO as a pretext for "fresh provocations."[94] E. Abartsumov, Chair of the Duma Foreign Affairs Committee, warned that the NATO bombing was a serious blow to cooperation with the West and violated the Russian-US agreement on military consultations.[95]

On May 13 Foreign Ministers from Russia, the US, and West Europe met in Geneva to discuss the Bosnian crisis, but failed to overcome their differences, although they did agree on a proposal to relaunch peace negotiations while a four-month ceasefire was in effect. The US accepted a West European proposal for a ceasefire, but did so reluctantly, fearing it would consolidate Serbian territorial gains. It was also proposed that Bosnia be divided up, giving Serbia 49% and the Muslims and Croats 51% of the Republic's territory. Kozyrev proposed, again unsuccessfully, that anti-Serb sanctions be lifted in recognition of the "positive" role Belgrade was playing in the peace settlement. Yeltsin, Kozyrev and other leaders rejected Parliament's demands that Russia use its veto against sanctions. Russia and the EU maintained their "stubborn" opposition to the US attempt to lift the arms embargo on the Bosnian government, however, which by May was the main bone of contention between the allies.[96]

In obvious retaliation against the May 12 vote in the US congress in favor of lifting the arms embargo on Bosnia, the Duma passed a resolution urging Yeltsin to unilaterally lift the embargo against Serbia if any other country sent arms to Bosnia,[97] yet Russia continued to adhere to its pro-Western tilt when at the July 6 Foreign Ministers meeting of the Contact Group Kozyrev acknowledged for the first time that the lifting of the arms embargo demanded by the US might be a "last resort" but "inevitable" if the parties to the conflict did not accept the plan of territorial division.[98]

On July 30 Kozyrev criticized the Bosnian Serbs for their rejection of the peace plan, and insisted that Russia "must stand by its Western partners," since it had "no alternative to unity with [its] partners in the Contact Group."[99] The next day Russia joined the US and the EU in tightening economic sanctions against Serbia, this time in reprisal for the

Bosnian Serb rejection of the West's peace plan the previous week. In fact, Russia had judged the Bosnian Serbs' "qualified yes" to the Contact Group's peace plan a positive response and the basis for further negotiation, whereas the other four Western members continued to insist on unconditional acceptance of the plan by the Bosnian Serbs. But when on July 26 the Bosnian Serb Assembly demanded that the Contact Group plan shut the roads in Sarajevo leading to the outside, Vitalii Churkin warned the Bosnian Serbs that if they rejected the peace proposal the Contact Group would, with Russia's consent, resort to "negative stimuli."[100]

During talks with Serb President Milosevic on August 1 Kozyrev guaranteed that all sanctions against Yugoslavia would be lifted if the Bosnian Serbs accepted the Contact Group's peace plan and pulled back to agreed borders. Milosevic accepted the Contact Group's plan and joined Russia in urging the Bosnian Serbs to accept it also.[101] When the latter refused, NATO initiated air strikes around Sarajevo. An August 5 RFM statement responded not by attacking the strikes but by weakly terming them "an outburst" and a potential setback to the peace process—a response *Izvestiia* characterized as "notably restrained"—then conceded the next day that the Bosnian Serbs had "given grounds" for the strikes. More, an RFM spokesperson on August 8 placed the entire blame for the situation on the Bosnian Serbs and insisted that they must accept the Control Group's peace plan. To many observers the Bosnian Serbs had thoroughly discredited themselves in the eyes of Russian policymakers,[102] so much so that the latter proceeded to sever diplomatic ties with them on August 8 and even pressed for further air strikes, insisting all the while that the reestablishment of ties was conditional on their approval of the Contact Group peace plan.[103]

West Europe and the US continued in August to oppose the lifting of UN sanctions against Belgrade proposed by Russia, who pointed to Belgrade's closing its borders to the Bosnian Serbs as justification for such a lenient attitude. But this did not satisfy the Western allies, who insisted that Belgrade must accept international observers to ensure it did not aid the Bosnian Serbs. To make matters worse, France and Germany declared the Bosnian Serb vote rejecting the peacekeeping plan illegal.[104]

The Duma Council turned up the heat on September 6 by agreeing to hold a special session on the Yugoslav situation in three days. It urged Yeltsin to sign the law it had passed in August calling for Russia to unilaterally withdraw from the PfP and from UN sanctions against Belgrade. It also called on Russia to coordinate Yugoslav policy with

Belarus and Ukraine and urged Yeltsin to fire Kozyrev. Yeltsin responded by launching into an anti-NATO tirade the very next day at a meeting with Spanish Prime Minister Gonzalez and European Commission President Jacques Santer, accusing NATO of appointing itself "judge and executioner" in Yugoslavia. In the vaguest and most unconvincing terms Yeltsin warned that Russia might have to "take an adequate response" to NATO's actions in the form of unspecified "aid" to the Bosnian Serbs or a reassessment of relations with NATO.[105]

Kozyrev met in Paris on November 17 with French Foreign Minister Juppe, who voiced "serious concern" that the new supply of arms to the Bosnians threatened France's blue helmets, but also joined Russia in warning the US that its tilt toward the Bosnian Muslims could jeopardize the chances for a settlement in the region. Russia hailed the unfolding solidarity with West Europe on this issue and on the long-standing shared opposition to US demands to lift the arms embargo against Bosnia. To one Russian journalist the November 14 Foreign and Defense Ministers meeting of the WEU at Noordwijk was unprecedented in that it revealed West Europe's loss of faith in the US and criticized it in a way not heard for some time.[106]

For its part, Russia hailed the cooperation of France, in particular, as a major blow to US hegemony: "France's public agreement with Russia's position on the Bosnian question [i.e., refusal to lift the arms embargo] is important because it demonstrates to the US that its European partners will not act solely according to its wishes," was the way one Russian observer put it. This was indeed so significant that analysts trumpeted it as the first time in postwar history Europe prevailed over the US on a major policy.[107] While still in Paris Kozyrev met with French and British Foreign Ministers on November 18 where they agreed on the need for a peaceful settlement in Yugoslavia; an invigorated Kozyrev urged his Western partners to reduce their reliance on the US.[108]

As usual, the euphoria did not last long and the balloon was punctured on November 21 when UN-backed NATO jets, in the largest military operation in NATO history, bombed a Krajina Serb airfield (in Croatia) in retaliation for Serb attacks on the Bosnian Muslim enclave of Bihac. Two days later NATO pounded the Bosnian Serbs near Bihac. Not only did Russia refuse to criticize the air strikes at the outset, but Yeltsin even condoned them as a "necessary response" to Serb aggression while expressing only "profound reservations" and mildly warning that future strikes could provoke Russia to remove its peacekeeping troops. The RFM gave "guarded support" for the strikes and condemned the Serb actions as unjustified.[109] RFM spokesperson Karasin, forced to respond to reports that his Ministry had struck a deal with France and Britain to support the strikes in exchange for their promise to apply pressure on the US not to lift the arms embargo on the Bosnian Muslims, protested that he did "not like the word 'deal' "—thus all but admitting it.[110]

The US lifting of the Bosnian arms embargo on November 12 was of concern to Kozyrev, as were observations that the Krajina air strikes had goaded the West into a unity lacking since the cold war. Kozyrev responded on November 19 by imploring West Europeans to allow their "autonomous voice" to be heard.[111] But Russia's Westernizers still had the issue of lifting the arms embargo to count on. At the WEU Parliamentary Assembly on December 1 Kozyrev again sided with the British and French against a US proposal to lift the arms embargo. In a clear reference to resurfacing divisions between West Europe and the US at the Brussels NATO Foreign Ministers' meeting that same day Kozyrev pursued the theme of European partnership, pleading that "we Europeans must first tend to our own interests, since it is we ourselves who must be concerned with European unity."[112] V. Nadein (whose stark by-line in the December 3 issue of *Izvestiia* read "A Black Week for American Diplomacy Places US Leadership in Doubt") rejoiced that Defense Secretary Perry now referred to the Balkan conflict as a "civil war" and refrained from characterizing Serb conduct as "aggression." "Unthinkable" until recently, this signaled a veritable sea change for US policymakers, an admission that the use of force had failed. Evidence of this, Nadein contended, could be found in the long-awaited speech on NATO on November 29 by Secretary of State Christopher, who accepted the use of diplomacy against the Bosnian Serbs rather than force, and did not oppose a "greater Serbia."[113]

One consequence of the shortsighted" positions of the US, Nadein argued, was the manifestation of sharp differences between the US and its allies. For the first time since the 1956 Suez crisis, the US and West Europe were fundamentally divided: the US had "impudently" accused France and Britain of betrayal after both expressed skepticism over US leadership and refused to adopt a "hard line" on Bosnia. France and Britain had also rejected Clinton's advocacy of harsh military reprisals against the Bosnian Serbs as they closed in on Bihac. Indeed, things had gotten so bad between the US and West Europe, Nadein contended, that Christopher's advisers urged him not to attend the Budapest summit, thus turning what had been predicted would be a major event into a "diplomatic Dunkirk."[114]

Tensions with the West not only did not dissipate but, if anything, mounted as Russia "cast a long shadow" over the December Budapest CSCE summit, vetoing resolutions it deemed unfair to the Serbs, including one condemning the Bosnian and Croatian Serbs for attacks on the Muslim-held enclave of Bihac, although the CSCE Executive Secretary Istvan Gyamati revealed that Russia was not the only country "having problems" with the resolution. French President Mitterand, in particular, criticized the US for its call for NATO strikes on the Bosnian Serbs in Bihac and other UN safe areas while it refused to commit ground troops.[115]

Just prior to the December Budapest CSCE summit and the day after NATO's vote approving expansion—and for only the second time since the collapse of the USSR—Russia, in an otherwise ineffectual move, vetoed a December 2 UNSC resolution blocking fuel shipments from Serbia to Serb-held areas of Bosnia and Croatia (it had *not* vetoed the more crucial resolution on NATO air strikes, however).[116] This was the apogee of Russia's attempts, however minimal, to display an assertive posture vis-à-vis the West during 1994-95, in the last phase of the Yugoslav conflict. Although it seemed anti-Western, as shown above and as time would soon prove, it was yet another act of the leadership's charades to demonstrate Russia's "independence" from a West which it remained dependent on.

Notes

[1] *Nezavisimaia gazeta*, August 23, 1994, p. 3. See a similar criticism of Western "reform" which links the "shift" in Russia's policy towards the West with those reforms, in Alexei Arbatov, "Russian National Interests," in Robert D. Blackwill and Sergei A. Karaganov, eds., *Damage Limitation or Crisis? Russia and the Outside World* (Washington, D.C.: Brassey's, 1994), p. 59.

[2] V. Muronov, *Nezavisimaia gazeta*, September 9, 1994, p. 5. Similarly, Communist Party chief Ziuganov said that Russia is "by conviction a left [i.e., collectively-oriented] country." See *Nezavisimaia gazeta*, November 4, 1994, p. 5.

[3] Georgi Arbatov, "Eurasia Letter: A New Cold War?" *Foreign Policy*, No. 95, Summer 1994, pp. 90-3. Arbatov was then Director of ISKRAN. Even the conservative Yu. Kondrashov resented the fact that Russia was compared to Poland and Latin America because they had also been subjected to IMF dictates. Russians,

he pointed out, had a "different and unique mentality." See *Izvestiia*, April 10, 1992, p. 7.

[4] Michael Mihalka, "Restructuring European Security," *Transition*, Vol. 1, No. 11, June 30, 1995, p. 4.

[5] ITAR-TASS, February 13, 1995, in *FBIS*-SOV-95-031, February 15, 1995, p. 44.

[6] Mayak Radio, March 23, 1994, in *FBIS*-SOV-94-057, March 24, 1994, p. 12.

[7] ITAR-TASS, December 9, 1994, in *FBIS*-SOV-94-238, December 12, 1994, p. 28.

[8] *Rossiiskie vesti*, October 21, 1994, p. 2. See a speech by Glaz'ev in *Nezavisimaia gazeta*, August 16, 1994, pp. 1, 4.

[9] *Izvestiia*, May 4, 1994, p. 4; Vera Tolz and Julia Wishnevsky, "Election Queries Make Russians Doubt Democratic Process," *RFE/RL Research Report*, Vol. 3, No. 13, April 1, 1994, pp. 1-3; *Sovetskaia Rossiia*, May 7, 1994, p. 2.

[10] *RFE/RL Daily Report*, No. 246, December 27, 1993, p. 1.

[11] Alexander Rahr, "New Focus on Old Priorities," *Transition, 1994 in Review*, Part II, February 15, 1995, p. 9.

[12] *Kommersant-daily*, January 19, 1994, p. 3; Leszek Buszynski, "Russia and the West: Towards Renewed Geopolitical Rivalry?" *Survival*, Vol. 37, No. 3, Autumn 1995, p. 109; S. Neil MacFarlane, "Russian Conceptions of Europe," *Post-Soviet Affairs*, Vol. 10, No. 3, July-September 1994, pp. 252-3; Eugene B. Rumer, *Russian National Security and Foreign Policy in Transition* (Santa Monica: Rand, 1995), p. 41.

[13] *Rossiiskaia gazeta*, February 25, 1994, p. 2; Reuters, February 24, 1994.

[14] *Nezavisimaia gazeta*, March 2, 1994, p. 4.

[15] *Rossiiskaia gazeta*, April 29, 1994, p. 3.

[16] A. Grachev, *Moscow News*, No. 51, December 23-29, 1994, p. 7.

[17] *Nezavisimaia gazeta*, August 16, 1994, p. 5.

[18] Ibid., February 23, 1994, p. 4.

[19] Ibid., May 27, 1994, pp. 4-5. See also Rumer, *Russian National Security*, p. 35-6.

[20] *Kommersant-daily*, December 8, 1994, p. 4.

[21] *The New York Times*, October 18, 1994, p. A16.

[22] *Novaia geopoliticheskaia situatsiia v Evrope, pozitsii Zapada i interesy bezopasnosti Rossii* (Moscow: Institut Evropy, 1994), p. 21.

[23] *Novaia ezhednevnaia gazeta*, November 16, 1994, p. 1. For a Western analysis, see Buszynski, "Russia and the West," p. 110. For similar Russian analyses, see *Nezavisimaia gazeta*, March 30, 1994, p. 4, and V. Kremeniuk, "Amerikanskaia strategiia 'rasshireniia' i Rossiia," *SShA*, No. 7, July 1994, pp. 3-6. Kremeniuk, Deputy Director of ISKAN, inveighed against US dreams of "global leadership" and its acting "as if the world is at [its] feet."

²⁴ A. Zagorskii, "Rossiia i Evropa: formulirovanie 'bol'shoi Evropy'," in *Ot reformy k stabilizatsii . . . vneshniaia voennaia i ekonomicheskaia politika Rossii (analiz i prognoz), 1993-5* (Moscow: MGIMO, "Promyshlennyi vestnik Rossii," 1995), p. 42. See also *Izvestiia*, February 16, 1994, p. 3.
²⁵ *RFE/RL News Briefs*, May 30-June 3, 1994, p. 1.
²⁶ Zagorskii, "Rossiia i Evropa," p. 41.
²⁷ *Rossiiskaia gazeta*, March 25, 1994, p. 6.
²⁸ Zagorskii, "Rossiia i Evropa," p. 42. See also *Izvestiia*, February 16, 1994, p. 3; Peter Shearman, "Russian Policy Toward Western Europe: The German Axis," in Peter Shearman, ed., *Russian Foreign Policy Since 1990* (Boulder: Westview, 1995), p. 102; *Rossiskaia gazeta*, August 6, 1994, p. 6.
²⁹ I. Lagunina, "Pochemu ne ustraivaet partnerstvo?" *Novoe vremia*, No. 14, April 1994, pp. 28-9.
³⁰ *Nezavisimaia gazeta*, March 2, 1994, p. 4.
³¹ *Christian Science Monitor*, January 7, 1994, p. 1; *The Washington Post*, October 6, 1993, p. A24.
³² *Rossiiskie vesti*, August 17, 1994, pp. 1, 2.
³³ *Rossiiskaia gazeta*, December 8, 1994, p. 1.
³⁴ Reuters, January 12, 1994.
³⁵ Ibid., February 6, 1994.
³⁶ The Reuter European Community Report, February 5, 1994.
³⁷ Richard L. Kugler and Marianna V. Kozintseva, *Enlarging NATO: The Russia Factor* (Santa Monica: Rand, 1996), p. 36.
³⁸ *Nezavisimaia gazeta*, March 2, 1994, p. 4. See also Alexander Konovalov, "International Institutions and European Security: The Russian Debate," in Marco Carnovale, ed., *European Security and International Institutions After the Cold War* (New York: St. Martin's Press, 1995), p. 133.
³⁹ *Rossiiskie vesti*, October 19, 1994, p. 3.
⁴⁰ *The New York Times*, December 2, 1994, p. A14.
⁴¹ *International Herald Tribune*, December 13, 1994.
⁴² Alexei Pushkov, *Moscow News*, No. 51, December 23-29, 1994, p. 6. For similar statements of major divisions within the western alliance, see *Nezavisimaia gazeta*, December 2, 1994, p. 1. Also see a similar example of wishful thinking in B. Kazantsev, "Pervye shagi k partnersvu Rossii s NATO," *Mezhdunarodnaia zhizn'*, No. 10, October 1994, p. 24. Kazantsev was Deputy Director of the Department of All-European Cooperation in the RFM.
⁴³ Michael Mihalka, "Continued Resistance to NATO Expansion," *Transition*, Vol. 1, No. 14, August 11, 1995, pp. 36-7.
⁴⁴ *Financial Times*, December 3, 1994, p. 2; *RFE/RL Daily Report*, No. 227, December 2, 1994; Michael Mihalka, "Creeping Toward the East," *Transition*, Vol. 1, No. 1, January 30, 1995, p. 85; *Segodnia*, September 13, 1995, p. 5.

Oznobishchev was the Director of the Center for International Security Problems of ISKRAN.

[45] *RFE/RL Daily Report*, No. 229, December 6, 1994; *Financial Times*, December 6, 1994, p. 1; Reuters, December 4, 1994.

[46] Alexei Pushkov, *Moskovskie novosti*, No. 63, December 11-18, 1994, p. 6.

[47] Reuter North American Wire, December 3, 1994.

[48] *Sovetskaia Rossiia*, December 8, 1994, p. 3, and *Rossiiskaia gazeta*, December 8, 1994, pp. 1-2.

[49] *OMRI Daily Digest*, Vol. I, No. 14, Part I, January 19, 1995; Reuters, January 19, 1995.

[50] *Rossiiskie vesti*, December 7, 1994, p. 3.

[51] Emphasis mine. Agence France Presse, December 7, 1994.

[52] Michael Mihalka, "European-Russian Security and NATO's Partnership for Peace," *RFE/RL Research Report*, Vol. 3, No. 33, August 26, 1994, p. 38.

[53] Mihalka, "Continued Resistance," p. 36.

[54] Zagorskii, "Rossiia i Evropa," p. 41.

[55] I. Lagunina, *Novoe vremia*, No. 14, 1994, p. 28.

[56] Hannes Adomeit, "Russia as a 'Great Power' in World Affairs: Images and Reality," *International Affairs* (London), Vol. 71, No. 1, January 1995, p. 49; *Nezavisimaia gazeta*, April 5, 1994, p. 1; *RFE/RL Daily Report*, No. 64, April 5, 1994, p. 1, and No. 55, March 21, 1994 p. 1; Agence France Presse, March 16, 1994.

[57] Zagorskii, "Rossiia i Evropa," p. 43; *The Houston Chronicle*, May 20, 1994, p. 28.

[58] *RFE/RL Daily Report*, No. 102, May 31, 1994.

[59] Ibid., No. 103, June 1, 1994.

[60] Mihalka, "European-Russian Security," p. 45; I. Lagunina, *Moscow News*, No. 26, July 1-7, 1994, p. 3.

[61] *RFE/RL Daily Report*, June 23, 1994.

[62] Ibid.

[63] Shearman, "Russian Policy Toward Western Europe," pp. 101-2.

[64] Reuters, June 18, 1994; *Segodnia*, July 9, 1994, p. 1.

[65] *RFE/RL News Briefs*, July 11-15, 1995, p. 1.

[66] *Rossiiskaia gazeta*, July 12, 1994, p. 1; *Segodnia*, July 9, 1994, p. 1. See a similar statement by Deputy Foreign Minister S. Krylov, who in 1994 had welcomed the APC signing as evidence of the "de facto economic unification of Europe's two parts." *Rossiiskie vesti*, July 7, 1994, pp. 1, 3. The APC was an agreement with the EU long sought by the Russian leadership which gave certain—minimal—trade advantages.

[67] Arbatov, "Russian National Interests," pp. 67-8; I. Zhinkina, "Mirotvorcheskie aktsii: nekotorye voprosy teorii i praktika," *SShA*, No. 10, 1994, p. 12.

[68] N. Arbatova, "Uroki Iugoslavii dlia Rossii i Zapada," *MEMO*, No. 2, 1995, p. 49. The Russian delegation had exercised its first and only other veto since the cold war on May 11, 1993 to defeat a resolution reforming financing for UN peacekeepers in Cyprus. See *The Guardian* (London), May 13, 1993, p. 9.

[69] Pia Christina Wood, "France and the Post Cold War Order: The Case of Yugoslavia," *European Security*, Vol. 3, No. 1, Spring 1994, p. 148; Stephanie Anderson, "EU, NATO and CSCE Responses to the Yugoslav Crisis: Testing Europe's New Security Architecture," *European Security*, Vol. 4, No. 2, Summer 1995, p. 349; Mihalka, "European-Russian Security," p. 39.

[70] Russian Television, February 14, 1994; Agence France Presse, February 13, 1994.

[71] *Krasnaia zvezda*, January 13, 1994, p. 3; *The New York Times*, February 11, 1994, p. A7; *The Washington Post*, January 23, 1994, p. A22.

[72] Agence France Presse, February 10, 1994.

[73] Ibid.

[74] *RFE/RL Daily Report*, No. 28, February 10, and No. 29, February 11, 1994; *Moscow News*, No. 8, February 25-March 3, 1994, p. 4; Inter Press Service, February 10, 1994; *The Washington Post*, February 11, 1994, p. A36.

[75] *The Guardian* (London), February 11, 1994, p. 11.

[76] *RFE/RL Daily Report*, No. 32, February 16, 1994; ITAR-TASS, February 15, 1994, in *FBIS*-SOV-94-031, February 15, 1994, p. 3; *The Independent* (London), February 16, 1994, p. 1. See also *Kommersant*-daily, February 16, 1994, p. 4, and *Segodnia*, November 23, 1994, p. 1, which similarly observes that Russia tended to object less to NATO air strikes than to not being consulted about them beforehand.

[77] Mihalka, "Europe-Russian Security," p. 39; *Izvestiia*, February 24, 1994, p. 3; V. Churkin, *Moscow News*, No. 8, February 25-March 3, 1994, p. 4; V. Kostikov, in *Trud*, February 22, 1994, p. 5; Arbatova, "Uroki Iugoslavii," p. 54; Agence France Presse, February 17, 1994.

[78] Inter Press Service, February 21, 1994.

[79] Hamburg, *Welt am Sonntag*, February 20, 1994, p. 2, and Berlin N-TV, February 22, 1994, in *FBIS*-WEU-94-035, February 22, 1994, p. 22.

[80] Associated Press, February 24, 1994; *Nezavisimaia gazeta*, February 26, 1994, p. 1. German Foreign Minister Kinkel called Yeltsin's summit proposal "premature." See also AP Worldstream, February 23, 1994 and *Kommersant-daily*, February 26, 1994, p. 3.

[81] *Sueddeutsche Zeitung*, March 1, 1994, p. 4, in *FBIS*-WEU-94-041, March 2, 1994, p. 20; Agence France Presse, February 28, 1994.

[82] *Financial Times*, March 1, 1994, p. 1; Belgrade, Tanjug, March 1, 1994, in *FBIS*-SOV-94-041, March 2, 1994, p. 10; *Izvestiia*, March 3, 1994, p. 3.

[83] Mihalka, "European-Russian Security," pp. 41-2.

[84] *RFE/RL News Briefs*, April 11-15, 1994, pp. 1-2, 4-5, 12.

[85] *Izvestiia*, April 13, 1993, pp. 1, 3.

[86] *Sovetskaia Rossiia*, April 19, 1994, p. 3.

[87] *RFE/RL News Briefs*, April 18-22, 1994, pp. 1, 3-4.

[88] *Financial Times*, April 21, 1994, p. 1.

[89] Mihalka, "European-Russian Security," p. 43. See also ITAR-TASS, April 19, 1994, *Izvestiia*, April 20, 1994, p. 1, and ITAR-TASS, April 19, 1994.

[90] *RFE/RL Daily Report*, April 21, 1994, p. 1; Mike Bowker, *Russian Foreign Policy and the End of the Cold War* (Aldershot: Dartmouth, 1997), p. 238.

[91] The Associated Press, April 21, 1994; *Segodnia*, April 20, 1994, p. 1.

[92] *RFE/RL News Briefs*, April 25-29, 1994, p. 1; *The Boston Globe*, April 24, 1994, p. 11.

[93] Associated Press, April 23, 1994.

[94] I. Nekrasov, *Moscow News*, No. 15, April 15-21, 1994, p. 1. See also Arbatova, "Uroki Iugoslavii, p. 54; "Russia" TV Channel, April 20, 1994.

[95] I. Nekrasov, *Moscow News*, No. 15, April 15-21, 1994, p. 1.

[96] *Izvestiia*, May 17, 1994, p. 3, and August 31, 1994, p. 3; *Kommersant*, May 14, 1994, pp. 1, 3; *Financial Times*, May 14, 1994, p. 2.

[97] *Financial Times*, May 14, 1994, p. 2.

[98] ITAR-TASS, July 5, 1994.

[99] Agence France Presse, July 30, 1994.

[100] *The New York Times*, July 31, 1994, Sect. 1, p. 1; *The International Herald Tribune*, July 25, 1994.

[101] ITAR-Tass, August 1, 1994.

[102] *RFE/RL News Briefs*, August 8-12, 1994, p. 1; *Izvestiia*, August 9, 1994, p. 3.

[103] *Moscow Times*, August 9, 1994.

[104] *Izvestiia*, August 31, 1994, p. 3.

[105] *RFE/RL Daily Report*, No. 174, Part I, September 7, 1995.

[106] *Rossiiskie vesti*, November 23, 1994, p. 3.

[107] *Nezavisimaia gazeta*, November 18, 1994, p. 1; The Associated Press, December 1, 1994.

[108] ITAR-TASS, November 18, 1994, in *FBIS*-SOV-94-224, November 21, 1994, p. 5; Interfax, November 20, 1994, in Ibid., p. 6.

[109] *RFE/RL Daily Report*, November 23, 1994, p. 1; *Financial Times*, November 22, 1994, p. 1; S. Samuilov, "SShA, NATO, Rossiia i bosniiskii krizis," *SShA*, No. 7, 1995, p. 27.

[110] United Press International, November 22, 1994.

[111] Samuilov, "SShA, NATO," p. 28; *Financial Times*, November 24, 1994, p. 23; Agence France Presse, November 20, 1994.

[112] *Nezavisimaia gazeta*, December 2, 1994, p. 1.

[113] *Izvestiia*, December 3, 1994, p. 3.

[114] Ibid., December 3, 1994, p. 3. See also *Izvestiia*, December 7, 1994, p. 1.

[115] *The Daily Telegraph*, December 7, 1994, p. 15; *The New York Times*, December 7, 1994, p. A12; Agence France Presse, December 5 and 6, 1994.

[116] *The New York Times*, December 4, 1994, Sect. 1, p. 21. See also John B. Dunlop, "The 'Party of War' and Russian Imperial Nationalism," *Problems of Post-Communism*, Vol. 43, No. 2, March-April 1996, p. 31.

6 1995: Russia Loses to the West

The Domestic Setting

The disastrous effects of Russia's "reforms" were by 1995 horrifically apparent. Deputy Director of ISKRAN S. Rogov fretted that Russian machine-building would need a minimum of 15-20 years just to reestablish positions lost since the economic collapse, that GNP had fallen to 20% of that of the USSR.[1] This grim perspective was underscored by the impoverishment of even the intelligentsia, who had been the Westernizers' main social base of support and the main beneficiary of their policies.[2] And a study by the World Bank published in mid-September 1995 revealed that income disparities in Russia were approaching those of Third World countries,[3] with 52 million Russians now living below the poverty line.[4]

Demands from Privatization Minister Polevanov to suspend the second stage of privatization were, not surprisingly, rejected by the government in early 1995 on the grounds that such a policy would only deepen the crisis. Clearly feeling that Polevanov had gone far enough and outlived his usefulness as an anti-Westernizing figurehead and a lightning rod to divert attention from the *zapadniki*'s pro-Western designs, Yeltsin sacked him on January 24.[5] In another move which kept Russia firmly on its pro-Western policy trajectory officials in early 1995 signed a secret "Statement of the Government and Central Bank of the Russian Federation on 1995 Economic Policy" with the IMF, described by one analyst as "an act of complete and unconditional capitulation" to the IMF. It was made especially opprobrious by the government's almost exclusive reliance on IMF loans totaling $12.7 billion for its 1995 budget.[6]

The Foreign Policy Setting

Emblematic of the anger aroused by the leadership's continuing pro-Westernism in the face of Russia's protracted downward slide was the accusation in July by leading foreign policy adviser S. Karaganov that the RFM persisted in its pro-Western, "whatever-you-say" diplomacy of the early post-Soviet years, even *"to this day under a cover of militant-nationalistic philippics."*[7] In November A. Pushkov raised a similar objection to Kozyrev's policy of "obediently" following the US lead in order to ensure Russian integration into the Western community. Kozyrev's "mistake" of expecting a reward of bountiful US financial aid for his subservience was a particular point of emphasis.[8] Kozyrev nevertheless continued to feign a "militant" posture vis-à-vis the near abroad by threatening on April 19 to use any means, even force, to protect Russians there.[9] And although he repeated the threat at the Inter-Tajik talks in Moscow several days later,[10] his forceful rhetoric only demonstrated to V. Lukin that he was playing to the home audience as part of his campaign strategy for a parliamentary seat.[11] *Krasnaia zvezda* added that Kozyrev's pseudo-militant[12] tone had become especially shrill since NATO's December 1994 decision to expand.

The ball of duplicity was kept rolling by Yeltsin's October address to the fiftieth anniversary session of the UN in which he chided those who pushed the UNSC "onto the sidelines of events" in Bosnia and warned that no regional organization (i.e., NATO) should circumvent the UNSC by resorting to the unilateral use of force. Tough-sounding as they were, Yeltsin's pronouncements struck his listeners as empty words "intended . . . for domestic consumption . . . aimed at voters whose patriotic feelings have been offended."[13]

Russian Relations with Non-Western States

Russia joined West Europe in refusing to comply with the US-initiated trade boycott and isolation of Iran, clearly in part because projections of an increase of $4.5 billion in Russian exports to Iran by the next decade seemed assured by the December visit to Teheran of Deputy Premier O. Davydov, who pronounced Iran Russia's "strategic partner, neighbor and friend," and also signed several protocols.[14] Russian-Cuban prospects also seemed to brighten with the arrival of Cuba's Foreign Minister in Moscow in June, the first such visit since 1991.[15] In mid-October Deputy Prime Minister O. Soskovets paid a return visit to Havana, where he signed eight protocols, including an agreement to supply Cuba with oil in exchange for Cuban sugar.[16] Military-technical cooperation was discussed, and Russia pledged $350 million to complete the Juragua nuclear power station.[17]

Russia and NATO

Russia's leaders apparently felt by early 1995 that not only had their militant tone exhausted itself but it was now safe to make amends to the West by negotiating NATO expansion in earnest. Sensing Russia's receptiveness the West responded by preparing a charter that would enshrine Russia's consent to NATO expansion. In direct contradiction to its declared hostility to NATO, Russia worked closely with it by, among other things, continuing to participate in NATO-sponsored maneuvers and finally agreeing in Noordwijk, Holland to sign the two documents on the individual partnership of the PfP on May 31, one on the PfP military cooperation program, the other an enhanced dialogue with NATO.[18]

The Russian leadership devised a new tactic for the NATO deception in 1995 by threatening to form an anti-Western alliance with other "anti-Western" states, including China, Iran, and India, a supposed counter to NATO expansion. But events would quickly prove the threat an empty one, since Russia's Westernizers would not jeopardize relations with the West for the sake of an alliance with partners whose international clout was minimal, whose allegiances were questionable at best and, above all, who had little or no money to give them.

Russian Relations with NATO

The idea of a Russia-NATO charter was first introduced by French Foreign Minister Alain Juppe in January 1995 and pushed consistently thereafter by French President Chirac. In February Juppe proposed a special NATO-Russia treaty, a kind of compensation for Russia's inevitable consent to expansion of NATO and the EU, but Russia immediately rejected it as detrimental to its interests. German Defense Minister Ruehe followed up Juppe's initiative on February 15 with an announcement to a Bundestag Defense Committee that a formal exchange of letters between Russia and NATO could take place within six months.[19] On that same day the US and Germany issued a draft charter which explicitly ruled out any special status or a veto right over expansion for Russia; it also rejected the proposal to elevate the OSCE to the status of main guarantor of European security. Russia responded with a proposed non-aggression pact, sought as a guarantee that NATO policy was not directed at it.[20]

Western pressure showed almost immediate results. As if in anticipation of a major breakthrough with NATO, and evidently in response to the West's probing, Yeltsin denounced NATO expansion in his State of the Union Address on February 16 while assuring the West that partnership remained Russia's key policy direction.[21] Kozyrev also cautioned NATO against a "hasty expansion" but simultaneously urged that relations be "repaired."[22] In light of such statements—which seemed unusually conciliatory under the circumstances—it came as no surprise that the RFM in late February began to negotiate an acceptable formula for NATO expansion. By so doing it repudiated its own previous ironclad prohibition against accepting or negotiating NATO expansion.

Just as Yeltsin's August 1993 acquiescence to NATO expansion had followed—and been an apparent response to—NATO's campaign to win Russian assent for expansion, Russia likewise gave in to Western pressure to negotiate NATO expansion on February 23-24 when Deputy Foreign Minister G. Mamedov told US Deputy Secretary of State Strobe Talbott at a Washington meeting that Russia would agree to expansion on the condition that NATO refrained from stationing troops or nuclear weapons on new members' territory and if Russia and NATO established a permanent consultative body.[23]

Although he surely had been aware of Mamedov's plans beforehand Yeltsin, claiming to have just "found out" about Mamedov's willingness to negotiate, denied approving these proposals and "suggested" that Kozyrev, as head of the RFM, renounce the actions of his Ministry—a suspiciously mild reproach for an action which bordered on selling out Russia's most vital security interests. The repercussions of this supposed "blunder" were not lost on A. Pushkov, who pointed out that a recent article by Zbigniew Brzezinski in the journal *Foreign Affairs* had alluded to Russia's changed position on NATO expansion.[24] Pushkov was of course right, for the February negotiations proved to be a kind of trial balloon, a testing of the waters for Russian agreement to NATO expansion. Within months Russia would give its formal consent to NATO expansion.

The perception that Russia was in essence a dependency of the West and would not contradict the West's dictates was now widespread, and it was common knowledge that "at bottom, Moscow is not completely opposed to the expansion of the [NATO] alliance, provided this is not accompanied by reinforcements of ground troops and nuclear arms."[25] It was therefore fitting that in late March Kozyrev continued the cave-in to

NATO by affirming that expansion would be acceptable if NATO deepened its ties with Russia (he no longer insisted on full Russian membership) and suggested that this be based on the formulation of a "general security concept" to include political consultations, military cooperation, and joint design of weapons systems.[26] On March 23 Kozyrev and Secretary of State Christopher met in Geneva for talks where, according to Kozyrev aide S. Karaganov, Kozyrev agreed to NATO expansion, this time on the condition that NATO shelve the idea for several years and rely on a formal consultation mechanism with Russia.[27]

Throughout 1995 the West craftily maneuvered in pursuit of its goal of NATO expansion. Britain and Germany reassured Moscow in April that the allies had no plans for hasty NATO expansion—whatever "hasty" meant.[28] A month later Clinton told Yeltsin at their May summit that the US government wanted to keep its options open for NATO membership for Russia—who "one day may become interested." Clinton made no formal proposal, although it was common knowledge that Russian membership was a virtual impossibility.[29] Russian officials nevertheless played along: on June 9, Vitalii Churkin expressed "deep concern" over NATO expansion while he welcomed NATO's "consideration" of Russian membership—even as he knew full well that it was an impossibility. "We will have to wait and see," Churkin declared, since "history is moving quickly now."[30]

The Russian-US summit held in Moscow on May 7 gave Kozyrev an opportunity once again to reassure the US and NATO that expansion to Russia's borders would be acceptable as long as it was not hasty,[31] which explained why it was by now frequently observed that Yeltsin "does not want to be embarrassed by his political opponents on nationalist grounds," that he displayed "far less opposition in private than he does in public . . . [His] tirades against NATO are '90% for domestic consumption,' if the goal is placating nationalists who see the alliance as a threat."[32] Perennial critic A. Migranian added that May 31 was a most unpropitious time for Russia to agree to sign the PfP individual agreement, given that NATO was bombing Serb positions without consulting Russia. Migranian derided the Foreign Minister for having "long won a reputation among Western partners as a politician whose entire aggressiveness is intended only for domestic consumption."[33]

Further reinforcing Russia's pro-Western policy direction was the publication of yet another of the CFDP "Theses" on Russia and NATO in June, whose principal thrust was embodied in a warning which echoed

CFDP director S. Karaganov's previous statement that the crescendo of "Soviet-style rhetoric" threatened to dangerously reverse the pro-Western tilt of Russia's initial post-Soviet years. The "Theses" repeated the oft-heard contention that NATO expansion was not so much a threat to Russia as a political-psychological factor furthering Russia's isolation, and concluded by advocating Russia's adoption of a strategy of compensating for NATO expansion *not* by increasing pressure on the West but by stepping up military-political ties with the EU, WEU and Western states.[34]

Yeltsin also played the "anti-Western" card, responding to NATO air strikes in Bosnia so "angrily," by warning on September 8 that NATO expansion could be the cause of war in Europe,[35] that the hapless Kozyrev was forced once again to lead the shovel brigade and reassure the West that Yeltsin's statement should be interpreted simply as a warning of what could happen if "other forces" took over in Russia. Kozyrev then soothed Western concerns with the assurance that Yeltsin's statement was in no way a "political preference" of the government.[36] NATO Secretary General Solana also wrote off Yeltsin's sputtering about air strikes as "a domestic element closely linked to the elections in December and pressure from the 'nationalists',"[37] and a NATO statement in September cautioned against exacerbating Russia's "genuine or faked outrage" over NATO expansion.[38]

Chair of the US Joint Chiefs of Staff Shalikashvili's statement in late September that Slovakia should be prepared to deploy nuclear weapons on its territory if NATO accepted it as a member was immediately attacked as "shameless impudence" by P. Shirshov, Head of the Federation Council Defense and Security Committee.[39] NATO seemed oblivious to Russia's concerns, however, issuing a memorandum reserving the right to station nuclear weapons on new members' territory and requiring that new members participate in its collective defense doctrine.[40] And despite NATO's mid-October announcement that it did not *plan* to deploy nuclear weapons on the territory of CEE states if they became members[41] Hungary directly challenged Yeltsin's October 19 warning that Russia would not permit CEE states to carry out such deployment by vowing on October 24, as Poland and the Czech Republic had before it, that it would deploy nuclear weapons if NATO asked it to do so.[42]

Russian Defense Ministry officials announced on October 2 that Russia would protest NATO's policy on expansion and the Balkans by refusing to participate in a NATO-sponsored PfP exercise in the Czech Republic, despite the fact that the exercise had been in the planning stages for eight months. Ten states had originally been included, but the Visegrad states—those most likely to join NATO and therefore most objectionable to Russia—were added at the last minute without notifying Russia or allowing it to screen the candidates.[43] Even when confronted with such a humiliating state of affairs, however, Russia remained committed to alliance with NATO, announcing on October 12 that it would still participate in Peacekeeper-95 exercises on US territory,[44] while Kozyrev welcomed as a "positive step" NATO's October 5 decision to delay expansion until 1997—and contradicting the totally different slant on the decision by a RFM spokesperson who insisted that Russia would be satisfied with nothing less than a total cancellation of expansion.[45]

Intimidation of the West was what evidently motivated Grachev's warning in November that NATO expansion would provoke Russia to form a defensive bloc of former Warsaw Pact members and Asian states.[46] A. Manannikov, Deputy Head of the Federation Council Committee for International Affairs, promptly dismissed this as "bluff,"[47] which only seemed to compel Grachev to qualify his remarks with the promise that Russia was "not talking about any immediate steps, since actual NATO expansion . . . is not a question of today, tomorrow, or even the day after tomorrow."[48] Grachev was then taken to task by Kozyrev, who contrasted his Ministry's cooperation with NATO with Grachev's Defense Ministry, which he accused of seeking confrontation.[49] As if competing with Kozyrev to prove who was more pro-NATO, Grachev, in turn, rebutted Kozyrev's allegations with the claim that no differences existed between the two Ministries and cited joint Russian-German-US military exercises scheduled for May 1996 to prove it. He also urged that additional documents on cooperation be signed with NATO.[50] Grachev's pro-Western sentiment was further confirmed by a November 29 announcement of Russian and US Defense Ministers of an agreement to step up military cooperation.[51]

NATO enlargement looked increasingly inevitable now, in spite of the proclaimed opposition from the Russian government. German Defense Minister Ruehe stated categorically in November that it was an "irreversible" process but that NATO would offer Russia a privileged and strategic partnership (whatever that meant) albeit with no right to veto or meaningful input into the decision to expand.[52] Still trying to put the best light on the issue, RFM spokesperson Demurin affirmed that Russia was ready for constructive cooperation with NATO and rejoiced that the "RFM and the Russian public" had prevented expansion.[53]

Russia and Yugoslavia

Russia continued its rhetorical broadsides against Western policies in Yugoslavia even as it supported the policies in practice. It did so by voting for or abstaining on UNSC resolutions imposing sanctions against the Serbs, creating the rapid reaction force and even supporting NATO air strikes. What is more, leaders maintained the Yugoslav charade by pretending that Russia was still a major player there when it had been reduced to the role of "errand person" for the West right up to the final peace agreement in Dayton. Russia's claims of an independent role in NATO-controlled peacekeeping were laughed off by Russian analysts, who called the whole operation a "fig leaf." When all was said and done, Russia continued to object to the West's policy in Yugoslavia not so much on principle as on the grounds that it was not consulted beforehand. This was made plain by Foreign Minister Ivanov in 1998 when he disparaged proposed NATO air strikes against Serbia on the grounds that "the point isn't that a strike is dangerous in and of itself. The dangerous thing is that people are starting to talk about using force in circumvention of the Security Council, something that we categorically oppose."[54]

Russian Perspectives on Yugoslavia

By 1995 all Russians save the most extreme pro-Westerners were harshly critical of Western—and Russia's pro-Western—policies in the former Yugoslavia. USA-Canada Institute (ISKRAN) researcher S. Samuilov argued with particular vigor that the West applied a "double standard" by initiating a "propaganda campaign" against Serbian "brutality" while ignoring the equally brutal policies of Croatia and its pro-Nazi past. Samuilov also criticized the West for pressuring the Bosnian Serbs and Russia for hewing to the West's line.[55]

Samuilov's charges were substantiated by Western journalist Tony Barber, who accused the Council of Europe in 1996 of taking a decision which "does not do justice to its generally well-earned reputation as a promoter of human rights and democracy" when it agreed to admit Croatia on the very week President Tudjman ordered the remains of Ante Pavelic, Croatia's notorious World War II fascist leader and a "murderous fanatic," returned to Croatia. Tudjman also renamed the Croatian currency the "kuna"—the same as during Pavelic's fascist regime—and suggested replacing fascist Croatia's "most horrific concentration camp," Jasenovac, with a combined anti-fascist and anti-communist memorial, thereby obscuring the fascist Ustashi's murderous historical record.[56]

Yugoslavia: Russian Relations with the West

Alleging "substantial differences" with "a number of Western partners" over the lifting of sanctions against Belgrade, Kozyrev in February accused them of roiling relations. *Le Monde* reminded Russia that it had approved the Contact Group resolution which declared that economic sanctions would be lifted only on the condition that Belgrade agreed to recognize the international borders of Croatia and Bosnia.[57] On February 28 Kozyrev's support of a French initiative to call a meeting between the Contact Group and the three Presidents of former Yugoslavia prompted a French Foreign Ministry spokesperson to welcome the "merger" of France's and Russia's positions.[58] Cooperation deepened in late April when Russia joined France in threatening to withdraw from the former Yugoslavia if the UN-brokered four-month-old truce, whose deadline was set at May 1, was not extended. The truce extension was under threat because the Bosnian Serbs had refused to reopen Sarajevo's airport.[59]

On April 24 Russia abstained on a UNSC vote on Resolution 981, supported by West Europe and the US, which temporarily extended and tightened sanctions against the Serbs. Russia favored the lighter sanctions regime extending sanctions indefinitely as a reward for a UN report of good behavior by President Milosevic, but a 75-day extension was finally voted on.[60] In fact, Russia had little choice but to support the indefinite extension of the lighter sanctions regime because failure to extend would have automatically reimposed the stricter sanctions formerly in effect.[61]

The speed of the retractions of policy statements on Yugoslavia by Russian officials had now become bewilderingly fast. On May 25 a RFM statement protested NATO air strikes against the Bosnian Serbs, who had failed to comply with a UN ultimatum to return heavy guns stolen near Sarajevo, but the next day Yeltsin reversed course and justified NATO's action while gloating that the Bosnian Serbs "got it" because they refused to desist in their military actions.[62]

Western officials accused Russia in late May of undermining a US mission to Belgrade sent to convince President Milosevic to recognize Bosnia in return for lifting some economic sanctions against Yugoslavia.

Russia reportedly advised Milosevic to hold out for a total lifting of sanctions before recognition.[63] This was not sufficient, however, to dispel military analyst Pavel Felgengauer's image of Russia as a willing pawn of the West. To Felgengauer Russia's influence in the Balkans was negligible. Other analysts alluded to Yeltsin's charade of taking "offense" at the NATO decision to bomb the Bosnian Serbs without consulting Russia.[64] Still other Russian observers knew well that Yeltsin's bombastic utterances were by now "tirades not for foreign consumption but for the domestic audience."[65]

On Prime Minister Major's initiative NATO finally agreed on June 3 to deploy a Rapid Reaction Force (RRF) in Bosnia composed of French, British, and Dutch troops. Although members of the RFM, including Kozyrev, slammed the RRF on June 5 as a dangerous and unilateral NATO scheme to derail the draft of the Contact Group's peace plan and hinted that Russia might veto the UNSC proposal to deploy the RRF,[66] Western observers scoffed at this obvious posturing: "even if the question [of the RRF] did come to a vote [in the UNSC]," one wrote, "Russia would probably not use its power of veto to scrap the plan and risk sparking a major row with its Western partners and creditors just one week ahead of the summit of the G-7." French Foreign Minister Juppe similarly found Russia's opposition to the RRF "distorted and exaggerated."[67] Such skepticism was borne out by Kozyrev's refusal to "rule out" Russian participation in the RRF on June 8.[68] Indeed, as far back as June 1992, when the Helsinki CSCE conference adopted a resolution in support of the creation and deployment of the RRF, Yeltsin categorically supported the idea of the RRF, although he carefully avoided mentioning Serbia by name, and even though it was well known that he intended for that country to be the force's target.[69] Military analysts fretted that such a force could be used indiscriminately, possibly even in the FSU.[70]

Krasnaia zvezda also upbraided Kozyrev for displaying such vehement opposition to the RRF while remaining, at the same time, responsive to British Foreign Minister Hurd's arguments that the RRF was consistent with the UNPROFOR mandate and was not an "intervention force." Kozyrev quickly caved in to Hurd's arguments, assuring him that Moscow did not object to an increased UN military component in Bosnia and promising that Moscow would not veto the UNSC resolution to reinforce UN peacekeeping forces in Bosnia with the RRF. He even suggested that Russian forces might join it.[71]

Such behavior placed Kozyrev's very credibility in question, so much so that the pro-government *Izvestiia* had doubts about his allegiances. It expressed "surprise" that the issue of NATO's bombing of the Bosnian Serbs was "not even raised" at the Kozyrev-Hurd meeting, and complained that Kozyrev had lamely commented that he "simply hope[d] that NATO has learned the lessons of the last such bombing."[72] In the event, Russia abstained on the June 16 UNSC vote authorizing the RRF, although it was widely known that the RFM approved the thrust of the motion in principle. Russia's UN delegation, it seems, had originally planned to vote for the RRF but "at the last minute . . . got the order [from Yeltsin] to abstain," according to French President Chirac, in retaliation against the G-7 for issuing a statement on Bosnia on June 15, one day before Yeltsin's arrival in Halifax. Russia's UN representative Lavrov tried to explain away Russia's abstention on the grounds that the resolution had been passed hastily and did not reflect amendments proposed by Russia, but this fantasy was shattered when Yeltsin agreed to the G-7's final statement supporting the RRF. When NATO dispatched RRF troops to Bosnia in late June, moreover, Russia made no protest.[73]

For its part, the West conducted adroit public relations on the issue: Karl Bildt, the EU's new mediator in the former Yugoslavia, visited Moscow in mid-June to ease Russian concerns that NATO might take military action against the Bosnian Serbs without consulting it, as it had during the previous month's air raid in Pale. Russia was also asked to help mediate with the Serbs after UN peacekeepers were taken hostage.[74] On June 22 the RFM issued a statement regretting the UNSC's failure to take action against the blockade of UN peacekeeping forces by Bosnian government forces. Russia twice called for an emergency session of the UNSC to discuss the Bosnian actions but, rebuffed both times, issued a statement questioning the UNSC's impartiality, then gave up.[75]

During the emergency session of the London Contact Group in late July the Russian delegation displayed its skill at deception diplomacy by "not rais[ing] serious objections to the Western allies taking a tough line" against the Bosnian Serbs for their attacks on Gorazde, the last remaining Muslim enclave in eastern Bosnia, even though Russia claimed to be "strongly opposed" to NATO air strikes (the BBC correctly noted that neither Kozyrev nor Grachev opposed NATO's use of force in principle; *Sovetskaia Rossiia* accused both of giving NATO a mandate to use massive force against the Serbs). Russia's position at the conference prompted a "quite positive" reaction from the West, who knew that this was the best that could be expected under the circumstances, since open Russian support for the motion was simply out of the question and would mean political suicide for Russian leaders. Indeed, although it was "not seriously believed that Yeltsin" would break with the UN embargo or "give effective diplomatic or military support to the Bosnian Serbs," the Western powers were careful nevertheless "not to offend Russian sensibilities" in the hopes that Moscow could "induce [Belgrade] to moderate Bosnian Serb behavior."[76] Although Kozyrev and Grachev both boasted that Russia had "turned back" air strikes and the proposed deployment of the new RRF in Gorazde in Bosnia at the London conference, the West warned on July 23 that further attacks on the safe areas by the Bosnian Serbs would be met with "unprecedented levels" of military force.[77]

In an attempt to resuscitate Russia's position in Yugoslavia Yeltsin called a meeting of Presidents Milosevic of rump Yugoslavia and Tudjman of Croatia. The meeting, needless to say, was a pathetic failure: Bosnian Muslim leader Izetbegovic ignored the invitation[78] and Croatian President Tujdman quickly backed out, citing the failure to invite Izetbegovic, although to Russian observers Tujdman was really acting in response to pressure from the US "and some Western European capitals." When the meeting was finally held on August 11 Yeltsin met with Milosevic alone and proceeded to "openly side with the Serbs." Yeltsin warned that if UN sanctions were not lifted against Belgrade Russia might unilaterally withdraw from sanctions, but critics belittled his "empty" threats, which rang hollow in light of his previous resolute opposition to Duma resolutions calling for the unilateral lifting of sanctions.[79] Indeed, Yeltsin refused to break ranks with the West on September 14 when he vetoed a bill the Duma had approved at its special August 12 session urging Russia to withdraw from international sanctions against Yugoslavia. He also vetoed a bill imposing a trade embargo on Croatia.[80]

When Milosevic's reception in Moscow was trumped by US National Security Adviser Lake's apparently deliberate omission of Russia from the itinerary of his upcoming visit to European capitals to work out a joint approach on Yugoslavia this seemed the final insult. In the end, the meeting proved to be another empty attempt at bolstering Yeltsin's image and indicated yet again the depth of Russia's marginalization.[81]

In his diplomatic machinations Yeltsin was nothing if not persistent. He condemned the Bosnian Serbs on August 30 for their role in a mortar attack on a Sarajevo market that killed forty people and NATO for responding with air strikes against the Bosnian Serbs. He also proposed as a solution another Moscow meeting with the presidents of the former Yugoslav republics in October.[82] Fearing a Russian veto in the UNSC, however, the Western powers had the UN Secretariat approve the air strikes, although a Russian veto would have been futile in any case, since Resolution 836, adopted in June 1993 with no principled objection on Moscow's part, gave NATO the right to use force if requested by UN officials.[83]

Although Moscow learned of the strikes only after the fact, an RFM statement directly contradicted Yeltsin's criticism of NATO by approving of its "not unjustified" actions given that the Bosnian Serbs had "total responsibility for such acts of barbarism for refusing to accept the peace proposals supported by the international community, including Yugoslavia." Another complained that the bombing went beyond the framework of UNSC resolutions, although it did not directly object to it.[84] And although RFM spokesperson Karasin appealed to the UNSC to immediately assess the situation and implement a political decision, Deputy Director of the Department of International Organizations of the RFM I. Shcherbak attacked the "barbaric Serb shellings" in Sarajevo and termed NATO's strikes justified. He did, however, have reservations about the scale of the response, which was "quite another matter."[85]

Enraged Duma deputies voted on September 6 to hold a special session three days hence on the Yugoslav situation. On the eve of the session Yeltsin predictably leveled vitriolic broadsides at NATO, criticized Kozyrev and the RFM, called NATO air strikes unacceptable and promised Russian aid to the Bosnian Serbs.[86] But ITAR-TASS showed Russia's deception to be wearing thin on September 4 when it made the familiar allegation that Russia's voice in the Balkans had been reduced from "a thunderous roar" to a "mutter," and that NATO air strikes against the Bosnian Serbs proved that Moscow had become an observer of events, "despite its repeated declarations of support for its Orthodox brothers." NATO, it asserted, had simply brushed off Russia's stern warnings and declarations of support for the Serbs as "oriented toward domestic consumption."[87] The reality was that Russia refused to aid the Serbs not only out of weakness; Russia's leaders were hostile to the Serbs on ideological grounds and willingly subscribed to the West's anti-Serb line.

Kozyrev proceeded to validate this view by mentioning briefly and almost in passing on September 7 that Russia opposed NATO's military operation, while adding the qualification that the situation was "very complicated" since the air strikes had been carried out on the "direct request" of the UN. Having thus given himself a convenient pretext to dispense with criticism of NATO, he quickly moved on to the main focus of his statement: an explanation of why Russia would not oppose NATO. The UNSC's rejection of Russia's request for a special session to discuss the air strikes, he pointed out, confirmed that the international community favored the strikes, thus making Russia's voice "rather lonely." "We can see the reality around us," Kozyrev went on, "We are advocating our position but we are not going into confrontation with the whole world around us."[88]

Yeltsin was equally deferential toward the West, cautioning Russians to tone down their criticism of NATO and approach the issue of "threats to the West" with a "cool head." On that same day he paraphrased Kozyrev's remarks by pledging that Russia would not engage in "confrontational actions with the West"[89] and condemned NATO air strikes as "unacceptable," warning—albeit in typically vague fashion—that if NATO persevered in its use of force, Russia would help the Serbs and things could "get hotter." He and Grachev also threatened on the same day to withdraw from the PfP if air strikes continued.[90] But the Germans gave what had by now become the typical yawning response: they "took note" of Yeltsin's criticism while promising that his words would be "studied carefully."[91]

The official representative of the UN Secretary-General admitted on September 11 that a secret memorandum on NATO military operations in Bosnia had been passed behind the backs of the UNSC without informing Russia or China. But the text of the memorandum—and this was not widely known—had reportedly been communicated to Kozyrev during the London Contact Group meeting in July which meant that, while distancing Russia rhetorically from NATO air strikes, Kozyrev "did in fact give [NATO] the go-ahead." German Foreign Minister Kinkel denied the existence of such a memorandum and Russian officials criticized the role of the UN and NATO in the affair[92] in an apparent effort to deflect attention from their complicity. But if past experience was any guide, the charges of Russian complicity and operating in secrecy were more than plausible.

French President Chirac announced on September 10 that NATO air strikes against the Bosnian Serbs had been suspended for several hours to permit a meeting between the commanders of the Bosnian Serb and UN forces. The pause, Chirac warned, was just that; strikes would be resumed if the Bosnian Serbs, "who are the aggressors . . . fail to fulfil the demands of the world community."[93] Following talks on the former Yugoslavia with Kozyrev on September 11 and 12 French Foreign Minister de Charette rejected Russia's proposal for an immediate cessation of the air strikes, insisting that the bombings would end only if the Serbs lifted their siege of Sarajevo and withdrew their heavy weapons.[94] The proposal, translated into a UNSC resolution, was never voted on.[95]

Russian officials noticeably toned down their anti-Western rhetoric on September 14 at a meeting with Clinton adviser Strobe Talbott, who expressed US alarm at the increasingly strident rhetoric emanating from Russia and the firing of a bazooka at the US Embassy in Moscow. To one Western analyst Russia was "clawing its way back to a role in the peace settlement" by acquiescing to the US peace plan to partition Bosnia[96]— although he could have substituted "crawling" for "clawing." The level of the rhetoric was also influenced by the announcement at the end of the Moscow meeting that NATO had suspended air strikes and given the Bosnian Serbs six days to withdraw from areas around Sarajevo. Kozyrev came out against the strikes, but reportedly "stopped short of warning NATO against resuming punitive actions" against the Serbs.[97]

In the meantime, as government critics were intensifying their assault on the leadership's policy even Western sources belittled Russia's behavior at the September 15 Contact Group meeting: "for all its sound and fury," it scoffed, "Moscow remain[ed] willing to cooperate with the West" on Yugoslavia.[98] And, true to his pro-Western colors, Kozyrev told Italian Foreign Minister Agnelli in September that despite strong differences with NATO over air strikes in Bosnia, Moscow intended to join its Western partners in the search for a political settlement in the region.[99] One October analysis typically accused the RFM of "passivity" for voting in favor of sanctions against the Serb Republic and urged Russia to use its veto to defeat NATO proposals.[100] Russia, it was clear, was following its pattern of raising the anti-Western rhetoric to a fever pitch only to squelch such sentiment when things became too uncomfortably anti-Western.

A principal line of Western analysis candidly acknowledged the Yeltsin government's strategy of intentionally overstating its friendship with Serbia for domestic political gain—to bolster Yeltsin's chances in the upcoming 1996 presidential election. Under "tremendous domestic political pressure" and facing potentially "dangerous" consequences from an enraged Russian public tired of his pro-Western policies, the leadership's *public* support for

Serbia would remain only that, for Moscow still needed "major Western financial support to continue its economic reforms."[101]

The long-awaited agreement on a Bosnian ceasefire came in early October. Yeltsin welcomed it as a "major step toward peace" while urging the UN to lift economic sanctions against rump Yugoslavia. As part of the attempt to project an image of "evenhandedness" RFM Spokesperson Karasin upbraided NATO for its "double standard" of bombing Bosnian Serb missile sites on October 4 but doing nothing after Bosnian Muslims launched an attack on the Serbs near Sarajevo.[102]

Preparations were in the works to hold an October meeting in Moscow of the leaders of the former Yugoslavia. Part of the West's "charm offensive" and public relations to "assure Russia of a central place in a Bosnian settlement," the meeting was, much like the phony "nuclear summit" in April 1996 (see Chapter 7), first broached by Yeltsin, this time at his summmit with Clinton in Hyde Park, New York on October 23. So as to allow Yeltsin his day of theatrics for the home audience the West agreed to delay by a day the opening of the real talks in Dayton, Ohio, which were scheduled for October 31. RFM spokesperson Karasin boasted that the Moscow meeting would be a "breakthrough," a "qualitatively new stage" in the peace process, and would "give a powerful impetus to further talks in the United States."[103]

But few were fooled. D. Trenin in September scoffed at the proposal and predicted that Russian officials would try make it *appear* that their demands for a peaceful settlement in Bosnia had been adopted by the West in order that Russian voters could see that their President was firmly "in charge" of Russia's diplomacy with the West. Trenin also predicted that Russia's behavior at the upcoming Contact Group conference would be "basically a theatrical performance."[104] In fact, Western officials made clear the October Moscow meeting's essentially empty, fraudulent character when they laid down the line that it was under no circumstances to be a negotiating session. Since US Ambassador to Russia Pickering would be there to supervise this "vehicle for making 'public Russia's strong support for the peace process' " whose script was written by the US, it was clearly a put-up job from start to finish.[105]

Consonant with the above, Russia's Contact Group partners stepped up their "charm offensive" by paying tribute to Russia's role in the peace process and thanking it for restoring natural gas shipments to Bosnia. "Salve to wounded Russian pride" was the apt description of France's "tactful support" of the Moscow talks, which were envisioned as a vehicle for Russia to project if not power then at least the image that it was involved, however marginally, in the peace process. US officials praised Russia for backing the US-led peace process, which Yeltsin had endorsed at Hyde Park. One Western diplomat even made the hardly enthusiastic—let alone convincing—announcement that there was a "genuine feeling that Russia's contribution is really valuable."[106] Karl Bildt, the EU representative to the Contact Group, similarly termed the Moscow meeting an "utterly important" preparation for the Washington meeting of October 31.[107] Clearly they did praise too much. In a pathetic postscript, the Mosow talks were cancelled and quickly forgotten after Yeltsin was taken ill days before the three-power talks were scheduled to take place.[108]

In an effort to finesse the reconciliation of Yeltsin's adamant refusal to place Russian troops under NATO command with NATO's objective of having Russia participate in a NATO-dominated peacekeeping force, France came up with an ingenious compromise proposal on October 21 which made it possible for Russia's leaders to safely comply. The plan stipulated that Russian troops would serve in a joint French-Russian division theoretically under NATO command, but because of France's "special relationship with NATO," which gave it a "certain autonomy," Russia was actually lured into accepting NATO's policies—*on NATO's terms*—and under the guise of a French moderating force aimed at sweetening Russia's bitter pill of dependence.[109] Russian diplomats were obviously not so naïve as to not know what NATO was up to. They therefore welcomed the French strategem as a clever means of disguising their cave-in to the West.

Worried that placing Russian forces under NATO command would be seen as an open surrender to the West, Yeltsin announced on October 19 that Russia was willing to send several regiments to join the Bosnian peacekeeping force but insisted that it was not a NATO operation and that Russian troops would not serve under NATO.[110] Grachev gave his assurance that Russia's brigade in Bosnia would be "independent" by virtue of the November 23 arrangement with NATO by means of which Russia agreed to participate in the planning of operations and the elaboration of the rules of engagement. But this was dismissed as sheer fantasy by RFM military expert General Boris Gromov, who insisted that NATO would dictate Russia's tasks in the operation down to the last detail.[111]

Mid-November talks in Brussels between Kozyrev and Secretary of State Christopher, aptly dubbed "operation fig leaf," ended with Russia's eventual consent to contribute a motorized brigade for Bosnian peacekeeping, despite its having no input in decisionmaking.[112] And a fig leaf it was, as Yeltsin announced categorically that Russia would not serve under NATO command, while Grachev thundered that Russia could "slam the door" on NATO's proposal—although for obvious reasons he "refused to go into detail" since the position Russia finally agreed upon, which was "passed off as a success" by the Russian leadership, entailed Russia's subordination to a US general and therefore to NATO, since he was also a NATO officer. The farcical deception was embodied in the stipulation that Russia would get "NATO orders, but not on official NATO forms."[113]

As happened so often, Yeltsin had kowtowed to the West then tried to conceal it with deception. Even *Izvestiia's* arch-Western political analyst S. Kondrashov asked whether Russia's participation in peacekeeping "really means a knee-jerk reaction and the acceptance of any terms, including unequal ones." And what, he asked, does this "imply from the standpoint of [Russia's] interests and the persuasiveness of its objections to NATO's expansion?" By this and other such actions, Kondrashov concluded, Russia was acting as the West's "errand boy,"[114] a singular honor which would again be bestowed on Russia for helping the West pull its chestnuts out of the fire in 1999. The Duma immediately raised objections to the NATO-Russian agreement on peacekeeping: N. Bezdorogov, Deputy Head of the Duma Defense Committee charged that the creation of a Russia-NATO consultation mechanism, worked out by Defense Minister Grachev and US Defense Secretary Perry to control the operation, left Russia in a position of complete subordination.[115]

Yeltsin, as noted above, had already vetoed a Duma law unilaterally terminating Russia's participation in sanctions against Yugoslavia.[116] Once the Balkan peace agreement was signed in Dayton on November 1, however, he hailed it and called for the swift removal of international sanctions on Serbia.[117]

Even after Dayton Russian officials continued to promote the fiction that Russia played a key role in the Balkans. To an interviewer's claim on November 23 that it was the Americans who ended the war, Kozyrev retorted "we did it together . . . None of us can do anything on our own."[118] But A. Golts of *Krasnaia zvezda* cut to the heart of the matter when he observed that Russia had lost, that along with other Contact Group representatives it had been sidelined in Dayton as the US dominated the negotiations and NATO's position in Europe was enhanced.[119] Its Balkan policy in disarray, Russia was marginalized as a player in Bosnia, indeed in most of the world, so much so that "none of the parties to the [former Yugoslavia] conflict now look[ed] to Russia to solve their difficulties."[120] Jubilant claims that Russia had been "restored to the heart of European diplomacy" and that the US badly "needed" Russia now sounded so absurd that P. Kandel of the Institute of Europe was prompted to make the observation that even though one could "objectively" say that Russia's Bosnian policy had been a "failure," Russia could only make its influence felt by "not playing a negative role."[121]

Notes

[1] S. Rogov, "Rossiia i Zapad," *SShA*, No. 3, March 1995, pp. 5-6. See also A. Utkin, "Posle protivosostoianiia," *SShA*, No. 11, November 1995, pp. 7-11.

[2] . Utkin, "Posle protivosostoianiia," p. 6. On the effects of "reforms" on the Russian intelligentsia, see *Literaturnaia gazeta*, November 16, 1994, p. 11.

[3] *Financial Times*, August 19, 1995, p. 2.

[4] A. Bekker, *Moscow News*, No. 2, January 19-25, 1996, p. 7.

[5] *Kommersant-daily*, January 26, 1995, p. 3; *Segodnia*, January 25, 1995, p. 1.

[6] *Nezavisimaia gazeta*, April 14, 1995, p. 2.

[7] Italics mine. S. Karaganov, *Moskovskie novosti*, No. 47, July 9-16, 1995, p. 5.

[8] *Nezavisimaia gazeta*, November 16, 1995, pp. 1, 5.

[9] Michael Mihalka, "Trawling for Legitimacy," *Transition*, Vol. 1, No. 11, June 30, 1995, p. 19.

[10] Alexei Pushkov, *Moscow News*, No. 17, May 5-11, 1995, p. 2; *Krasnaia zvezda*, April 22, 1995, p. 2.

[11] Y. Bykovsky, *Moscow News*, No. 15, April 21-27, 1995, p. 2. Bykovsky was Editor-in-Chief of *Moscow News*.

[12] *Krasnaia zvezda*, April 22, 1995, p. 2.

[13] *Izvestiia*, October 24, 1995, p. 1.

[14] S. Strokan, *Moscow News*, No. 1, January 12-18, 1996, p. 6; *Kommersant-daily*, May 3, 1995, pp. 1, 4.

[15] S. Bausin, *Moscow News*, June 2-8, 1995, p. 7.

[16] *OMRI Daily Digest*, No. 200, Part I, October 13, 1995.

[17] Ibid., No. 201, Part I, October 16, 1995; *Financial Times*, October 12, 1995, p. 6.

[18] *The Daily Telegraph*, June 1, 1995, p. 12.

[19] Paris, *Le Point*, June 2, 1997 p. 21, in *FBIS*-WEU-97-156; *OMRI Daily Digest*, No. 35, Part 1, February 17, 1995.

[20] The Reuter Economic Community Report, February 16, 1995; *The Times* (London), March 13, 1995.

[21] Reuters, February 16, 1995.

[22] *OMRI Daily Digest*, No. 35, Part 1, February 17, 1995.

[23] Michael Mihalka, "Continued Resistance to NATO Expansion," *Transition*, Vol. 1, No. 14, August 11, 1995, p. 38; Alexei Pushkov, *Moscow News*, No. 11, March 24, 1995, p. 2.

[24] Alexei Pushkov, *Moscow News*, No. 11, March 24, 1995, p. 2.

[25] Agence France Presse, March 6, 1995. However obvious this contention may have been, Westerners and others continued to insist that Russia was hardening its line, especially against NATO expansion. See, for example, Taras Kuzio, "NATO Enlargement: The View from the East," *European Security*, Vol. 6, No. 1, Spring 1997, pp. 50-2.

[26] Agence France Presse, March 22, 1995.

[27] *Financial Times*, March 23, 1995, p. 3.

[28] Reuters Financial Service, May 9, 1995, p. 9.

[29] *Sueddeutsche Zeitung*, May 12, 1995, p. 1, in *FBIS*-WEU-95-093, May 15, 1995, p. 13.

[30] Russian NTV, June 9, 1995, in *FBIS*-SOV-95-112, June 12, 1995, p. 7.

[31] *The New York Times*, May 8, 1995, p. A6.

[32] Ibid., March 27, 1995, p. A6.

[33] A. Migranian, *Moia gazeta*, June 21, 1995, p. 9, in *FBIS*-SOV-95-120, June 22, 1995, pp. 4-5.

[34] *Nezavisimaia gazeta*, June 21, 1995, p. 2.

[35] Scott Parrish, "Twisting in the Wind: Russia and the Yugoslav Conflict," *Transition*, Vol. 1, No. 20, November 3, 1995, p. 31.

[36] *OMRI Daily Digest*, No. 179, Part I, September 14, 1995.

[37] Madrid, *El Pais*, September 10, 1995, p. 3, in *FBIS*-WEU-95-176, September 12, 1995, p. 4.

[38] *Liberation*, September 21, 1995, p. 9, in *FBIS*-WEU-95-186, September 26, 1995, p. 1.

[39] ITAR-TASS, September 29, 1995, in *FBIS*-SOV-95-190, October 2, 1995, pp. 16-7.

[40] *Rossiskaia gazeta*, October 4, 1995, p. 7; *Financial Times*, September 28, 1995, p. 2.

[41] *OMRI Daily Digest*, No. 204, Part I, October 19, 1995.

[42] Reuters, October 19, 1995, October 24, 1995; *OMRI Daily Digest*, No. 204, Part I, October 19, 1995.

[43] October 2, 1995, in *OMRI Daily Digest*, No. 192, Part I, October 3, 1995.

[44] ITAR-TASS, October 12, 1995, in *FBIS*-SOV-95-197, October 12, 1995, p. 23.

[45] *OMRI Daily Digest*, No. 6, Part I, October 9, 1995.

[46] ITAR-TASS, November 15, 1995, in *FBIS*-SOV-95-221, November 16, 1995, p. 13.

[47] Interfax, November 20, 1995, in *FBIS*-SOV-95-224, November 21, 1995, p. 16.

[48] *Segodnia*, November 16, 1995, p. 2.

[49] Agence France Presse, December 6, 1995.

[50] Russian Public Television, December 3, 1995, in *FBIS*-SOV-95-233, December 5, 1995, p. 22.

[51] Reuters, November 29, 1995.

[52] Deutsche Presse-Agentur, November 6, 1995.

[53] Interfax, December 5, 1995, in *FBIS*-SOV-95-234, December 6, 1995, p. 22.

[54] *Trud*, September 26, 1998, p. 3.

[55] S. Samuilov, "SShA, NATO, Rossiia i bosniiskii krizis," *SShA*, No. 7, 1995, pp. 19-22. Even some Western analysts conceded that Russian policy toward the former Yugoslavia not only did not challenge the West in the region, but may even have helped the West to achieve its objectives there. For an example of such an analysis, see Paul J. Marantz, "Neither Adversaries Nor Partners: Russia and the West Search for a New Relationship," in Roger E. Kanet and Alexander V. Kozhemiakin, eds., *The Foreign Policy of the Russian Federation* (New York: St. Martin's, 1997), p. 89.

[56] *The Moscow Times*, May 13, 1996, p. 8.

[57] ITAR-TASS, February 19, 1995, in *FBIS*-SOV-95-034, February 21, 1995, p. 7; *Le Monde*, February 21, 1995, p. 17, in *FBIS*-WEU-95-037, February 24, 1995, p. 24.

[58] Agence France Presse, February 28, 1995.

[59] *Financial Times*, April 27, 1995, p. 2.

[60] *Die Welt*, April 25, 1995, p. 6, in *FBIS*-WEU-95-080, April 26, 1995, p. 14; Agence France Presse, April 21, 1995.

[61] Agence France Presse, April 21, 1995.

[62] ITAR-TASS, May 25, 1995; *OMRI Daily Digest*, No. 102, Part I, May 26, 1995. See a similar statement by a RFM official in Interfax, May 26, 1995.

[63] United Press International, May 24, 1995.

[64] *Segodnia*, May 30, 1995, p. 1. *The Washington Post*, September 7, 1995, p. A19, termed Yeltsin's response to the air strikes "tepid," and asserted that "Russia's cultural and strategic ties to the Serbs have been exaggerated."

[65] *Izvestiia*, June 8, 1995, p. 3.

[66] *The Moscow Times*, June 6, 1995; Agence France Presse, June 6, 1995.

[67] Agence France Presse, June 6, 1995.

[68] *OMRI Daily Digest*, No. 122, Part I, June 9, 1995.

[69] *The New York Times*, July 11, 1992, Sect. 1, p. 1; *The Washington Times*, July 11, 1992, p. A6.

[70] *Krasnaia zvezda*, June 5, 1992, p. 3.

[71] Ibid., June 8, 1995, p. 3; *Izvestiia*, June 8, 1995, p. 3; *Kommersant-daily*, June 8, 1995, p. 4; *Segodnia*, June 8, 1995, p. 2.

[72] *Izvestiia*, June 8, 1995, p. 3.

[73] United Press International, June 17, 1995; ITAR-TASS, June 16, 1995; Agence France Presse, June 14, 1995; June 20, 1995, in *FBIS-SOV-95-119*, June 21, 1995, p. 2.

[74] *The Times* (London), June 12, 1995.

[75] *OMRI Daily Digest*, No. 122, Part I, June 23, 1995.

[76] *Sovetskaia Rossiia*, July 25, 1995, p. 3, and September 9, 1995, p. 1; Agence France Presse, July 25 and 26, 1995; *The Herald* (Glasgow), September 8, 1995, p. 9.

[77] Parrish, "Twisting in the Wind," p. 29.

[78] *Kommersant-Daily*, October 11, 1995, p. 1.

[79] *Krasnaia zvezda*, August 12, 1995, p. 2; *Segodnia*, August 11, 1995, p. 1; *Kommersant-daily*, August 11, 1995, p. 1.

[80] *OMRI Daily Digest*, No. 180, Part I, September 15, 1995.

[81] Parrish, "Twisting in the Wind," p. 30.

[82] *OMRI Daily Digest*, No. 170, Part I, August 31, 1995.

[83] Agence France Presse, April 11, 1994.

[84] *Izvestiia*, September 1, 1995, pp. 1, 3; *OMRI Daily Digest*, No. 171, Part I, September 1, 1995; Interfax, August 30 and 31, 1995, in *FBIS-SOV-95-169*, August 31, 1995, p. 11; ITAR-TASS, August 31, 1995, in Ibid., p. 12; p. 14; Agence France Presse, August 30, 1995.

[85] *Segodnia*, August 31, 1995, p. 1.

[86] *OMRI Daily Digest*, No. 176, Part I, September 11, 1995.

[87] The Associated Press, September 1, 1995. For another criticism of Russia's pro-Western policy in the Balkans, see *Krasnaia zvezda*, September 1, 1995, p. 3.

[88] Russian Public Television, September 7, 1995.

[89] Mayak Radio, September 8, 1995, in *FBIS-SOV-95-175*, September 11, 1995, p. 13.

[90] *Rossiiskie vesti*, September 9, 1995, pp. 1, 3; ITAR-TASS, September 11, 1995; Agence France Presse, September 8, 1995.

[91] Berlin DDP/ADN, September 8, 1995, in *FBIS-WEU-95-174*, September 8, 1995, p. 19. Others pointed out that Russia, as a member of the UNSC, had approved of the decision for air strikes in the first place. See Agence France Presse, September 8, 1995.

[92] ITAR-TASS, September 12, 1995, in *FBIS*-SOV-95-177, September 13, 1995, p. 4; Radiostantsiia Ekho Moskvy, September 12, 1995, in Ibid., p. 4; ITAR-TASS, September 13, 1995, in *FBIS*-SOV 95-178, September 14, 1995, p. 4.

[93] ITAR-TASS, September 11, 1995.

[94] Xinhua News Agency, September 12, 1995.

[95] *OMRI Daily Digest*, No. 178, Part I, September 13, 1995, pp. 1-2; Agence France Presse, September 13, 1995.

[96] Parrish, "Twisting in the Wind," pp. 31, 70; *Segodnia*, September 14, 1995, p. 1.

[97] *The Los Angeles Times*, September 16, 1995, p. A11.

[98] *Financial Times*, September 18, 1995, p. 17.

[99] ITAR-TASS, September 7, 1995. See also Alexei Arbatov, "Russian Foreign Policy Thinking in Transition," in Vladimir Baranovskii, ed., *Russia and Europe: The Emerging Security Agenda* (Oxford: SIPRI, Oxford University Press, 1997), p. 153, who argues that Russia followed the West's lead in the former Yugoslavia.

[100] *Nezavisimaia gazeta*, October 11, 1995, p. 2.

[101] Inter Press Service, September 18, 1995.

[102] *OMRI Daily Digest*, No. 195, Part I, October 6, 1995.

[103] Xinhua News Agency, October 25, 1995.

[104] Agence France Presse, September 21, 1995. Trenin was a researcher for the Carnegie Institute for Peace.

[105] United Press International, October 25, 1995.

[106] Reuters North American Wire, October 25, 1995; *The Herald* (Glasgow), October 21, 1995; Reuters World Service, October 17, 1995.

[107] ITAR-TASS, October 17, 1995.

[108] United Press International, October 25, 1995.

[109] *The Independent* (London), October 21, 1995, p. 16.

[110] Mayak Radio, October 19, 1995, in *FBIS*-SOV-95-202, October 19, 199, p. 17; *Rossiiskie vesti*, November 10, 1995, p. 3.

[111] *Komsomol'skaia pravda*, November 28, 1995, p. 6.

[112] *Izvestiia*, November 11, 1995, p. 3.

[113] *Kommersant-daily*, October 24, 1995, pp. 1, 3; *Krasnaia zvezda*, November 10, 1995, p. 1; *Izvestiia*, October 25, 1995, pp. 1, 3. *Pravda*, October 26, 1995, pp. 1, 3 had predicted that peacekeeping would be a "purely NATO exercise."

[114] *Izvestiia*, November 21, 1995, p. 3. The charge that Russia was the "errand boy" for NATO would come up again during the Kosovo crisis in 1999. Russia's behavior during the crisis in fact gave grounds for the charge.

[115] Reuters, November 29, 1995.

[116] Official Kremlin International News Broadcast, November 10, 1995.

[117] United Press International, November 21, 1995.

[118] Russian NTV, November 23, 1995, in *FBIS*-SOV-95-226, November 24, 1995, p. 18.

[119] *Krasnaia zvezda*, November 25, 1995, p. 2.

[120] Parrish, "Twisting in the Wind," pp. 31, 70.

[121] Reuters World Service, November 22, 1995.

7 1996: Yeltsin Victorious

The Domestic Setting: The Economy

The success of the Russian Communist Party in the December 1995 parliamentary elections made it the largest bloc in the State Duma and was a measure of the unpopularity of Yeltsin's policies among increasingly larger segments of the Russian people. Economic corruption was rampant, evidenced by the "loans-for-shares" program, a scheme giving first crack at Russia's most valuable industries at fire sale prices to a consortium of leading banks in exchange for $2 billion in loans to the government to fill its budget gap. Prime Minister Chernomyrdin angrily chastized the perpetrators of the scheme once the details were widely known, but this only made the farce all the more absurd because it was he who floated the idea for it in the first place.[1] And while the super-rich gorged themselves on the people's wealth the government's economic policy of spring-summer 1994 reduced the people's real income another 18% by February 1995.[2]

The Domestic Setting: Political Developments

Kozyrev's replacement as Foreign Minister in January by the reputedly more "hard-line" Yevgenii Primakov began a new phase in Russian politics which alarmed many, especially Western, observers, who assumed that Russia would move in a "more anti-Western and anti-reform direction" and would display "extreme aggressiveness" toward Western "democracies." And when in mid-February Yeltsin dismissed the last of the prominent "reformers," the alarm bells went off for worried Westerners and "liberal-minded" Russians.[3] But 1996 occasioned no watershed, no "hard-line" shift in Russia's foreign policy—quite the contrary, the government's pro-Western orientation in 1996 which *seemed* to give way to a harder-line direction actually heralded, as in December 1993 and 1995, a more pro-Western thrust. And as always "economic interests . . . trumped geopolitical interests . . . Powerful interest groups such as Gazprom, LUKoil and Uneximbank made sure of it."[4]

The highlight of 1996, Russia's presidential election was by any measure a closed, highly undemocratic affair, assiduously promoted by the government-controlled media. Reports on the war in Chechnya, for example, were monopolized and given out by the Defense Ministry with commentaries by ITAR-TASS. Indeed, by its actions the media seemed to take a cue from the US government's control of the information flow after the Vietnam war, especially during the Grenada and Panama invasions, and including the 1999 Kosovo conflict when NATO relied on its spokesperson Jamie Shea and the US State Department as a principal source of disinformation.[5] Another government tactic was to give scant exposure to candidates other than Yeltsin. As reported by the European Institute of the Media, not only were the elections rigged but candidates had been substantially less free to get their views across and the voters given even less information than in the 1991 Soviet presidential election.[6] And on the day Yeltsin announced his candidacy he sacked the head of independent Russian television, O. Poptsov, to better manipulate the media—even after he had already barred television station NTV from the Kremlin for criticizing his policies.[7]

The West's affection for Russia's "democrats" was not only not diminished by the aforementioned violations of democracy—it seemed to actually welcome them with unqualified support to the Yeltsin regime. In May European Commissioner for Foreign Affairs van den Broek warned Russia's Communists that "what will determine our willingness to cooperate with Russia is whether the policy of political and economic reform is pursued." This was particularly timely, coming as it did at a worrying time for the West as the Communists seemed poised to unseat the "reformers" from power. Van den Broek expressed the EU's "preference" for Yeltsin's reelection, because "that gives the best guarantee of the continuation of reform."[8] IMF Director Michel Camdessus similarly gave notice that the proposals of Communist Party leader Ziuganov to nationalize enterprises "contradicts the reached agreements between the IMF and Russia," and assured Russia's leaders that the IMF had every confidence in their readiness "to assume responsibility for the country's switchover to a market economy."[9]

But *Time* magazine revealed that the West's backing for the Yeltsinite "reformers" went far beyond mere declarations of support by detailing in an unusually candid July article how US political consultants—not coincidentally, conservative Republicans—had designed the "aggressive anti-communist strategies that propelled Yeltsin to victory." Among other things, they played on the people's fear of civil war and orchestrated the April 1996 Yeltsin-Clinton meeting so that the former could "sound tough on the West . . . without sparking a rebuttal from Clinton," a tactic aimed at coopting a Ziuganov campaign theme. The pro-Yeltsin campaign covered by state-owned television station received "detailed instructions on how each Yeltsin event could be covered." The US advisers acknowledged that they were forced to operate in secret, aware that if they were found out this would only add fuel to the opposition claim that Yeltsin was an "American tool." To top it all off, the advisers laughed off Yeltsin's campaign as "nonsense . . . a lie."[10] Lies, deception—Russia's leaders, with Western complicity, were thus willing to use any means to insure that Russia remained dependent on the West.

It was further reported that the US government had given $500 million in March 1996 to Russian banks to finance Yeltsin's 1996 re-election campaign, in spite of a ban on candidates accepting foreign money (and which, among other things, made laughable outraged cries from US Republicans that the Clinton administration had accepted money from foreign donors for the Democratic Party campaign).[11] The IMF signaled its support for Yeltsin by approving his promise to pay off public sector wage arrears by May 31, 1996. The budget later ran over target, but the IMF, predictably, suspended its loan facility in July 1996 "after Yeltsin had been safely elected President,"[12] and which aroused understandable concern among Russian election officials that the IMF's tacit consent to Yeltsin's excessive electoral spending and its undisguised pressure on Russia would be exploited by the opposition.[13] After holding out, the IMF finally voted in August to grant the next tranche of credit to Russia—$330 million—while it congratulated Russia for continuing to adhere to a policy "consistent with the macroeconomic objectives of the joint program."[14]

Leonid Abalkin, who had been Gorbachev's economic adviser and was now Director of Russia's Economics Institute, argued from the opposite standpoint that the scale of the Russian government's financial dependence had been exaggerated, given that the IMF loan of $10.3 billion over three years was easily covered by Russia's favorable external trade balance from exports of more than $10 billion (not including capital flight). To Abalkin, this proved that Russia's leaders were exploiting relations with the IMF to gain support for their pro-market policies. Criticizing the IMF demand, among others, that Gazprom be broken up, Abalkin accused the IMF of "trying to impose conditions on us that go beyond the framework of economic policy and affect our national interests."[15]

The West extended assistance to its Russian government allies in other ways. At the end of April the Paris Club rescheduled Russia's $40 billion debt and gave it 25 years (instead of the usual 18) to repay; and on May 1 the World Bank approved a $200 million loan to shore up Russia's social services. But the anti-"reformist" former Minister of Foreign Economic Relations Sergei Glaz'ev stated the obvious: that the money from the West—and its unusually rapid disbursement—was aimed at helping Yeltsin's candidacy by temporarily increasing social spending prior to the election. Glaz'ev also found it "extraordinary" that the money was given for government dicretionary spending rather than being linked to specific goals, as was normal practice. And Yeltsin himself said it all in an unusually candid admission of Russia's dependency on Western money when he maintained that the money was "nothing less than [my] due after years of cooperation with the US-designed economic reforms."[16]

The spiraling chaos and decimation from the "reforms" resulted in "widespread but uncoordinated" strikes in November of "hungry employees whose jobs are financed by the budget" and led by local strike committees.[17] The Russian people were restive, and their anger seemed to be reaching a point of mass action.

The Foreign Policy Setting

Throughout 1996 specialists remained gloomy about Russia's foreign policy prospects: S. Kortunov of ISKRAN cautioned that naïvely playing the European card by trying to win West Europeans over to Russia's side against the US was futile, since the West Europeans would never prefer a weak and unpredictable Russia to its US partner.[18] D. Trenin similarly cautioned that Russia-EU and Russia-NATO relations had "no reliable foundation for partnership" and were even approaching a "critical state"— ecstatic claims by Russian officials about the success of such relations notwithstanding.[19] Iu. Borko and B. Orlov, both of the Institute of Europe, argued that the assumption that the cold war and military confrontation were over simply because the Soviet Union ceased to exist was misplaced, given that the only real result of the cold war was the irreversible collapse of "real socialism." The world, they warned, was approaching the prologue to a new confrontation.[20]

The G-7 endeavored mightily to help Yeltsin's election campaign by agreeing to hold an April meeting in Moscow—the so-called "nuclear summit"—a "photo op," where the West pledged $14 billion in credits, thereby "dropp[ing] any pretense at impartiality" in the election. The meeting, which was "long on ceremony and short on concrete results," was used by Yeltsin as an occasion to assume the role of a "dynamic leader of a still-powerful nation." Yeltsin's performance did little to boost his image as a leader in charge, however, especially when, during a post-summit press conference, he awkwardly fumbled through his notes trying to come up with something—anything—he could list as an achievement of the meeting. After taking an inordinately long time, he quipped that he was "just trying to give journalists time to take notes." The joke, needless to say, fell flat. The fact was that he had such a hard time listing any achievements because there were none—unless duping the Russian and world public about the true aims of the Russian and Western elites is considered an achievement.[21]

Some Russian analysts managed to keep a straight face as they put a positive spin on the summit by referring to it as the "G-8" and contended that not only had Russia's positions been accepted but "constructive measures for cooperation" were discussed. But behind this false front was a very different picture: Western participants had in reality *ignored* Russia, especially its centerpiece proposal that nuclear weapons be deployed only on the territory of their owners. Pretense was indeed the modus operandi here, for Russia did not even dare to table another of its core proposals, the creation of a nuclear-free zone in CEE (to head off NATO expansion), in part because German Chancellor Kohl refused to discuss it, objecting that it was "too early" to do so, but mainly because, as even Westernizers admitted, the meeting "was primarily intended for public effect."[22]

This facile blowing off of Russia's most vital concerns made it obvious that no serious discussion took place here, that the summit, as *Pravda* correctly characterized it, was a put-up job solely for public consumption and orchestrated by the West to help foster an image that Yeltsin was an equal participant in the G-7/8 (it was, of course, really a G-7; Russia's utter weakness made even the suggestion of a "G-8" laughable) shortly before Russia's president election. World leaders, it noted, had agreed to "go through the motions" to support the Yeltsin government and its "democratic reforms."[23] And *Sovetskaia Rossiia* noted the irony that just when the West was rejecting Russia's chief proposal at the summit not to station nuclear weapons on new members' territory Russia was withdrawing missiles from Belarus and Ukraine.[24]

In fact the timing of the meeting had been "no accident," for it was Yeltsin himself who conceived of this forum at the previous G-7 meeting in Halifax to enhance his electability and "for which an opportunity to heighten his profile as a world statesman on home ground would be a welcome boost." Yeltsin risked overstepping the bounds set by his Western overseers, however, when he aroused their ire by referring to the summit as the "G-8," thus implying full Russian membership.[25] At the summit the Western participants made sure Russia's behavior was closely monitored, much as a parent oversees an unruly child. Thus, the summit's signal achievement was the signing, on Yeltsin's urging, of a pact to prevent the smuggling of nuclear materials originating mainly from Russia.

An equally farcical deception took place weeks later with the arrest of nine Britons for spying in Russia. Few were fooled, however, by this obvious attempt "to show the [Russian] voters that [Yeltsin] is a good President who takes forceful action to protect Russia's national interests, even if it threatens friendly relations with the West."[26] The government's blasé attitude about the incident reeked of a put-up job, as RFM spokesperson G. Karasin revealed: "such things happen sometimes," he admitted; "the main thing now is not to succumb to emotions and to avoid hasty decisions," even as he pledged that the RFM would try to "ensure that the incident does not damage the cooperation that has been developing between the two countries in recent years."[27]

Russian Relations with Non-Western States

Improved Russian-Iranian relations dissuaded the US from even trying to convince Russia to follow the trade boycott and political isolation of Iran. Even pro-Western analysts resented Washington's "unconcealed pressure" on Moscow to prevent its deal with Iran to build the Bushehr atomic power station from going through.[28]

In March Oleg Davydov visited Tripoli, where he handed Libyan President Khaddafi a message of support from Yeltsin. Two Libyan delegations had just returned from Moscow to boost trade and economic ties and to discuss repayment of Libya's $3.8 billion debt.[29]

Russia and NATO

The leadership evidently agreed with Western officials that March was a propitious time to explore negotiations on a treaty with NATO, for steps were taken to draw up a charter on Russia-NATO relations not long afterwards. With the issue thus joined the NATO expansion deception continued and even intensified, since this naked acquiescence to NATO expansion contradicted Russia's previously expressed "opposition" and made it all the more necessary for the leadership to fend off the frequent accusations of selling out to the West. One of the stratagems of deception they came up with was the worn-out threat to form a bloc of states which were supposedly anti-NATO. But the leadership's continuing close ties with NATO agencies and its consent to participate in NATO military exercises aroused extreme skepticism about such anti-NATO moves, a skepticism fully justified in December by Primakov's agreement to negotiate NATO expansion.

Russian Relations with NATO

Guile was now the watchword for Western leaders when they dealt with Russia. In February German Foreign Minister Kinkel denied that Chancellor Kohl had visited Moscow to boost Yeltsin's election chances, despite Kohl's having rushed off to Moscow days after Yeltsin announced his candidacy.[30] Nor was Yeltsin averse to dissimulation, as when he told Kohl on February 19 that the two leaders' positions on NATO expansion differed only in "shading," despite Kohl's having advocated merely a *delay* in expansion to forestall conflict with Russia. Kohl's urging the Western powers to soften statements on NATO expansion to help Yeltsin's chances in the Russian Presidential election[31] was not enough to paper over Russian Deputy Foreign Minister S. Krylov's acknowledged differences with Germany over NATO expansion or Russian Federation Council Speaker Shumeiko's complaint that Russia did "not want the process of NATO expansion beginning at all. Germany plays a huge role in this."[32]

If Kohl and other Western leaders urged a delay in NATO expansion to avoid undermining Yeltsin in the Russian presidential elections, they could afford to do so, since a hiatus in the NATO expansion process would not significantly influence NATO's expansion timetable in any case, given that the next expansion steps were not to be even considered until the December

Foreign Ministers meeting in Brussels. This explains why commentators in February noted that Germany (and Britain), normally "energetic champion[s] of [CEE] membership of NATO," had become "lukewarm" over the idea—"*at least until after the Russian election.*"[33]

Kohl was therefore more forthcoming after the elections, warning at his August meeting with Yeltsin at Zavidogo that Russia must not veto NATO expansion even as he assured Russia that its position would be "taken into full account and discussed at the highest level." The two also "disagreed" over US actions in the Persian Gulf.[34] In mid-September Chancellor Kohl proved that his government's stance on NATO expansion diverged fundamentally from Russia's stated position when he assured Polish President Kwasniewski that Germany sought to implement NATO expansion with "full determination" in June or July, and insisted that Polish membership in NATO was a "foregone conclusion."[35] No wonder *Sovetskaia Rossiia* berated Russia's "democratic" press in late March for harping on the idea that Germany took "a supposedly more flexible stand than its partners" on expansion and "heeded Yeltsin's arguments" on the issue. Such a view was deceitful, it complained, especially given Kohl's non-fulfilment of pledges to Gorbachev that NATO would not expand if the USSR acquiesced to Germany's unification.[36]

Analysts who labeled Foreign Minister Primakov a Russian "hard-liner" were surely surprised in early March when he announced that Russia was willing to consent to NATO expansion under certain conditions. Primakov's demarche evidently stemmed from the leadership's decision that now was the time to make a major concession to the West. But this solicitude to Western concerns on Primakov's part was so discrepant with the conventional image of him as a staunch "anti-Westerner" that analysts could only explain it by means of the implausible assertion that Russia had really advocated such a concession to NATO all along but that Kozyrev, as Foreign Minister, had failed to "explain it properly."[37] In reality the move, which was inevitable, was probably part of the Yeltsin leadership's probing the West for support for the upcoming Presidential election.

The demarche, a milestone in Russia's policy toward NATO and the West, came during a March 11 meeting with Hungary's Foreign Minister Kovacs, where Primakov proferred the important concession—ironically, not long after he had declared that Russia's opposition to NATO expansion had not changed and would not change—that the key criterion for compromise in the expansion controversy was the non-movement of NATO military structures towards Russia's borders. Russia, in other words, could live with a scenario—however farfetched—in which new members joined only NATO's *political* structures.[38] Primakov repeated this new line on March 23 and 28.[39] Indeed, the scenario's very impossibility suggested that it was a tactical ploy to set in motion the process of Russia's eventual agreement to NATO expansion.

Just days after a March 21 meeting with NATO Secretary General Solana where he had publicly reiterated Russian disapproval of NATO expansion and also chided Primakov for objecting "too mildly" to NATO expansion,[40] Yeltsin also abruptly changed his line on NATO expansion— ironically again, only months after Kozyrev ruled out "horse-trading" on NATO expansion—by announcing in Norway on March 25 that it was now acceptable for new members to join NATO's political committee but not its military structure, much like France had done. Presidential Press Secretary Medvedev tried to reinterpret Yeltsin's comments as meaning Russian acceptance of cooperation within the framework of PfP and the NATO Council only, and not territorial expansion of NATO.[41] But Yeltsin's modification of his stance on expansion was bad timing, to say the least, and this was not lost on Russian observers who were surely well aware that NATO had just completed military maneuvers, named "Operation Battle Griffin 96," in Northern Norway. Unmoved by Russia's concession, NATO Secretary General Solana reminded Russia on April 16 that there was "no such thing" as political membership in NATO, because in NATO "you are [either] part of a whole of it or you are not part of it."[42]

During the latter stages of the expansion controversy NATO promised not to deploy military hardware on the territory of new members, but this was taken with a very large grain of salt by military analyst Pavel Felgengauer who argued that the precedent of German unification, during which Gorbachev had made the mistaken assumption that a verbal agreement would suffice in dealings with the West, proved that the West could not be trusted to adhere to *oral* agreements.[43] German Defense Minister Ruehe confirmed Felgengauer's suspicions when he affirmed in June that although NATO had no plans to station nuclear weapons or troops on Russia's borders after expansion new members would be integrated militarily with *the same rights and duties as others.*[44]

The Russian leadership's conciliatory attitude toward NATO complemented NATO efforts to support Yeltsin's bid for the Presidency. German Foreign Minister Kinkel, with an eye to the Russian presidential election, emphasized in January that EU and NATO expansion would be impossible if the West turned its back on Russia and affirmed that EU and not NATO expansion was now the order of the day.[45] But this was revealed to be just another deception strategem, given that the most compelling issue was obviously NATO expansion and because EU expansion could not feasibly precede NATO expansion, if only because it would involve a damaging loss of credibility for NATO and because EU expansion was a far more complicated affair requiring the alteration of deeply ingrained procedures and the mollification of powerful vested interests.[46]

Nor did the softened stand on NATO expansion by Russia's leaders go unchallenged in Russia. Yeltsin adviser A. Migranian was impelled to denounce the leadership's "illusions about a possible compromise" with NATO and their "caving in" under pressure from Western "partners," and rejected concessions on expansion by asserting that such a strategy would, like the PfP, only strengthen the hand of the West.[47] Other, equally hard-line warnings reverberated throughout Russia in response to the Yeltsin leadership's accession to NATO expansion: Chernomyrdin was compelled in early May to downplay threats from Russian defense analyst Anton Surikov and others that admittance of the Baltic states to NATO would force Russia to order a preemptive strike,[48] while Defense Minister Grachev warned that Russia and Belarus could strengthen their troop positions on Poland's borders if NATO expanded.[49] In the meantime, Primakov had his hands full denying that Russian "opposition" to NATO expansion had softened and tried to smooth over his recent capitulation by insisting that Russia "opposed" any movement of NATO's military infrastructure closer to Russia's border.[50]

Because the issue of NATO expansion to the Baltics was such a sensitive one for Russia Defense Minister Rodionov declined an invitation to a September NATO conference in Copenhagen on security in the Baltics, even as he expressed Russia's extreme displeasure over the prospect of further NATO enlargement to the Baltics.[51] Russian officials were also wary of NATO exercises, warning in March that NATO's aforementioned "Battle Griffin 96" exercises in Norway near the Russian border would "not pass unnoticed."[52] But Russian opposition to NATO was not so far-reaching as to preclude Rodionov from attending an informal meeting of NATO Defense Ministers in Norway on September 26 where, according to one observer, he made it plain that Russia was reconciled to NATO expansion when he agreed to discuss a Russia-NATO charter. Rodionov also stated that Russia could "in time" support expansion, thus coming "very close to" the consent on expansion the West sought from him.[53]

Russia's leaders, including "hard-line" Foreign Minister Primakov, also came under attack by *Pravda* for signing the total nuclear test ban treaty on September 24. Since the Western powers possessed advanced computer technology which enabled them to upgrade their nuclear weapons without actually testing them (testing was something Russia, which lacked such technology, had no choice but to do), Russia's acquiescence was viewed as a "surrender" to the West.[54] And in contrast to the enthusiasm of Western officials who had hailed the signing of the PfP as a "turning point in post-Cold War history," Russia was roundly criticized for having participated in PfP, which brought "mostly disappointments" by 1996. Cooperation with the West nevertheless moved forward as Russia agreed to participate in the IFOR brigade in Bosnia and—in a first—a PfP peacekeeping exercise, "Peace Shield 96," to be held in the Ukraine in June.[55]

Until now Russia's policymakers had declined to participate in PfP peacekeeping for fear that active cooperation with NATO could be interpreted as a "recognition of the inevitability of the alliance's eastward expansion." For this reason, too, Russia's participation in joint Russian-US peacekeeping exercises at Russia's Tomsk range and in Fort Riley, Kansas in 1994-5 were purely token and pointedly bilateral, and not part of the PfP. But the charade of Russian hostility to NATO came to an abrupt end when Moscow, fearing that the boycott of the PfP looked somewhat "offensive" to NATO, agreed to take part in the aforementioned "Peace Shield 96," to be held on June 15 as a token of the leaders' gratitude to their Western "friends" for having kept their promise to postpone NATO expansion until after the 1996 presidential elections.[56] Further Russian cooperation with NATO was forthcoming in the agreement by Grachev to set up a permanent Russian mission in the Supreme Headquarters Allied Powers Europe and his suggestion that Russian liaison officers be placed in other NATO commands in Europe.[57] NATO did not reciprocate, and even conspicuously failed to invite Russia to the preparations for the PfP's "Cooperative Partner 96" naval exercises from July 22-8 in Romanian territorial waters.[58]

Primakov continued his pursuit of a rapprochement with NATO in early June when he celebrated the fact that the ice which had frozen Russia-NATO relations for so long was "beginning to crack," and offered as an example the recent NATO Council meeting where participants had urged a dialogue with Russia and the working out of a mutually acceptable formula on NATO expansion, something Russia had previously ruled out.[59] Several days later, however, Primakov advanced a new argument against NATO expansion: it would result, he argued, in the deployment on the territories of new members of nuclear warheads with the same strike time as Pershing-2's and would violate agreements eliminating medium-range missiles.[60]

On October 2 Primakov dismissed as a "maneuver" the suggestion that Russia apply for NATO membership, although on October 30 newly-appointed Secretary of the Russian Security Council Rybkin openly proposed precisely that for Russia, a move regarded as a trial balloon for Russia's impending softened stance on NATO expansion. Primakov scolded Rybkin for talking out of turn, but this was clearly a ruse, given Rybkin's admission that it was Yeltsin himself who had "engineered" the proposal. Indeed, it was reported on October 30 that NATO Secretary General Solana's recent statement on the possibility of a charter with Russia had merely confirmed Yeltsin's own initiative on a charter, first proposed on September 28. What is more, Primakov himself had stated openly on October 2 that Russia would sign a charter with NATO on the condition that it "substantially" address Russia's security concerns. Within two months Russia would agree to sign such a charter even in the absence of the fulfilment of such conditions by NATO.[61] That Russia's kowtowing to NATO was now an open secret was made clear when even Russia's ultimate "hard-liner," Aleksandr Lebed, recently appointed by Yeltsin as adviser to the Russian Security Council, mollified Western concerns about Russia's response to NATO expansion in the fall with the assurance that Russia would not "get hysterical" over such a development.[62]

Primakov made a tour of Asian countries in November with the objective, according to the RFM's official statement, of reaffirming Russia's Eastern priority "as a counterbalance to the Eastern priorities" of the West—that is, NATO's determination to expand eastward. But any hope that Russia would succeed in swaying its Asian neighbors to join an anti-NATO coalition was practically nil given that Russia held "no economic trump cards to further her interests in the Orient." Nor could the "strategic" partnership with China which Russian officials projected "in [any] way be regarded as a union or alliance."[63] Indeed, as argued by one leading political analyst, because Beijing's "interest in economic relations with the U.S. outweighs its interests in relations with Russia, its political alliance with Moscow is impossible in the near future."[64] The vaunted anti-NATO alliance with China and others was, like so much else in Russian foreign policy, another ploy in the elaborate game of deception.

In order to ease Primakov's task of "lulling Russian public opinion" against NATO expansion, *Sovetskaia Rossiia* contended, the final communique of the December 10 NATO Ministers meeting included a statement on the "three noes," a pledge that the alliance had "no intention, plans, or reason to deploy nuclear weapons on the territory of the new member countries." Some Russian analysts revealed their gullibility by terming the pledge a "pleasant surprise"; others noted, more realistically, that the pledge was meaningless because it was not juridically binding and because the West's intentions could change at any time,[65] a view at once validated by a US State Department spokesperson who assured his listeners that he was "not certain that the United States gives any commitments forever or any nation does . . . circumstances can always change."[66]

Another watershed in Russia-NATO relations came on December 10 when Primakov communicated to NATO Secretary General Solana Russia's acceptance at long last of NATO's offer to open negotiations on a charter—and despite that fact that he had only recently reiterated Russian "opposition" to NATO expansion at the Lisbon OSCE conference. In the view of US officials the Yeltsin government realized that NATO expansion could not be stopped and sought a dialogue with the West to acquire a bigger voice in European security,[67] although it was clear that the West would accept a dialogue only on its own terms. At the same time Defense Minister Rodionov outlined publicly and for the first time Russia's "military response" to NATO expansion, including strengthening its armed forces and possible retargeting of missiles at CEE states in NATO.[68]

Russia and Yugoslavia

After Dayton the Balkan issue lost its immediacy and Russia became an onlooker in a game run and played exclusively by Western players. Perhaps the most contentious issue was Russia's peacekeeping contingent. In spite of its insistence that its troops would never serve under NATO, it was obvious that there was no way around subordination to NATO and that Russia would inevitably give in to NATO's demands. The show Russia's leaders put on to make it seem that they were standing up to the West ended with their complete cave-in to NATO's demands, including their replacement of an officer NATO deemed too friendly to the Serbs.

Yugoslavia: Russian Relations with the West

Having been marginalized in the former Yugoslavia by the Dayton agreement of the previous year, Russia now played the role of an onlooker who, having no control over actual events, could only scream at perceived infractions from the sidelines. The leftist newspaper *Zavtra* sought to debunk the government-promoted myth that Russia conducted its own independent policy in Bosnia by belitting the Russian force stationed there as miniscule and terming Bosnian "peacekeeping" an "occupation" of the Bosnian Serbs under NATO auspices. NATO's unilateral initiative to replace the commander of Russia's forces, Maj. Gen. N. Staskov, by the more pro-Western Maj. Gen. Sigutkin was pointed to as evidence of Russia's lack of independence.[69] As it turned out, because Russian troops had been slated to deploy in areas controlled by the Bosnian Serbs, Staskov decided to meet with Bosnian Serb commander Ratko Mladic, and was promptly sacked by the Russian government on February 14 for his display of apparent pro-Serb sentiment. Despite the Defense Ministry's insistence that his removal was part of the normal rotation of commanders, Russian sources knew that "he was removed because of his meeting with Mladic, as the incident had become an 'irritant' in relations with the other participants in IFOR"—i.e., the US and the West.[70]

Russia thus showed itself to be willing once again to knuckle under to the West, a development which was not lost on even Western analysts, who depicted Russian officials as "gamely striv[ing] to maintain the illusion that their country is an equal partner in the [Balkan peace] process" when in reality Russia played a "notably minor role in the Dayton process" (Dayton was the Ohio city where the Yugoslav peace agreement was finally signed on November 1, 1995). To perpetuate the illusion Russian and Western officials claimed ad nauseum that Russia was an "important player" in the Bosnian settlement "to help Russia maintain its image as a great power, especially in the runup to the Russian presidential election," but "an enormous gulf divide[d] the rhetoric about the Russian role from reality." Indeed, Western observers openly acknowledged that Russia had been accorded a visible role in the negotiations only to prevent its public humiliation.[71] Western officials also came up with the brainstorm that the "strategic partnership" pro-Western Russian officials so fervently sought could somehow be built from cooperation which developed out of Balkan peacekeeping. Russia's leaders concurred, exulting that "for Russia, the Bosnian operation [was] a kind of proving ground for honing technical cooperation with NATO in the area of peacemaking."[72] And yet in one sense Russia was a not insignificant player in the Yugoslav drama—it had, as one Russian put it, been the "facilitator of Western policy" in the region, its role ridiculed as the West's "postman" or "errand boy."[73]

On February 15 Primakov called on the Contact Group to discuss a "delay" in the suspension of sanctions against Belgrade. Russia claimed to favor an end to sanctions but the US insisted on lifting sanctions only on the condition that Bosnian Serb forces withdraw and also that IFOR establish "zones of separation." On February 23 Yeltsin seemed to prove his mettle by finally signing a decree withdrawing from UN sanctions against Belgrade but this move, like so many others, proved to be merely a "theatrical gesture" so typical of Yeltsin, aimed at enhancing his flagging domestic popularity, especially since the UNSC was in any event scheduled to lift sanctions within four days.[74] Russian "opposition" to NATO's policies in the former Yugoslavia "quieted" dramatically after it joined NATO's peacekeeping operations.[75]

The issue of Yugoslav "war criminals" was now a major bone of contention in Russian-Western relations. A summit hastily called in Geneva by the US on March 18 succeeded in formulating a twelve-point plan to support the Croatian-Muslim federation in Bosnia and completed agreements to hand over suspected war criminals for prosecution. The US-coordinated summit upstaged Contact Group talks to be held five days later in Moscow, surprising West Europeans and angering Russia, who initially threatened to boycott but typically backed down and agreed to send an observer to the talks.[76] Russia also backed the G-7's threat to impose sanctions against the Bosnian Serbs if their leader, Radovan Karadzic, did not quit public life immediately, and also urged that Bosnian elections be held on schedule on September 14,[77] but in July Russia accused the international tribunal for the former Yugoslavia of becoming an "over-politicized and partial structure" for having issued a warrant for the arrest of Bosnian Serb leaders Karadzic and Mladic.[78]

Serbian sources practically damned Russia with faint praise in early October when they declared that, however contradictory its behavior, Russia remained the sole channel through which the Bosnian Serbs could at least "declare their interests to the world community";[79] Russian Deputy Foreign Minister Afanasievskii nevertheless declared Russia's willingness to maintain cooperation with its Western partners in Bosnia by assenting to Moscow's "tak[ing] part in forming the political concept for the next stage of the operation in Bosnia and in [its] military planning."[80]

At long last the UNSC on October 1 adopted Resolution No. 1074 lifting sanctions against Belgrade. Russia, with France and Britain, had fought "until the last minute" to include in the Resolution a recommendation that the UN General Assembly allow Belgrade to resume its participation in the UN but was rebuffed by the US,[81] although Russia's supposed "support" for Serbia's UN status was diminished by its 1992 refusal to uphold Belgrade's right to the former Yugoslavia's UN seat (see Chapter 3). In any case, once Resolution 1074 was adopted NATO and the WEU immediately terminated their joint naval blockade in the Adriatic—even as the UNSC reserved the right to reimpose the sanctions if the Dayton peace accord was broken. Russia threatened to block such a move.[82]

NATO ambassadors met at the alliance's headquarters to discuss proposals for the new force, which was to replace the NATO-led Implementation Force (IFOR) and whose mandate would end in December. Russia agreed to send troops.[83] At the December OSCE summit in Lisbon Russia insisted that the final draft declaration calling for "democratization, independent media, free and fair elections" in Serbia be removed.[84]

Notes

[1] *International Herald Tribune*, January 29, 1996, p. 11. Alarmed by the success of the Communists in the Duma elections, Western analysts warned that Russian public opinion was moving in the "wrong" direction on key issues. See Peter Reddaway, *The New Republic*, January 29, 1996, pp. 15-16.

[2] A. Bekker, *Moscow News*, No. 2, January 19-25, 1996, p. 7.

[3] Peter J. Stavrakis, "Russia After the Elections: Democracy or Parliamentary Byzantium?" *Problems of Post-Communism*, Vol. 43, No. 2, March-April 1996, pp. 16, 20; John B. Dunlop, "The 'Party of War' and Russian Imperial Nationalism," in Ibid., p. 34; Deutsche Presse Agentur, February 19, 1996.

[4] Michael McFaul, *The Moscow Times*, February 10, 1998.

[5] For a good example of US and NATO disinformation on Kosovo see *The New York Times*, November 11, 1999, p. A6.

[6] L. Telen, *Moscow News*, No. 15, April 18-24, 1996, p. 2; Margot Light, "Two Cheers for Russian Democracy," *The World Today*, Vol. 52, Nos. 8-9, August/September 1996, p. 201.

[7] Peter Truscott, *Russia First: Breaking with the West* (London: I.B. Tauris, 1997), p. 189.

[8] Reuters World Service, May 31, 1996.

[9] Agence France Presse, May 13, 1996.

[10] *The Moscow Times*, July 9, 1996, p. 4.

[11] *Moskovskii komsomolets*, February 11, 1998, p. 3.

[12] Truscott, *Russia First*, p. 191.

[13] *Segodnia*, July 25, 1996, p. 1.

[14] Ibid., August 23, 1996, p. 2; ITAR-TASS, August 22, 1996.

[15] *Rossiiskaia gazeta*, November 29, 1996 (Weekend Edition), p. 27.

[16] Fred Weir, "Betting on Boris: The West Antes Up for the Russian Elections," *CovertAction Quarterly*, No. 57, Summer 1996, pp. 40-1. The Paris Club was a group of international government creditors led by the wealthy Western powers.

[17] *Moskovskie novosti*, no. 44, November 3-10, 1996, p. 4.

[18] S. Kortunov, "Rossiia ishchet soiuznikov," *Mezhdunarodnaia zhizn'*, No. 5, 1996, pp. 18-19.

[19] D. Trenin, "Russia and the West: Avoiding Complications," *International Affairs* (Moscow), Vol. 42, No. 1, January-February 1996, p. 30. Trenin was a leading research associate at the Institute of Europe.

[20] Iu. Borko and B. Orlov, " . . . I mozhno li vinit' Evropu?," *MEMO*, No. 6, 1996, p. 69.

[21] *The New York Times*, April 1, 1996, p. A17, April 21, 1996, Sect. 1, p. 1; *Journal of Commerce*, May 1, 1996, p. 7A.

[22] *Moscow News*, No. 16, April 25-May 1, 1996, p. 4; *The New York Times*, April 21, 1996, Sect. 1, p. 1.

[23] *Pravda*, April 23, 1996, p. 1. To get a sense of the artificial nature of the summit, see the "special issue" in *Mezhdunarodnaia zhizn'*, 1996, especially the article by I. Ivanov, First Deputy Foreign Minister, p. 29, the joint press conference of Yeltsin and French President Chirac, pp. 13-17, and *The Irish Times*, April 22, 1996, p. 11. Because Russia does not belong in the world's exclusive club of the wealthy and powerful nations and because it was obviously granted "membership" only as a sop for acquiescing to NATO expansion and to help its besieged leaders keep power, I refer throughout this study to the G-7 and not the G-8, even after Russia was supposedly made a member. Most observers seem to agree, as the organization is even by the year 2000 still widely referred to as the "G-7" by observers who clearly feel that the term "G-8" is simply too absurd.

[24] *Sovetskaia Rossiia*, April 23, 1996, p. 3.

[25] Reuters, in *The Moscow Times*, April 18, 1996, p. 5.

[26] *Nezavisimaia gazeta*, May 8, 1996, p. 2.

[27] *Rossiiskaia gazeta*, May 8, 1996, p. 7.

[28] Iu. Mel'nikov and V. Frolov, "Iranskii vopros vo vzaimootnosheniakh Moskvy i Vashingtona," *Mezhdunarodnaia zhizn'*, No. 7, 1995, pp. 15-16.

[29] *Izvestiia*, March 30, 1996, p. 3; *The Moscow Tribune*, March 28, 1996, p. 7.

[30] Agence France Presse, February 16, 1996.

[31] *International Herald Tribune*, February 20, 1996, p. 6.

[32] ITAR-TASS, October 10 and 20, 1995.

[33] Italics mine. *The Times* (London), February 5, 1996.

[34] *Rossiiskaia gazeta*, September 10, 1996, p. 7.

[35] TV Polonia, Warsaw, September 12, 1996, in BBC Summary of World Broadcasts, September 14, 1996.

[36] *Sovetskaia Rossiia*, March 23, 1996, p. 3.

[37] *The Washington Post*, March 27, 1996, p. A13.

[38] ITAR-TASS, March 11, 1996; *Financial Times*, March 12, 1996, p. 2. See also *The Angeles Times*, April 15, 1996, p. A5.

[39] *The Washington Post*, March 23, 1996, p. A23; Interfax, March 28, 1996.

[40] *Financial Times*, September 22, 1995, p. 2; *Kommersant-daily*, March 22, 1996, p. 4; *OMRI Daily Digest*, No. 59, Part I, March 22, 1996.

[41] *Izvestiia*, March 27, 1996; *Segodnia*, March 27, 1996, p. 1.

[42] *The Moscow Tribune*, April 17, 1996, p. 5.

[43] *Segodnia*, June 5, 1996, p. 1.

[44] Italics mine. The Reuter European Community Report, June 8, 1996.

[45] *Frankfurter Allgemeine*, January 22, 1996, p. 2, in *FBIS*-WEU-96-015, January 23, 1996, p. 14.

[46] *Financial Times*, December 18, 1996, p. 22.

[47] *Moskovskaia pravda* (*Moia gazeta*, Supplement No. 17), May 15, 1996, p. 1.

[48] *The Moscow Times*, May 5, 1996, p. 4.

[49] Agence France Presse, May 23 1996.

[50] *Obshchaia gazeta*, September 19, 1996, p. 4.

[51] Agence France Presse, September 23, 1996.

[52] ITAR-TASS, February 26, 1996, in *FBIS*-SOV-96-039, February 27, 1996, p. 10; Ibid., February 29, 1996, in *FBIS*-SOV-96-042, March 1, 1996, p. 11. See also *Segodnia*, June 5, 1996, p. 1.

[53] *Kommersant-daily*, September 28, 1996, p. 4. *Nezavisimaia gazeta*, September 27, 1996, p. 2 contended that Rodionov adopted a hard-line stance against NATO expansion at the meeting.

[54] *Pravda*, October 1, 1996, p. 1.

[55] *The Moscow Times*, May 30, 1996, p. 9.

[56] *Segodnia*, May 28, 1996, p. 2.

[57] *The Moscow Tribune*, June 15, 1996, p. 3.

[58] ITAR-TASS, July 23, 1996.

[59] *Izvestiia*, June 8, 1996, p. 3.

[60] Rome, LIMES, June-September 1996, pp. 53-6, in *FBIS*-SOV-96-115, June 13, 1996, p. 24.

[61] *Nezavisimaia* gazeta, November 1, 1996, p. 1; *Segodnia*, November 1, 1996, p. 1; *OMRI Daily Digest*, No. 192, Part I, October 3, 1996; ITAR-TASS, October 30, 1996; Agence France Presse, September 30, 1996.

[62] *The New York Times*, October 10, 1996, p. A16.

[63] *Izvestiia*, November 11, 1996, p. 4. Noted political analyst D. Trenin stated categorically that there could be no question of an alliance with China against NATO. See *Segodnia*, March 29, 1996, p. 9.

[64] *Nezavisimaia gazeta*, December 28, 1996, p. 1.

[65] See *Sovetskaia Rossiia*, December 15, 1996 p. 7, *Segodnia*, December 11, 1996, p. 1; *Nezavisimaia gazeta*, December 10, 1996, p. 2, and December 15, p. 2.

[66] M2 Presswire, December 11, 1996.

[67] *International Herald Tribune*, December 11, 1996; *Segodnia*, December 15, 1996, p. 2.

[68] *The Guardian* (London), December 2, 1996, p. 10.

[69] *Zavtra*, No. 10, March 1996, p. 4.

[70] Scott Parrish, "Russia's Marginal Role," *Transition*, Vol. 2, No. 14, July 12, 1996, pp. 22-3.

[71] Ibid., p. 21.

[72] *Financial Times*, September 27, 1996, p. 2; *Segodnia*, March 29, 1996, p. 9; *Nezavisimaia gazeta*, January 17, 1996, p. 2; *Segodnia*, December 18, 1997, p. 4. See a similar optimistic perspective on Russian participation in the Bosnian peacekeeping operation in *Krasnaia zvezda*, December 1, 1995, p. 1.

[73] *Nezavisimaia gazeta*, December 8, 1995, p. 5.

[74] Parrish, "Russia's Marginal Role," p. 23; Agence France Presse, February 24, 1996.

[75] United Press International, February 13, 1996.

[76] Agence France Press, March 22, 1996; AP Worldstream, March 17, 1996.

[77] The Reuter European Community Report, June 29, 1996.

[78] Agence France Presse, July 17, 1996.

[79] Interfax, October 2, 1996, in *FBIS*-SOV-96-193.

[80] Ibid., October, 3, 1996, in *FBIS*-SOV-96-194.

[81] *Segodnia*, October 3, 1996, p. 8.

[82] The Associated Press, October 2, 1996.

[83] Agence France Presse, November 11, 1996.

[84] Reuters Financial Service, December 3, 1996.

8 1997: Russia Accedes to NATO Expansion

The Domestic Setting

Despite claims by pro-government economists in 1997 that signs finally
pointed to a reversal of the downward economic spiral—and which, if true,
would be a turning point in Russia's quest for a viable capitalist economy—
the economic situation in fact continued to go from bad to worse. In May
Iurii Masliukov, a leading Communist and Chair of the Duma Economic
Committee, pointed out that the *real* sector of Russia's economy had
declined 4% for industry and 6% for agriculture, and that capital
investments had continued to fall.[1] Within a year Russia's economic
meltdown would prove Masliukov's analysis accurate. Accompanying the
decline in growth was a fall in the standard of living for the average
Russian, which Yeltsin promoted by criticizing the Duma in October for
rejecting the government's reduction of social benefits, which were already
at an abysmally low level.[2]

The people responded with an increasing receptivity to socialism even
as their hostility to Russia's "reforms" deepened. One poll showed that only
6% of Russians believed their country was moving in the right direction;
54% felt it was moving in the wrong direction, and 58% opposed privatization.[3] Another poll revealed that only 29% felt that the socialist system in
principle could not create conditions for Russia's development; 60% said
they had lived better under socialism (although 52% did not want a return to
"communism");[4] and 61% regretted the breakup of the USSR, compared
with 33% in December 1992.[5]

After being temporarily grounded by a reported bout of pneumonia
Yeltsin returned to the political scene to oversee Russia's disintegration by
removing all but two government officials as a precursor to a March cabinet
shakeup. Anatolii Chubais was elevated to the post of Deputy Prime
Minister, which gave banking interests even more direct entree to the
uppermost levels of government. After having strayed somewhat from the
path of free-market reforms in 1996 (part of his strategy of appeasing
burgeoning anti-Western sentiment before the election) Yeltsin announced

to Parliament in early 1997 that "reforms" would be accelerated through an overhaul of the tax code, pensions, budget, subsidies, natural monopolies, and the military.[6] The new program also included the sequestration of $19 billion from the budget.[7]

But foreign policy was another matter, and the crucial nature of issues which required more immediate resolution, above all, NATO expansion, dictated a less ingenuous approach. Accordingly, prior to his highly-awaited March summit with Clinton, Yeltsin threw down the gauntlet to the West on a wide range of foreign policy issues, including his complaint about antidumping restrictions against Russian goods. This proved to be bombast, however, in light of his appointment to high office of arch-Western "reformers" Anatolii Chubais (who was also appointed Head of the Presidential Administration in late August, contrary to Yeltsin's post-election vow that he would not do so) and Boris Nemtsov as Deputy Prime Minister,[8] both of whom encouraged high levels of Western imports to Russia and were taken to task by the opposition for their failure to support Russian industry. Yeltsin also named the latter two officials to the Security Council on May 23 simultaneous with his sacking Defense Minister Rodionov in an effort to comply with the aforementioned IMF demands, and proving to one Russian observer that Russia was willing yet again to bend over backwards to accommodate the West.[9]

The IMF's partiality toward Chubais made perfect sense in light of US dominance of the IMF and the heavy funding of Chubais' State Privatization Committee by the USAID.[10] Western business circles, in fact, loved Chubais so much so that the pro-business *Euromoney* magazine named him "Finance Minister of the year" in late 1997,[11] and Yeltsin had a similar honor bestowed on him by a Western group, the Media Control Institute of Europe, which strained incredulity by naming him "man of the year" for his "effective influence on the media" during the 1996 election campaign and his pursuit of "partnership" with the West, deemed "a strong link in the reform process."[12] In light of the anti-democratic, even criminal behavior of the Yeltsin clique during the 1996 campaign this showed the West's true colors on Russia and its "democracy."

In his address to the Russia people one year after his reelection Yeltsin boasted of his great accomplishments, including his bringing "young and dynamic people," like Chubais and Nemtsov, into government. He also promised to ensure the payment of pension arrears by June 30, and for those who did not receive them he set up a "hot line." The sorry state of the

Russian telephone system alone was enough to arouse skepticism on this score, however. Yeltsin also bragged that Russia was now a member of the "G-8," but acknowledged with not a little understatement that Russia did not "measur[e] up" in this forum in some areas—even as he gave reassurances that this was only a temporary condition. He ended with the promise that prosperity was "not far off."[13]

Chubais proved to be no less averse to deception than Yeltsin. Quite the contrary, almost immediately after boasting that Russia had seen the last of its economic difficulties and would no longer require foreign assistance, he met in early December with heads of Western banks to request $2 billion in emergency loans to cover the budget deficit and pay public-sector wage arrears.[14] The government also appealed to the IMF and to private bankers in December for economic help to replace the withdrawal of billions of dollars by foreign investors in the wake of the Asian economic turmoil,[15] prompting a letter from IMF chief Camdessus to Chernomyrdin in December detailing twenty-one conditions the Russian government must meet for assistance. To *Sovetskaia Rossiia* this proved that Russia's government was essentially an apparatus to monitor the fulfillment of instructions from Western financial institutions.[16] Even more telling was Yeltsin's signing a decree lifting restrictions on foreign ownership of Russia's oil companies which annulled a November 1992 decree prohibiting foreign ownership in more than 15% of such companies. The decree aimed at bids for upcoming sales of such Russian companies as Rosneft, LUKoil, and the Tyumen Oil Company.[17]

Meanwhile, the Russian military continued to get short shrift. Russian and US Defense Ministers agreed on December 3 to "boost Washington's support for Moscow's push to slash and reform its Soviet-style armed forces" hours after Yeltsin had promised to make large cuts in the military and, not coincidentally, while the Russian government was in the process of "scrambling" for a $2 billion loan and additional help from the IMF.[18]

The Foreign Policy Setting

The year's most significant foreign policy event was the signing of the Russia-NATO Founding Act on May 27. For its willingness to comply with Western demands on the issue Russia was rewarded with "full" membership in the "G-8," widely touted as a "victory" by Russia's Westernizing leadership but laughed off by most everybody else as "ludicrous for a country with a collapsed and corrupt economy" and a "geopolitical joke," although Foreign Ministers Ikeda of Japan and de Charette of France seemed not to be amused when they made sure in late May that Russia was shut out of all important G-7 discussions, including those on international finance, macroeconomic adjustments, and development issues.[19] Russia was also excluded from the session on economic and financial issues at the June meeting in Denver.[20] In any case, G-7 meetings, which no longer made authoritative decisions, had lost their luster long ago; it is thus no wonder the idea of their discontinuation had been raised at the Tokyo summit four years earlier.[21] Indeed, precisely because the G-7 had come to be a yearly ritual, an almost meaningless display by and for the world's wealthiest nations, Russia's paramount objective of membership in such an organization seemed to conform nicely with the leadership's strategy of deception. At the June G-7 session in Denver Yeltsin told French President Chirac that Russia would side with Europe in "future disputes" with the US.[22] This supposedly dramatic shift in Russia's focus toward West Europe, part of its campaign to counterbalance the US, was belittled as just another Russian maneuver by observers who knew that West Europe would never jeopardize its relations with the US for Russia's sake.[23]

Russian Relations with Non-Western States

In early October Gazprom, with its French and Indonesian partners, agreed to a $2 billion gas deal with the National Iranian Oil Company. During the ensuing political flap deep rifts emerged between the US on one side and its European allies and Russia on the other. Yeltsin chastized the US for "dictating" its will on the question, for imposing sanctions on countries, including Russia, who traded with Iran and who were, like Iran, "independent and freedom-loving countries."[24]

For all its seeming resistance to US domination during the controversies over Russian and European relations with Iran and Iraq, and contrary to the assumption by many Russians that it was Russia's chief "ally" in the West, France was actually strongly supportive of the US. Most generally, with respect to Iraq, it offered Saddam Hussein carrots while relying on the credibility of the US military stick.[25] Amid the public squabbling Russia continued to lean towards the US, quietly sharing sensitive intelligence with Washington to prevent Russian technology from reaching Iran.[26]

Russia's policy toward Iraq tended to follow a similar pro-Western trajectory. On June 23 Russia's UN delegation voted for a US- and British-inspired anti-Iraq resolution on the personal instruction of Yeltsin who, having initially threatened a Russian veto, agreed with President Clinton at the Denver G-7 summit to take joint measures against "aggressor states" and promised to vote in favor of the resolution. The resolution gave Iraq until October 11 to cooperate with UN inspections but would bar Iraqi officials from entering other countries if Baghdad remained in defiance.[27]

Russia pulled off its most striking display of diplomatic independence in late November by brokering a deal which stipulated an end to Iraqi sanctions if Iraq complied with UN resolutions on arms inspections, and thereby averted US air strikes against Iraq. Congratulations were immediately forthcoming from French President Chirac and German Foreign Minister Kinkel, among others, for this "major success," including a note to Yeltsin welcoming "the very spectacular return of Russia" to Mideast politics. As on previous occasions, however, they did praise too much, for the hullabaloo reached its peak just as others were questioning the prospects for success of Russia's long-term aim of lifting sanctions on Iraq, a necessary precondition if the latter were to repay billions of dollars in Soviet-era debts. The chances seemed even more remote when one took into account continued opposition by the US, Britain, and France to the lifting of sanctions.[28] And Primakov himself deflated any optimism on this score when he refuted claims that Russia had promised Iraq that sanctions would be immediately lifted once UN inspectors were readmitted into Iraq by urging that sanctions be lifted only in proportion to Iraq's compliance with UN resolutions.[29]

Although analysts concluded from Russia's alleged success in resisting the West on the Iraq issue that Russia was strongly anti-Western, former Reagan administration official Helmut Sonnenfeldt put a different cast on things by pointing out that Russia's "defiance" was in reality a ploy by "the Russians, and Primakov personally" who, while faithfully doing the West's bidding, "have been looking for ways to sort of disassociate themselves from the US [and West] from time to time *to show that they don't always knuckle under so easily.*"[30]

While extolled as anti-Western, moreover, Russia's policies toward Iran and Iraq were generally in accord with those of West Europe, China, and indeed most nations, who likewise objected to the imperious behavior of the US. Britain demonstrated West Europe's sympathy for Russia on the Iraq and Iran issues by terming US proposals to punish companies for trading with Iran "wholly unacceptable." Russia joined the EU in refusing to comply with the Helms-Burton Act, which punished US and foreign companies investing in oil and gas sectors in Iran and Libya. Russia's behavior, moreover, did not run completely counter to the US on the Iraq question, as the US, realizing that its unwillingness to bend on the issue would alienate most of the world, signaled in mid-November that it wished to avoid a military confrontation with Iraq, and used Russia's good offices to press Saddam Hussein to back down on the weapons inspections issue.[31]

Russia and NATO

As the deception on NATO expansion was being perpetuated by Russian and Western leaders the West, adamantly refusing to yield on the basic issues, also realized that it must protect Russia's Westernizers by modifying certain elements of its NATO expansion strategy, especially its timing. The West carried its campaign of deceit to considerable lengths, including making the claim that expansion would not lead to an increase in NATO military forces. During and after the negotiations on the Russia-NATO treaty Russian and Western leaders made frequent reference to the contemplated quid pro quo: in exchange for Russian acquiescence to NATO expansion, the West would make such "concessions" as Russian membership in the G-7 and the Paris Club, additional financial aid, etc. Yeltsin even threw in some gratuitous concessions, including approving anti-ballistic research programs and his "spectacular" announcement that Russia's missiles targeted at Western cities would be disarmed—a meaningless gesture, since retargeting could be accomplished in no time.

Just as the controversy over eastward expansion was in full swing NATO declared its intention to admit the Baltic states, prompting Russia to warn that its new line against expansion was now drawn at the Baltics.

Russian Relations with NATO

Chancellor Kohl visited Moscow in early January where he denied that NATO expansion meant a massive military shift toward the Russian border, and insisted that Germany had "no intention to move our military machine closer to the Russian border . . . I can't see who would want that. That is partly propaganda." He neglected to specify what the other part was.[32]

But the West, ever oblivious to Russian interests, forged ahead with NATO expansion. In early January German Foreign Minister Kinkel disclosed that Russia could not stop NATO expansion, and Russia's leaders knew it. What is more, Chancellor Kohl and President Clinton had apparently agreed after the August 1996 Yeltsin-Kohl meeting at Zavidogo (see Chapter 7) that Russia's opinion on NATO expansion would no longer be taken into account,[33] that all that was needed was a "wide range of reassurances" to Russia that NATO would not threaten it. For this Kinkel suggested the familiar but utterly meaningless remedy of a consultative body, in this case, a permanent one with "equal" rights for Russia, to discuss global issues and confidence-building measures with NATO with respect to the SFOR (NATO-led Stabilization Force) peacekeeping forces in Bosnia. This would, he claimed, convince Russia of NATO's "good intentions."[34] Kinkel also proposed what had become the generally accepted quid pro quo for expansion: IMF assistance, Russian membership in the G-7, minor changes in the CFE treaty, and NATO's assurance that it would not deploy nuclear weapons in CEE countries.[35]

The Russian government also pretended to be hard at work formulating a position on NATO expansion when Yeltsin ordered the preparation of an "action program" in early January to implement the government's "opposition" to NATO expansion. Touted as the one mechanism that would prevent NATO expansion, it was soon quietly dropped and forgotten,[36] a measure of the Westernizing leadership's lack of seriousness in their "opposition" to the West, of their willingness to resort to empty shows of defiance in the face of this most serious threat to Russia's security.

When US Secretary of State Albright came to Moscow to try to reconcile Russia to NATO expansion in late February the public had been so softened up by the above trickery of Russia's leaders that acceptance of her new proposals, which proved to be merely old wine in new bottles, was considerably smoothed. Albright's proposals: rejected Russia's demand for a ban on construction of new NATO installations on the territory of new members; refused to agree to a binding treaty and insisted on a non-binding "charter"; proposed a joint Russian-NATO brigade patterned on Bosnian peacekeeping; refused to promise that the Baltics would not be admitted to NATO; and pledged the "three noes"—that NATO had "no plan, no need and no intention to station nuclear weapons on the territory of new members," in essence sidestepping a direct answer as to whether NATO would ever station such weapons.[37]

No matter how much she assured Russia that NATO was no longer its enemy Albright could not get around the fact that in the final analysis NATO's expansion was aimed at heading off a resurgent and above all left-leaning Russia—in spite of the fatuous claims of Russians that the "three noes" were rendered insignificant by laws in "a number of [CEE candidate] countries" which forbade nuclear weapons on their territory and by strong public sentiment against such deployment in those countries.[38] Albright all but acknowledged that NATO expansion was directed against Russia when she affirmed in July that if the situation in Russia did not "work out the way that we are hoping it will . . . NATO is there."[39] And NATO adopted a disingenuous negotiating posture by posing as the paragon of moderation, assuring Russia that it had no intention of increasing its military forces while neglecting to mention that its proposals *did not require* a decrease in the number of weapons because budget cuts had already forced bigger reductions than required under the CFE treaty. Moreover, because the treaty entitled the US to 4,000 tanks in Europe, the US' current level of 1,500 enabled it to lower the allotment without actually reducing its forces.[40] And the proposed "joint brigade" was simply not serious—British Defense Minister Portillo dismissed it as "a kind of brand name."[41]

Western reassurances notwithstanding, most Russians were apprehensive about NATO expansion—but not, apparently, Russia's NATO-friendly leaders. And the people's apprehension was understandable, given that Russia's military budget for 1997 was 2.5 times lower than 1996—itself a "most difficult year" for the military. Observers warned that non-fulfilment of even the minimal budget in 1997 would spell the "complete destruction of the national defense potential"[42]—even as NATO's combat potential would increase some 15-20% after expansion.[43]

The not inconsiderable benefits NATO would derive from expansion were documented by Deputy Head of the General Staff Nikolai Pishchev: the additional 3,400 tanks from the new CEE states would more than cancel out the disarmament of 1,300 US tanks; in place of the withdrawn 511 US combat jets, 731 aircraft would be added, as well as 290 airfields and 5,500 weapons depots; and the shifting of NATO's outer borders by 650-740 kilometers to the east would, after the withdrawal of medium-range missiles, give the West the capability to carry out attacks on Russia directly from Europe with fully loaded fighter planes. Norway and Turkey, located on NATO's flanks, would now have equipment significantly more modern than before while the US, with the capability to be in Europe in full strength within sixty days, could maintain weapons dumps there for six armored US brigades.[44] Finally, expansion would enlarge the depth of NATO's zone of responsibility, greatly reducing the Russian ABM defense warning period. The troops of the Kaliningrad Special Military Area would now directly face NATO troops, while the Baltic Fleet would lose its room for maneuver altogether.[45]

The political left once again saw most clearly through NATO's machinations: V. Safronchuk of *Sovetskaia Rossiia* pointed out that Russia would get virtually nothing from NATO in the proposed treaty, that NATO would dictate terms;[46] leader of the Communist Party Duma faction V. Iliukhin observed that Yeltsin's "tough pose" during expansion negotiations was a ploy "to trick the public into believing that Russia would join the bargain in exchange for advantages,"[47] a view validated by US Deputy Secretary of State Talbott's assurance that NATO's pledge not to station nuclear arms and "substantial troops" in new member states could be changed the moment a new threat developed. "The alliance," Talbott maintained, "reserves the unilateral right to reassess the security environment at any time and, if it felt there was a new challenge, to change deployments accordingly."[48]

From the opposite end of the political spectrum four State Duma members from the right-wing Yabloko, *Nash Dom Rossiia* political parties, as well as independents, set up a pro-NATO group,[49] a response to an anti-NATO formation in the Duma which by late March counted 243 members (46 members of the Duma's upper house also joined).

Although the RFM's formal reaction to the West's proposals on NATO expansion was "negative," Yeltsin assured the West on March 17 that he sought to avoid confrontation, that he remained optimistic he and President Clinton would reach a compromise at their upcoming summit in Helsinki—despite his having insisted just a few days earlier that "Russia will not change its position on NATO . . . our diplomats have made enough concessions to the United States. We can't give any further." Adopting his familiar adversarial pose, Yeltsin warned that if attacked by NATO, Russia "would simply hit back."[50] The "militant" pose was soon exposed by, of all people, the putatively "hard-line"[51] Foreign Minister Primakov, who on February 20 surprised observers with the announcement that Russia would ask for only "a voice, not a veto" in NATO, something NATO had insisted on all along.[52] In May the RFM—again led by the "hard-line" Primakov—made another notable concession when it agreed to open an office at NATO headquarters with an ambassador and military staff.[53]

Yeltsin's February 23 statement that Russia's key task in its relations with NATO was compromise and the avoidance of confrontation essentially complied with NATO's terms of expansion and represented a sea change compared with statements Yeltsin had made since August 1993. He had apparently been brought around to such a position by Madeleine Albright just days before during her February visit to Moscow where he had also agreed that he would compromise with President Clinton at their upcoming March summit in Helsinki.[54] Days later Yeltsin met with Dutch Prime Minister Wim Kok (then chair of the EU) and European Commission President Jacques Santer in Moscow, where Kok predicted that the new concept of NATO would differ significantly from the old one and emphasized, "without going into details," that the changes would conform to the new realities, *above all the fact that the Warsaw Pact was a thing of the past*. Kok voiced his "understanding" of Russia's objections to NATO's expansion, but warned that Moscow had no right of veto and that a decision to admit new members would be taken at the NATO summit in Madrid on July 9 (the new members officially signed the accession protocols in December).[55] NATO was not even making a pretense of "equality" and mutuality with respect to Russia. It set an ironclad agenda, dictated terms—which consisted almost entirely of Russian concessions to the West—and brooked no disagreement.

Even in the face of imminent NATO expansion, Russian officials continued to feign a posture of toughness toward the West, clearly as part of a strategy to soften the sharp edges of their open giveaway to NATO. At a May 27 press conference Primakov expressed satisfaction that Russia's relations with China, as with other Asian countries, were "developing well,"[56] as if to imply that this powerful anti-NATO alliance would always be there if NATO stepped out of line and got too aggressive. Some steps were taken to help this process along—an invitation to Chernomyrdin to visit India coincided with the arrival of the Indian Prime Minister and Chinese Foreign Minister on March 25,[57] and in early May Russia assured Iran it would not let Iran's political crisis with the EU affect Russian-Iranian relations.[58]

The Yeltsin-Clinton summit in Helsinki, held on March 21, was a dress rehearsal for the signing of the Founding Act in May, which would enshrine Russia's acquiescence to NATO expansion. Russia's spin doctors were at the ready in Helsinki—and their "slick media operation" came in very handy, given Yeltsin's exaggerated assessments after the summit, which had yielded, he boasted, "positive results" for Russia. He claimed, falsely, that progress had been made on the strictly binding nature of the charter as well as on NATO pledges not to station troops or bases on new members' territories. In reality, Yeltsin gave in to Clinton without a fight on the central issue of whether the agreement would be internationally binding (Clinton insisted that it would not). Yeltsin defended against charges that he had not been "sufficiently tough" in standing up for Russia's interests with the familiar but weak claim that a harsher tone would have "isolated" Russia and jeopardized its security.[59]

The Communist version told a far more accurate story of "crushing defeat," of how Yeltsin had surrendered by dropping Russia's long-standing demand that relations with NATO be made legally binding.[60] Indeed, Yeltsin's acceptance of all of Clinton's proposals with scarcely any change was so unexpected that US policymakers, having gotten from Yeltsin "virtually everything they hoped for" were "stunned by the victory that fell in [their] lap." By taking care to "restrain their rejoicing and to emphasize instead a tie game in which friendship triumphed," however, "they hoped to avoid distressing Yeltsin or making life harder for him at home."[61]

By also submitting to US demands that it be allowed to proceed with all six programs to develop a theatre anti-missile defense Yeltsin made it possible to break a three-year impasse over the 1972 ABM Treaty.[62] For its easy agreeability Russia received the miserly reward of a promise from Clinton to "upgrade" Russia's presence at G-7 meetings and to increase US investment in Russia—although even this was contingent on the chimerical scenario of a radically reformed Russia. He also pledged to help Russia join the WTO by 1998, but it was evident that Russia still had much to do to harmonize its legislation with WTO standards, and that WTO rules would not be bent to allow Russia easy entry.[63]

Yeltsin pulled another rabbit out of his hat at the summit, pledging that he would ask Parliament to ratify the START-2 treaty, which stipulated the elimination of land-based multiple-warhead missiles by 2003. Many Russian politicians opposed this on the grounds that these missiles were the backbone of Russia's nuclear force and had ensured nuclear parity with the

US. In exchange for ratification the US offered the paltry concession of extending by a year the deadline for dismantling nuclear warheads and set 2007 as the date for destroying missiles and silos.[64]

Yeltsin sought to reassure the West of Russia's benign intentions by cautioning Russians just after the summit that they should not provoke a major rift over NATO expansion. What Russia really needed, Yeltsin argued in a revealing statement implying he had caved in for monetary compensation, was economic cooperation with the West: I could have banged my shoes on a table at the summit as Soviet leaders did during the cold war, he declared, but "our choice is partnership, especially economic."[65] In similar fashion, the US' categorical refusal to make further concessions on NATO expansion forced Primakov, during talks with US Secretary of State Albright on May 2, to admit that "being realists, we understand that we need to have a relationship with NATO."[66] *Komsomol'skaia pravda* was unforgiving toward Yeltsin for his sellout, pronouncing the Helsinki summit a total "loss" for Russia, contrary to Yeltsin's starry-eyed claim that it had "opened prospects of establishing strategic stability and security in the 21st century" and that it forged an "equal partnership between Russia and the US." It asked rhetorically—and with incredulity—whether Yeltsin believed his own words.[67]

In a most revealing statement about the Russian leadership's motives, French Defense Minister Millon wholeheartedly welcomed the summit on the grounds that NATO and Yeltsin were "on the right track," above all *in defusing Russian opposition to expansion.*[68] Yeltsin and the Russian leadership, in other words, were, contrary to their anti-NATO rhetoric, *pro-NATO*. But because this was tantamount to open capitulation to the West, obfuscation was called for. Accordingly, Russian officials resorted to the worn-out tactic of claiming that Russia was fortifying its "anti-Western" alliances, this time with France. On the eve of President Chirac's visit to Moscow in early February, Russian officials proclaimed "special relations" with Paris and affirmed that the " 'closeness of positions' of both states on the problem of European security, and hence the question of NATO's expansion," would resolve Moscow's strategic dilemmas.[69] Primakov visited Paris—and Minsk—in April for the purpose of setting up an "anti-NATO" coalition, but some Russian analysts immediately saw the folly of trying to play the French card: "for all its anti-NATO sentiments," they pointed out, "France is returning to the alliance's military structure and will have to comply with the opinion of a majority of its members."[70]

France nevertheless remained Russia's privileged ally. Thus, in contrast with Chancellor Kohl's January 4 visit to Moscow, which "flopped," Chirac's February visit was said to have "opened up possibilities of greater cooperation between Russia and NATO." Chirac's announcement that a compromise could be found prior to the alliance summit in July[71] gave some Russians to assume that France displayed "an understanding of Russia's objections to NATO expansion,"[72] that Chirac favored a "middle option," an "interim solution" to a Russia-NATO charter between a purely political document sought by Washington and a purely legal one sought by Moscow. But others saw through this deceit, aware that while Chirac may have preferred "a gentler way of dealing with Moscow" on NATO expansion at February talks between Yeltsin and Chirac in Novo-Ogarevo, France would, as a member of NATO, act "within the framework of a long-established consensus." In this light, it was telling—and contrary to Primakov's assertion in October 1996 that France favored a binding Russia-NATO treaty—that Chirac declined to take a "definite position" on the binding nature of the NATO-Russian document.[73] By leaving it to NATO to dictate terms, France showed itself to be a proponent of NATO expansion.[74]

In an obvious attempt to prove his mettle against an aggressive NATO Primakov predicted that his upcoming meeting with NATO Secretary General Solana in late April would be "pretty tense."[75] But Primakov proved himself a paper tiger once again when he announced on April 11 that Russia would sign the agreement establishing relations with NATO, and confirmed what one *Segodnia* correspondent knew well: that NATO posed no threat to Russia *under its current leadership*, whose "threatening anti-NATO rhetoric" was intended solely for "Russian domestic consumption."[76] Indeed, as talks between Primakov and NATO General Secretary Solana on the finalization of the terms of the Russia-NATO treaty were wrapping up on May 14 Yeltsin termed NATO expansion the "most acute issue between Russia and the USA and NATO since the Cuban missile crisis," but also expressed his determination to sign the treaty, despite "misgivings" from senior Russian officials, journalists, and attacks from the left. So eager was Yeltsin to promote the West's agenda, in fact, that he urged that the date for the charter's signing be *moved up* to May 27, a move eagerly sought by NATO since this would allow the signing to be dispensed with well in advance of NATO's July meeting, where the alliance was to invite CEE nations to begin the accession process. The agreement to finalize the treaty, Western analysts noted, showed the "huge importance"

Russia placed on relations with the West; "at crucial times in the bargaining process, the personal intervention of [Yeltsin] . . . and his apparent desire to remain close to his Western friends, pushed the talks forward."[77]

Yeltsin nevertheless continued to advance the standard and hardly convincing argument that NATO expansion was inevitable and that Russia had no choice but to sign and minimize the risks. To political analyst Andrei Kortunov this argument proved that Yeltsin was interested not in Russia's security but only in retaining the support of Russia's financial oligarchs, who "want to keep the door open to Western investments and business." The role of the "IMF and the West in general" was thus "unmistakable, if unspoken" in Yeltsin's position on NATO expansion.[78]

On May 27 the Founding Act was initialed by Russia and NATO. By defining mutual relations it closed the book on the drawn-out expansion controversy and marked the Russian leadership's formal acquiescence to enlargement. That the actual signing went so smoothly came as a shock to most Western analysts who had long held that, particularly since late 1993 when Russia's foreign policy line putatively hardened vis-à-vis the West,[79] NATO expansion would catalyze "fierce opposition" within the Russian leadership. Others argued more realistically that Russia was too weakened to effectively block NATO expansion, although this only partly explained the cave-in,[80] for it was not mainly weakness that prevented Russia's Westernizers from opposing NATO. The fact was that they were in essence supportive of NATO and its policies and did not really oppose expansion.

Yeltsin resorted to more double-dealing at a meeting with parliamentary party leaders following the signing of the Founding Act by terming it a great victory that ensured the non-deployment of nuclear weapons on the territories of new NATO members and the non-use of the former Warsaw Pact's stores for this purpose. "Even a year ago NATO openly said Russia had no right to resist the enlargement plans," Yeltsin bragged. But "we changed this tendency."[81] How Russia did this, and how Russia had gotten the better of NATO was never specified.[82] Yeltsin also claimed that NATO had offered Russia attractive compensation in the form of political membership in the new "G-8," the planning of START-3 talks on reducing strategic weapons, and more IMF loans in the offing—all of which "*seem* to have convinced Mr. Yeltsin that Russia's status as a great power [wa]s being respected."[83]

Aware that this was meaningless recompense for Yeltsin's giving away the store, his Western overseers sought to make sure their ally in Moscow saved face, especially in view of President Clinton's explicit denial of Yeltsin's false claim that decisions opposed by Russia would not be adopted by NATO. Clinton laid down the line: Russia would cooperate with NATO but not work in it; only the North Atlantic Council would have the "prerogative of working out NATO's policy and strategy."[84]

The Founding Act was the culmination, as it were, of the NATO expansion charade, epitomized by Yeltsin's spurious boast that Russia had won the battle with NATO over expansion.[85] What is more, Russia continued to look "mostly to the West" and its financial institutions, as was underscored by Chubais' flight to Washington to win IMF financing for Russia's economic "reforms" even as the treaty talks were going on. P. Felgengauer's bitter observation could not have been more apt: Russian officials, he grumbled, were "so eager to clinch economic and financial rewards from the West—including an IMF commitment of continuing support—that they are ready to sign any vague 'Charter' [on NATO]. Then, after the signing, Yeltsin can 'give in' to political pressure and send the document to the State Duma for ratification."[86] Unlike most pro-Western analysts Felgengauer was not taken in by the declarations of opposition to NATO expansion from Russian policymakers.[87]

As if to confirm Felgengauer's analysis, just two days after the signing of the Founding Act the IMF made public its agreement to make available a long-delayed $700 million installment of a three-year, $10 billion credit to Russia—payment for its consent to NATO expansion. For their part, Gazprom officials anticipated stepped-up contracts in the West following the agreement, happy that "the enlargement of NATO to the East will be more than compensated by the enlargement of Gazprom to the West." What is more, financial deals, some of them directly linked to expansion, "would have been riskier, costlier or impossible had Mr. Yeltsin turned his back on the alliance and threatened a new confrontation with the West."[88] Here was an unadorned demonstration of how Russia's foreign policy was run in the interests of its financial oligarchs in collaboration with Western elites.

Among Russians the response to the Founding Act was immediate and varied. V. Lukin, who had expressed a wariness of PfP and NATO duplicity, praised the agreement as the "best that could be expected" under the current circumstances. A. Shokhin agreed, while director of ISKRAN S. Rogov, ecstatic over the "great success of Russian diplomacy," accepted Yeltsin's claim that Russia now had a "decisive say" in NATO decisions, that the Founding Act allowed Russia to "shape European security" and expressed confidence that NATO would not expand its military infrastructure.[89] Even Chief of the International Military Cooperation Section of the Defense Ministry Gen. Leonid Ivashov, a reputed anti-Western "hard-liner," welcomed the document and the "three noes" because they "reflect Moscow's greatest concerns related to . . . enlargement."[90]

Many who would be considered pro-Western, on the other hand, expressed dissatisfaction with the Act and with Yeltsin's conduct in Paris, among them a group of leading politicians and lawmakers which included Vice Chair of the Duma Defense Committee A. Arbatov, S. Karaganov, and V. Nikonov, President of the Politika Foundation.[91]

The claim of a "strategic partnership" with China was flaunted yet again by the leadership after the Founding Act in an attempt to counteract the effects of Yeltsin's sellout. But this, too, proved baseless, for the partnership was neither strategic nor a partnership: Russian-Chinese trade was on the decline, border agreements had stalled, and confidence-building measures were "more theater than substance." Russians were even worried that military technology purchased by China could be used against Russia itself.[92] What was advertised as an alliance with China was in reality a pseudo-alliance based on empty rhetoric, according to S. Oznobishchev of the Center for Strategic Assessments. Not only was Russian-Chinese trade declining but, Oznobishchev cautioned, Russia "must remember that China is a potential enemy . . . we must proceed with caution."[93] The reality was that Chinese leaders, "for economic and strategic reasons . . . see no good alternative to cooperative relations with the United States in the years ahead." For its part, a crisis-ridden, dependent Russia "could hardly afford an anti-Western stance."[94]

There were, moreover, obvious limits to the effectiveness of Russia's cooperation with other Asian nations. Analysts saw Iran and Iraq as weak counterweights to the West and viewed a strategic alliance with them, as with China, as more posturing than substance. The leadership exploited such relations in its deception as a vehicle to placate the opposition in Russia and to "demonstrate Russia's independence from the West." Despite hints of an anti-Western Russian-Iranian condominium, Moscow assured Washington in 1997 that it would limit its military cooperation with Iran, pledging in April 1997, for example, not to provide Iran with more submarines once its current contract with Teheran had expired.[95]

One of the most farcical episodes in the NATO expansion affair took place in May when US Secretary of State Albright, seeking to assuage

Russian concern that NATO states were lining up against it, announced that Russia's presence at the upcoming Denver G-7 meeting in June "should prove . . . to Russia and the world" that Russia's position had actually been enhanced, and promised that Yeltsin would be accepted at the meeting as "virtually" a "full participant." Why? "Part of this is a sense of being part of the group, of being there, having a discussion, being in a class photo, that is, being part of a family of nations that in fact makes decisions," Albright declared. And although the "ultimate act of inclusion" for Russia would be to be made a full member, US officials would only be "looking at that." Albright made no recommendations and refused to say whether Clinton would propose permanent membership for Russia, but she did make a promise that he would push to have Russia "more and more a part of our institutional systems." Even if Yeltsin did not become a member, Albright said, "the fact that he's here is a big deal."[96]

Clinton's Special Adviser on Russian affairs Strobe Talbott used similarly deceptive, overblown language in November of the following year when describing what he termed Russia's "achievements" in Europe. Talbott listed Russian membership in the ineffectual "G-8," Council of Europe, Arctic Council, Council of Baltic Sea States, Permanent Joint Council of the NATO-Russia Founding Act, and Control Group on the Balkans,[97] all part of the calculated effort by the West to portray Russia's weakness as strength. This was also small consolation for Russian diplomacy, and Western diplomats thus surely understood all too well Yeltsin adviser Migranian when he pointed out that the G-7 "has no serious significance for Russia," that Russian "membership" served merely to maintain the illusion that it was a great power. Because it was so weak, Russia, Migranian lamented, would be isolated in the G-7, "forced to play by the rules presented to it, rules worked out without its participation."[98]

As if this were not farcical enough, Yeltsin made the "sensational" announcement at the May 27 signing ceremony that Russian missiles targeted at the West would be disarmed. Here was yet another gratuitous— albeit totally meaningless—gift to his Western patrons. And as with similar instances in the past, steps had to be taken to minimize the damage: Yeltsin's spokesperson Yastrzhembsky immediately added the "correction" that the missiles would not be disarmed but would merely be targeted away from the Western states.[99]

Russian and Western leaders nevertheless seemed interested in pursuing the farce in as many directions as possible. In the aftermath of the Russia-

NATO summit, the OECD joined in the deception by signing a cooperation pact with Russia agreeing to help it liberalize its economy and meet OECD membership conditions "without," significantly, "giving a target date for Russia to join." Although the OECD accepted the principle of Russian membership, it admitted that formal membership was "some ways off" since Moscow would need time to "adapt to the group's free-market ideology"—and even though the OECD had already embraced CEE states. The upshot was a hollow agreement to establish two high-level meetings a year.[100] While Russian leaders placed a high priority on joining the OECD (and other organizations), OECD officials admitted that, as with the aforementioned "victories," it was not clear that Russia stood much to gain in the OECD beyond "symbolism of being part of the exclusive 'club'." Russian membership, they conceded, was a "distant prospect" at best.[101]

The chicanery continued in late May when Yeltsin warned just prior to his departing Moscow for Ukraine that any attempt by NATO to incorporate former Soviet republics would undermine East-West cooperation. But Western sources knew that "behind the bluster was a retreat from similar sentiments previously expressed about Poland and Hungary." Relations with Ukraine were another issue of vital strategic importance to Russia, and one which would also fall victim to the Russian leadership's dependence on the West, as one Western newspaper acknowledged when it called Yeltsin a "Russian President made in heaven for NATO." NATO expansion, moreover, was succeeding faster than its designers dared hope: one week after resigning itself to NATO expansion, Russia acknowledged Ukraine's independence, and an independent Ukraine, seen by the West as the "best single guarantee against any return of Russian imperialism," was "just the sort of stabilization of new and wannabe democracies that NATO ha[d] hoped to promote" in CEE. Of course, it was Yeltsin and his fellow "democrats" who saw to it that this all came about. The admission that Ukraine would not return to Russia's lap after all, as Russian elites expected after the split-up of the USSR, came when Yeltsin visited Kiev in May and signed agreements recognizing Ukraine's territorial integrity and sovereignty over the disputed Black Sea naval base of Sevastopol. Yeltsin had planned six times to visit Kiev and sign a friendship treaty but cancelled each time that Russian nationalists laid claim to Sevastopol. This time Yeltsin accepted the Ukraine's terms: a 20-year lease for continuing to base the Russian Black Sea Fleet in Sevastapol with rental payments acknowledging Ukrainian sovereignty and with berths in Sevastopol for the Ukrainian Black Sea Fleet.[102]

Although Ukraine's goal of NATO membership would cross Yeltsin's declared "bottom line" against NATO membership for Ukraine, the Baltic states, or any other part of the FSU,[103] even as Yeltsin issued "powerful" threats NATO made it "absolutely clear that the Baltic States continue to be eligible for . . . membership,"[104] thus demonstrating that they took neither him nor his "threats" seriously. Indeed, two days after the signing of the Founding Act Madeleine Albright urged the participants at the NATO Ministerial meeting at Sintra, Portugal to make sure that NATO expansion would continue and embrace European "democracies." The July NATO summit in Madrid which formally accepted the new members also agreed that five states (including the Baltics) would be the next group of prospective members.[105]

Primakov shifted the locus of Russian opposition to NATO expansion from CEE to the Baltics in late February when he gave notice that Baltic membership in NATO would "undermine Russia's relations" with NATO, and even threatened to end all relations with NATO and build up Russia's defenses if the Baltics were granted membership.[106] But in October Yeltsin proceeded to nullify Primakov's threats by signing a border treaty with Lithuania, the first such treaty between Russia and a Baltic country. He also offered the Baltics Russian security guarantees and warned that "if anyone decides to threaten Lithuania, he will have to deal with us." It is unlikely that many took him seriously, although the Duma, aware that the treaty would help pave the way for Lithuania's accession to NATO, had appealed to Yeltsin not to sign it.[107] At the November 10 Baltic summit in Palanga, Lithuania, the Baltic states formally rejected Yeltsin's offer of security guarantees[108]—but such enmity had not discouraged Russia from taking part in a U.S.-led NATO exercise the previous June, "Baltops 97," in the Baltic Sea, which involved NATO countries, the Baltic states, and Poland.[109]

Prime Minister Chernomyrdin also voiced Russia's objection to Baltic NATO membership in early September, repeated Moscow's concern over the mention of the Baltics in the July Madrid NATO Declaration on NATO expansion, and warned that Russia would not tolerate a revision of Kaliningrad's status.[110] But A. Fodorov, Head of the Center for Political Technologies, discerned the real direction of Moscow's policy in the Baltics when he predicted that the Russian government, as it had with NATO's expansion to CEE, would merely express its negative attitude toward

NATO expansion to the Baltics then take no action to stop it because "we are realists now"[111]—a sentiment Primakov seemed to echo in December when he asserted that Russia would not "keep on harping" about NATO expansion to the Baltics, that it was "not [the issue] uppermost in his mind."[112] Others, however, expressed concern at a report that Latvia was told at an August meeting between the military staffs of the Baltics and Denmark that its tiny defense budget threatened Baltic NATO membership. In addition, NATO was making regular inspections of Latvia's air force.[113]

Already worried about NATO expansion to the Baltics, the Duma in fall 1997 was watching even more anxiously Western military maneuvers in Kazakhstan and Uzbekistan, where 500 marines from Fort Bragg landed during the military exercise "Central Asian Batallion 97." In early October the Duma called on the Russian government to end its silence on the issue, notify NATO of its concern over activity so close to Russia's borders, and make it known with "appropriate action" that Russia would regard such maneuvers as hostile.[114] At a session of the Russia-NATO joint permanent military committee on December 4 Russian delegates also expressed concern that NATO had a secret agenda for bases and exercises near Russia's borders.[115]

Meanwhile, Russian-Ukraine relations were made even more tense by the NATO bulldozer, which continued on its unstoppable path, oblivious to Russia's March threat to boycott NATO-led exercises scheduled for August in the Crimea. Dubbed "Sea Breeze 97," the operation was almost entirely funded by the US and was reviled by Russian officials as "anti-Russian" and "provocative."[116] The objective of the maneuvers was to plan for a potential attack from an "ethnically-based party"—obviously a code name for Crimean Russians—and the neighboring country which backed them—obviously Russia.[117] By late August the exercise's theme had been revised to make it less obviously anti-Russian, but Russia's fears were not entirely allayed.[118] When they were finally held in late August Russian's Defense Ministry refused to send observers and Defense Minister Sergeev even postponed a scheduled visit to the Black Sea fleet so he would not be in Sevastopol on the day the exercises began.[119]

Russia and Yugoslavia

After the Dayton Accord Russia continued to grumble about the West's Balkan policy, which included objecting to the arrest of purported "war criminals," almost all of them Serbian—although once again Russian leaders were primarily concerned that the West had not consulted with them beforehand. Such implicit pro-Westernism was made explicit by Russia's support of the Western-backed candidate in the elections for President of the Bosnian Serbs.

Yugoslavia: Russian Relations with the West

Because the Yugoslavia issue lost its immediacy after the 1995 Dayton Accords, Russian officials in 1997 were reduced, as in 1996, to complaining that they had been left out of deliberations and other perceived slights. They did, however, join with the Western allies in delivering a "stern written message" to Croatian President Tujdman in late May warning that they would postpone the transfer to Croatian control of UN-administered enclaves unless Croatia lived up to its commitments in the 1995 peace agreement to allow exiled ethnic Serbs to return.[120]

Primakov complained to British Foreign Minister Cook in July that NATO raids to arrest accused Bosnian Serb war criminals were hindering peacekeeping in the region and reprimanded NATO for failing to consult with Russia on the matter.[121] The RFM again objected in August to US and British attempts to arrest Bosnian Serbs accused of war crimes, but Russia could do nothing in the face of NATO's power.[122] The next month Primakov conferred with French Foreign Minister Vedrine on the Bosnian situation and emphasized that the Dayton accords should not be at the expense of the dissolution or partition of Bosnia's Republika Srpska (Serb Republic).[123] The RFM also expressed unhappiness over NATO plans to jam "inflammatory" Bosnian Serb broadcasts.[124] There was nothing new in these protests against Western treatment of the Serbs, since Russian officials were merely pursuing their strategy of appearing to be "evenhanded" as they kowtowed to the West's anti-Serb policies.

In spite of Western accusations that Russia was blocking OSCE plans to supervise parliamentary elections in Serbian-controlled territory in Bosnia and undermining efforts to shore up the Dayton peace accord,[125] Moscow adopted a flexible position at the August 21 OSCE meeting in Vienna, supporting the Western-backed Bosnian Serb President Plavsic and thus mitigating Western fears that Russia would impede OSCE supervision of the October parliamentary elections.[126] Weeks later the NATO-Russia Permanent Council met to form a working group to elaborate the principles and tasks of peacekeeping, including those in Bosnia. Fearing that NATO might try to detain indicted war criminals in Bosnia without prior Russian approval, Primakov reiterated Russia's position that UNSC or OSCE approval (for the use of force in peacekeeping operations) must be requested in advance.[127] Russian troops nevertheless participated, at least as observers, in the early October NATO-led SFOR operation, which took control of Bosnian Serb transmitters near Sarajevo.[128]

Notes

[1] RIA Novosti, May 19, 1997; *OECD Economic Surveys 1997-1998: Russian Federation* (Paris: OECD, 1997), p. 5.

[2] Reuter, October 7, 1997.

[3] *Segodnia*, October 18, 1997, p. 3.

[4] Interfax, November 6, 1997.

[5] Ibid., December 25, 1997.

[6] *The Independent* (London), March 12, 1997, p. 12.

[7] Interfax, May 21, 1997.

[8] Reuters World Service, March 17, 1997. As a sign that the international financial community was "wedded to Chubais," the IMF had in early 1995 demanded that he, the mastermind of Russia's dash to a Western-style system and "point man" for Russia in the West, be put in charge of economic policy as one of the conditions for extending a $6.4 billion loan. See Peter Reddaway, *The Washington Post*, August 24, 1997, p. C1, and *The eXile*, September 3, 1997.

[9] *Sovetskaia Rossiia*, April 29, 1997, pp. 1-2; *Financial Times*, May 23, 1997, p. 2; *The New York Times*, May 22, 1997, p. A1.

[10] The *eXile*, November 20, 1997.

[11] *Nezavisimaia gazeta*, September 19, 1997, pp. 1-2, in *CDPSP*, Vol. 49, No. 38, October 22, 1997, p. 7.

[12] *Kommersant-daily*, April 18, 1997, p. 3.

[13] *Rossiiskie vesti*, July 5, 1997, p. 3.

[14] *RFE/RL Newsline*, No. 172, Part I, December 4, 1997.

[15] *The Washington Post*, December 4, 1997, p. A22.

[16] *Sovetskaia Rossiia*, December 20, 1997, p. 1.

[17] ITAR-TASS, November 5, 1997.

[18] AAP Newsfeed, December 4, 1997.

[19] Tokyo Kyodo, May 27, 1997, in *FBIS*-WEU-97-146.

[20] *Segodnia*, June 21, 1997, p. 3.

[21] Yoshikazu Sakamoto, "Democratization, Social Movements, and World Order," in Bjorn Hettne, ed., *International Political Economy: Understanding Global Disorder* (London: Zed Books, 1995), p. 130.

[22] *RFE/RL Newsline*, No. 58, Part I, June 23, 1997.

[23] Reuters, October 14, 1997.

[24] *RFE/RL Newsline*, No. 131, Part II, October 3, 1997; *The New York Times*, November 11, 1997, p. A10.

[25] *The New York Times*, November 11, 1997, p. A27.

[26] *Boston Globe*, October 23, 1997, p. A2.

[27] *Kommersant-daily*, June 24, 1997, p. 3; *International Herald Tribune*, June 23, 1997, p. 2.

[28] Reuters, November 21, 1997; *Nezavisimaia gazeta*, November 21, 1997, pp. 1, 4.

[29] Russian NTV, November 23, 1997.

[30] Emphasis mine. *RFE/RL Newsline*, No. 165, Part I, November 21, 1997; Julie Moffett, *RFE/RL*, November 21, 1997.

[31] *The New York Times*, November 17, 1997, p. A1, and October 16, 1997, p. A1.

[32] *Interfax*, January 4, 1997, in *FBIS*-SOV-97-003. Bruce D. Porter, "Russia and Europe After the Cold War: The Interaction of Domestic and Foreign Policies," in Celeste A. Wallander, ed., *The Sources of Russian Foreign Policy After the Cold War* (Boulder: Westview, 1996), p. 127, characterizes post-Soviet Russia's threat environment, including NATO, as negligible.

[33] *Izvestiia*, January 9, 1997, p. 3.

[34] Reuter European Community Report, January 7, 1997.

[35] ITAR-TASS, January 8, 1997.

[36] *Interfax*, January 4, 1997, in *FBIS*-SOV-97-003; *Rossiiskie vesti*, January 9, 1997 p. 1.

[37] *The Daily Telegraph*, February 22, 1997, p. 12; *The New York Times*, February 19, 1997, p. A1.

[38] *Denver Rocky Mountain News*, February 27, 1997, p. 36A; Munich *Sueddeutsche Zeitung*, October 8, 1996, p. 4, in *FBIS*-WEU-96-196; Alexei Pushkov, "A Compromise with NATO?" *International Affairs* (Moscow), No. 3, March 1997, p. 17.

[39] *Los Angeles Times*, July 7, 1997, p. B5. See also United Press International, October 7, 1997, and a similarly ominous warning to Russia by Robert Smith, the US representative to the Russia-NATO Council, that the US could come to the defense of Europe within a day, and that if Russia ever threatened Europe, the US could quickly expand NATO. Truth in Media, April 29, 1998.

[40] *The New York Times*, February 21, 1997, p. A6.
[41] Reuters North American Wire, February 3, 1997.
[42] *Nezavisimaia gazeta*, May 23, 1997, pp. 1-2.
[43] Ibid.
[44] *Die Welt*, May 7, 1997, in *FBIS*-WEU-97-127, May 7, 1997.
[45] *Sovetskaia Rossiia*, May 17, 1997, p. 1.
[46] Ibid., February 27, 1997, p. 7.
[47] Interfax, May 15, 1997. See also the piece by S. Baburin, State Duma Deputy Speaker and Chair of the Anti-NATO Commission, in *Pravda-5*, May 22, 1997, p. 3.
[48] Reuters North American Wire, May 20, 1997.
[49] ITAR-TASS, April 9, 1997; *Kommersant-daily*, February 12, 1997, p. 2.
[50] *Kommersant-daily*, March 18, 1997, p. 1.
[51] Even *Sovetskaia Rossiia*, April 29, 1997, p. 2, fell for the line that Chubais' position on NATO expansion was "fundamentally at variance" with Primakov, who insisted that Russia would "never and not for any price reconcile itself to NATO expansion."
[52] AP Worldstream, February 22, 1997.
[53] Ibid., May 15, 1997.
[54] *Christian Science Monitor*, February 24, 1997, p. 1.
[55] Emphasis mine. Interfax, March 3, 1997, in *FBIS*-SOV-97-062; Iu. Davydov, "Rossiia i NATO: 'posle bala'," *SShA*, No. 1, January 1998, p. 3.
[56] Official Kremlin International News Broadcast, May 24, 1997. See also *Kommersant-daily*, April 12, 1997, p. 4.
[57] Official Kremlin International News Broadcast, March 27, 1997, p. 1. See also *Kommersant-daily*, March 26, 1997, p. 5.
[58] Agence France Presse, May 4, 1997. The EU states had recalled their ambassadors from Iran following the implication by a German court of senior Iranian officials in the 1992 assassination of four Iranian Kurdish dissidents in Berlin.
[59] *OMRI Daily Digest*, No. 57, Part I, March 21, 1997, and No. 61, Part I, March 27, 1997.
[60] *Nezavisimaia gazeta*, March 27, 1997, p. 1; *The Washington Post*, March 22, 1997, p. A1. Even arch-Westerner Stanislav Kondrashov belittled the summit, terming it "Yeltsin's fiasco," in *Izvestiia*, March 27, 1997, p. 2.
[61] *Izvestiia*, March 28, 1997, p. 3.
[62] *The Boston Globe*, March 22, 1997, p. A1.
[63] *Financial Times*, March 22, 1997, p. 1; *The Moscow Times*, April 16, 1997; *Journal of Commerce*, April 3, 1997, p. 2A.
[64] *The New York Times*, March 22, 1997, Sect. 1, pp. 1, 6.
[65] Agence France Presse, March 26, 1997.

[66] *Financial Times*, May 2, 1997, p. 2.

[67] *Komsomol'skaia Pravda*, March 28, 1997, p. 3.

[68] Agence France Presse, March 22, 1997.

[69] *Moskovskii komsomolets*, January 31, 1997, p. 2.

[70] *Kommersant-daily*, April 9, 1997, p. 1. For a similarly realistic view of France's position on NATO expansion, see Reuters World Service, February 6, 1997, and Interfax, January 31, 1997, in *FBIS-SOV-97-022*.

[71] Les Echos, February 1997, p. 52, in *FBIS-WEU-97-023*.

[72] *Rossiiskiie Vesti*, February 4, 1997, p. 1.

[73] *Nezavisimaia gazeta*, February 4, 1997, pp. 1-2.

[74] Other analyses which saw France as an "enthusiastic proponent of both EU and NATO expansion" include *The Irish Times*, February 28, 1997, p. 12, and Interfax, October 8, 1996, in *FBIS-SOV-96-197*.

[75] Brussels *Le Soir*, 14 April 1997, p. 6, in *FBIS-WEU-97-104*.

[76] *Segodnia*, May 15, 1997, p. 4.

[77] *Financial Times*, May 15, 1997, p. 3; ITAR-TASS, May 7 and 23, 1997. See also the analysis of Vladimir Nadein in *Izvestiia*, May 6, 1997, p. 3, which stressed Russia's cave-in on virtually every issue.

[78] *International Herald Tribune*, May 27, 1997, p. 1.

[79] Suzanne Crow, "Russia Asserts Its Strategic Agenda," *RFE/RL Research Report*, Vol. 2, No. 50, December 17, 1993, pp. 1-2, 7; Idem, "Why Has Russian Foreign Policy Changed?" *RFE/RL Research Report*, Vol. 3, No. 18, May 6, 1994, p. 1; Michael McFaul, "Revolutionary Ideas, State Interests and Russian Foreign Policy," in Vladimir Tismaneanu, ed., *Political Culture and Civil Society in Russia and the New States of Eurasia* (Armonk, NY: M.E. Sharpe, 1995), p. 27. Even Yuri N. Afanasyev, "Seems Like Old Times? Russia's Place in the World," *Current History*, Vol. 93, No. 585, October 1994, pp. 305-7, bemoaned Russia's imperialist impulses.

[80] Michael Mandelbaum, *The Dawn of Peace in Europe* (New York: The Twentieth Century Fund, 1996), p. 59.

[81] Interfax, 19 May, 1997, in *FBIS-SOV-97-139*; Agentsvo informatsionnoe Ekho Moskvy, May 29, 1997.

[82] See Josef Joffe, *Sueddeutsche Zeitung*, 27 May 1997, p. 4, in *FBIS-WEU-97-147*.

[83] Emphasis mine. *The Economist* (US edition), May 17, 1997, p. 55.

[84] *Segodnia*, May 16, 1997, p. 3.

[85] Agentsvo informatsionnoe Ekho Moskvy, May 29, 1997. The editorial in *The New York Times*, May 15, 1997, p. A28, admitted that Russia gained nothing from the May 14 Primakov-Solana negotiations which finalized an agreement on Russia-NATO relations. Another "dissimulator" on the nature of the Russia-NATO treaty was S. Rogov, Director of ISKRAN. See RIA Novosti, May 29, 1997. One analysis

which acknowledged that NATO sought to keep Russia in its "proper place" was Alexei Pushkov, *Rossiiskaia gazeta*, August 13, 1997, p. 7. *Moskovskii komsomolets*, May 29, 1997, pp. 1, 3, termed the Founding Act Russia's "surrender"; *Pravda*, May 29, 1997, p. 1, said that the Founding Act gave NATO a "tremendous unilateral advantage."

[86] *St. Petersburg Times* (Russia), May 19, 1997.

[87] *Segodnia*, June 23, 1995, p. 9. See a similar position in *Sovetskaia Rossiia*, October 25, 1997.

[88] *The International Herald Tribune*, May 27, 1997, p. 1. See also Tokyo Kyodo, May 27, 1997, in *FBIS*-WEU-97-146; *St. Petersburg Times* (Russia), May 26, 1997.

[89] Interfax, May 15, 1997; *Izvestiia*, May 27, 1997, p. 4; *The Moscow Times*, May 16, 1997; *Nezavisimoe voennoe obozrenie*, No. 1, January 11-18, 1997, p. 4.

[90] Interfax, May 19, 1997.

[91] Baltic News Service, May 14, 1997.

[92] Reuters, May 9, 1997. See also *The New York Times*, May 1, 1997, p. A3, BBC News, November 9, 1997, and *Literaturnaia gazeta*, April 16, 1997, p. 5.

[93] *The Hindustan Times*, November 11, 1997. See also Interfax, October 1, 1999.

[94] *The New York Times*, September 13, 1999, p. A7. Some pro-Yeltsin observers swallowed the "strategic partnership" line. See *Nezavisimaia gazeta*, March 22, 1997, p. 1. See also Inter Press Service, August 26, 1999.

[95] *The New York Times*, April 12, 1997, p A5.

[96] *The Denver Post*, May 18, 1997, p. A21.

[97] *RFE/RL Newsline*, Vol. 2, No. 211, Part I, November 2, 1998.

[98] *Nezavisimaia gazeta*, May 27, 1997, pp. 1-2.

[99] *RFE/RL Newsline*, Part I, No. 40, May 28, 1997.

[100] Reuter, May 27, 1997.

[101] *RFE/RL Newsline*, No. 133, Part I, October 8, 1997.

[102] *The Baltimore Sun*, May 28, 1997, p. 8A, and June 4, 1997, p. 21A.

[103] Ibid.

[104] Baltic News Service, May 27, 1997; See also a statement on the inevitable accession of the Baltic states to NATO by German Defense Minister Ruehe in The Reuter European Community Report, May 8, 1997.

[105] Jonathan Deane, "NATO Enlargement: Coping With Act II," in Ted Galen Carpenter and Barbara Conry, eds., *NATO Enlargement: Illusions and Reality* (Washington, D.C.: The Cato Institute, 1998), pp. 121-2.

[106] *The Moscow Times*, February 28, 1997, p. 4; *Pravda-5*, March 4, 1997, pp. 1, 3.

[107] *RFE/RL Newsline*, No. 144, Part I, October 27, 1997.

[108] *Segodnia*, November 12, 1997, p. 3; *RFE/RL Newsline*, No. 157, Part I, November 11, 1997.

[109] Deutsche Presse-Agentur, June 5, 1997.

[110] Interfax, September 3, 1997.

[111] Reuters, November 10, 1997.

[112] BBC News, December 16, 1997. During a March press conference with British Foreign Minister Rifkind, Primakov termed NATO expansion to the Baltics "absolutely unacceptable," and threatened to take several steps in response. See *Pravda-5*, March 4, 1997, p. 1. See also *Izvestiia*, December 23, 1997, p. 3.

[113] *Rossiiskaia gazeta*, November 13, 1997, p. 7; ITAR-TASS, September 19, 1997.

[114] *Rossiiskaia gazeta*, October 8, 1997, p. 6.

[115] Reuters, December 5, 1997; ITAR-TASS, December 4, 1997. The relative inactivity in the face of such a massive intrusion by NATO into the territory of the FSU makes statements to the effect that Russia increasingly demanded acceptance of its great power role in NATO, the former Yugoslavia, the near abroad, and the Middle East, "even if this leads to a clash of interest with the West," clearly unsubstantiated. See Peter Truscott, *Russia First: Breaking with the West* (London: I.B. Tauris, 1997), p. 36.

[116] Agence France Presse, March 25, 1997.

[117] *Sunday Times*, March 20, 1997.

[118] Reuter, Associated Press, August 23, 1997.

[119] *Segodnia*, August 27, 1997, p. 4.

[120] *The New York Times*, May 28, 1997, p. A9. On Croatia's role in the Balkan conflict see the paper presented by Danir Mirkovic to the AAASS, Seattle, November 20-3, 1997.

[121] *The Scotsman* (Glasgow), July 15, 1997, p. 12.

[122] *Rossiiskaia gazeta*, August 13, 1997, p. 7.

[123] *RFE/RL Newsline*, No. 113, Part I, September 9, 1997.

[124] *RFE/RL*, September 15, 1997.

[125] *Financial Times*, August 22, 1997, p. 2.

[126] *The Independent* (London), August 22, 1997, p. 15.

[127] *RFE/RL*, September 29, 1997.

[128] *RFE/RL Newsline*, No. 130, Part I, October 2, 1997.

9 1998: Economic Crisis and Mounting Anti-Westernism

The Domestic Setting

As Russia's economy continued to slide, a disturbing report was issued in early 1998 by Finance Minister Livshits which expressed concern that practically all growth in 1997 (however miniscule) had been in raw materials—"not a very good sign," as he put it.[1] This put a real damper on the government's jubilant claims that the economy was finally entering a period of sustained growth. Similarly gloomy reports came out in May which revealed that Russia's GDP had declined a staggering 83% between 1991 and 1997—triple the losses sustained in WWII. Industrial output plummeted 81%, agriculture 63%, and capital investment fell 92%. Housing commissions were down by 44% from 1990 to 1997, retail trade fell 36%, and the services market turnover declined by 46%.[2] This was an economic crisis of catastrophic proportions, but Yeltsin announced optimistically in September 1997 that the "stabilization" of the financial sphere and the naming of his leading adviser, Chubais, "world's best finance minister" by the Europeans were successes which in tandem made it possible for Russia to "gradually decline" IMF assistance. Westernizers interpreted this as proof Russia was "once again laying claim to the role of a world power."[3]

Yeltsin dismissed the government in late March 1998 then announced plans to sack over 200,000 state employees and slash $6.7 billion in spending, both part of the Kudrin-Fischer program agreed with the IMF, the Fischer being Stanley Fischer, First Deputy Managing Director for the IMF. Deputy Finance Minister Kudrin legitimized the cuts on the ground that they would "actually brighten the national mood" by making possible government payments to those employees who remained on government payroll.[4] Yeltsin and Kudrin quickly denied that the government had approved the program, however, prompting Martin Gilman, IMF representative in Russia, to insist that the job cuts formed a "critical part of IMF support for the 1998 program."[5]

Then in August 1998 Russia became a victim of the global economic crisis as its economy underwent a virtual meltdown. In its wake mass layoffs hit all sectors, including highly-paid professions. For the first time in post-Soviet Russia's short life the savings of the top one-third of Russians were wiped out with the collapse of the ruble.[6] Russian agriculture was decimated, its output having already declined 64% in 1997 from its 1990 level as total agricultural capital investment had fallen sixteen times in terms of 1991 prices.[7] During 1998 alone the already staggering number of Russians below the poverty line rose another 25%.[8]

Immediately following the August crash Chubais rushed to Washington purportedly to discuss business connected to United Electrical Systems, the company Yeltsin had recently named him to head, but it was quickly made known that the real purpose of the trip was to plead for money from the West—which directly contradicted Chubais' recent boast that Russia no longer needed financial assistance.[9] Yeltsin had also appointed Chubais special presidential envoy to influence financial organizations[10] which meant, to one observer, that Russia was now "to be run by the International Monetary Fund for the benefit of the Russian oligarchy."[11] Russia's subordination to the West was also reflected in the fact that Yeltsin was not invited to the main discussion at the Birmingham G-7 meeting on Southeast Asian financial problems—for obvious reasons, given that Russia itself was still reeling from the economic crisis in Asia, and contrary to the insistence of Russian officials and some Western analysts that Yeltsin participated on an "equal footing" in the G-7.[12]

Western observers no longer apologized for the Yeltsin leadership, whose incompetence and greed had clearly become a liability and an embarrassment to world capitalism—although Western capital did continue to support Yeltsin as the best alternative to the communists. The robber capitalists may have been "sons of bitches," but "at least they're our sons of bitches" was one characterization of the West's support. Western observers also attacked Yeltsin's "strong-arm tactics" in support of "sham" regional elections conducted in June 1998.[13]

The cataclysmic economic and other shocks in 1998 engendered an exceeding pessimism about the country's fate: over 90% of the Russian people foresaw social upheavals in Russia in the near future,[14] a sentiment which spurred M. Shmakov, Chair of Russia's main trade union organization and a long-time champion of the Yeltsin leadership, to call for mass action against the government's social measures, which he attacked as a violation of the "social partnership."[15] In some respects, Yeltsin's post-Soviet edifice seemed to be disintegrating in ways reminiscent of the latter

Gorbachev years. Indeed, the threat of unrest was so palpable by early July that Yeltsin was compelled to warn openly against attempts by military "extremists" and "fascists" to seize power.[16]

Yeltsin had to respond to the alarming set of events with extraordinary measures. Accordingly, on a September day he without warning replaced Prime Minister Kiriyenko with Foreign Minister Primakov, who had been supported by the left opposition, including the Communists. In the ensuing outcry predictions abounded that Primakov and his associates, a number of them Communists (including Masliukov, who was named Finance Minister)—albeit with a social democratic orientation—would institute hard-line and anti-market measures. This proved grossly inaccurate, however, and a more reasoned assessment of Primakov's government recognized that his principal aim was to stabilize Russia's market economy "without upsetting the existing interests on which Mr. Yeltsin's power base has existed for the past seven years. He will seek stabilization. The politically influential bankers [will] be rehabilitated."[17]

The Foreign Policy Setting

Apart from NATO and Yugoslavia, the principal issues for Russian foreign policy were relations with non-Western regimes, above all, Iran and Iraq. A Russian journalist trenchantly characterized Yeltsin's foreign policies in early 1998 as having served "American interests" on "such controversial issues" as NATO expansion, Iraq and the sale of nuclear technology to Iran.[18] This trend was maintained in 1998.

The issue of Russian-Iranian relations continued to dominate Russia's agenda in 1998, flaring up in March when Russia held firm to its refusal to comply with US demands that it cancel the Bushehr nuclear power project in Iran which was, the US charged, being used for non-peaceful purposes.[19] But even as Russia denied such charges Russians welcomed West Europe's sympathy for their opposition to the US line in Iran and applauded West Europeans for their willingness to hold a "critical dialogue" and engage in trade with Teheran.[20]

Nevertheless, Russia sought to avoid unduly antagonizing the US, and Chernomyrdin issued a decree in January 1998 tightening controls on the export of military and civilian technologies to Iran.[21] Russia also acquiesced to US dictates on Iran in early March when it fired Energy Minister V.

Mikhalkov, who was extremely unpopular in Washington for engineering Russia's nuclear ties with Iran and for calling for nuclear competition with the US. Mikhalkov had, not coincidentally, been locked in a power struggle with Chubais and Nemtsov.[22] In May the US welcomed Yeltsin's "helpful comments" on the enforcement of export controls to deter Russian companies from selling missile technology to Iran.[23] And Russia (with the EU) agreed to tighten controls over the export of weapons technology to Iran after the Clinton administration waived sanctions against foreign companies doing business in Iran and pledged that it would seek legislation to head off sanctions against businesses that operated in Cuba.[24]

As with Iran and other issues, when dealing with Iraq Yeltsin found himself in the familiar position of "trying to appease nationalist sentiment at home without causing too much damage to relations with Russia's . . . Western partners" since Western—above all, IMF—support remained crucial to Russia's "reforms."[25] West Europeans joined Russia in criticizing US policy toward Iraq as dangerously shortsighted and far too prone to resort to military force,[26] although Primakov rejected a non-binding Duma resolution in early February asking Yeltsin to review Russia's adherence to UN sanctions on the issue.[27] Russia and West Europe both had serious misgivings about lifting sanctions against Iraq, as they feared the sale of Iraqi oil would flood the world market, lower world oil prices and drastically reduce Russia's export sales, especially since lower oil prices were already decimating Russia's hard currency earnings.[28]

Yeltsin aides in February were again called on to minimize the fallout from another of his diatribes, this time involving his warning that a US attack against Iraq could cause World War III. Officials gave their familiar assurances to the US that Yeltsin would never consider military measures if such an attack took place.[29] Nevertheless, in early November the RFM issued a statement of "deep concern" about Iraq's October 31 decision to end cooperation with UN inspectors and warned Iraq to "weigh scrupulously" the consequences.[30] But when asked whether Russia would call a UNSC meeting if the US attacked Iraq over its refusal to allow inspections, Russian UN Ambassador Lavrov was characteristically evasive: "I am not in the 'if' business . . . We want information now. On the basis of this information we would be taking our position."[31] Moscow was "resigned to the US attack on Iraq" and "too preoccupied" with its own economic troubles to focus on the issue in any case.[32]

After the US and British bombing of Iraq in December commentators predicted that the "close ties Russia and the [West] have enjoyed since the collapse of the Soviet Union in 1991" would be damaged. Moscow recalled its ambassador from Washington, something it had not done even during the Soviet period, promised to cancel joint military exercises, and reportedly put its nuclear fleet on alert.[33] But the inevitable backtracking ensued, aimed at assuaging Western apprehensions and returning to the path of "stable relations" with the West: reports that Russian submarines had been put on alert were flatly denied and interviews stressed "positive developments" in relations with the West. And Russia continued to oblige the West when it initially objected to US-backed plans to strengthen Bosnia's central government then "accommodated" the West at the December Madrid meeting of the Peace Implementation Council for Bosnia by giving it "everything [it] wanted."[34]

A week later Primakov clarified his threat to form a "strategic triangle" with China and India by affirming that he had not made a "formal proposal" to either and insisted that his threat had simply been intended to explain how a "partnership between the three powers could reliably stabilize the situation in the [South Asian] region." He admitted that such an alliance was problematic at best, given that "a lot depends on the politics of India and China," and gave assurances that a "military bloc," which would "in no case . . . be directed against a third country," was not Russia's objective.[35]

The reality was that Moscow had displayed such a supposedly militantly "anti-Western" posture at this time because it had to, given the level of rage and frustration at the Yeltsin government's Westernizing "reforms," which had ruined so many Russian lives—especially after the August economic crash. Anti-Western, anti-Yeltsin sentiment was at an all-time high; the leadership's pretense at independence vis-à-vis the West was therefore *directly proportional* to the mounting disquiet. And the essence of Yeltsin's policies remained pro-Western through and through.

Russia and NATO

The salience for Russia of NATO's expansion to the Baltics increased in 1998 at the same time as the controversy over the expansion to CEE wound down. In January a "new chapter" in the Baltic expansion saga was written, capped by the signing of a Charter of Partnership between the Baltic states and the US which affirmed the objective of Baltic integration into Western institutions, including NATO. Apart from this, however, in its official statements the US, clearly mindful that overly hasty action could antagonize Russia, adopted a noncommittal approach to the question of Baltic membership in NATO.[36] And well it should, for the Duma sounded the alarm by characterizing the Partnership Charter as a step toward Baltic NATO membership and incompatible with the Founding Act.[37] Primakov nevertheless played down the Charter days later in a speech in Stockholm by characterizing it as a "normal development" which did not contradict Russian interests. He also cautioned, however, (as did Yeltsin in May) that Baltic membership in NATO could damage relations with Russia.[38]

Nevertheless, Yeltsin aide S. Prikhodko put NATO on notice in late August 1998 that Moscow drew a "red line" for expansion at the former Soviet states and would "revise relations" with NATO in the event of such expansion, even as he reassured the West that "we do not have the slightest wish to return to confrontation," a statement which surely caused no quaking in NATO boots. Prikhodko also expressed satisfaction that "the most pressing and rather complicated questions are now seen by Russia's partners through a prism of cooperation with Moscow."[39] In the same vein, Foreign Minister Ivanov insisted two months later that Russia's foreign policy goal was continuity, with no "radical changes," and neutralized Prikhodko's warning by assuring NATO that "when Russia says that there is some kind of red line, it should not be thought that tomorrow it will be putting an ultimatum to somebody." If a threat to Russia arose, he noted, it would be assessed "through a different prism."[40] This was put into practical effect in early June 1998 with the creation, on Russia's initiative, of the Euro-Atlantic Disaster Response Coordination Center, viewed by Russia as the most "significant step toward 'productive cooperation' between Russia and NATO since the signing of the Founding Act."[41]

NATO expansion to the Baltics took on a special urgency for Russia's leaders in July of 1999 after the second annual meeting of the US-Baltic Partnership Commission. Already stung by NATO's steamroller tactics in Kosovo, they were forced to endure the humiliation of Strobe Talbott's pronouncement that Baltic NATO membership was practically "inevitable," thereby "dismiss[ing] Russia's opposition as unlikely to prevent the three nations from joining the alliance." Talbott then rubbed Russia's nose in it, blithely asserting that NATO had already expanded and carried out military strikes against Yugoslavia in the face of Russian "opposition."[42] This was an obvious provocation, but Russia's leaders uttered not a word in protest.

NATO's humiliation of Russia continued unabated. In mid-June 1998 Defense Minister Sergeev took NATO to task for notifying him of the start of military exercises held in the former USSR only after they had begun. In response, Russian officials hurriedly summoned V. Zavarzin, Russia's representative to NATO, back to Moscow—although they refused to say directly whether it was in protest against the exercises.[43] British Foreign Secretary Cook and US Defense Secretary Cohen were insistent, however, that both Zavarzin and Sergeev had been "aware of the discussions that took place" on the issue, and Chair of the US Joint Chiefs of Staff Hugh Shelton maintained that Russia had expressed concern not over the exercises but over their timing.[44]

Russia's Defense Ministry ignored an August 1998 invitation from the Lithuanian Defense Ministry to observe PfP exercises named "Baltic Challenge 98" in Klaipeda, Latvia,[45] although Russia did agree to participate in other PfP exercises, including "Cooperative Assembly 98" in Albania in August—but only on the condition that NATO promised to keep it "politically sterile"[46]—and "Sea Breeze 98," PfP maneuvers in the Ukraine. Some Russian officials legitimized Russian participation on the grounds that it was a "depoliticized" and "strictly humanitarian" operation,[47] but less sanguine officials observed ironically that when NATO claims that its exercises are depoliticized and aimed at training troops against drug trafficking, terrorism, and the like, "all we can do is smile."[48]

Others were concerned that NATO's influence in other parts of the FSU was increasing, especially in Central Asia and the Transcaucasus where US peacekeeping exercises and training of military specialists, aimed at blocking Russia's presence in the region, were taking place right under Russia's nose. Such apprehension seemed justified in light of NATO Secretary General Solana's tour of the Caucasian republics in late September, even as the flagship US Sixth Fleet patrolled the Black Sea.[49]

The military's concerns over NATO apparently were not serious enough to prevent Russia from sending a military unit in May to NATO exercises in Denmark, a first for Russian troops.[50] Indeed, the exercises elicited Western congratulations to the Joint Permanent Council for having "played its role to perfection" in toning down Russian belligerence toward NATO, and to Russia for "playing the game" which NATO dictated.[51] Nor did Russian diplomats display much antagonism toward NATO Council officials in late February with whom they were meeting to arrange joint Russia-NATO anti-terrorism teams.[52] Quite the contrary, Defense Minister Sergeev praised the Council for "allowing Russia's voice to be heard."[53]

Russia and Yugoslavia

In direct contradiction to its professed affinity for Milosevic and the Serbian people Moscow continued to support anti-Serb sanctions in the UNSC, even as it protested against NATO's one-sidedly ignoring Kosovar Albanian transgressions. Aware that it had to toe the Western line or be deprived of financial aid, however, the Russian government delivered a message from NATO to Belgrade: end the war or face air strikes. Russia's pro-Western policy in 1999 was capped by its voting for UNSC Resolution 1199, which in essence sanctioned NATO force against Belgrade.

Yugoslavia: Russian Relations with the West

In response to the unrest in Yugoslavia's Kosovo region, US Secretary of State Albright urged the Contact Group in late March to pressure Serbia to restore Kosovo's autonomy, but Russia, along with the other four West European Contact Group states, was reluctant to impose sanctions on Belgrade only two days after it had made the concession of allowing Albanian language instruction in the region.[54] Nevertheless, in early April Russia made the "extremely difficult" decision to support the West by voting for an arms embargo on Belgrade which could be lifted only if the Milosevic government agreed to enter into talks with Kosovo on its political status. According to one source Moscow hoped that this action would persuade Milosevic, who had specifically asked the Russian delegation to veto the resolution, to "take this warning to heart." *Sovetskaia Rossiia* criticized Russia's leaders for "delud[ing] Russian public opinion" on the issue since, the newspaper argued, Kosovo was an internal affair and not within the purview of the Contact Group.[55]

The Duma achieved a historic first in mid-June with the passage of a resolution praising Yeltsin for his recent meeting with Milosevic while it chided "several Western countries" on the issue. They were referring to Yeltsin's mid-June meeting with Milosevic in Moscow which produced a joint statement reaffirming the principle of preservation of the territorial integrity and respect for the sovereignty of Yugoslavia, and deploring terrorism, separatism and armed actions affecting the civilian population.[56] The statement was a response to heavy fighting in Kosovo which had resumed on June 14, the eve of NATO's "Operation Determined Falcon" exercise scheduled to take place in Albania and Macedonia and which was aimed at deterring a Serb crackdown on Kosovo separatists. The exercise was deliberately timed to step up pressure on Milosevic ahead of his upcoming Moscow talks with Yeltsin.[57]

The anti-Yeltsin forces and "hard-liners" also sounded off on the subject of Kosovo. General L. Ivashov, for example, warned in June that a new cold war could erupt if NATO intervened militarily in Kosovo without UN approval.[58] In early October the Duma approved a resolution condemning the use of force in Kosovo as "an illegal, aggressive action" which it cautioned could prompt a review of Russia's agreements with NATO. The Defense Ministry also warned that air strikes in Kosovo would hold back Duma ratification of START-2.[59]

The Kosovo crisis escalated on June 14 with the aforementioned resumption of heavy fighting. US Secretary of State Albright expressed the hope that the "close relationship" between Russia and Yugoslavia would produce an agreement at the upcoming Moscow meeting where Russia, it was clear, would play the role of NATO's intermediary with Milosevic. Indeed, although NATO hoped that Yugoslavia would capitulate to its demands without a resort to violence, NATO Secretary General Solana warned that the alliance would not allow Kosovo to degenerate into another Bosnia and that NATO would not hesitate to launch air strikes.[60]

Yeltsin now found himself impaled on the horns of a tricky dilemma. In the throes of a financial meltdown, Russia was in desperate need of a standby loan from the IMF even as US Defense Secretary Cohen informed it that it risked "isolation" (i.e., deprivation of financial aid) if it blocked NATO action against the Serbs in Kosovo. On the other hand, openly backing the West would mean a "speedy end" for Yeltsin, who would have to disregard the overwhelming sentiment against NATO and its use of force in Kosovo.[61] Moscow's leaders therefore undertook a delicate balancing act, trying to appear firm on Kosovo while giving their wholehearted backing to their Western allies.[62] It was in this context that Foreign Minister Ivanov and Defense Minister Sergeev delivered an October message from Yeltsin to Milosevic which essentially paraphrased the NATO line that Milosevic must take immediate measures to end the Kosovo crisis or risk NATO air strikes.[63]

In evident collaboration with their Western overseers, Russian leaders devised a policy toward Kosovo which made their capitulation to the West just gradual and subtle enough to avoid the appearance of an open sellout to the West. An important act in this drama was Russia's agreement to participate in two NATO exercises, one dubbed "Cooperative Assembly 98," to take place in Albania beginning on August 10, and the other in Macedonia two weeks later. One analyst indicted Russia's leaders for agreeing to participate in this "first step" toward Russia's defeat in the Balkans which would "enhance the legitimacy" of NATO's intervention in the Balkans. Observers found Russia's willingness to participate "bewildering, to say the least," given the "sharp" opposition it had displayed in June to the Albanian maneuvers. But the demarche was perhaps not so strange when viewed through the prism of Russia's ultimate objective of solidarity with NATO in Kosovo, an end which seemed especially cynical in light of the Pentagon's "making no secret of the fact that the exercises are meant to show the Yugoslav President that the US is prepared to take decisive and forceful action in the region."[64]

The drama continued as Russia voted on September 23 for the explicitly anti-Serb UNSC Resolution 1199, which called on Belgrade to agree to an immediate ceasefire, withdraw its special forces from Kosovo, allow refugees to return, and begin a political dialogue with Kosovo's ethnic Albanians. However much Foreign Minister Ivanov insisted the resolution was not a legal basis for the use of force, he could not deny that it made specific reference to the UN Charter's Chapter Seven, which authorized the use of military force "to maintain peace and security." Russia's vote for the resolution could therefore not but be interpreted as a hardening of its line toward Belgrade.[65] The vote was historic, for it set the stage for Russia's step-by-step cooperation with the West to secure Milosevic's capitulation to NATO demands, an objective which the West would finally attain in June 1999.

Russian officials were successful in their scheme to make it *appear* that they were hostile to NATO policy in Kosovo even as they treated NATO with kid gloves. This was borne out by analyses of US and NATO officials which expressed the conviction that Russia's policymakers favored an assertive policy in Kosovo but had to be reined in by Foreign Minister Primakov.[66] ISKRAN Director S. Rogov pointed out that on the issues of

Kosovo and the Middle East, at least, Primakov was, contrary to the above, "rather successful in trying to pursue a more independent foreign policy [from the West] despite [Russia's] financial and economic dependence." Russia, which had "already fallen into line over NATO expansion [by] signing a Founding Act with [NATO] in a tacit acceptance of NATO's plans to 'expand eastwards' " (and which Rogov himself had greeted as a Russian victory) had now, Rogov asserted, finally broken the bonds of dependence on the West on the Kosovo issue. Even Communist Duma Speaker Seleznev praised the RFM for not giving grounds to the accusation that it was "dancing to somebody else's tune."[67]

But a contrary—and by all accounts more persuasive—perspective was hammered home by head of the Russian Institute of Political Studies S. Markov, who lamented that "for all the tough talk," Russian foreign policy as directed by Primakov "in practice always ends up toeing the West's line when it comes to the crunch."[68] Western analysts also took note of Primakov's inclination to cooperate with the West, including his dutiful implementation of the Dayton Accords on Bosnia.[69] Primakov himself as much as conceded this in his September confession to the Duma that he would work to avoid confrontation with the West, favored the ratification of START II, "refused to be goaded into a denunciation of NATO enlargement," and defended Russia's signing of the Founding Act, all of which indicated that "Western support remain[ed] crucial" to Russia's leaders.[70] Indeed, Primakov's policies, including his "complian[ce] in negotiations" with Secretary of State Albright and his reliance on "foreign capital as the instrument for stimulating growth," were so unabashedly pro-Western as to strike one Russian analyst as nothing less than "strange."[71]

Talks between Yugoslav President Milosevic and US envoy Richard Holbrooke concluded with an agreement on October 12 that entailed a pullback of Serbian forces from Kosovo in accordance with UNSC Resolution 1199, an OSCE "verification force," and surveillance flights to check on Belgrade's compliance. NATO put its troops on alert and issued an ultimatum to Belgrade that it comply with the resolution or face air strikes, which in turn prompted a warning from Primakov that NATO strikes against Yugoslavia could prompt Russia to adjust its attitude toward NATO, freeze relations, and halt arms negotiations—a seeming revival of the cold war. Russia's Ambassador and military representative to NATO were recalled for "consultations" and Foreign Minister Ivanov outlined Russia's bottom line on Yugoslavia: it opposed both the use of NATO forces without UNSC sanction and NATO actions which went beyond its sphere of responsibility. Aware that Russia was incapable of effective action in the Balkans, however, analysts typically noted that such "militancy" would not last long in light of the reality that Russia simply could not afford a *permanent* rift with the West. Temporary difficulties did not run counter to the long-term objective of partnership with the West pursued by Kremlin officials, who refused to affirm that Russia would supply S-300 missiles to Yugoslavia, as some officials had threatened. Indeed, Foreign Minister Ivanov explicitly ruled out the use of force against NATO, and even mollified the West by affirming that Russia had "no strategic disagreements" with it.[72] The next day the Defense Ministry issued a statement that it would disregard pledges by Russian military officials to give aid to Belgrade if NATO attacked, since only Yeltsin and the Foreign Ministry could make official policy.[73]

NATO then extended its ultimatum for another 96 hours, inciting Russia's leaders, practically beside themselves with joy, to boast that, like the 1995 Bosnian crisis and the 1997 crisis in Iraq, it was their warning not to launch air strikes or face a drastic transformation of Russia's attitude which had cowed NATO into postponing the strikes. But the arch-Western *Kommersant-daily* took the wind out of Russia's sails by pointing out that while "celebrating its diplomatic victory in the Balkans, Moscow avoided the question of why Milosevic considered US envoy Holbrooke the principal peacekeeper on the issue—and not the Russian representative, and also completely ignored the possibility that NATO might order air strikes after its ultimatum had expired." The reality was, as Richard Holbrooke pointed out, that NATO was "keeping the trigger cocked over the Serbian head." NATO extended by deadline by ten days on October 16.[74]

Russia (with China) abstained on an October 24 vote for a UNSC resolution authorizing ground and air monitors in Kosovo on the grounds that Belgrade was complying with UN decisions.[75] In a significant admission, however, Ivanov hinted on October 27 that Russia might approve the use of force in Yugoslavia if "the necessary measures" were not taken (by Belgrade) in Kosovo. Russia did just that on October 24, voting for UNSC resolution 1203, which granted the UNSC the power in an emergency to take measures to protect the safety of observers, and thus gave NATO legal grounds to launch air strikes.[76]

Despite all its tough talk, Russia's leaders continued to cave in to the West, agreeing in late November to participate in "control flights" over

Kosovo, part of NATO's Operation "Eagle Eye," in which Russian crews would monitor the scene from the air. Russia's Westernizers were ecstatic that, having been left out of air reconnaissance operations during the Iraq and Balkan crises, they were now allowed to join their NATO "allies." The overtly anti-Serb plan entailed the deactivation of anti-air defense systems deployed by Serbs in Kosovo and the shutdown of radar installed in Serbia on the border with Kosovo.[77]

Notes

[1] *The Hindu,* February 4, 1998.
[2] *RusData DiaLine—BizEkon News,* June 1, 1998.
[3] *Nezavisimaia gazeta,* September 19, 1997, pp. 1-2.
[4] *Financial Times,* March 26, 1998, p. 30.
[5] *RFE/RL Newsline,* Vol. 2, No. 64, Part I, April 2, 1998.
[6] *The Jamestown PRISM,* No. 20, Issue 4, October 16, 1998.
[7] Reuters, October 19, 1998.
[8] *The Moscow Times,* October 20, 1998.
[9] *RFE/RL Newsline,* Vol. 2, No. 103, Part I, June 1, 1998.
[10] Ibid., Vol. 2, No. 115, Part I, June 17, 1998.
[11] *The St. Petersburg Times* (Russia), June 19, 1998.
[12] *The Moscow Times,* May 28, 1998; *Christian Science Monitor,* June 5, 1998, p. 6. One Western analyst made the inaccurate assertion that "after seven years of being a marginal participant in international economic institutions, in May 1998, Russia became a full participant at the Birmingham G-8 summit." See Angela E. Stent, *Russia and Germany Reborn. Unification, the Soviet Collapse, and the New Europe* (Princeton: Princeton University Press, 1999), p. 176. Stent's assertion in Ibid., p. 175, that by having Russia associated with the G-7 the West was "sending an important political signal to Yeltsin" is equally questionable.
[13] *The Boston Globe,* June 16, 1998, p. A2.
[14] *RFE /RL Newsline,* Vol. 2, No. 140, Part I, July 23, 1998.
[15] *Nezavisimaia gazeta,* July 14, 1998, p. 3.
[16] The Charlie Rose Show, PBS Television Station, interview with Stephen Cohen, July 13, 1998.
[17] *Journal of Commerce,* October 26, 1998, p. 5A.
[18] Melor Sturua, *Nezavisimaia gazeta,* January 15, 1998, p. 3.
[19] ITAR-TASS, March 5, 1998.
[20] *Nezavisimaia gazeta,* March 6, 1998, p. 6; Agence France Presse, February 23, 1998.
[21] The Associated Press, January 30, 1998.

[22] Ibid., March 6, 1998; *International Herald Tribune*, March 3, 1998, p. 5.

[23] *RFE/RL Newsline*, Vol. 2, No. 92, Part I, May 15, 1998.

[24] *The New York Times*, May 19, 1998, p. A6.

[25] Reuters, February 2, 1998.

[26] *The Los Angeles Times*, January 31, 1998, p. A10.

[27] *RFE/RL Newsline*, Vol. 2, No. 23, Part I, February 4, 1998.

[28] Interview with Andrei Kortunov in *Die Woche*, Hamburg, February 20, 1998.

[29] *RFE/RL Newsline*, Vol. 2, No. 23, Part I, February 4, 1998.

[30] Ibid., Vol. 2, No. 211, Part I, November 2, 1998.

[31] Reuters, November 11, 1998.

[32] *The New York Times*, November 13, 1998, p. A14.

[33] *Nezavisimaia gazeta*, December 19, 1998, pp. 1, 6; The *Boston Globe*, December 19, 1998, p. A2.

[34] *The Washington Post*, December 19, 1998, p. A19.

[35] *RFE/RL Newsline*, Vol. 2, No. 245, Part I, December 22, 1998. See the statement by Press Spokesperson Rakhmanin playing down Primakov's proposed deepening of relations with China and India in Ibid., Vol. 3, No. 44, Part I, March 4, 1999. See also *Kommersant-daily*, June 3, 1999, p. 4, which quoted a Russia official who asserted that there would be no strategic axis or triangle with China. One noted analyst argued that China and India were "firmly opposed" to any strategic alliance with Russia. See *Nezavisimaia gazeta*, June 4, 1999, p. 3.

[36] *RFE/RL Newsline*, Vol. 2, No. 8, Part I, January 14, 1998; RIA Novosti, January 14, 1997.

[37] Susan Eisenhower, *The Los Angeles Times*, February 1, 1998, p. M5. *Krasnaia zvezda*, February 26, 1998, p. 3, took a similar position.

[38] *RFE/RL Newsline*, Vol. 2, No. 13, Part II, January 21, 1998; *Rossiiskaia gazeta*, May 12, 1998, p. 7.

[39] ITAR-TASS, August 18, 1998.

[40] Jan de Weydenthal, *RFE/RL Newsline*, October 29, 1998.

[41] *Izvestiia*, June 4, 1998, p. 1.

[42] Agence France Presse, July 16, 1999.

[43] Reuters, June 15, 1998.

[44] *RFE/RL Newsline*, Vol. 2, No. 114, Part II, June 16, 1998; Reuters, June 15, 1998; *Segodnia*, June 18, 1998, p. 3.

[45] *RFE/RL Newsline*, Vol. 2, No. 156, Part II, August 14, 1998.

[46] Ibid., Vol. 2, No. 156, Part II, August 18, 1998.

[47] *Kommersant-daily*, August 8, 1998, p. 3.

[48] *Nezavisimaia gazeta*, May 27, 1998, p. 3.

[49] *The Independent* (London), September 30, 1998, p. 15.

[50] *RFE/RL Newsline*, May 20, 1998.

[51] Agence France Presse, December 7, 1998.

[52] *RFE/RL Newsline*, Part I, February 26, 1998.

[53] Ibid., Vol. 2, No. 111, Part I, June 10, 1998.

[54] Ibid., Part II, March 25, 1998.

[55] *Kommersant*-daily, April 3, 1998, p. 5; Sovetskaia *Rossiia*, March 12, 1998, p. 4; *RFE/RL Newsline*, Part II, April 1, 1998.

[56] *RFE/RL Newsline*, Vol. 2, No. 116, Part I, June 18, 1998; Federal News Service, Moscow, June 17, 1998.

[57] Agence France Presse, June 14, 1998.

[58] Reuters, June 22, 1998.

[59] *RFE/RL Newsline*, Vol. 2, No. 192, October 5, 1998, Part I, October 2, 1998.

[60] Agence France Presse, June 14, 1998.

[61] *The Moscow Times*, June 18, 1998. Reuters, October 5, 1998, reported that Moscow was waging a "fierce campaign" against NATO action, but sought to avoid a confrontation with its former cold war foe that would threaten its ties with Western creditors.

[62] Reuters, October 6, 1998.

[63] *RFE/RL Newsline*, Vol. 2, No. 192, Part II, October 5, 1998.

[64] *Izvestiia*, August 19, 1998, p. 3; *RFE/RL Newsline*, Vol. 2, No. 207, Part I, October 26, 1998; *Novye izvestiia*, August 8, 1998, p. 3.

[65] *The Washington Post*, October 6, 1998, A20. Even pro-Western sources implied that the leadership had acceded to the West when it voted for Resolution 1199. See *Izvestiia*, September 25, 1998, p. 3; *Sovetskaia Rossiia*, April 1, 1999; Press Association Newsfile, October 6, 1998; Agence France Presse, October 14, 1998.

[66] *RFE/RL Newsline*, Vol. 2, No. 156, Part II, August 14, 1998.

[67] Reuters, August 27, 1998. Rogov, it will be recalled, had praised the Founding Act.

[68] Ibid.

[69] *The Christian Science Monitor*, September 11, 1998, p. 8.

[70] *The Jamestown Foundation Monitor*, Vol. 4, Issue 167, September 14, 1998.

[71] Interfax, No. 48, December 1-7, 1997, pp. 1, 6.

[72] *Nezavisimaia gazeta*, October 13, 1998, pp. 1, 6; *RFE/RL Newsline*, Vol. 2, No. 197, Part I, October 12, 1998; *Segodnia*, October 13, 1998; *Kommersant-daily*, October 13, 1998, p. 4. In May Primakov had stated unequivocally that the use of force must be authorized by the UNSC. See *Nezavisimaia gazeta*, May 30, 1998, pp. 1, 6.

[73] Reuters, October 13, 1998.

[74] *Izvestiia*, October 14, 1998, p. 1; Agence France Presse, October 14 and 18, 1998; *Kommersant-daily*, October 15, 1998, p. 4; *The Daily Telegraph* (London), October 14, 1998, p. 15.

[75] *RFE/RL Newsline*, Vol. 2, No. 207, Part I, October 26, 1998; *Novye izvestiia*, August 8, 1998, p. 3.

[76] *Izvestiia*, October 28, 1998, pp. 1, 6; *Nezavisimaia gazeta*, October 27, 1998, p. 6.

[77] *Izvestiia*, November 27, 1998, p. 1; ITAR-TASS, November 26, 1998; Agence France Presse, November 19, 1998.

10 1999-Early 2000: Kosovo Farce and Political Scandal

The Domestic Setting

By 1999 Russia's policy of deception had become so obvious that reference to it in the media was almost commonplace, including in the West. One report, for instance, disparaged IMF funding of Yeltsin and the "reformers" for making possible the "pretense" that Russian leaders made believe they were carrying out reforms and the IMF pretended to believe them.[1] The deception seemed all the more necessary in light of the social unrest produced by the "reforms," which had reduced Russia's population by 5.6 million people, the result of higher infant mortality rates and lowered life expectancy relative to 1990 rates.[2] Equally shattering revelations of the devastation wrought by "reforms" came to light with the April disclosure that not a single new jet fighter plane had been put into production since 1992 and that none was scheduled until 2001.[3] Understandably worried, A. Voloshin, Head of the Presidential Administration, echoed Yeltsin's 1998 warning against displays of unrest in the military with his own admonition that officers whose "militant" remarks were "inconsistent with Yeltsin's positions" would be dismissed.[4]

The onset of NATO's bombing campaign over Kosovo heightened Russian leaders' concern that relations with the West would suffer, as anti-Western and specifically anti-American and anti-NATO sentiment in Russia rose to a pitch not heard even during the Soviet years. This was clearly cause for worry for the Westernizers, who lamented that "in one stroke" NATO's campaign erased all the "progress" the West had achieved in its relations with Russia.[5] An April 1999 survey told the tale: 50% of Russians disliked the US (compared to less than one-third in December 1998);[6] two-thirds even believed that NATO's armed intervention in Kosovo would soon be replicated in Russia.[7] Underpinning the mounting anti-Westernism were the horrific effects of the "reforms," documented by a UN Development Program report which revealed that the number of people living in poverty in the former socialist bloc exploded from 14 million in 1988 to 147 million in the mid-1990s. The 1998 economic crash further worsened the standard of living of another 25-30% of Russians and threw 22 million more into poverty.[8]

In what seemed to be a reprise of the infamous 1996 meeting in Davos, Russia's leading oligarchs met with top Yeltsin advisers in early August 1999 in the south of France to plot their political strategy and strengthen Yeltsin's (or his successor's) position in the 2000 presidential elections.[9] Weeks later the biggest scandal in post-Soviet Russian history erupted with the sensational revelation of a $15 billion money laundering scheme by Russians working for the Bank of New York. During the ensuing cascade of revelations observers made mocking reference to the "Claude Raines routine" (from the film "Casablanca") performed by Western (primarily US) officials who feigned shock upon learning that "corruption was going on" in Russia. The crisis forced Russia's once well-concealed dependency, its deception and its corruption still further into the open.

The Foreign Policy Setting

At the November 18 OSCE summit in Istanbul Yeltsin adopted a militant posture, attacking NATO's campaign against Serbia and defending Russia's actions in Chechnya, and even made a display of anti-Western pique by leaving the summit a day early. Typically, however, just hours after Yeltsin's "tough" talk Russian negotiators made "potentially significant concessions on the international agreements under discussion at the summit," leading one observer to muse that Yeltsin's performance was "theatrics aimed at his domestic audience. But while playing to the gallery at home, he also likes to maintain some support in the West. Hence the concessions . . . " President Clinton went especially easy on Yeltsin.[10]

Mutual recriminations escalated throughout late 1999, primarily over Western criticism of Russia's conduct in the war in Chechnya, to such an extent that by February 2000 analysts were forecasting an imminent return to the cold war. But as they had on numerous occasions in the past Russian leaders made sure that the harsh rhetoric was kept within strict limits: after Russia criticized the US for denouncing Russia's policy in Chechnya, President Putin sent a message to Clinton stressing their mutual interests and the coincidence of their strategic goals. Relations with the US, Putin assured Washington, were a Russian foreign policy priority.[11]

Russia and NATO

A NATO conference in early February was the setting for a diplomatic tongue-lashing delivered by Russian Deputy Foreign Minister Gusarov to NATO for its new strategic doctrine. Gusarov also demanded guarantees that the UNSC, not NATO, take on responsibility for international peace and security and for NATO cooperation with the OSCE.[12] But his security concerns seemed misdirected. The real danger evidently lay not outside Russia's borders but within the ranks of the leadership itself, for in his eagerness to mend ties with the West after relations soured over NATO's bombing campaign in Yugoslavia, Yeltsin agreed on June 20 to consider a revision of the ABM treaty, a move many regarded as an outright sellout to the West. Yeltsin's consent made it easier for President Clinton to respond positively to Congress' increasingly insistent demand that the ABM Treaty and its limits on a national missile defense be scrapped and a US missile defense be deployed.[13] As shocking as this cave-in to the West was, it should be borne in mind that Yeltsin had proffered a similar concession on the ABM Treaty at his 1997 Helsinki summit with Clinton, which prompted an amazed US arms control official to call his giveaway " 'extraordinary' because it legalized anti-missile systems under the ABM by defining limits on target missiles used in testing."[14]

The Russia-NATO Council met in Brussels on July 24, 1999 for the first time since Russia suspended relations in retaliation for NATO's air campaign against Yugoslavia. The thaw was slow to develop, however, and Foreign Minister Ivanov took the initiative to further warm frozen relations by declaring in mid-February 2000 that NATO's presence in Europe was a reality and must be taken into account. It was also announced that NATO Secretary General Robertson would visit Moscow to resume relations, although commentators were aware that this was in fact the prelude to a major demarche by NATO, namely, its preparation for a "second wave of eastward expansion." Russia's Westernizing leadership knew this meant that "relations [would] have to be established sooner or later." Moscow was even willing to restore ties in spite of the fact that on the eve of Robertson's visit to Moscow he and his NATO colleagues stopped in to visit Ukraine, Bulgaria, Moldova, and the Baltics, where he declared NATO's intention to further expand.[15]

Russia and NATO Expansion to the Baltics

The expansion to CEE having been finalized in 1997, NATO's expansion focus shifted to the Baltics, picking up from where it left off in 1998. NATO let it be known that it would not be deterred in its determination to expand—not only to the Balkans but, as Clinton adviser Strobe Talbott made clear in his pronouncement at the session of the US-Baltic Commission, to the Baltic states who were now "not only eligible for [NATO] membership but desirable."[16] As the overseer of US policy toward Russia, Talbott continued on his anti-Russian path in the Baltics six months later in Tallinn when he promised the grateful Baltic states that the US would make sure that the doors of NATO were kept open. Talbott, never one for pulling punches as far as Moscow was concerned, literally taunted Russia by assuring the Baltics that Russian opposition would be no obstacle to their membership in NATO. Talbott clearly had good reason to be so bold, for Russia's recent softer tone on the issue had given grounds for the widespread assumption that it had reconciled itself to Baltic membership, in spite of stern government denials.[17]

Russia and Yugoslavia

Kosovo was Russia's foreign policy focal point in 1999. Russian officials followed their familiar pattern of warning of measures to counter NATO "aggression" in the region then issuing retractions and apologies. A sequence of events was set off in early June which culminated, as in 1995, in Russia's dutiful fulfillment of its role as NATO's "messenger" charged with the task of getting Belgrade to capitulate to NATO's demands. As they also did in 1995, Russia's leaders agreed, after a period of brief but token resistance, to NATO's terms for Russian participation in Kosovo peacekeeping. And as with the NATO expansion issue, Russia's leaders in the end received the anticipated payoff for assisting the West.

Yugoslavia: Russian Relations with the West

Russia's policy vis-à-vis Yugoslavia in 1999 was a confused cacaphony of threats and denials. As early as late January Foreign Minister Ivanov warned the West that the use of force in Kosovo could aggravate regional stability and lead to a wider Balkan war, although while these very words were uttered his own Foreign Ministry was warning Yugoslavia that its threat to expel William Walker, the Western head of the OSCE mission in Kosovo who had blamed Belgrade for the "mass murder" of Kosovar Albanians, would undercut Russian support for Yugoslavia. On January 22 Belgrade suspended its decision to expel Walker, crediting messages sent by Yeltsin and Primakov to President Milosevic for the change of heart.[18]

Although Russian public opinion was almost universally opposed to NATO's actions in Yugoslavia, a small number applauded NATO or, what was virtually the same thing, treated it with the same kid-gloves gentleness they had displayed toward NATO expansion. Father of Russian "reforms" Egor Gaidar, for example, did not so much attack NATO's actions as bewail its "mistaken hypothesis" and "erroneous decisions," while *Izvestiia* straightforwardly attacked the government for "conniving" with Milosevic and ignoring his "ethnic cleansing."[19]

On February 10 Deputy Prime Minister Masliukov denied statements by his press spokesperson that Russia was "being pressured to soften its policies vis-à-vis Kosovo and Iraq in order to receive IMF support,"[20] but days later Russian officials all but confirmed the charge when they agreed not only not to oppose the stationing of a NATO force in Kosovo but to join it.[21] Yeltsin made a familiar attempt to camouflage Russia's capitulation on the issue with militant rhetoric on February 18 during a Russia-EU summit. Responding to NATO's impending use of force against Belgrade Yeltsin growled that Russia would "not allow Kosovo to be touched," that bombing would "not do." But his bluster only prompted yawning analysts to recall previous Russian threats against NATO's bombing of Iraq which had been followed by Moscow's recalling its ambassadors to Western countries and which culminated ineluctably in a Russian cave-in.[22]

Prime Minister Primakov happened to be en route to Washington for a meeting with the IMF when NATO commenced its bombing campaign against Serbia on March 24. He immediately ordered the plane turned back to Moscow in a demonstration of Russian displeasure at NATO's audacity. Or so it seemed. In reality, Primakov's order proved to be just another chapter in the deception game—and smacked of Kozyrev's phony "anger" at NATO for its expansion decision in December 1994, since he had been informed of the bombing before his plane took off and orchestrated the plane's return to "appease an angry Russian public that sympathized with the Serbs." Contrary to what many expected from Primakov, with his reputedly "hard-line" orientation, moreover, analysts conceded, in a kind of paraphrase of the dependency thesis, that there was little he or "Russia [in general could] do about the West's plans" since it lacked the "military or economic might to impose its views and it is desperate for Western financial aid." He, like other Russian officials, was compelled to "maintain stable ties with [the West if he wanted] to have any hope of solving [Russia's] enormous economic problems."[23] Indeed, almost immediately after the airplane incident Primakov's refusal to rule out meeting with the IMF in a third country[24] caused observers to comment that "the flight by Russian ministers to the West seeking International Monetary Fund loans had become a symbol of the Boris Yeltsin years—a sign of Russian . . . moral and economic . . . weakness, of dependency."[25]

Russian officials immediately adopted a belligerent posture towards NATO's onslaught. Russia withdrew from the PfP, its offices at NATO headquarters were ordered closed, and Ambassador to NATO Kisliak suspended military—but not political—cooperation; Duma Speaker Seleznev gave notice that START-2 was in jeopardy and that Russia would "give powerful weapons" to Belgrade in its defense; Chief of Staff of the armed forces Kvashnin called a meeting of top military officials to discuss a possible military response to the air strikes and scrapped plans to cooperate with Washington on Y2K problems in Russian nuclear forces; Foreign Minister Ivanov threatened to lift the international arms embargo on Belgrade while expressing regret that West Europe was in lockstep with the US on Yugoslavia; Defense Minister Sergeev confirmed that Russia was considering the deployment of tactical nuclear weapons in Belarus, although he also conceded that Russia was "planning no military response to the NATO aggression"; and finally, Primakov affirmed in a note to US Vice President Gore that the strikes would only destabilize the Kosovo situation and damage relations with Russia.[26]

Another "militant" response to NATO air strikes included Russia's dispatching a frigate to the Mediterranean to "monitor" Western ships, although in the end this presented no threat to NATO, and was "more of a political than a military gesture"[27] given that Russia did not even have enough fuel for the mission. Russian officials, moreover, assured Washington they would not hand over reconnaissance to Belgrade in any case.[28] Other seemingly militant diplomatic actions which, it was clear, would never be put into effect or were totally ineffectual, and whose real design was to deflect attention from Russia's eventual surrender to the

West, included Russia's request to the World Court to make a determination on the legal consequences of NATO air strikes against Yugoslavia, submission to a UN General Assembly committee of a resolution declaring NATO's actions illegal on the grounds that the UNSC had not explicitly authorized it,[29] and the boycott of NATO's fiftieth anniversary summit in late April.[30]

Amid the clamor of threats and recriminations Duma Speaker Seleznev returned from Belgrade on April 9 with a message from Milosevic proposing that Yugoslavia join the Russia-Belarus union. In his "senseless" response aimed at appeasing the people's anger, Yeltsin "play[ed] largely to a domestic audience" by issuing thunderous verbal "detonations that had the world quivering" and voicing support for such a union, a position the State Duma had also been urging.[31] Yeltsin also instructed government officials to draft a relevant statement on the formation of such a union, although this proved to be merely symbolic.[32]

Yeltsin seemed enraged by the West's naked aggression against Serbia, and on April 11 he took the characteristically bold step of warning NATO not to push Russia toward military action and risk a "European war or maybe even a world war"[33]—this just just two days after having announced that Russian missiles were targeting NATO countries fighting against Yugoslavia. But commentators quickly unmasked this obvious fakery by pointing out that because it took only seconds to target a missile Yeltsin's words should be taken "largely symbolically."[34] What is more, in response to Yeltsin's threat to unleash a "world war" a top Primakov aide hastened to reassure US officials that Yeltsin had not been serious and was merely trying to "appease the increasingly militant nationalists at home."[35] Yeltsin was most concerned not about the harm NATO's bombing campaign was inflicting on Serbia and the Serb people—if he thought at all about them, he clearly felt more hostility or just plain annoyance than sympathy—but rather with the campaign's effect on Russian public opinion, which he realized was reaching dangerous anti-Western levels, and which could threaten his position and that of the entire robber capitalist elite.

In stark contrast, Interior Minister Stepashin (who would become Prime Minister in May) announced on March 25 that because Russia must live and work in Europe it should avoid being dragged into "outright confrontation with the West." This attempt to brake the mounting anti-Westernism in Russia was part and parcel of Russia's continued pursuit of close relations with the West, which also included the signing of a contract to ship highly enriched Russian uranium to the US and a memorandum of cooperation between the Russian Academy of Sciences and the US Department of Energy.[36] And Foreign Minister Ivanov reiterated his advocacy of Russian ratification of START-2, although he conceded that NATO's actions made "now not the best time" to do so from a political standpoint.[37]

Yeltsin nevertheless turned up the heat. In his March 30 speech to the Federal Assembly he pronounced Russia's "non-acceptance" of NATO expansion to be "well-founded" in light of NATO's activities in Kosovo, but this only caused one skeptical observer to dismiss his posturing and to point out that Yeltsin's prior warning that Kosovo must not be touched was made irrelevant by NATO's not only having touched Kosovo but by Russia's having "simply been ignored" by the West.[38] And the Duma, which had been anything but temperate until now, agreed to withdraw its threat to supply Belgrade with arms, but only after Primakov convinced it that such measures should be resorted to only in the event of an escalation of the conflict.[39] This was also dissimulation, since neither Primakov nor any top Russian official would dream of carrying out such a threat.

The deception continued all through the spring. As early as late March Yeltsin boasted that Russia was "above" the West's resort to military action, that "on the moral level we are superior to the Americans"—then proceeded to emphasize that Russia would under no circumstances take "extreme [anti-Western] measures."[40] Then, almost overnight, Russia's tone on Kosovo changed "dramatically" on April 6, the result of a telephone call from Vice President Gore to Primakov during which Gore urged Russia to play a key role in settling the conflict. Evidently sensing that it was now safe to make the inevitable climbdown, Russian leaders began to underscore the priority of cooperation with the West, symbolized by Yeltsin's April 14 removal of Primakov as emissary to Belgrade and his replacement by Chernomyrdin, largely on grounds that the latter was believed to be more receptive to the West and because Primakov had reportedly resisted the draconian conditions for the $4.5 billion the IMF had agreed to release.[41]

Yeltsin pressed on with his reconciliation with the West in late April. When he announced that the number one policy objective was to counter mounting anti-Americanism in Russia he implied a downgrading in the priority of the campaign to stop NATO aggression. And when he at the same time urged regional leaders to grab more power from the center the many Russians who suspected him of being an agent of the West saw this as a "CIA-devised plan to break up Russia the same way the Soviet Union was dismantled in 1991."[42] Yeltsin's aim was to neutralize the mounting anger at his utter disregard of Russia's interests and, apparently, to break up any crystallization of a united opposition.

Russian government television followed suit, reshaping its overwhelmingly anti-Western reportage on Kosovo into a more "balanced" mix which conspicuously included coverage of Serb-initiated "ethnic cleansing."[43] In conformity with the new emphasis Ivanov openly expressed compassion for the Kosovar Albanians and insisted on a halt to all violence and repression, while refusing to single out NATO as the principal transgressor in the conflict. The leadership nevertheless continued to draw the line at air strikes, which remained at the core of their criticism of NATO.[44]

As usual, Yeltsin's anti-Western threats proved to be mere "symbolic gestures" which aroused extreme skepticism as to his real motives. His goal of avoiding confrontation with the West at all costs[45] dovetailed with his strategy of utilizing "tough cold-war-style oratory" to keep him "abreast of the wave of anti-American feeling that . . . swept Russia. Nevertheless, as the NATO bombing continue[d], limiting Russia's opposition to just words" would prove increasingly difficult.[46]

A "decisive step away from the specter of a wider conflict" between Washington and Moscow was taken in early May when Russia agreed with the G-7 foreign ministers in Bonn on the need for an international military presence in Kosovo—and not merely unarmed observers, as had been insisted on previously. This demonstrated to one observer that Moscow was "not ready to turn its back on the West" and support Milosevic.[47] Western sources acknowledged that the Bonn agreement was a major victory for the West, since it approved the continuation of air strikes, put pressure on Milosevic to agree to NATO's terms, and rejected Russia's proposal that US and British troops be excluded from the peacekeeping force. Although a "concession" was made to Russia in the omission from the text of the agreement of any reference to NATO as a component of the peacekeeping force in Kosovo, this was just one more tactic in the deception, since "everyone agreed" that "a strong military force with *NATO at its core*" was precisely what was needed.[48]

Defense Minister Sergeev also made a show of opposing the West by warning that if NATO air strikes continued Russia might insist on a revision of the CFE treaty and refuse to sign several military cooperation agreements with Norway.[49] And Foreign Minister Ivanov pulled another fast one when he cancelled a planned visit to Britain on May 8, purportedly in protest over NATO's bombing of the Chinese embassy in Belgrade. The true depths of his "anti-Western" passions were made clear, however, when he and British Foreign Secretary Cook agreed over the telephone to meet at "the earliest opportunity"; the meeting date was eventually reset for July 23, and when they finally did meet both Cook and Ivanov seemed "pleased." Ivanov emphasized the need not only to establish full-scale cooperation but to give relations a "new impetus."[50]

In what seemed the most serious response to NATO's use of force to date, the Russian military conducted "high-profile" war games in June and also flew military jets close to the Icelandic and Norwegian coasts. Yeltsin blunted this seeming bellicosity, however, with the assurance that Russia viewed its principal threat of "large-scale military aggression" not "from abroad" (the West) but from regional conflicts. The "threatening" flights, moreover, were dismissed as having little political meaning, while Russian leaders played them up "as a big deal to boost morale and boost the military's profile [at home]," especially given mounting dissatisfaction in the Russian military over the perceived sellout of Russia's interests by the leadership.[51]

That Russia was in fact playing by the West's rules now was made clear when Chernomyrdin, who was scheduled to appear in Belgrade at a May 9 ceremony celebrating the anniversary of the ending of WW II in Europe—and where he was also to speak with Milosevic about a peace settlement—met instead with top Clinton adviser Strobe Talbott in Moscow. Such perfidy confirmed to the Serbs what their government had been saying privately, namely that "Moscow, despite its professions of support for Belgrade, is largely doing Washington's bidding in the hopes of gaining more financial aid from the West."[52] Russia's leaders were in fact now so amenable to the West that on May 20 they "cordially received" the head of the US Cooperative Threat Reduction Program, whose visit had been cancelled in March when NATO's campaign against Belgrade began.[53]

As emissary to Belgrade, Chernomyrdin knew that the nature of Russian politics was such that it would be too much to expect him to openly "negotiate on NATO's behalf"—even though this was his real intention—without being seen as a Western stooge. So a clever solution was devised in clear collaboration with the West: Finnish President Ahtisaari, the token Western diplomat, would accompany him to Belgrade and thus relieve him of the "unwelcome role of serving as NATO's postman,"[54] a charge that brought back uncomfortable memories of the 1995 war in Bosnia. NATO officials now openly acknowledged, as did the Russians and Ahtisaari himself, that Ahtisaari's role was—*on Russia's own suggestion*, no less—to make clear to Milosevic that he must accept NATO's strictly non-negotiable terms, including a withdrawal of all Serb forces from Kosovo, rather than the May 6 statement drawn up by Russia and the allies which was largely vague and contained, in deference to Russia, no mention of the withdrawal of all Serb forces from Kosovo.[55]

The Russian government's scrupulous efforts to obfuscate Chernomyrdin's role of "postman" for the West came unceremoniously undone with the publication of a May 23 op-ed piece in *The New York Times* by President Clinton which brazenly described Chernomyrdin's mission as helping to "work out a way for Belgrade to meet our conditions."[56] Regardless of whether this was deliberate or an inadvertent blunder Chernomyrdin, clearly worried that the mask had been ripped off, was compelled days later to issue his own op-ed piece in *The Washington Post*, a rejoinder to his US patron which emphasized that Russia did not share NATO's goal of a "protectorate" in Kosovo. He threatened to end his mission and veto Western proposals in the UN, and raised the old bogey of an anti-Western "triangle" of Russia, China, and India.[57]

But the cat was out of the bag, and no amount of duplicity could conceal the deception. Within days and without protest Russia conceded NATO's position that "all Yugoslav forces . . . should withdraw from Kosovo and that the withdrawal be substantially under way before any pause in NATO bombing." The capitulation was made close to complete on June 2 when a Russian spokesperson advised the Yugoslav leaders that they must accept all NATO's demands.[58] Like Warsaw in August 1993 where he gave the green light to NATO expansion and, to one prominent Western journalist, like Russia's "tilt our way"—that is, toward the West—which had been "crucial against . . . Iraq," it was Yeltsin and company who had made the "critical" move "over to NATO's side of the table"[59] to further the West's aims in the former Yugoslavia. In the process the lie was put to Russian "threats" against NATO and to Chernomyrdin's intimations of opposition just days earlier.

A climax of sorts came on June 4 when Chernomyrdin succeeded in convincing Milosevic and the Serbian parliament—now diplomatically isolated—to accept NATO's terms. According to US officials, Russia played a "crucial role" in showing the Serbs the "united front" of Russia and the West.[60] It was also significant that Russia's arch-capitalist leaders had called on the services of a London investment banker, Peter Castenfelt, with whom they had close ties and who had been instrumental in sealing accords between Russia and the IMF, to spend the days preceding Milosevic's final capitulation persuading the Yugoslav President to accept NATO's terms.[61]

On June 12 Russian troops made their now fabled "mad dash" to the Pristina airport in Kosovo, "triumphantly" occupying it before NATO had given its approval and without NATO's authorization or knowledge. But this was in fact just another tactical maneuver by the West, who had apparently refused to challenge the action in Pristina with the aim of protecting Yeltsin—especially given that the action had little political or military value.[62] It was perhaps understandable that pro-Western sources were taken in by the "mad dash"—one article made the erroneous claim, much like the false belief that the "three noes" had pledged never to site nuclear weapons on new members' territory, that Russia had been given "its own sector" in Kosovo as an "obvious result" of the Pristina incident, and that Russian troops were subordinate not to NATO but to the UN.[63] But the duping of left-wingers—as manifested in Communist Chair of the Duma Seleznev's lauding "our boys" for doing "the right thing" and Italian communist Armando Cossetta waxing rhapsodic over the Pristina "mad dash" and praising Foreign Minister Ivanov for his role in the Kosovo conflict—was surely difficult to comprehend.[64]

The "triumph" at the Pristina airport, undertaken either with the concurrence of Russia's leaders or at least used to good advantage by them once it had taken place (*Segodnia* termed the episode a "bluff" for "domestic consumption"[65]) was understandably the object of widespread ridicule. The argument by many Russians that Russia's "resolute" position at the "G-8" meeting in Cologne, its forceful staking out a claim to a military presence in the Balkans, and its "weighty and equal participation in UN peacekeeping" were somehow all the result of the mad dash[66] was demolished by French Foreign Minister Vedrine, who dismissed the incident as nothing more than an attempt by a humiliated Russia to "show that it was not a complete cipher." *Moskovskii komsolets* poked fun at the Russian troops at the Pristina airport who, in their hour of "heroism," neglected to bring enough underwear (and food and gasoline), thus necessitating a humanitarian rescue mission by a British convoy who flew in fresh supplies to save the "heroes."[67]

The ease with which NATO for all intents and purposes "grounded" the Russian paratroopers who were to rescue their comrades at the Pristina airport by securing, in one fell swoop, agreement of the Hungarian, Romanian, and Bulgarian governments to deny permission for Russian supply flights to Pristina over their air space was equally pathetic.[68] Yet even after all the humiliation, once NATO reestablished its control of the airport Yeltsin, acknowledging its "strategic importance," graciously suggested that the airport could be used jointly with other peacekeepers and offered Russian "assistance" at the airport to any state needing it.[69] As comic as it was, his gesture was meant to show he was "in control."

Russian officials and their supporters nevertheless rejoiced in their diplomatic "success," supposedly brought about by the "mad dash." To ISKRAN Director Rogov (who had also praised the Russia-NATO Founding Act as a victory for Russia) "Moscow's place at the head of the table has been reaffirmed." In fact, the "mad dash" was used as a political ploy to quell mounting opposition to Yeltsin's sellout of the Serbs by strengthening Yeltsin's position and Russia's international standing— Yeltsin even decorated the participants in August (see below).[70] CPRF leader Ziuganov, however, not deceived, accused the leaders of "selling Yugoslavia the way they sold and betrayed" Russia. Even the pro-Western Sergei Karaganov bemoaned the "moral and political losses" caused by Russia's leaders who had acted in furtherance of NATO's interests.[71]

The next episode in the Kosovo farce centered around the status of Russian peacekeeping forces in Kosovo. June talks with US and Finnish generals on the issue stalled over Russia's insistence that it be given charge of its own sector. Leonid Ivashov, head of the Russian military delegation, warned that if an agreement were not reached Russia would "announce a sector that will be agreed upon with the Yugoslav side and will meet our interests." But US negotiator Strobe Talbott laid down the law: there would be one peace force in Kosovo and NATO alone would be in charge of all sectors.[72] Russia would not dare to transgress these boundaries.

A June decree by NATO officials ordered—amid Russian protest—that Russian peacekeeping forces would be placed under NATO command "even if," Western sources noted, "the alliance has to devise some sort of fig leaf to disguise the fact that Russian troops are reporting to a NATO officer." Shades of 1995. This most unfortunate choice of words was made doubly ironic by the fact that—like the earlier "errand boy" charge—it was an almost word-for-word paraphrase of the description of Russia's subservient role in the 1995 controversy surrounding NATO peacekeeping in Bosnia (see the discussion of "operation fig leaf" in Chapter 6).[73] As if this were not enough, the Kosovo peacekeeping deception was taken to even more absurd lengths by a draft UN resolution, hammered out by the Western powers and Russia in Cologne on June 9 and paralleling the Bonn agreement on Kosovo peacekeeping in its omission of any direct reference to NATO command of the Kosovo peacekeepers. The resolution was "little more than a sop to Moscow," since the Kremlin was "under no illusion about the allies' plans" to subordinate Russian troops to NATO.[74]

On June 18 Russia finally paved the way for a restoration of relations with NATO by agreeing to integrate its forces into KFOR. Completely contradicting what they had sworn they would never do (Yeltsin had "firmly instructed" Defense Minister Sergeev to insist on a separate Russian sector, and had "categorically [refused to] agree" to placing Russian troops under the control of other countries) Russian officials now consented—for reasons and with a docility "still not clear to the non-Russian participants"—to the division of its troops among three sectors, each led by a NATO member. And as always after such Russian capitulations Yeltsin declared that the compromise met his "requirements." The agreement placed Russia's troops, like those of any participating nations, under a commander from their country while NATO retained overall command of the mission and real tactical control over all forces.[75] And contrary to Russia's previous categorical refusals to be subordinated to NATO, to Russian complaints in August that the West was revising the agreement on Russian participation in peacekeeping and, finally, to its concern over the hostility its peacekeepers encountered in Albanian Kosovar areas such as the town of Orahovac, where Albanians put up roadblocks to prevent the entrance of Russian peacekeepers, observers reported in September that Russian peacekeeping troops in Kosovo had "excellent relations" with NATO, due in large part to the "strong lobby in the Russian Defense Ministry which thinks it's a great idea to cooperate with NATO." Russia's leaders, the source asserted, were "playing a 'political game' " by "refus[ing] to be seen holding meetings with NATO, but [we]re holding seminars and meetings with individual NATO member states."[76]

In an obvious effort to head off potential opposition to his NATO-friendly policies Yeltsin ordered Defense and Interior Ministry officials assembled at the Kremlin on July 8 to "follow one line in life—the line of the president." Russia, he insisted, will "not clash with NATO, but neither will we flirt with it. We shall closely follow NATO's activities and develop our tactics jointly." Rumors of a Russian military "collapse," he assured his listeners, were "nonsense" and he pointed to the Pristina airport incident as proof, even suggesting that the troops involved be decorated. On August 5 he signed a decree to that effect.[77]

Yeltsin's bombast that Russia's policy in Kosovo had been "brilliantly executed" was such an obvious attempt to hoodwink the public that Westernizer Alexei Arbatov wondered whether Yeltsin was living in an "imaginary world, having lost all ties with reality" or simply regarded Russians as "absolute idiots." Russia, Arbatov accurately pointed out, had "suffered a . . . possibly irreparable defeat" from its leaders' policy of issuing threats against NATO then making "one concession after another," and finally agreeing to "foist NATO's terms on the Yugoslav leadership."[78]

Those were strong words, and they were an indication that there was real cause for concern by the leadership. This applied with special force to the military, as was made clear when, following Chernomyrdin's return from his mission to Belgrade, Russia's military attache, sent as an observer to Macedonia for military talks, encouraged the Serbs to rebuff NATO's demands. It was also reported that the Deputy Foreign Minister had announced his Ministry's disassociation from the agreement, as did Col. Gen. Leonid Ivashov, Director of the Defense Ministry's Chief Administration for International Military Cooperation, and Viktor Zavarzin, Russia's representative to NATO. Defense and Foreign Ministry officials sent to the Duma to explain the Kosovo agreement had attacked it more than they defended it, and representatives of the Defense Ministry who participated in the delegation which negotiated the peace plan in Bonn openly objected to Russia's "excessive" concessions to the West.[79]

Almost as quickly as it appeared, however, the leadership's feigned animus toward NATO had largely faded by summer. In late July RFM spokesperson Rakhmanin stated at a Moscow briefing that relations with the US were still central to Moscow, "which intends to broaden them in all areas," and praised the Clinton-Yeltsin talks in Cologne for "help[ing] overcome the alienation that appeared during the Kosovo crisis"—as if mere talks could make the grounds for the purported tensions somehow magically disappear. And he assured NATO that Russia's freezing relations did not apply to bilateral relations with NATO member countries—especially since it was, after all, this relationship which "made it possible to halt the war in Yugoslavia."[80] Of course a prime factor in overcoming the alienation, and one which went largely unmentioned, was that Russia (or at least its elites) counted on—and salivated over—money funded by the West for "lucrative reconstruction contracts" after the hostilities in Kosovo.[81]

On August 2 Yeltsin's reception of Montenegran President Djukanovic, whose anti-Serb statements were described as "music to the ears" of Westerners, indicated that Moscow was now willing to bestow its blessing not on Milosevic but on those who opposed him. And it was of a piece with Prime Minister Stepashin's recent statement disparaging Milosevic and blaming him for the suffering of the Serbian people, a demarche which "bewildered" many Russians by "devaluing" the leadership's supposed support for Milosevic.[82] It also shattered the illusions of Yugoslavs who had assumed that Russia was Belgrade's staunchest ally—and proved to ISKRAN Director S. Rogov that Russia was now interested in participating in the settlement of the Balkan conflict and "not in being associated with anti-Western regimes."[83]

Other developments made the situation seem even more absurd—if that was possible. Even as they pretended that their country was an independent power which acted in its own interests in Kosovo, Russia's leaders in practice complied with Western dictates by working behind the scenes in late May to convince parliament to pass laws demanded by the IMF as conditions for its disbursing $4.5 billion in funds.[84] And the quid pro quo relationship of dependency between Russian and Western capitalist elites was made even more glaringly manifest in late June when the Cologne G-7 summit agreed on a plan for debt relief for Russia, said by a German official to be just a " 'little thank you by the West' for Russia's role in resolving the Kosovo crisis."[85] A more fitting end and a more open acknowledgement of the Yeltsin leadership's dependence on the West could hardly have been possible. Nor could the validity of Marx's class analysis and of dependency theory have been more plainly affirmed.

Postscript: Putin and Russian Policy Toward the West

From late 1999 to February 2000 several developments took place which had a dramatic impact on Russia's foreign policy. On August 9 Yeltsin fired Prime Minister Stepashin and replaced him with Vladimir Putin, a former official in the KGB, who was now clearly the heir apparent. In late August and September explosions rocked Moscow and other cities of Russia, officially said to be the work of Chechens, a charge which seemed to be reinforced by the invasion of Dagestan by Chechen forces in early August. But those responsible for the bombings were never identified, in spite of the government's flimsy claim months later that it had a videotape in its possession which "categorically" proved the culprit was a Chechen. Indeed, many strongly suspected that the government itself had masterminded the bombings to create a new "enemy" in the Chechens. If so, this was arguably a stroke of genius, for it provided the current rulers with a convenient opportunity to extricate themselves from their political difficulties and to divert the people's wrath away from the Westernizers and toward the Chechens. A military campaign was launched against Chechnya on September 30 (air and artillery attacks had begun on September 23).[86]

Although Western leaders criticized Russia for its behavior in Chechnya at the November OSCE summit in Istanbul and a December statement by EU leaders in Helsinki chided Russia's Chechnya campaign as "totally unacceptable" while demanding that Russia begin a "political dialogue," the Chechnya campaign proved to be a boon for pro-government forces for it would propel them—first and foremost Putin, the anointed savior of those Russians who saw him as the long-awaited "firm hand" against the enemies of the people—to victory in the State Duma election.[87]

The Duma elections, held on December 19, resulted in the first pro-Kremlin majority since the Duma's creation in 1993; for the first time the Communists did not control it, although it must also be borne in mind that the 24% of the vote they garnered this time exceeded even that of the 1995 elections. This "great victory" by the "reformers" was in part the result of campaign violations by the Kremlin who, according to the European Institute for the Media, ran a considerably more corrupt campaign than even that of 1995. Adviser to German Chancellor Michael Steiner disgustedly dismissed the Russian elections as a "dirty campaign offensive [that] paid off," and one Western observer called Russia's political process "criminalized," complaining that "a large number of candidates who allegedly have committed illegal acts or have ties to organized crime are seeking election. Victory will ensure their immunity from prosecution." *The Economist* described the election as "a matter of dirty money, wild promises, defamation of character and the promotion, with varying degrees of slickness and sophistication, of personalities devoid of politics." The US and Britain, on the other hand, hailed Russia's electoral "democracy."[88]

But the biggest surprise came on new year's eve when Yeltsin unexpectedly resigned and named his Prime Minister, Vladimir Putin, to replace him. Putin retained his post of Prime Minister. This apparent political master stroke seemed to insure that Yeltsin's hand-picked successor would win the presidential election, which had been moved up three months to March 2000, especially given that Putin's popularity was far greater than that of any other candidate at the time of his appointment—and assuming, of course, that no major mishaps occurred in Russia's Chechnya campaign, which was Putin's political trump card.

During his first months as President most thought Putin's stand on the issues inscrutable, although some—even left-wing—analysts foresaw the possibility that Putin could become a Russian Pinochet and pursue a "more assertive" policy "opposing the expansion of US influence."[89] On the other hand, in late February 2000 the authoritative voice of the liberal sector of the US ruling class and of the Clinton administration, *The New York Times*, pronounced Putin a politician who was "steering to reform, but with Soviet discipline."[90]

Glimmers of where Putin stood on the issues could be gleaned from the press, and the picture which took shape diverged sharply from the alarmist perceptions. In the first place, although Putin acted quickly to remove some Yeltsin cronies once he assumed office, he left enough in place to indicate that the changes were merely "cosmetic." Indeed, Putin had been originally recruited into the political leadership in his native St. Petersburg by the right-winger Anatolii Sobchak and was brought to Moscow by Chubais who, along with Gaidar, was Putin's economic adviser. Chubais and Gaidar were also known to have "played an important role" in the fall 1999 presidential election campaign, during which Chubais' financial backer, the notorious oligarch Boris Berezovskii, reportedly worked closely with Chubais and the Yeltsin forces to generously fund ORT television, which gave special coverage to the Unity bloc supported by Putin, and whose scurrilous reporting almost single-handedly caused the eclipse of Unity's main rival, the Luzhkov-Primakov coalition.[91]

Anders Aslund predicted that Putin would act even more boldly on economic "reform" than Yeltsin had by pushing for increased foreign investment, tax reform and the privatization of land, which Putin pointedly urged the Duma to support in an unprecedented speech before that body in mid-January 2000. And early statements signaled that Putin favored the implementation of "very radical and unpopular" neo-liberal policies once he won the election in March.[92]

The "deal" Putin worked out on January 18 to control the State Duma with Russia's Communist Party (CPRF) by dividing up Duma committee leadership posts says something not so much about his political leanings as where the CPRF itself stands. If anything, it was a maneuver by Putin to ensure that his "reform" agenda would sail through the parliament more easily than it did under Yeltsin, especially because he saw not the Communists but the Luzhkov-Primakov forces as his main political threat. Putin was banking on the CPRF's support—or at least its neutralization— for the most right-wing proposals, especially pro-capitalist land "reform," which he openly pushed. Judging by past experience it is not clear that the alliance will last for long, particularly since the CPRF still identifies—at least to some degree—with the interests of the Russian working class.[93]

As of February 2000 Putin's foreign policy seemed no less pro-Western than his predecessor—if anything, he indicated the reverse, affirming in late December that the Russian economy must integrate into "world [i.e., Western capitalist] economic structures," in particular, the WTO,[94] and in talks with Strobe Talbott on December 22 argued for quick ratification of START-2. In December Putin perfomed damage control in response to Yeltsin's "ferociously hard-line" statement of December 9 that Clinton "appears to have forgotten . . . what Russia is. Russia has a full arsenal of nuclear weapons, but Clinton decided to flex his muscles" (itself a response to Clinton's criticism of Russia's military incursion in Chechnya) with the comment that he (Putin) was "sure" both Presidents did not intend to cool relations and that no such cooling was taking place. In another revealing action Putin's stern warning to CIS Ministers in September that bombings and "international terrorism" were aimed at undermining the CIS was itself undermined by his own machinations to that end, which came to light in the reports of Belarusian officials that immediately after he came to office a distinct "slowdown" was detected in the Belarus-Russia rapprochement pushed by Yeltsin, and despite efforts by Belarus' "hard-line" President Lukashenko to "heal relations" with the US on a range of issues. Belarusian officials also took note of Putin's order to slow the establishment of supranational bodies called for in the CIS Treaty.[95]

Perhaps most important, although Putin, like virtually all the other top leaders, affected a "hard-line" anti-Western stance (clearly as a pre-election ploy) by criticizing the West in December for its use of the "language of force" with Russia—he even paraphrased Yeltsin's December 9 threat with the warning that Russia had "everything to guarantee its security" and that if the US changed the ABM treaty Russia's "answer will be adequate"—all expectations were that Putin's ascension to the presidency would actually help to push Russian policy in a direction more congenial to US and Western interests. This seemed to be confirmed in early January when Clinton administration officials asserted that Putin's ascension would not only not "dramatically alter" relations for the worse but could even "improve the chances" that Washington's proposals for the 1972 ABM Treaty would be negotiated on terms favorable to the US, given that the new leader would be able to "negotiate with authority." Putin thus seemed poised in the early days of 2000 to do the bidding of the West, as much as or even more than Yeltsin had before him, to give away the store at the expense of the interests of the Russian people.[96]

This became yet more apparent in February 2000 when the controversy over NATO expansion to the Baltics flared up sharply, and Putin made conciliatory gestures toward NATO, declaring Russia's interest in a "more profound integration" with the alliance, and even joining it "as a political organization" (as long as Russia was regarded as an "equal partner" whose interests were taken into account)—*"though he seemed to struggle to state what those interests were."* Putin also admitted that he found it hard to "visualize NATO as an enemy."[97]

These words were of great import for the strategic objectives of both Russia and the West. And the general reaction was not favorable for Putin, for he was attacked almost universally by politicians and political analysts alike, including Grigorii Yavlinskii, for making possible "unrestricted NATO expansion": "How can Russia object to Baltic membership when Putin himself says Russia may join?" one noted political commentator asked with obvious alarm. It was no surprise, therefore, that the Latvian Foreign Ministry immediately alluded to Putin's statement as further proof Russia did not oppose Baltic membership in NATO. Most ominously for Putin, parallels were made with Yeltsin's August 1993 capitulation in Warsaw, which "led to the start of NATO expansion . . . [Putin] has decided to support and follow Yeltsin's undertaking." This was not high praise. Indeed, by his acquiescence to NATO Putin seemed, like his mentor and precedessor, to be playing the comprador role to the hilt and selling his own country out. Russian policy toward NATO by early 2000, it was now clear, had since August 1993 come full circle.[98]

Notes

[1] *The Moscow Times*, January 30, 1999.

[2] Reuters, March 6, 1999.

[3] AP Online, April 20, 1999.

[4] Interfax, April 8, 1999.

[5] *Nezavisimaia gazeta*, April 16, 1999, p. 8.

[6] Interfax, April 9, 1999.

[7] *The Gazette* (Montreal), April 10, 1999, p. B3.

[8] World Socialist Web Site, August 5, 1999; *RFE/RL Newsline*, Vol. 3, No. 159, Part I, August 17, 1999; *The Times* (London), August 23, 1999.

[9] *Financial Times*, August 26, 1999, p. 2.

[10] Ibid., November 20, 1999, p. 10.

[11] The Associated Press, February 18, 2000.

[12] *RFE/RL Newsline*, February 8, 1999.

[13] The Associated Press, June 22, 1999. See another such reproach by Sergei Baburin, left-wing Chair of the Duma Anti-NATO Commission in *Pravda-5*, May 22, 1997, pp. 1, 3.

[14] *The Washington Times*, June 3, 9197, p. A3.

[15] NTV International, February 16, 2000; *Nezavisimaia gazeta*, February 16, 2000, p. 1; The Associated Press, February 18, 2000, and March 5, 2000; *Kommersant*, July 24, 1999, p. 2.

[16] *The Chicago Tribune*, December 15, 1999.

[17] BNS News Agency (Tallinn), January 27, 2000; Agence France Presse, January 24, 2000.

[18] *RFE/RL Newsline*, Vol. 3, No. 15, Part I, January 22, 1999; *Kommersant-daily*, January 20, 1999, p. 4 and January 23, 1999, p. 2; *Nezavisimaia gazeta*, January 19, 1999, pp. 1, 6.

[19] *The Jamestown Foundation Monitor*, Vol. 5, Issue 172, April 14, 1999; *Izvestiia*, April 4, 1999.

[20] *RFE/RL Newsline*, Vol. 3, No. 29, Part I, February 11, 1999. Masliukov was on the defensive with respect to Russia's relations with the IMF and the West. According to a Western observer, the US White House had concocted an "elaborate scheme to buy the Kremlin's neutrality in the Balkan war" and sought to "pay for a softer voice from Moscow." See *The Chicago Sun-Times*, April 12, 1999, p. 31.

[21] *RFE/RL Newsline*, Vol. 3, No. 32, Part II, February 16, 1999; *The New York Times*, February 18, 1999, p. A14.

[22] *Segodnia*, February 19, 1999, pp. 1-2; AP Online, February 18, 1999.

[23] *The New York Times*, June 6, 1999, p. A16.

[24] *RFE/RL Newsline*, Vol. 3, No. 58, Part I, March 24, 1999.

[25] *The Observer* (UK), March 28, 1999, p. 21.

[26] *RFE/RL Newsline*, Vol. 3, No. 58, Part I, March 24, 1999; The Associated Press, March 24, 1999; Reuters, March 24, 1999; *RFE/RL Newsline*, Vol. 3, No. 59, Part I, March 25, 1999; Reuters, March 25 and April 1, 1999.

[27] Agence France Presse, April 1, 1999.

[28] Reuters, April 1, 1999.

[29] AP Worldstream, April 12, 1999.

[30] *Kommersant-daily*, April 24, 1999, p. 2.

[31] *The Sunday Times* (London), April 11, 1999.

[32] AFX News, April 12, 1999; ITAR-TASS, April 9, 1999; *The International Herald Tribune*, April 13, 1999, p. 1.

[33] *RFE/RL Newsline*, Vol. 3, No. 70, Part I, April 12, 1999.

[34] Reuters, April 9, 1999.

[35] *The Sunday Mirror*, April 11, 1999, p. 5. Some Russian analyses gave credence to Yeltsin's threats as, for example, *Izvestiia*, April 13, 1999, p. 1.

[36] *RFE/RL Newsline*, Vol. 3, No. 59, Part I, March 25, 1999.

[37] *Kommersant-daily*, March 29, 1999.

[38] *Nezavisimaia gazeta*, March 31, 1999, p. 3.

[39] *Kommersant-daily*, March 27, 1999, p. 2. To be sure, Duma leaders agreed that extreme measures should be used, but only if softer ones failed.

[40] Reuters, March 25, 1999.

[41] *U.S. News and World Report*, May 3, 1999, p. 33; *Sovetskaia Rossiia*, August 3, 1999, p. 1.

[42] Pavel Felgengauer, *The Moscow Times*, April 22, 1999.

[43] *RFE/RL Newsline*, Vol. 3, No. 66, Part I, April 6, 1999.

[44] *The Moscow Times*, April 21, 1999.

[45] Reuters, March 25, 1999.

[46] *The New York Times*, April 10, 1999, p. A8. Reuters derided Yeltsin for his propensity to be "strong on anti-NATO rhetoric" but "short on actions that could lead to a confrontation." See Reuters, April 25, 1999.

[47] *The New York Times*, May 7, 1999, p. A1.

[48] Emphasis mine. *The Boston Globe*, May 7, 1999, p. A28.

[49] *The Washington Post*, May 5, 1999, p. A26.

[50] Agence France Presse, May 8, 1999; *Segodnia*, July 23, 1999, p. 3.

[51] *The Los Angeles Times*, July 3, 1999, p. A5.

[52] *The New York Times*, May 11, 1999, p. A10.

[53] P. Felgengauer, *The Moscow Times*, May 20, 1999.

[54] *The New York Times*, June 4, 1999, p. A22. Alexei Arbatov warned that Russia should avoid being the "messenger boy" for NATO and Belgrade. See *Novye izvestiia*, April 28, 1999, pp. 1-2.

[55] *The New York Times*, June 2, 1999, p. A14.

[56] Ibid., May 23, 1999, Sect. 4, p. 17.

[57] *The Washington Post*, May 27, 1999, p. A39.

[58] *The New York Times*, June 3, 1999, p. A1; The Chinese observed that the Russian-US agreement at Helsinki showed that "Russia actually approves the European security path in which NATO is the pillar and Russia is a participant." See Beijing, *Renmin Ribao*, June 29, 1999, in *FBIS*-CHI-1999-0629.

[59] Thomas L. Friedman, *The New York Times*, June 8, 1999, p. A27.

[60] Ibid., June 4, 1999, p. A22.

[61] *The New York Times*, June 15, 1999, p. A15.

[62] *The Washington Post*, June 12, 1999, p. A1.

[63] *Moskovskii komsomolets*, June 14, 1999, pp. 1-2. See Chernomyrdin's statement that Russia would have an independent military contingent in Kosovo, in ITAR-TASS, June 19, 1999.

[64] *The New York Times*, June 13, 1999, Sect. 1, p. 29; Milan, *Corriere della Sera* (Internet version), June 13, 1999, in *FBIS*-WEU-1999-0614, June 14, 1999.

[65] *Segodnia*, June 14, 1999, p. 1.

[66] *Rossiiskaia gazeta*, June 22, 1999, pp. 1, 7; *Krasnaia zvezda*, June 19, 1999.

[67] *The New York Times*, June 19, 1999, p. A6; *Moskovskii komsomolets*, June 19, 1999, p. 3; London Press Association, June 15, 1999, in *FBIS*-EEU-1999-0615, June 15, 1999.

[68] *The New York Times*, July 6, 1999, p. A1; *International Herald Tribune*, July 5, 1999, p. A1.

[69] ITAR-TASS, June 28, 1999.

[70] *The Wall Street Journal* (European edition), June 14, 1999.

[71] *The New York Times*, May 8, 1999, p. A8; Associated Press, May 5, 1999. In an interview with *Komsomol'skaia pravda*, May 15, 1999, p. 4, Sergei Karaganov ruled out partnership with NATO for the next few years, and even recommended that the Final Act be "terminated."

[72] Reuters, June 11, 1999. Knowing that an open admission of their agreement to subordinate Russian troops to NATO risked a political backlash, the leaders resorted to double-talk on the issue, as exemplified by Chernomyrdin's statement that "if Russia is represented in Kosovo, it would be necessary to speak about a zone of responsibility. For our group will not just stay in one place. It must bear responsibility for a certain sector." See ITAR-TASS, June 10, 1999. Chernomyrdin also asserted that "for Russia, our presence is under our command, and only under ours." In June he denied Russian troops were subordinated to NATO, prompting an assurance by a German official that Chernomyrdin's words "should not be taken at face value," since "obviously each politician has his constituency that has to be satisfied." See *The New York Times*, June 3, 1999, p. A14.

[73] *The New York Times*, June 13, 1999, Sect. 1, p. 28. The absurd lengths of the farce was embodied in the proposal, aimed at answering Russia's demand that the UN have "some say" in peacekeeping, which stipulated that Supreme Commander of

NATO Wesley Clarke make a written report to the UNSC over specific periods. See Ibid., June 8, 1999, p. A16.

[74] Ibid., June 9, 1999, p. A14.

[75] Ibid., June 19, 1999, p. A6; *The Washington Post*, June 25, 1999, p. A1.

[76] Reuters, September 23, 1999; Agence France Presse, August 29, 1999; The Associated Press, August 25, 1999.

[77] *RFE/RL Newsline*, Vol. 3, No. 131, Part I, July 8, 1999; Agence France Presse, July 8, 1999; *RFE/RL Newsline*, August 6, 1999.

[78] *Nezavisimaia gazeta*, July 15, 1999, p. 6.

[79] *The New York Times*, June 9, 1999, p. A14; *Izvestiia*, June 4, 1999, p. 1; *Kommersant-daily*, June 5, 1999, p. 1 and June 8, p. 1.

[80] Interfax Russian News, July 20, 1999; *Kommersant-daily*, July 24, 1999, p. 2.

[81] Agence France Presse, July 26, 1999. First Deputy Prime Minister Avdeyev set forth the "most acceptable scenario for Russia" after NATO's war against Belgrade: Russian participation in restoring Kosovo, "financed by international organizations." Interfax, June 24, 1999. See also ITAR-TASS, June 29, 1999.

[82] *Kommersant-daily*, August 3, 1999, pp. 1, 3; *Nezavisimaia gazeta*, July 30, 1999, pp. 1, 6.

[83] *RFE/RL Newsline*, Vol. 3, No. 150, Part I, August 4, 1999. Other observers continued to maintain that Russia was Belgrade's "ally," that it had "expressed strong support for Belgrade during the conflict with NATO." See The Associated Press, June 25, 1999.

[84] Reuters, May 26, 1999.

[85] *The New York Times*, June 21, 1999, p. A8.

[86] Ibid., August 9, August 31, September 23, October 1, 1999.

[87] Ibid.

[88] *The Boston Globe*, December 20, 1999; *RFE/RL Newsline*, December 21, December 23, 1999; *RFE/RL*, December 16, 1999; The *Economist* (UK), December 18-24, 1999; *The New York Times*, March 13, 2000, p. A6.

[89] *The Nation*, January 24, 2000, p. 4. The argument that a Pinochet would be more anti-Western was invalidated by the fact that the dictator Pinochet had been in many ways the creature of the US CIA. A similar apprehension about the anti-Western tone of Russia's leaders, particularly with respect to the recently signed Belarus-Russia treaty, was signaled by Deputy Chair of the Media MOST company, Igor Malashenko in *Newsweek International*, December 20, 1999, and *RFE/RL Newsline*, Vol. 3, No. 243, Part I, December 16, 1999, and especially *The Times* (UK), February 10, 2000.

[90] *The New York Times*, February 20, 2000, Sect. 1, p. 1.

[91] Ibid., January 1, 2000, p. A11, and January 4, 2000, p. A3; *Moscow Times*, December 16, 1999, and January 1, 2000; *The Times* (UK), January 19, 2000.

[92] *Moscow Times*, December 16, 1999; Bloomberg, January 18, 2000.

[93] See *The Gazette* (Montreal), January 20, 2000, p. B1, and *Manchester Guardian Weekly*, February 2, 2000, p. 27.

[94] *Irish Times*, December 31, 1999.

[95] *RFE/RL Newsline*, September 16, December 10, 1999; January 14, 16, 2000.

[96] The *New York Times*, January 1, 2000, p. A19.

[97] Emphasis mine. *The New York Times*, March 6, 2000, p. A8; Agence France Presse, March 6, 2000.

[98] Interfax/BNS (Riga), March 6, 2000; *Kommersant-daily*, March 11, 2000, p. 1; Interfax, March 12, 2000; *Nezavisimaia gazeta*, March 7, 2000, pp. 1-2.

11 Conclusion

Consonant with its Marxist perspective this study has aimed to move beyond mere description of its principal objects of analysis, in this case political phenomena involving states, institutions, and individuals, to penetrate to the underlying motive force of Russian foreign policy. By so doing it has set as its objective the affirmation of Engels' thesis that socioeconomic class is, in the final analysis, the determining factor in the explanation of social phenomena. To be sure, non-class factors, including history, political culture (the absence of democracy throughout tsarist history and the reliance on a strong leader), psychology (the personal idiosyncrasies of Yeltsin and other leaders), what I call "economic culture," i.e., the legacy of pre-Soviet capitalism, ideology and the role of ideas (the influence of neo-liberalism on "reform"), have been shown to impact on Russian foreign policy—but only to the extent that they are, as it were, the handmaidens of what is the *chief* and overarching determinant: the dynamics of class relations between capitalists and workers and between different international capitals with respect to the ownership, production and distribution of the material wealth.

Linking class and foreign policy is always a difficult proposition, but it is especially so when the analytical focalpoint involves deception, as in the case of Russia, when the culprits are not likely to openly acknowledge their true roles, and particularly given that their strategy entails the concealment of their aims to insure their political survival. Problematic too is the fact that the link between economic and political power is largely an indirect one in that the political elites act as *agents* for the former. In Russia, moreover, the two have enjoyed a uniquely close relationship which has often blurred the lines between them, as the oligarchs themselves occupied and continue to occupy the pinnacle of political power. Conversely, members of Russia's political class have appropriated for themselves a portion of the spoils and become capitalists. But a Russian bourgeois class proper simply did not exist until the latter stages of the Yeltsin regime. Until that time the capitalist class existed as a class-in-creation, with its proxy, the political elites, taking on the task of transforming a socialist society into a capitalist one and creating a capitalist class from the remnants of socialism.

Further tracing the link between class and policy, this study has

265

demonstrated that Russia has been and remains dependent on the West, that the nations of Russia and the West are intimately linked on a bilateral and multilateral basis (the G-7, NATO, the EU, the WEU, etc.). In the context of this mutual assistance the West has been "paid back" for the monetary aid and political support it extended to Russia's elites in the form of the latter's compliance with the dictates of Western policymakers on such foreign policy issues as the war in Yugoslavia, NATO expansion, Iraq, arms control, etc.

The opposition to the capitalist West which emanated from the USSR and the socialist bloc has been extinguished, giving the West a largely free hand around the world. By seeing to their country's military incapacitation Russia's leaders have willingly neutralized any geostrategic threat the West would otherwise face, especially but not exclusively in the Eurasian region. In the Caspian region the West has been able to seize huge energy reserves, something unthinkable only ten years ago. Western capitalists have, in the long run, indeed derived incalculable benefits from their quid pro quo deal with Russia. With Russia's assistance the scope of the capitalist West's geopolitical dominance, fortified by an aggressive NATO, has been expanding eastward, broadening the range of markets and sources of raw materials, actual or potential, sought by international capital. As long as Russia's Westernizers remain in power and continue their decimation of the Russian economy and military it may be only a matter of time until, as they did in the former Yugoslavia, NATO and the West advance to and dominate states of the FSU.

For the Western ruling classes the economic payoff is in the final analysis much the same as for Russia's elites, economic enrichment, but it is a more indirect and long-term one in that the principal objective remains, at least for the moment, to prevent the reemergence of communism in Russia, which would cut Western business off from potential markets in Eurasia, and to make these areas safe for capitalist investment. To be sure, Western investment has found its way to Russia, but the economic payoff is still some way down the road for this still largely untapped and unstable market. In any case, the preservation and expansion of capitalism's world dominance can only be accomplished if Russia's Westernizers retain power; hence the Western ruling classes' largely unqualified support for Russia's "reformers," even if that means—following the West's practice of supporting despots around the world—sanctioning corruption, harsh exploitation, even wide-scale killing in the name of anti-communism.[1]

Western leaders made common cause with the Russian ruling class in support of a regime that has been anything but democratic, thereby validating one observer's comment that "while paying lip service to [Russian] democracy, Western governments actually favored authoritarian policies."[2]

The advantages of the quid pro quo are all the more attractive for Russia's elites in view of the peculiarly mercenary nature of Russian capitalism and the overweening greed that it embodies.[3] Like their tsarist predecessors, Russia's economic elites consume conspicuously, work unproductively, and give little thought to the needs or wishes of Russia's working people. Their activity is heavily skewed toward the *indirect* appropriation of rental value of natural resources and energy from the Western market. They are dependent on the West for hard currency, the bulk of which is obtained from the sale of Russian raw materials and energy, and for credits and loans—a policy which drives the Russian government deeper into debt dependence on the West and enables wealthy Russians to evade contributing to society and amass vast personal fortunes.

Russia's elites—the mafia-oligarchy and their political agents, the pro-Western Yeltsinites—have enriched themselves by corrupt means and with the connivance of Western elites who, as the Bank of New York and other scandals have shown, have encouraged the widespread greed and criminality pervading Russia. With their obsession with personal enrichment the elites—economic as well as political—salivate at the prospect of the billions of dollars in Western assistance they largely pocket for themselves; they welcome Western support which helps make it possible for them to send billions to the West in capital flight, all of which provides powerful confirmation of Lenin's characterization of Russia's capitalists as a comprador bourgeoisie willing to go to almost any lengths to sell out their country's interests, of which Russia's acquiescence to NATO expansion is perhaps the most telling example. Michael Mandelbaum captured the essence of this relationship when he imputed Yeltsin's caving in to the West on Kosovo in 1999 to his desire to "get paid; [Yeltsin] sells out Russia's national interest to get a new loan."[4]

If we accept the proposition advanced in the Introduction that explanation derives from the discovery of regularities, then the main thesis of the link between class and policy has been confirmed in this study. The evidence is overwhelming that Russia's leaders complied time and time again with the West's policy dictates—it was a rare case, in fact, when they did not. This alone should be sufficient proof of the main thesis. But this study has gone further by presenting additional evidence in the admission of a leading architect of the Western strategy toward Russia, Lawrence Summers, that the West literally bought off Russia's leaders in return for their acquiescence to Western foreign policy. This is precisely the smoking gun which proves this study's theses—of deception, of Russia's dependency on the West, and of the mutality of purpose of the international capitalist class. Another "smoking gun" presented in this study is the published secret communications between Russian and Western elites which exposed to public view Russia's obeisance to Western dictates.

Although the central truths about Russian domestic and foreign policy have—or should have—been obvious ever since the USSR's "democrats" surfaced as a political force in the late 1980s, it was not until 1997 that the term "robber capitalism" was first introduced by the World Bank, a sign that the West recognized—grudgingly and half-heartedly—the realities of Russia's grotesquely failed "reform." Indeed, only by the late 1990s did Western analysts and politicians acknowledge that "all those years [Russia's] leadership—from Yeltsin and Chernomyrdin down the ladder— whined and moaned about flight capital, about how the nation was bleeding hard currency by the billions, yet they and their cronies were doing the exact same thing—with the nation's strategic reserves with money that belongs to the citizens of Russia."[5] A principal source of that capital, one might add, came from the West, whose "consultants," especially during the early post-Soviet years, made many of the decisions for Russia's leaders, in secret and with the collaboration of Russia's elites.

The quid pro quo relationship between Russian and Western elites has therefore entailed Russia's implementation of policies favorable to Western elites *and* has benefited Russia's Westernizers. One of the chief favors Russia's elites have performed for the West in return for its funding and political support is compliance with the foreign policy scripted by Western policymakers. Russia's foreign policy history vis-à-vis the West is summarized in the following section.

Russia's Strategies of Deception

Western observers have, to a much greater extent than Russian, either been unconscious of or reluctant to discuss the real nature of Russia's relationship with the West, a fact which likely derives from political-ideological considerations in that the mainstream Western position on post-Soviet Russia has tended to echo the voice of the Western ruling classes, who have generally supported the Russian elite's efforts to nudge their country along the path of a market-oriented, allegedly "democratic" society. It has been a sine qua non among Westerners (including Western specialists on Russia) that Russia's elites should be supported, given that their mortal enemies, the Communists, are waiting in the wings to take power. This reality gives special resonance to the thesis of Marx and Engels that the ideas of the ruling class are the ruling ideas of a society. It also means that those most active in unmasking the deception tend to be on the political left, both in Russia and the West, whose views will be given little exposure in these societies so thoroughly controlled by the capitalist classes and where left-wing opinions are largely excluded.

As has been argued, in Russia's early years the policies of the "democratic" leaders were characterized with few exceptions by an open obsequiousness toward the West. They worshipped NATO, the EU, the IMF, the World Bank, the Paris Club, the CofE, and virtually everything about Western capitalist society and made no secret of it, which points up the glaring disjunction between Russia's capitalist elites and the working masses (including the intelligentsia, the original social base of "reform" but whose deteriorating situation has only deepened their feeling of alienation from the Westernizers). As the "reforms" gradually *deformed* Russian society the masses reacted to the West and all things Western in increasingly negative fashion, linking the West and the devastating "reforms" associated with it with the downfall of the USSR and Russia's decimation. And because the masses were leary of the "giant confidence trick"[6] played by Russia's Westernizers, it was politically dangerous for the leaders to appear too conciliatory toward the West.

As the gap between the masses and the top leaders lengthened the maneuvering and dissimulation to make it seem that the leaders were protecting Russia's interests in the face of an "aggressive West" became more far-reaching. The disjunction between their allegiance to the West and the need to appear anti-Western became so serious that the leaders were forced to devise varied means to perpetuate the grand deception. Russia's elites could not and would not curtail their worship and support of the West, however—and why should they, when the West has remained the chief buttress against the communists, their mortal enemies? Even Chubais admitted that when during the early post-Soviet period he had to choose between communism and robber capitalism he chose the latter without hesitation.

To be sure, although Marxists argue that all capitalists act in this fashion, that all capitalist polities similarly deceive, they (Marxists) also accept that there is a range of behavior displayed by capitalists from different nations. Historical and cultural factors, for instance, have created a Norwegian capitalist class which accepts as its civic duty that it should share the wealth. As a result, Norway is a relatively egalitarian capitalist society that affords its workers a comparatively comfortable standard of living (huge North Sea oil profits, of course, have also been a major factor in Norway's enduring postwar prosperity).

By late 1993 things began to change so dramatically in Russia that Russian leaders, in concert with their Western counterparts, were compelled to create a panoply of methods to perpetrate the pretense that suffused their relations with the West (to be sure, deception had existed before late 1993, but on a much smaller scale). Their strategies of deception have included the following:

1) In the most basic sense Russia's leaders have expressed outright opposition to Western policies—on NATO expansion, the former Yugoslavia, Iraq and Iran, etc.—when deep down they have been generally supportive. As part of this strategy they have on many occasions condemned Western policy in one breath only to follow with expressions of support in the next. Western officials have generally worked with them by pretending that they are not aware of the deception.

This strategy of deception, in turn, has been especially manifest with respect to the former Yugoslavia. In February 1994 Russia criticized NATO air strikes against the Bosnian Serbs for their alleged bombing of the Sarajevo market, but within hours approved of the strikes and retracted its demand that a UNSC vote be taken before such strikes. This scenario was revisited again in August of that year when Russia at first weakly criticized NATO for launching air strikes against the Bosnian Serbs then quickly "justified" the strikes. Yeltsin warned the West in April 1999 that a "world war" could break out if NATO drew Russia into Kosovo, which prompted Russian officials to issue immediate disclaimers that he was not "serious" and was only appeasing his critics.

The above "rapid retraction" syndrome was modified during the 1999 NATO bombing campaign in the former Yugoslavia, when Russia did not disavow its displeasure with NATO's campaign in one fell swoop—except on certain occasions, such as at the 1999 Bonn G-7 summit where Yeltsin approved *all* of the West's decisions on Kosovo—but retracted *gradually*, over a period of several months. Within weeks of the onset of the campaign a more subtle shift began, reflected in reportage on the war which went from being largely pro-Serb to striking a more "balanced" position. In late April Yeltsin instituted a campaign to counter burgeoning anti-US and anti-Western sentiment in Russia. For one, he replaced Primakov with Chernomyrdin as emissary to Belgrade because the latter was perceived in the West as more "amenable." In this role Chernomyrdin would willingly convey NATO's demands to Yugoslav President Milosevic.

2) A companion strategem of the preceding, also used especially with respect to the former Yugoslavia, is Russia's attempts to portray its policies as "evenhanded," whereby officials (claim to) take sides not with Belgrade, their supposed ally, but display "nonpartisanship," siding with both sides. In practice, however, Russia has almost invariably sided with the West, especially on important decisions and on UNSC resolutions, and has stood up for Belgrade generally only at lesser forums (e.g., Russia's blocking a resolution marking Belgrade as a pariah at the CSCE meeting in May 1992) and with respect to relatively inconsequential decisions. One analyst captured the essence of this strategy when he observed that Russia's warning that it might seek sanctions against Croatia in January 1993 fit its "long-standing advocacy of an evenhanded approach towards warring parties in the former Yugoslavia," although more rational voices knew that "Russia's fundamental alignment with the West on Yugoslavia is unlikely to change as long as pro-Western reformers remain in power."[7]

Russia tried to portray itself as an "ally" of Belgrade by mitigating the force of a September 1992 UNSC resolution banning Belgrade from voting in the UN, but immediately nullified the seemingly pro-Serbian sentiment of its initiatives by rejecting the latter's claim to be the successor to the former Yugoslavia on the grounds that post-Soviet Russia and post-Yugoslav Serbia were "incomparable." With friends like Moscow, as they say, Belgrade needed no enemies.

3) Another Russian strategy has been to portray itself as a great power with ongoing international influence—in reality, a means of diverting attention from the fact that Russia's leaders have, through their pro-Western policies, destroyed their country's economy and military and left Russia largely impotent internationally. A particularly obvious example of this has

been the campaign, first begun in 1996, by Russian and Western leaders to inflate the significance of Russian membership in the G-7 with the fraudulent claim that it placed Russia among the ranks of the wealthiest and most powerful countries in the world. More sober assessments of Russia's role in the G-7 termed Russia's "membership" a "joke" and a "pretense"[8] (this is why throughout this study I have referred to the G-8 and not the G-7). Another example was the leadership's contention that Russia played a major role in the conflicts in the former Yugoslavia when in fact it played a notably marginal role, one of "errand boy" for the West. Russia's hosting the G-7's "nuclear summit" in Moscow in April 1996 was another obvious ploy, conducted to advance Yeltsin's presidential candidacy just prior to Russia's 1996 presidential election by portraying him as an equal of the leaders of the most powerful Western nations at a gathering which was a thinly-disguised sham.

4) Russia's strategy of deceit has included the outright resort to secrecy, coverup, and fabrication. This study documents a number of such practices by Russian officials, some of which were exposed by the newspaper *Den'*, including: (a) the publication of a secret letter by Russia's UN Ambassador Vorontsov acknowledging that his delegation had voted for sanctions against Serbia out of a desire to support the West; (b) secret instructions from US Secretary of State Baker to Kozyrev dictating what policies to carry out with regard to Yugoslavia; (c) secret transcripts of what were essentially demands from President Bush, including that Yeltsin retain Kozyrev as Foreign Minister, as well as the "suggestion" that Russia ratify START-2 in return for monetary payment; and (d) Kozyrev's reported secret consent to NATO air strikes in November 1995, which contradicted the RFM's allegation that the Western powers had acted behind Russia's back and without informing it in the UNSC of a secret agreement on military operations in Bosnia.

Still other forms of deception included: (a) the sham order by then Prime Minister Primakov to return his jet to Moscow, a supposed display of anger at the 1999 NATO bombing campaign but which he had known about beforehand; (b) numerous Russian threats issued after NATO's 1999 bombing campaign over Kosovo, almost all of which either proved to be empty (e.g., the sending of a "reconnaissance" ship to the Adriatic which conducted no reconnaissance and did virtually nothing to oppose NATO; the flight of Russian fighter jets close to the coasts of NATO members Norway and Iceland in June 1999, which was an equally empty gesture), all to conceal the obsequieousness of Russian leaders vis-à-vis the West; and (c) Kozyrev's feigned angry response to NATO's decision to expand at the December 1994 NATO Council meeting when he had known about the decision all along.

5) Russian leaders have appeased anti-Western and especially anti-US sentiment in Russia on the issue of NATO expansion by threatening to use armed force against NATO in defense of the Serbs and to form an "anti-Western" alliance consisting of various combinations of the usual suspects: China (always the principal ally in such an alliance), Iran, India, Belarus, France, Belgrade, etc. As documented at different points in this study, because the prospects for such an alliance have been virtually nil, given that none of the states has any intention of jeopardizing economic ties with the West, this proved just another empty Russian threat.

To illustrate this point, Russia's unwillingness to follow up on Defense Minister Grachev's proposed formation of a Joint Chiefs of Staff Committee of CIS armed forces in 1995 seemed "strange" to Russian observers, who speculated that Grachev did not really want to "tease the West once again" with a strategy it adamantly opposed.[9] In February 1996, just months before the crucial presidential election Yeltsin called for "unity" with Belarus after a meeting with Belarus President Lukashenko, prompting commentators to observe that he was just using "Lukashenko's visit to bolster his re-election campaign," to "deprive [his] communist and nationalist opponents" of their main trump cards, since he never had any intention of implementing the proposal. As *Izvestiia* remarked, "only the blind" could fail to see that the restoration of the USSR was used merely as a "bargaining chip" in the coming election.

Revised in early 1997, the treaty proposal was trotted out again as a "tactical move to bolster [Yeltsin's] claim that he was acting firmly against NATO expansion" just one month before his cave-in to NATO expansion. Yeltsin felt free to proffer this proposal because it would "not eventually lead to an alliance of much substance" in any case. The treaty proposal was revived yet again in early April 1999 when Yeltsin approved Yugoslav President Milosevic's request to admit Yugoslavia to the union of Russia and Belarus,[10] still another way to appear supportive of the Serbs in the face of NATO's bombing of Yugoslavia. Within months events would prove this, too, to be a maneuver, for on May 13, 1999 Russia's leaders "made it very clear" that they would under no circumstances change Russia's constitution to create a single state with Belarus—let alone Belgrade. And even when Belarus urged Russia in July 1999 to introduce a common union presidency and supranational bodies with extensive powers Russia "declined the proposal."[11] In October 1999 Yeltsin and Belarusan President Lukashenko signed yet another version of the treaty, said by one Russian analyst to evidence the increasingly "anti-Western" policy direction of the Yeltsin leadership, although the analyst neglected to point out that this was a pre-election ploy to create an anti-Western Russian image two months before the Duma elections.[12] As noted in Chapter 10, a "slowdown" in the Belarus-Russia rapprochement took place after the December 1999 accession of Putin, who ordered restraint in the creation of CIS supranational bodies.

6) Various diplomatic machinations have concealed Russia's dependence on and support of the West. Examples include: (a) the Balkan peacekeeping charade, in which Russian officials, during fall 1995 with respect to Bosnia and in July 1999 with respect to Kosovo, refused to place Russian peacekeeping troops under NATO command, then finessed the issue by means of a gimmick in which they consented to the subordination of Russian commanders to officers from individual states—but who were also NATO officials. Commentators aptly termed this subterfuge a "fig leaf"; (b) in January 1997 Yeltsin's order to formulate an "action program" opposing NATO expansion seemed a display of toughness against Western aggression, but its swift and quiet disbandment indicated that the leadership had no intention of really opposing the West; and (c) Russia's request of its Western allies in the UNSC to postpone two separate votes on Bosnia, one in March and the other in April 1993, in order that Russia's UN delegation might avoid voting on the pro-Western, anti-Serb resolutions just prior to the crucial 9th CPD and Yeltsin's April 25 referendum on his rule. Not only did the West gladly oblige, but Russia's leaders later expressed "regret" at Russia's abstention on the April resolution.

Russia used the tactic of abstaining on important proposals more broadly as a means of disguising its support of Western policy, especially in the all-important UNSC. Compelled by furious opposition to its knee-jerk pro-Westernism to scale back somewhat its overt support of the West, especially in the Balkans, Russia abstained on a Western-backed proposal for the first time in the aforementioned April 1993 vote and resorted periodically to the tactic of abstention thereafter. This did not in any case obstruct the West's ultimate objectives, however, especially given Russia's steadfast refusal—save in one isolated instance in December 1994—to use its veto in the UNSC.

Russia's Support for Western Policies: A Brief Review

The strategy of deception, of course, is carried out by Russian officials as a cover for the many instances of their outright support for Western policies, such as the repeated refusal to use Russia's UNSC veto on issues and even to vote for them, in particular the lifting of sanctions against Belgrade, while repeatedly rejecting parliamentary resolutions calling on them to do so. Instances of open Russian support for Western policies include:

With Respect to the Former Yugoslavia

1992 Russia (a) voted in May and November for anti-Serb sanctions in the UNSC; (b) backed Western opposition to the Socialists in the 1992 Yugoslav elections; (c) offered to send a warship in October to assist the West in monitoring sanctions against Serbia; (d) supported the Western-led anti-Serb October UNSC resolution creating a no-fly zone in Bosnia; and (e) voted in December in favor of the UNSC resolution which punished violators of the no-fly zone in Bosnia—that is, the Serbs.
1993 Russia agreed to participate in NATO's campaign against the Serbs by flying relief supplies for NATO airfields and approved the June UNSC resolution to send troops to protect Bosnian Muslims against the Serbs.
1994 Russia backed NATO's April ultimatum to the Bosnian Serbs to withdraw or face air strikes, while attacking the Serbs for their "criminal" actions; Russia supported stronger economic sanctions against the Serbs in July, and approved NATO air strikes against the Serbs in November.
1995 In May and again in September Russia approved massive NATO anti-Serb air strikes.
1998 Russian troops participated in NATO military exercises in Albania, clearly directed against the Milosevic government, and voted in September for UNSC Resolution 1190 which authorized force in Kosovo.
1999 Russia's envoy to Belgrade, Chernomyrdin, knuckled under to Western dictates by agreeing to persuade Milosevic to accept the West's terms to end the Kosovo crisis in June; Russia also caved in the West's insistence on its subordination to NATO control of Kosovo peacekeeping.

With Respect to NATO

1992 Russian representatives attended the NATO conference in Banff, a first for Russia.

1993-94 The most consequential instance of outright support for Western policy by Russia's leaders came in August 1993 when Yeltsin consented to CEE membership in NATO; Russia also agreed to participate in PfP military maneuvers in 1994 in spite of its repeated threats against NATO expansion throughout 1993-94.

1995 In February the Russian Foreign Ministry launched a trial balloon for its eventual consent to NATO expansion by negotiating with NATO on the issue; the next month Kozyrev declared expansion acceptable under certain conditions; Russia signed the PfP agreements with NATO in June and consented to participate in NATO military exercises in December.

1996 In March Yeltsin and Foreign Minister Primakov openly broached the idea of negotiating a treaty with NATO for the first time; in December Primakov officially agreed to begin negotiations on the treaty.

1997 Yeltsin capitulated to the West on virtually every issue related to NATO expansion at his summit with Clinton in Helsinki in March, then Russia agreed to enshrine this on May 14 in the finalized draft of the Russia-NATO charter; the Founding Act was signed on May 27, termed a "victory" by Yeltsin, although in reality Russia suffered a disastrous defeat.

Russia's Declared Opposition to Western Policies

Russia has frequently expressed opposition to Western policies: it steadfastly refused—as did West Europe—to give in to US urgings that sanctions against Bosnia be lifted, and has been for the most part (rhetorically) antagonistic to NATO's eastward expansion; Russia secured an agreement by the Bosnian Serbs in February 1994 to withdraw from Sarajevo in the face of threats of NATO air strikes; Kozyrev suddenly and unexpectedly refused in December 1994 to sign the PfP agreement, although this was exposed as a sham; perhaps the highpoint of Russia's anti-Westernism was, in conjunction with the above refusal to sign the PfP, its veto in December 1994 of a UNSC resolution toughening sanctions against the Serbs, Russia's second and last veto since the USSR's demise (the first was in May 1993 over the minor issue of reformed financing for

UN peacekeepers in Cyprus); Russia pushed through a UNSC resolution preventing NATO air strikes against Iraq in November 1997.

Although they seem to demonstrate the anti-Western inclinations of Russia's leaders, the aforementioned in fact can be read in two ways. On the one hand, they are manifestations of Russia's tendency to display a certain independence, however minimal, from the West (see below). On the other, they prove just how pro-Western Russia has really been since, as former US foreign policy official Helmut Sonnenfelt has noted, a key strategy of Russia has been to disassociate itself from the West from time to time to show its "independence." Seen in this light, the few instances of "independence" actually play a central role in the strategy of deception by making it *seem* that Russia really "opposes" the West while it covers up its pro-Westernism.

That this is, as a rule, sheer posturing has been repeatedly demonstrated by Russia's open support for air strikes against the Serbs just months after its adoption of a "tough" stance on anti-Serb sanctions in December 1994. What is more, the following month Polevanov and other "anti-Western hard-liners" in the government were dismissed by Yeltsin, and two months after that the government consented to negotiate NATO expansion. Yeltsin's December 1994 threat of a "cold peace" was immediately disavowed by Kozyrev, who clearly feared it might be misinterpreted in the West as a display of genuine anti-Western sentiment. In any case, Russia's policies of reconciliation quickly eased any tensions.

The above discloses still one more calculated strategy of deception of Russia's Westernizing leaders, that of making concessions to anti-Western sentiment at certain periods by temporarily placing in positions of authority figures considered to be less pro-Western, but removing them when the peak of the mass anti-Western mood has passed or, conversely, removing the most controversial Westernizers at strategic points in time and returning them to their positions when it is judged politically feasible. This happened when: (a) Primakov was installed as Prime Minister, and a number of Communists, including Masliukov, were named to government posts just weeks after the economic crash of August 1998; Primakov and the Communists were removed months later when the peak of the crisis had passed; (b) Polevanov became Privatization Minister during the apogee of Russia's anti-Westernism in late 1994 but was sacked in early 1995 during the campaign to reverse what was viewed as the dangerously anti-Western mood in Russia; (c) and Chubais was fired or demoted several times over the years by Yeltsin in response to the public outcry against his willingness to cater to the sleaziest forms of greed and criminality of Russian "capitalism." Because of his inestimable value to Russia's Westernizers and their Western partners, however, he was allowed to return to power in each instance once the controversies had blown over. As of this writing (March 2000) Chubais remains at the pinnacle of power.

Dependency and Russian Foreign Policy

The destruction of the USSR was not inevitable, even given the shortcomings of the Soviet system. But during the Gorbachev years pro-Western Soviet leaders acted in ways which at a minimum greatly accelerated the collapse. Vernon Aspaturian confirmed this when he accused Soviet officials at the end of the Soviet era of giving away "one unilateral concession after another in return for empty Western 'kudos' or illusory expectations of financial and economic aid . . . the Ministry of Foreign Affairs was indeed deceived, defrauded, outwitted, and hoodwinked by crafty bourgeois diplomats."[13]

But were the Soviets, as Aspaturian implies, unwittingly deceived? Evidence shows that pro-Western Soviet diplomats in fact *willingly accepted* policies which proved to be disastrous for their country's interests[14] and beneficial for the West—even before the collapse of the Soviet Union. Late Soviet and Russian Westernizing diplomats, in short, have been complicit with the West's goals, as even critics of the Soviet system Raslan Khasbulatov and Aleksandr Dubcek, both staunchly anti-Soviet, acknowledged when they bemoaned the "thoughtless destruction of everything positive that was created in Eastern Europe during the existence of the [socialist] totalitarian regime there." Similarly, Vladimir Lukin, himself a Westernizer, warned Russian "democrats" in fall 1992 against self-destructive policies which derived from the "self-loathing characteristic of the position of more radical Westernizers."[15]

An adjunct of their policy of dissimulation was the leaders's characteristically secretive, hasty actions aimed at insuring that their policies of placating the West could be rammed through without popular scrutiny. Indeed, they "stood to benefit personally by shielding their positions from democratic accountability . . . "[16] Thus in 1992 Yeltsin rushed through the signing of the START-2 treaty which many, including

Russia's top military brass, viewed as a boon to the West's strategic interests. Although a delay in signing would have protected Russia's interests, Yeltsin acted in great haste because an "early signing . . . insured [he] would have US support in the coming struggle in Moscow" (the parliament was preparing to impeach Yeltsin at the time).[17]

Many other examples of the Russian leadership's secretive style include Russia's publication in February 1992 of its Economic Policy Memorandum (issued *after* price liberalization, which itself was not put to a popular vote), addressed to the IMF and not to the Russian people; Privatization Minister Chubais' secret voucher plan, which contravened the one already approved by the Supreme Soviet—Chubais pushed through his secret plan because he knew that neither parliament nor the Russian people would countenance such an outright theft of the people's wealth; and contrary to the argument that, at least until fall 1993, Russian foreign policymakers have responded in a democratic fashion to domestic opinion,[18] the Russian government reached agreement in August 1992 with the IMF "in secret, overriding objections among government and Central Bank officials, and without consulting the Supreme Soviet," thus demonstrating the power of the IMF to compel the Russian government to sign agreements behind closed doors which it would not justify in public, and on "less than satisfactory terms."[19]

An important element of this study is its refutation of the commonly-held belief that as Russian Foreign Minister and later Prime Minister Primakov was "hard-line" and "anti-Western." In reality, it was Primakov's predecessor as Foreign Minister, Kozyrev, who instituted "hard-line" policies (if only rhetorical) beginning as early as late 1992.[20] The widely-held belief that Primakov was the exclusive author of Russia's purportedly "anti-Western" "Eastern" strategy (including the proposed Moscow-Beijing-Delhi "strategic triangle")[21] designed to counterbalance the West is also specious, belied by the fact that such a policy had been instituted in late 1992 with the "double-headed eagle" policy which emphasized warmer relations with China (and was accompanied by the restoration of ties with Cuba).[22] Even *Pravda* columnists observed in 1995 (although they vastly overstated the case) that Kozyrev's views had changed in a "very important way during the past few years," so that he no longer advocated "degrading, copycat approaches" of the West.[23] Finally, in line with the disconnect between his hard-line rhetoric and his soft-line practice,[24] Primakov acquiesced to the West on key issues including the most critical one, NATO expansion. It was Primakov who first expressed Russia's official acceptance of NATO expansion, which only provoked Yeltsin to accuse him in March 1996 of objecting to NATO expansion "too mildly."

The Extent and Nature of Russia's Dependency on the West

This study concludes that Russia is dependent on the West. As documented in Chapter 2, Russia conforms to all of the economic and political criteria of a dependent state with the exception of foreign investment. Having said that, it must be pointed out that its dependency is not a totally harmonious, smooth, and mutually coordinated affair, but entails bargaining for advantage, give-and-take, even threat among the various parties. The following discussion of Russia's relationship with the West seeks to elucidate the complex nature of Russia's dependency.

Dependency theorists recognize that no universal truths exist across states. Rather, state-level factors, including size, colonial history, the nature of foreign penetration, and other factors condition the effects of dependence on economic growth and inequality within the dependent state.[25] Studies employing what is more properly termed the "dependency approach" have focused primarily on relatively small, poor and weak states mainly in Latin America and Africa. But post-Soviet Russia shares a number of features of dependent states and meets the criteria for a dependent state in that it is primarily a raw materials exporter, has huge and rising inequalities of wealth, lacks real democracy, has experienced a significant "brain drain," etc. Nevertheless, when considering whether Russia is a dependent state certain qualifications must be borne in mind to avoid oversimplification.

Boris Kagarlitsky has correctly pointed out that as they "integrate themselves into the Western system, the former Communist countries [including Russia] have increasingly become part of the [capitalist] periphery." With its significantly higher social development Russia is at the same time set apart from third world dependent states.[26] It thus conforms to dependency theory, but the nature of that dependency must be qualified in light of its unique features, which include the fact that its predecessor, the USSR, had: (a) the most entrenched state-run command economy of any socialist society; (b) little or no historical experience with capitalism or (Western-style) democracy; (c) virtually no foreign investment; (d) a socialist system that was the longest-lasting and the most legitimatized and institutionalized of all the European socialist states; and (e) lacked a societal consensus in favor of Western democracy or capitalism. The USSR also differed from all other societies in history for which the introduction of capitalism entailed the destruction of pre-capitalist structures to make way for modernization. Finally, Russia's old structures are technologically and organizationally on a far higher level than the new, post-Soviet ones.[27]

Post-Soviet Russia's dependency also cannot be appraised without taking account of its predecessor state's autonomy from the capitalist core and its unwavering opposition, ideological and otherwise, to capitalism. Indeed, it was precisely because of its opposition to monetary control and fiscal discipline that macroeconomic stabilization in Russia could not be sustained after mid-1992. And unlike most third world societies, where only a small minority is employed regularly in wage labor (and where an even smaller percentage are members of trade unions),[28] the USSR had a large, well-defined, and well-organized working class.

Finally, the USSR was the heart of an entire world system, the socialist bloc. As such, it was a superpower in its own right whose military might was on a par with the US. This, plus its vast size and population and the aforementioned extended isolation from the West, imbue post-Soviet Russia with certain features more common to a core than to a dependent state, and make it possible for Russia's elites to blunt somewhat the leverage exerted by the advanced capitalist states.[29] This is particularly manifest in post-Soviet arms transfers, which remain extensive. According to traditional dependency theory, the advanced core powers transfer arms to the poorer and weaker peripheral states. The USSR, a core state, was one of the world's leading arms suppliers, and Russia has gone to great lengths to retain this advantage.[30] In April 1996, for example, Russia played hardball in the international arms market by refusing to notify signatories of the Wassenaar Agreement (signed in December 1995 to replace Cocom) of its global arms sales for fear of losing its top customers and its key sources of hard currency revenue—Cuba, North Korea, and Iran—with whom Moscow enjoyed a market monopoly thanks to Western export restrictions.[31]

Analysis of Russia's dependency on the West must be modified in light of the above. Other considerations include the following:

1) Russia's dependence on the West derives as much from political as from economic criteria based by the beginning of the new millennium not so much on direct foreign ownership and control of the economy via investment (as in Latin America) as, in the case of South Korea, for example, on Western economic aid and political support of its capitalist

system to fend off a potential communist takeover[32]—a point all but admitted by the principal ideologists of Russia's privatization, who urge the West to continue aid because it "change[s] the political equilibrium [in Russia] by explicitly helping free-market reforms to defeat their opponents." Aid helps reform, they argue, "not because it directly helps the economy—it is simply too small for this—but because it helps the reformers in their political battles."[33] By the late 1990s Russia had in fact become the IMF's biggest recipient of economic assistance.

What is more, a distinct, albeit assymetrical, mutuality characterizes the relationship between Russia and the West. Each strongly needs—and therefore depends on—the other for specific purposes: the West needs Russia's Westernizing leadership as an anti-communist bulwark to carry out the policies desired by the West, and Russian leaders need the West to give them and their policies legitimacy—not to speak of international moral, political, and above all financial support.

Thus far, the West has been willing to accept that it cannot buy up the Russian economy and has remained content with the Russian elite's success in having slain the Soviet communist dragon and ensuring that the dragon does not rise again. But Russia's dependence derives more from (immediately) political than economic factors, as has been argued by leading analysts Leonid Abalkin and Stanislav Menshikov.[34] In their view the Russian government has exaggerated the scale of its financial dependence on the West because it simply does not need such aid, given its highly favorable external trade balance, which in 1996, for example, amounted to more than $10 billion (not including the hundreds of billions of dollars in capital flight) even as the IMF approved a $10.3 billion loan that year.[35] This proves, they argue, that the leadership exploited its relations with the IMF to plunder the state.[36] Sergei Glaz'ev similarly noted that Western money dispensed just prior to the 1996 election was to be used only temporarily to increase social spending, *thereby to bolster Yeltsin's shaky political position.* Glaz'ev noted how "extraordinary" it was that the money was given for government dicretionary spending, to be disbursed any way the Russian government saw fit, rather than being linked to specific goals, as was normal practice. The West's $22 billion bailout of Russia in summer 1998 revealed a similar endgame of Western financial "assistance" to Russia—to prop up an increasingly unpopular, politically shaky regime.[37]

2) Resistance by dependent countries against the preferences of dominant states may not actually reduce ties of dependence but rather

serves a symbolic function, assuring the dependent governments a better chance of survival in office as their leaders feel "duty-bound" to act in "the national interest" by resisting the positions of dominant countries, at least on minor issues.[38] The dominant country's elites are as a rule interested in compliance mainly on salient issues in any case,[39] so that contrary to the claims of "vulgar compliance theorists" dependent states can and do exhibit a certain degree of autonomy vis-à-vis core states. Dependent states are expected to "satisfy the obligation of their assymetrical [economic or political] exchange by supporting the foreign policy of the dominant country to a greater extent than do other, nondependent countries, without being totally obeisant."[40]

This study has shown that Russia has certainly complied with Western demands on the most salient *domestic* issues in its creation of an economic "market" via monetarist "reforms" and ballooning disparities of wealth and impoverishment of the masses, the brain drain and, closely connected with the latter, a downscaling of the Russian military. The ultimate consequence of these policies is Russian impotence in the international arena. Russia has at the same time resisted the West's instructions on a few issues, including the military campaigns in Chechnya in 1994-5 and 1999-2000, certain developments with respect to Iraq and Iran, etc. This is a reflection of Russia's minimal independence vis-à-vis the West, but it also reflects Helmut Sonnenfeldt's thesis that Russia's Westernizers seek to legitimize their pro-Western policies with occasional displays of independence. It is, of course, an all but impossible proposition to try to definitively ascertain in certain cases whether Russia's leaders were motivated out of the need to make a display of independence or were genuinely resisting the West.

3) In one sense Russia's dependence should be assessed not so much in terms of its absolute subordination to the West as on the basis of the distance it has moved along the continuum with respect to its former Soviet isolation and autarky. The USSR was indeed autarkic: 67% of its foreign trade in 1987 was with other socialist countries, although this trade accounted for only 4% of world trade.[41] For the Soviet Union foreign trade was in fact an almost negligible factor for its enormous economy.

4) The history of capitalist Russia also sharpens our understanding of Russia's position in present-day capitalism. Tsarist Russia's position in world capitalism reflected dual tendencies which still manifest themselves today. Until the first World War Russia was highly dependent on Western capital, but foreign finance capital could not complete Russia's

284 Capitalist Russia and the West

"enslavement" without the aid and support of Russian finance capital itself, without the transformation of the big Russian bourgeoisie into a comprador class. On the other hand, tsarist Russia was an imperialist power *in its own right,* with its own system of financial-monopoly capital and its own imperialist interests,[42] and it at times insisted on pursuing its own foreign policy, even if that meant contradicting the dominant West.

This dual nature of Russian power became manifest in the 1990s with the reemergence of Russian capitalism. Especially since 1993 the Russian leadership has sought, within its overall dependence, to stand up, albeit minimally, for Russia's economic and political elites. On *balance,* however, Russia's modest refusals to comply with the West pale by comparison with the far more significant agreement to obliterate post-Soviet Russia's economic and military potential, with its subservience to NATO expansion, Western policy in the former Yugoslavia, and other issues.[43]

5) It must be borne in mind that, within the framework of the social contract, Russian opposition to the Westernizers has grown in proportion to the societal devastation the failed "reforms" of the Yeltsin regime have caused. One response of the Russian leadership has been to assuage popular unrest by means of a "show" of assertiveness on the international arena—generally rhetorically and within the limited confines of its dependency—by resisting, however minimally, the dictates of the West; total acquiescence to the West would be the political kiss of death and threaten the popular explosion so feared by Russia's Westernizers.[44]

Although Western elites are increasingly disenchanted with Russia's Yeltsin-Putin forces, they continue to support Russia's Westernizers because they form the chief bulwark against a radical, above all left-wing regime in Russia. The West has tolerated the Russian leadership's seeming bellicosity on certain issues, realizing that this is a price it must pay for appeasing anti-Westernism in Russia and because it forestalls the far more serious danger of a return to the "bad old Soviet times." This is why the West is willing to write off Russia's behavior, especially on issues linked more directly to financial gain for Russia's capitalists such as profitable nuclear sales to Iran, and why it allowed Russia into the G-7 in exchange for its acquiescence to NATO expansion. Minor concessions by Western elites, in other words, have been made to salvage the entire project.

6) Dependent states may be dependent on either a single core state or their dependency may be dispersed among several partners.[45] In Russia's case the latter is clearly more applicable, in that it is dependent on West

Europe and the US as a bloc. On a number of issues Russia has defied the US (including Iraq, Iran, and Cuba) but its policy has coincided with that of West Europe. In these cases Russia does not so much oppose the West as a whole as it does the more "hard-line" United States. Particularly since the 1994 election of the Republican Congress the US has, to a far greater extent than its West European allies, acted aggressively to stymie Russia in the world arena. The US decision in late 1996 to block Russia's purchase of US supercomputers, for example, was said to recall the cold war Cocom restrictions; and the Clinton administration was forced to go to great lengths in May 1998 to stop Congress from imposing sanctions on Russian business for allegedly permitting missile technology to leak to Iran.[46]

The foregoing explains why on some issues the West European allies have balked at US overassertiveness and linked arms with Russia (and others) against the US. In the former Yugoslavia the US undermined the Vance-Owen plan in 1993 and after November 1994 refused to monitor the arms embargo, as EU envoy David Owen criticized Washington for advocating a policy in Yugoslavia which would compromise peacekeepers on the ground and peace enforcement in the air.[47] And during the 1998 Iraq crisis Washington, "spoiling for a fight," was forced to alter its scenario of massive force against Iraq by "France, which, with its clever matchmaking, was helped by Russia and China."[48] It should be pointed out, however, that such behavior does not at all represent the return to anything like the Soviet exploitation of "interimperialist contradictions" between West Europe and the US during the cold war, but simply demonstrates the intersection of the policy trajectories of Russia and West Europe on individual issues.

Russia set about restoring economic ties with "pariah" states (Iran, Sudan, Iraq, Cuba, Libya, etc.) as early as late 1992, motivated not by ideology but by economics. Shut out from Western markets, it has been forced to return to its traditional markets—largely poor states unable to afford Western products, especially technology, making Russia's lower-priced goods attractive to them. As an indication that Russia's behavior is not politically motivated, even Western analysts acknowledge that Russia has largely observed UN sanctions against such "pariahs."[49]

Western Policy Toward Russia

This study has shown that the Western nations have steadfastly refused to integrate Russia into the West. They have resorted to temporizing, high-flown rhetoric, half-measures and half-truths in an effort to keep Russia at bay. This is why their agreements with Russia—from NATO's Founding Act to Russia's membership in the CofE, the G-7, the PfP, the APC, etc.—have, at least on paper, seemed to hold promise but in reality have been devoid of substance, let alone benefit to the people of Russia. Perceiving it to be a pariah state and above all fearing the appearance of a recidivist communist regime, the West has dealt with Russia at arms length with the aim of shutting it out of European and Western affairs. It was in this context that Yeltsin's statement at a March 1998 meeting in Moscow with German Chancellor Kohl to the effect that "Russia has become a part of Europe. Greater Europe will [now that Russia is a member] be a hegemonic force" was so ludicrous that Russian observers noted that Kohl "was barely able to suppress a laugh."[50]

The West knows at the same time that it must somehow integrate Russia into the West, but only to the extent that it can monitor and control Russian behavior. Accordingly, it has allowed Russia to join politically toothless bodies while slamming shut the doors of more meaningful organizations shut. And the West's imposition of heavy quotas and tariffs on Russian goods has helped to worsen Russian-West European trade and to weaken Russia economically.

In its relations with the West Russia has largely played the role of a supplicant begging for handouts, as in the 1991 episode when Western food aid was shipped to Russia to tide it over during its economic crisis as well as its shameful replay in the wake of the economic crisis of summer 1998. What is more, in practically all of its dealings with Russia, the West has aimed to weaken Russia economically and militarily by forcing it to cut its military arsenal. It has insisted that Russia pledge that its nuclear industry be protected and safeguarded against theft and subversion, etc.[51]

The West's Part of the Bargain

Believing that there is no good alternative to Russia's current crop of corrupt elites, Western elites have offered now the carrot and then the stick in their aid to Russia, brushing aside any doubts or hesitations about aid when the Yeltsin forces were threatened and becoming more demanding when the threats diminished. As one Russian analysis pointed out, the IMF agreed in 1996 to a $10 billion aid package for Russia even though it had complained about the latter's tax collection because "the election was drawing near, and the IMF simply had to support Yeltsin" in spite of Russia's failings. Once the "political danger" had passed, however, IMF representatives reverted to their typical hard line, again demanding that Russia be more stringent in its tax collection.[52]

Western aid to the Yeltsin government has taken many forms, including overt support during the spring and fall 1993 crises embodied by the West's justification of Yeltsin's October slaughter at the White House and its attribution of all blame to the opposition. In March 1993 the G-7, fearing Yeltsin's defeat by the parliament-led opposition, called an emergency meeting to discuss aid to the Yeltsin government. It finally came up with a $3 billion IMF loan for Russian "market reforms" on April 23, just two days before Yeltsin's referendum on his presidency—to be used, among other things, to pacify strikers and politically volatile regions. In conformity with the typical pattern, however, once the April 1993 crisis had died down the West dealt with Russian aid in a way which suggested a reduced sense of urgency by demanding that Russia step up "reforms." This in turn prompted Yeltsin, who apparently feared the loss of billions from the West, to use desperate measures, including sanctioning NATO membership for the Visegrad states in August 1993. In early 1995 the IMF had Russian officials sign a secret protocol, correctly termed a "capitulation" by critics. And the West pulled out all the stops in 1996, helping to insure Yeltsin's victory in the 1996 presidential election by agreeing to $14 billion in IMF credits, rescheduling some $40 billiion in debts in the Paris Club, agreeing to hold the sham "nuclear summit" in Moscow in April to boost Yeltsin's image (he himself had come up with the idea for the summit), playing along with the contrived arrest of nine Britons in the same month, contributing $500 million to Yeltsin's campaign, sending a group of US Republican Party operatives to run Yeltsin's campaign. And the West in 1999 approved some $4.5 billion in aid as a "thank you" gift for Russia's acquiescence during the Kosovo conflict.

Another crackdown on Western aid came in December 1999, when the IMF delayed disbursing credits to Russia even though the Russian leadership had adopted a "tough" budget in record time. Russian officials complained that the IMF delay was the result of political criteria—in this case opposition to Russia's military action in Chechnya.[53]

Dependency, The Russian Military, and Russian Security Policy

The legacy of Russia's Westernizers cannot be easily undone. Their "reforms" have rendered Russia impotent and insured that for some time to come it will be largely incapable of projecting its power around the world. Even when it had become clear that Russia's military was compromised to the point of collapse Russia's leaders refused to take steps to remedy the situation and even continued to pursue a dubious military "reform" which severely short-changed the military. Russian military spending declined by some 80% in 1992 alone, a stipulation of the first Russia-IMF agreement which imposed "stiff conditions" dictating huge defense cuts (Gen. Lev Rokhlin revealed not long before he was killed that the IMF had demanded that Russia allocate no more than 3.5% of its GDP for defense, "a sum," in his view, "small enough to completely destroy the army." That the disarming of the USSR/Russia had apparently succeeded even sooner than anticipated was confirmed by CIA Director Robert Gates when he declared in January 1992 that Russia was no longer a military threat to the US).[54]

In view of Yeltsin's directives to limit defense financing one can only assume that, as commander-in-chief he agrees with the IMF.[55] It is worthy of note in this regard that the Yeltsin government has expressed more concern about an internal than an external security threat.[56] Nor has the leadership taken any forceful action to stem the exodus of hundreds of billions of dollars in capital flight—money which could help revive Russia's military, among other things. In this light one could argue that the line between post-Soviet Russia's *inability* to oppose NATO's (and the West's) dictates due to its weakness—a weakness deliberately brought on by Russia's leaders—and the latter's *willing acquiescence* to the West is at best extremely thin.[57]

The weakening of Russia's military capability by Russia's leaders appears even more damaging when one bears in mind that NATO was and remains the military-political alliance which embodies the interests of the united mechanism of national and international monopolies and the bourgeois state by pursuing imperialist policies and "suppressing revolutionary forces by means of outside intervention."[58] This view is confirmed by Elizabeth Sherwood's documention of NATO's "shadow alliance," of Western military-political coordination in areas in Europe and beyond in order to respond to "a myriad of challenges to Western [capitalist] interests."[59] A principal motive for the hostility of the "US and other NATO members" toward Russia is the fear that an "extreme nationalist" and especially "Communist" regime could come to power. This has catalyzed the West to seek to maximize the security gains won since the end of the cold war.[60]

Russian Policy and Learning Theory

Conventional learning theory is conceptually flawed for the very reason that it is possible to conclude from its premises—establishing flexible but well-defined guidelines for resolving conflicts among goals and the reassessment of fundamental beliefs and values—that learning took place in Russian policy toward the West. It would be difficult, however, to legitimately argue that Russia's Westernizing leaders learned simply because they fundamentally reassessed their values—to the point where, in contrast with the Soviet period, corrupt and violent mafia groupings impoverish the masses by plundering the people's wealth, send enormous amounts of capital abroad so that little remains for investment in Russia, and adhere to a foreign policy of subservience to the West, thereby selling out the interests of their country.

What is missing is a truly meaningful definition of learning which takes into account *why* leaders learn and *for whom* the learning is taking place, that is, what groups or classes benefit or lose from their policies. Learning is in this sense normative; the values must be clearly spelled out to prevent its lapsing into fetishism. And it must avoid the assumption that the interests of Russia's Westernizing leaders are identical with those of its people. From one standpoint the tiny band of elites who hijacked Russian policy to run it exclusively in their own interests certainly learned relative to their Soviet counterparts, for they succeeded in fundamentally transforming values. But from the standpoint of the Russian state and its people no learning at all has taken place by Russia's leaders. Quite the contrary, they have "unlearned" from their Soviet predecessors, who at least maintained a strong defense and maintained a comparatively egalitarian society which also assisted the exploited masses worldwide.

The Future

As we reach the millennium Russia is being gradually encircled by NATO, it is shut out of the EU and other Western organizations, and Russian-Western economic relations are floundering. On the home front, Russia's own economic "reform" and march toward Western-style "democracy" both are stalled, the people progressively impoverished.[61] One would think this is particularly fertile ground for a social explosion, but Russia's working masses have remained passive to a degree that almost defies comprehension, and seem to confirm Marx's thesis that the proletariat is itself capable of a "false" or "vulgar" bourgeois consciousness.[62] It seems, therefore, that the ruling class has, at least for some time to come, little to fear, a conclusion bolstered by the success of the Westernizers in the December 1999 Duma elections and in the popularity of Prime Minister Putin and his use of a "strong hand" in Chechnya which made possible his accession to the Presidency. But if there is a limit to the Russian people's fabled patience then the Westernizers may someday be rejected.

A major test for Russia's Westernizing leadership in the near future will be NATO expansion to the Baltics and to other former socialist bloc states, which appears likely. In this regard one Western source, who obviously bought into the grand deception and thus lent credence to it, warned that Washington's "unilateral persistence [to admit the Baltics to NATO] might eventually lead to a fatal split in the [Western] Alliance," not to speak of a militant reaction from Moscow.[63] But she need not worry, at least as long as the Westernizers remain in power, for if their record of relations with the West is any guide, they will protest loudly but avoid actions that in the end cut them off from Western money. They, as a comprador elite, are far more concerned with their pocketbooks than with the well-being of their own people, and will continue to sell out their country at the drop of a hat. And this study has documented the acceptance of such expansion by Russia's Westernizers by early 2000.

As far as the Russian people are concerned, the solution to their current dilemmas seems to have eluded them. While a certain segment of the Russian people has been willing to put its trust in the robber capitalist-mafia-led Yeltsin-Putin-Chubais leadership, who rule in collaboration with Western capital, another very large sector of the people has become disenchanted with the government and with politics in general. Many, as one quickly learns in Russia, refuse to vote for the anti-Yeltsin opposition not necessarily because they disagree with them but out of fear of retaliation from the capitalist mafia and of the civil war which an opposition victory could provoke. Such is the sorry state to which Russian society has been reduced with the help of Russia's illustrious "democratic" leaders.

But capitulation and fear only beget worse oppression by tyrants. Russia, which has so much to be proud of in its history and its people and whose spirit of generosity—which itself stems above all from that most decent of all human traits, collectiveness—was manifested most concretely during the Soviet period, and despite the USSR's many failings and problems. Russia can regain its illustrious place in history only by casting off both the exploitative system of robber capitalism—or any form of capitalism, for that matter—and the oppressive relationship of dependency on the West. Only then can its star rise again in a collectivized but this time renewed and revitalized, more democratically socialist form.

Notes

[1] The appalling record of Western, especially US, support for brutal regimes around the world was brought into sharp focus in late February 1999 by reports which revealed the US government's central role in the genocide in Guatemala during its 36-year civil war, in which hundreds of thousands were killed by government forces. See *The New York Times*, February 26, 1999, p. A1. At about the same time, it was reported that important files documenting US support for the Chilean dictator Pinochet were sought in his extradition case. By contrast, another report surfaced in November 1999 which exposed the fraudulent nature of the West's campaign in Kosovo and its phony charge of "genocide" against the Serbs. NATO and Western sources fabricated the numbers of killings by the Serbs during the civil war in Kosovo—one US government source reporting as many as 500,000. In reality, the number was estimated by more objective sources to be perhaps several thousand—and even then, many were military casualties in the civil war. A Spanish forensic team, whose experience was said to be "typical," found only 187 bodies *in individual graves*, instead of the over 2,000 in mass graves they expected. Typical of the fraud was the statement of deputy chief prosecutor for the US- and NATO-created International Criminal Tribunal for Yugoslavia that it was "not really a numbers game to determine whether genocide has been committed." See *The New York Times*, November 11, 1999, p. A6.

[2] *The Guardian* (UK), December 16, 1999.

[3] *Sovetskaia Rossiia*, May 5, 1998, p. 2. Grigory Yavlinsky concurred, observing that Russia's "robber-baron market cannot tackle important social and

economic questions. It is primarily concerned with issues that affect its masters' short-term power and prosperity." See Grigory Yavlinsky, "Russia's Phony Capitalism," *Foreign Affairs*, Vol. 77, No. 3, May/June 1998, p. 69.

[4] Associated Press, June 22, 1999.

[5] *The Moscow Times*, March 9, 1999. It is a notable fact that the latter newspaper was for years, like almost all Western sources, one of Yeltsin's biggest cheerleaders. I attempted, in research begun as far back as the late 1980s, to explicate this tendency among Western specialists in my "Ligachev and Soviet Politics," *Soviet Studies*, Vol. 43, No. 2, 1991.

[6] *Financial Times*, September 18, 1995, p. 17.

[7] Ibid., January 26, 1993, p. 2.

[8] *The Washington Post*, December 13, 1999, p. A24.

[9] *Kommersant-daily*, November 3, 1995, p. 3.

[10] *Segodnia*, April 10, 1999, pp. 1, 2.

[11] *OMRI Daily Digest*, No. 43, Part I, February 29, 1996; *RFE/RL Newsline*, Vol. 3, No. 94, Part II, May 14, 1999, and No. 129, Part II, July 2, 1999.

[12] Reuters World Service, April 2, 1997; *OMRI Daily Digest*, No. 43, Part I, February 29, 1996, No. 66, Part I, April 2, 1996; *Newsweek International*, December 20, 1999.

[13] Vernon V. Aspaturian, "Farewell to Soviet Foreign Policy," *Problems of Communism*, November-December 1991, Vol. XL, p. 57.

[14] By "the country's interests" I mean those which benefit the Russian working masses, as opposed to only a small group of wealthy elites.

[15] ITAR-TASS, February 22, 1992; Vladimir P. Lukin, "Our Security Predicament," *Foreign Policy*, No. 88, Fall 1992, p. 65.

[16] Lynn D. Nelson and Irina Y. Kuzes, *Radical Reform in Yeltsin's Russia: Political, Economic, and Social Dimensions* (Armonk, NY: M.E. Sharpe, 1995), p. 40.

[17] *Moscow Times*, April 16, 1998.

[18] Bruce D. Porter, "Russia and Europe After the Cold War: The Interaction of Domestic and Foreign Policies," in Celeste A. Wallander, ed., *The Sources of Russian Foreign Policy After the Cold War* (Boulder: Westview, 1996), p. 121.

[19] J. Helmer, *Business Times*, (Singapore), August 28, 1992, p. 10.

[20] See Chapter 6, for example, on Russia's reestablishment of relations with Cuba in 1995. In addition, Russia was one of twenty-four nations abstaining in a 1995 vote criticizing Cuba of human rights violations in the UN Commission on Human Rights. Ten opposed it. See *Izvestiia*, April 18, 1997, p. 3.

[21] *Rossiiskaia gazeta*, December 22, 1998, p. 7.

[22] See Chapter 3 for details about the diversification of Russia's foreign policy directions in 1992.

[23] *Pravda*, July 26, 1995, p. 7. See also Coit D. Blacker, "Russia and the West," in Michael Mandelbaum, ed., *The New Russian Foreign Policy* (New York: Council on Foreign Relations, 1998), pp. 178-82.

[24] Blacker, "Russia and the West," pp. 184-5.

[25] Jeanne A.K. Hey, *Theories of Dependent Foreign Policy and the Case of Ecuador in the 1980s* (Athens, Ohio: Ohio University Press, 1995), pp. 224, 269.

[26] Boris Kagarlitsky, *The Mirage of Modernization* (New York: Monthly Review Press, 1995), p. 217.

[27] Idem., *Restoration in Russia: Why Capitalism Failed* (London: Verso, 1995), p. 88; Michael McFaul, *Post-Communist Politics: Democratic Prospects in Russia and Eastern Europe* (Washington, D.C.: CSIS, 1993), pp. xv, 91.

[28] Vicky Randall and Robin Theobald, *Political Change and Underdevelopment: A Critical Introduction to Third World Politics* (Durham, NC: Duke University Press, 1985), p. 182.

[29] McFaul, *Post-Communist Politics*, pp. 92-3.

[30] David R. Stone, "Rosvooruzhenie and Russia's Return to the World Arms Market," in John MicGiel, ed., *Perspectives on Political and Economic Transitions After Communism* (New York: Institute on Eastern Central Europe, Columbia University, 1997), pp. 85-6.

[31] *The Moscow Tribune*, April 4, 1996, p. 3. Cocom, or Consultative Group and its Coordinative Committee, was founded by the Western powers in Paris in January 1950 for the purpose of embargoing exports to the communist bloc.

[32] For an excellent analysis of this aspect of dependency, see Peter Evans, "Class, State, and Dependence in East Asia: Lessons for Latin Americanists," in Frederic C. Deyo, ed., *The Political Economy of the New Asian Industrialism* (Ithaca: Cornell University Press, 1987), pp. 206-11.

[33] Maxim Boycko, Andrei Shleifer, and Robert Vishny, *Privatizing Russia* (Cambridge, MA: The MIT Press, 1995), p. 143.

[34] Personal correspondence from Menshikov.

[35] *Rossiiskaia gazeta*, 29 November, 1996 (Weekend Edition), p. 27; Fred Weir, "Betting on Boris: The West Antes Up for the Russian Elections," *CovertAction Quarterly*, No. 57, Summer 1996, p. 40.

[36] *Rossiiskaia gazeta*, November, 29, 1996 (Weekend Edition), p. 27.

[37] Fred Weir, "Betting on Boris," pp. 40-1.

[38] Neil R. Richardson, *Foreign Policy and Economic Dependence* (Austin: University of Texas Press, 1978), p. 69.

[39] Hey, *Theories of Dependent Foreign Policy*, pp. 224, 269; Neil R. Richardson and Charles W. Kegley, Jr., "Trade Dependence and Foreign Policy Compliance: A Longitudinal Analysis," *International Studies Quarterly*, Vol. 24, No. 2, June 1980, pp. 198-9. See also Adrienne Armstrong, "The Political

Consequences of Economic Dependence," *The Journal of Conflict Resolution*, Vol. 25, No. 3, September 1981, pp. 422-3.

[40] Hey, *Theories of Dependent Foreign Policy*, p. 269; Richardson and Kegley, "Trade Dependence and Foreign Policy Compliance," pp. 198-9.

[41] Anders Aslund, "Adapting to the World Economy: Interests and Obstacles," in Stephen Sestanovich, ed., *Rethinking Russia's National Interests* (Washington, D.C.: Center for Strategic and International Studies, 1994), p. 83.

[42] Ia. Livshin, *Monopolii v ekonomike Rossii* (Moscow: Izdatel'stvo sotsial'no-ekonomicheskoi literatury, 1961), pp. 261-2.

[43] The Russian leadership's obvious attempt to cover up their destruction of Russia's military and to portray themselves as supporters of the military was demonstrated by Defense Minister Sergeev's claim in late February 1999 that Russia had begun to rebuild its armed forces and Yeltsin's implied endorsement when he conferred a military award on Sergeev. Others saw "obvious political reasons" for the government's claims of success in halting the deterioration of Russia's military, however, and painted instead "a depressing picture of a demoralized and destitute" Russian army. See *The Jamestown Foundation Monitor*, Vol. 5, Issue 40, February 26, 1999.

[44] Yeltsin was forced to replace Kozyrev with Primakov not because he disagreed with Kozyrev's policies—as Coit Blacker points out, Kozyrev "faithfully exercised the strategy that he and Yeltsin . . . developed jointly"—but because his foreign policy, like his domestic policies, "had become deeply unpopular with a Russian electorate disllusioned with reform." See Blacker, "Russia and the West," p. 188.

[45] Vincent A. Mahler, *Dependency Approaches to International Political Economy: A Cross-National Study* (New York: Columbia University Press, 1980), Chapter 7.

[46] *Moscow Times*, November 29, 1996; The Associated Press, May 20, 1998.

[47] Mike Bowker, *Russian Foreign Policy and the End of the Cold War* (Aldershot: Dartmouth, 1997), pp. 224-5.

[48] Daniel Singer, "Euroland vs. Dollarland?" *The Nation*, May 25, 1998, p. 22.

[49] *Moscow Times*, May 20, 1995.

[50] *Kommersant-daily*, March 27, 1998, p. 1.

[51] Michel Chossudovsky, *The Globalisation of Poverty: Impacts of IMF and World Bank Reforms* (London: Zed, 1997), pp. 225, 232, argues that international Western organizations aim to weaken Russia—above all, its military-industrial complex—to prevent its development as a rival capitalist power. This in my opinion takes second place to the prevention of the rebirth of communism as a motive for Western behavior toward Russia.

[52] *Kommersant-daily*, July 24, 1996, p. 1.

[53] *Financial Times*, December 13, 1999, p. 10.

[54] *Financial Times*, January 23, 1992, p. 6.

[55] Stephen Covington, "Moscow's Insecurity and Eurasian Instability," *European Security*, Vol. 4, No. 3, Autumn 1995, p. 443; *Pravda-5*, June 26, 1997, pp. 1-3.

[56] The Associated Press, December 2, 1997; Reuters, December 18, 1997.

[57] Michael Mandelbaum, *The Dawn of Peace in Europe* (New York: The Twentieth Century Fund, 1996), p. 59. As one observer noted, the "NATO-centric model of the new European and world architecture is being taken to its logical conclusions, and there is no place for Russia in that model. Weakness and a lack of national will have left their mark." See *Izvestiia*, October 13, 1998, p. 2.

[58] *Bol'shaia sovetskaia entsiklopediia* (Moscow: Izdatel'stvo "Sovetskaia Entsiklopediia," 1974), pp. 480-1. See also *Christian Science Monitor*, October 4, 1995, p. 20.

[59] Elizabeth D. Sherwood, *Allies in Crisis: Meeting Global Challenges to Western Security* (New Haven: Yale University Press, 1990), pp. 184-5.

[60] *Nezavisimaia gazeta*, December 31, 1994, p. 3.

[61] Even Yeltsin's proposed Prime Minister, Sergei Kiriyenko, admitted during his address to the Russian Parliament, delivered even before the August crash of April 10, 1998, that Russia spent 30% of its budget servicing a foreign debt of $122 billion, up from 13 percent in 1996, that GDP had stopped growing, and that almost one-third of Russians were living at or below the poverty line. Kiriyenko also responded to the government's claim that the economy was growing with the retort that not a single citizen had felt this. See *The Washington Post*, April 11, 1998, p. A9.

[62] Georg Lukacs, *History and Class Consciousness: Studies in Marxist Dialectics* (Cambridge, MA: The MIT Press, 1971), p. 69.

[63] *The Los Angeles Times*, February 1, 1998, p. 5. *Krasnaia zvezda*, February 26, 1998, p. 3, took a similar position.

Index